Contents

CHILDREN, RISK AND SAFETY ON THE INTERNET

Research and policy challenges
in comparative perspective

Edited by Sonia Livingstone, Leslie Haddon
and Anke Görzig

First published in Great Britain in 2012 by

The Policy Press
University of Bristol
Fourth Floor
Beacon House
Queen's Road
Bristol BS8 1QU
UK
t: +44 (0)117 331 4054
f: +44 (0)117 331 4093
tpp-info@bristol.ac.uk
www.policypress.co.uk

North American office:
The Policy Press
c/o The University of Chicago Press
1427 East 60th Street
Chicago, IL 60637, USA
t: +1 773 702 7700
f: +1 773-702-9756
sales@press.uchicago.edu
www.press.uchicago.edu

British Library Cataloguing in Publication Data
A catalogue record for this book is available from the British Library.

Library of Congress Cataloging-in-Publication Data
A catalog record for this book has been requested.

ISBN 978 1 84742 882 0 (paperback)
ISBN 978 1 84742 883 7 (hardcover)

Cover design by The Policy Press
Front cover: image kindly supplied by Nigel Stead.
Printed and bound in Great Britain by TJ International, Padstow

List of tables and figures

Tables

Figures

Acknowledgements

This book draws on the work of the EU Kids Online network funded by the EC (DG Information Society) Safer Internet plus Programme (project code SIP-KEP-321803). Project reports, questionnaires, information on participating countries and related materials are all freely available at www.eukidsonline.net. The editors warmly thank all members of the network for their lively and thoughtful collaboration on the EU Kids Online project over the past five years. We also thank the International Advisory Panel for the project, the Safer Internet Programme staff and the many colleagues, stakeholders and others who have worked with us – critiquing, advising, guiding and debating our work – over recent years. The Department of Media and Communications at the London School of Economics and Political Science (LSE) has provided a supportive home for the project since 2006. Finally, we are also grateful to our friends and families who have put up with many unanticipated absences as we deserted them to work on this hugely demanding but most rewarding project.

Notes on contributors

Monica Barbovschi is associate researcher at the Institute of Sociology, The Romanian Academy, and postdoctoral fellow at the Centre for Social and Educational Research at the Dublin Institute of Technology, Ireland. Her current research interests are in the area of information and communications technology (ICT) and children, the sociology of childhood and rights-based policy approaches to children's play.

Joke Bauwens is professor of media sociology in the Department of Media and Communication Studies, at the Free University of Brussels (Dutch-speaking part). Her research focuses on the social contexts and consequences of media use. She has published on young people's internet use, digital broadcasting and media and morality.

Lukáš Blinka is a research fellow and PhD candidate at the Department of Psychology at Masaryk University, the Czech Republic, and PhD candidate in the Institute of Journalism and Communication at the University of Tartu, Estonia. His research areas are internet addiction, online gaming and blogging.

Kürşat Çağiltay is professor of the Department of Computer Education and Instructional Technology at the Middle East Technical University (METU), Ankara, Turkey. He holds a double PhD in instructional systems technology and cognitive science from Indiana University, USA. His research focuses on social informatics, human computer interaction and sociocultural aspects of technology.

Miguel Ángel Casado has a PhD in journalism and is a researcher at the University of the Basque Country. He is an expert in audiovisual policy and in youth and new technologies. He has published several articles in the main Spanish and international communication journals.

Jos de Haan is head of the Time, Media and Culture research group at the Netherlands Institute for Social Research/SCP and professor at Erasmus University Rotterdam. He specialises in research on cultural interests and media use. His recent research on new media focuses on the digital divide, the digital generation and the rise of e-culture.

Leen d'Haenens is a professor at the Centre for Media Culture and Communication Technology, Catholic University of Leuven, Belgium. Her main research interests include media policy and governance, minority ethnic adults' and young people's (new) media use and diversity as a quality criterion of media contents.

Verónica Donoso is research fellow in the Centre for Media Culture and Communication Technology at the Katholieke Universiteit Leuven, Belgium. She is passionate about the internet and in particular social media and the impact they can have on (young) people's lives. Her work focuses on internet studies, social media, safer internet and user experience research.

Andrea Dürager is a research assistant, lecturer and a scholarship holder for her PhD in the Department of Communication at the University of Salzburg, Austria. She holds postgraduate degrees in communication (2006) and in education (2008). Her special interests are media studies, audience research (focusing in particular on children) and higher education research.

Anna Galácz is a sociologist, working on her PhD dissertation at Eötvös Loránd University, Budapest. In her work she focuses on the process of social embeddedness of information and communication technologies. She is a member of the Hungarian research group of the World Internet Project (WIP) and EU Kids Online.

Carmelo Garitaonandia is professor of journalism at the University of the Basque Country, Northern Spain. He holds a PhD in political sciences, a BA in law and a Master's in information and audiovisual communication (from the University of Paris VII). His interests are new technologies and their influence on children and teenagers.

Maialen Garmendia has a PhD in sociology (from the University of Deusto, Spain) and has been teaching at the University of the Basque Country since 1990. Her interests are in social research techniques, statistics and audience research and new communication technologies. She has been a member of the EU Kids Online Spanish network team since 2006.

Anke Görzig is research fellow in social statistics at the Anna Freud Centre/University College London and was the survey research officer of EU Kids Online II at the LSE. She has a background in psychology and has extensive experience in quantitative research in the social sciences. Her general research interests evolve around applying psychological theories and concepts to social policy and applied research with a specific focus on social inequality.

Leslie Haddon is a senior researcher and part-time lecturer in the Department of Media and Communications, London School of Economics and Political Science, and visiting research associate at the Oxford Internet Institute and the Institute for Social and Technical Research, University of Essex. His work focuses on the social shaping and consumption of information and communications technology. He is co-series editor for a collection of textbooks on new media by Berg and part of several European research networks.

Uwe Hasebrink is director of the Hans Bredow Institute and professor for empirical communication research at the University of Hamburg, Germany. His work focuses on patterns of media use, the concept of media repertoires, communication modes in converging media environments and instruments to strengthen the users'/citizens' role in media politics.

Ellen Helsper is lecturer in media and communications at the London School of Economics and Political Science. She is an academic adviser at the Pontificia Universidad Católica, Chile, visiting fellow at New York University's Media, Culture, and Communication Department, and research associate at the Oxford Internet Institute. Her research focuses on vulnerable groups and their use of technologies.

Veronika Kalmus is professor of media studies in the Institute of Journalism and Communication at the University of Tartu, Estonia. Her work focuses on socialisation and intergenerational relations in the information society. She has published in many international journals and collections, including *Childhood: A Journal of Global Child Research*, *Children & Society* and the *Journal of Computer-Mediated Communication*.

Türkan Karakuş is currently working as assistant professor in the Department of Computer Education and Instructional Technology at Ataturk University, Turkey. She has carried out several studies related to training instructional designers, game-based learning, human computer interaction, cognitive aspects of human learning system, multimedia learning and e-learning.

Duygu Kaşikçi is a PhD student and research assistant in the Department of Computer Education and Instructional Technology at the Middle East Technical University (METU), Turkey.

Lucyna Kirwil is affiliated with the Warsaw School of Social Sciences and Humanities. She studies media impact on children and parental mediation in youth's online behaviour. She was expert adviser on the internet uses and abuses by children for the Ombudsman for Children in Poland and co-authored the Polish system of TV-ratings.

Elodie Kredens is associate professor in the University of Savoie, Chambery, France. She is a member of the research laboratory IREGE and holds a PhD in information and communication sciences. Her main research relates to the reception of reality TV by teenagers. She has conducted several surveys with children and teenagers on their use of the internet in France.

Els Kuiper is researcher and lecturer at the Department of Pedagogical and Educational Sciences, University of Amsterdam. In 2007 she published her PhD thesis 'Teaching web literacy in primary education'.

Reijo Kupiainen is professor of theory of visual culture in the Pori Unit, Department of Art and Media at Aalto University in Finland. His research focuses on media literacy, media education, creative media practices and image theory.

Engin Kurşun is currently working as an assistant professor at the Department of Computer Education and Instructional Technology in Ataturk University, Turkey. His main research interests are open educational resources, human computer interaction, mobile learning, new media and learning environments.

Claudia Lampert is senior researcher at the Hans Bredow Institute in Hamburg, Germany. Her research interest is in the area of media socialisation and media education. In the context of various projects, she is working on the role of digital media in the everyday lives of adolescents and on the challenges for parental mediation.

Yiannis Laouris is a social and business entrepreneur, a neuroscientist and systems engineer, currently working as senior scientist and chair of the Cyprus Neuroscience and Technology Institute and as director of CyberEthics, the Cyprus Safer Internet Center. His team represents

EU Kids Online and runs two projects, SimSafety.eu and InetRisks. net, which explore children's and parents' attitudes towards new technologies.

Eva Laszlo is a doctoral student in sociology and teaching assistant in the Department of Social Work at Babes-Bolyai University, Romania. Her research is focused on domestic violence, sexual abuse and women trafficking.

Alfredas Laurinavičius is associate professor and head of the Department of Psychology at Mykolas Romeris University, Lithuania. His research areas are mainly in legal psychology. He is a member of a group of scientists working on the adaptation of risk assessment instruments in the Lithuanian penitentiary system.

Sonia Livingstone is professor of social psychology in the Department of Media and Communications at London School of Economics and Political Science. She is author or editor of 16 books and many academic articles and chapters, including *Young people and new media* (Sage Publications, 2002), *The handbook of new media* (edited, with Leah Lievrouw, Sage Publications, 2006), *The international handbook of children, media and culture* (edited, with Kirsten Drotner, Sage Publications, 2008), *Children and the internet* (Polity Press, 2009), and *Media regulation* (with Peter Lunt, Sage Publications, 2012).

Bojana Lobe is an assistant professor at the Faculty of Social Sciences, a member of the *International Journal of Multiple Research Approaches* editorial board and author of *Integration of online research methods* (Faculty of Social Sciences Press, 2008). Current research interests include mixed methods research, new technologies in social science data collection, systematic comparative methods and methodological aspects of researching children's experiences.

Valentina Marinescu is associate professor at the Faculty of Sociology and Social Work, Bucharest University, Romania. She teaches undergraduate and graduate courses in media and society, and methods of researching mass communication. Her interests lie in media and communication studies in Eastern Europe, particularly in Romania, and gender studies.

Gemma Martínez is a PhD student at the University of the Basque Country, Northern Spain. She has a research grant from the Spanish

Ministry of Education. Her research topic is parental mediation and children on the internet. She stayed for a year at the London School of Economics and Political Science (Department of Media and Communications) as a PhD visiting student.

Giovanna Mascheroni is lecturer of sociology of communication and culture in the Department of Sociology at Università Cattolica del Sacro Cuore, Italy. Her work focuses on the social shaping of the internet and mobile media, on online participation and digital citizenship. Her latest publications include 'Remediating participation and citizenship practices on social network sites' (*Medien Journal*, vol 3, 2010).

Maria Francesca Murru is a doctoral researcher at OssCom, Università Cattolica del Sacro Cuore, Italy. Her research focuses on children's media practices and online public spheres. She has published on young people's internet use and civic participation in the digital media environment.

Kaarina Nikunen is university researcher in the Swedish School of Social Sciences at the University of Helsinki, Finland. She is editor of *Media in motion: Cultural complexity and migration in the Nordic region* (with Elisabeth Eide, Ashgate, 2011) and *Pornification: Sex and sexuality in media culture* (with Susanna Paasonen and Laura Saarenmaa, Berg, 2007).

Christine Ogan is professor emerita from the School of Journalism and the School of Informatics and Computing at Indiana University, USA. She has written extensively on the role of traditional and new media in the lives of Turks and the Turkish people in the diaspora.

Kjartan Ólafsson is lecturer at the University of Akureyri in Iceland where he teaches research methods and data analysis. He has been involved in a number of cross-national comparative projects on children and was a member of the International Advisory Panel of the EU Kids Online II.

Brian O'Neill is head of the School of Media and Government of Ireland senior research fellow for 2011–12 at the Dublin Institute of Technology, Ireland. His research focuses on media literacy, policy making and information society issues for children. He co-edited *Digital radio in Europe: Technologies, industries and cultures* (Intellect Books, 2010).

Dominique Pasquier is research director at the National Centre for Scientific Research in France and member of the Social and Economic Sciences Department at Telecom Paristech. Her main research, as a sociologist of culture, deals with young people, media and the use of information and communications technology (ICT). She is the author of six books and many academic articles and chapters.

Ingrid Paus-Hasebrink is professor for audio-visual communication at the Department of Communication and dean of the Faculty of Culture and Social Science at the University of Salzburg, Austria. She is responsible for the Audio-Visual and Online-Communication programme and has conducted many research projects on children and adolescent's reception of media. She is currently head of a longitudinal study on the media socialisation of socially disadvantaged children.

Cristina Ponte is lecturer in journalism, communication and children and media studies in the Faculty of Social Sciences and Humanities at Universidade Nova de Lisboa, Portugal. She is vice-chair of ECREA's (European Communication Research and Education Association) Audience and Reception Studies Section and a member of the steering committee of the COST Action IS0906, Transforming Audiences, Transforming Societies (2010–14), where she coordinates the Working Group on Audience Transformations and Social Integration.

Pille Pruulmann-Vengerfeldt is associate professor and head of the Institute of Journalism and Communication at the University of Tartu, Estonia. She also works part time in the Estonian National Museum. Her research interests are focused on user-friendly online spaces as possible venues for participation in political and cultural life.

Antonis Rovolis is assistant professor of spatial and urban economics at the Department of Economic and Regional Development, Panteion University of Athens, Greece. His areas of expertise are spatial dimensions of new technologies, urban and regional infrastructure investment and urban and regional economic growth.

Pille Runnel is research director of the Estonian National Museum. Her main research areas are information society studies, media sociology and media anthropology, as well as inclusive and participatory practices in museum communication and museum audiences. She has recently published in the *Journal of Baltic Studies* and the *Journal of Computer-Mediated Communication*.

Bence Ságvári is a research fellow in the Institute of Sociology at the Hungarian Academy of Sciences, and managing director of ITHAKA Research and Consulting Ltd. His work focuses on the social aspects of information and communications technology (ICT) with special interest on the younger generations and on values in general. He is a member of the World Internet Project (WIP) research network.

Katia Segers is professor of media studies at the Vrije Universiteit Brussel and the University of Antwerp, Belgium. She is director of the Centre for Research on Media and Culture. Her research and publications focus on children, media and culture. She is president of the Flemish Regulator for the Media.

Andra Siibak is senior research fellow of media studies in the Institute of Journalism and Communication at the University of Tartu, Estonia, and part-time PhD research fellow in communication, media and IT at Södertörn University, Sweden. Her present research interests focus on generations and the mediation of children's new media use.

José Alberto Simões holds a PhD in sociology from the Faculty of Social Sciences and Humanities at the New University of Lisbon (FCSH-UNL), where he is an assistant professor in the Department of Sociology. He is also a researcher at CESNOVA (FCSH-UNL). His main research areas include the sociology of culture, youth cultures and communication and media.

Nathalie Sonck is senior media researcher in the Time, Media and Culture research group at the Netherlands Institute for Social Research/SCP, The Hague. She specialises in research on media use, and in particular the consequences of internet use by young people, their digital skills and the role of parental mediation.

David Smahel is associate professor at the Institute of Children, Youth and Family Research, Masaryk University, the Czech Republic. He is editor of *Cyberpsychology: Journal of Psychosocial Research on Cyberspace* and has co-authored *Digital youth: The role of media in development* (Springer, 2011).

Elisabeth Staksrud is a research fellow at the Department of Media and Communication at the University of Oslo, Norway, researching digital risks, rights and regulations. She has a long international track record in practical policy, awareness and dissemination work on internet safety, and has coordinated and participated in several European Union-funded awareness projects.

Gitte Stald is associate professor at IT University, Denmark. Her main research areas are digital media cultures and social change, with a focus on mobile media and on digital youth cultures. Her recent research projects include Global Media Cultures 1999-2001, Youth, Digital Media and Learning (MacArthur Foundation) 2006-07, Mobile Content Lab 2004-06 and EU Kids Online 2006-14.

Annikka Suoninen is senior researcher in the Research Centre for Contemporary Culture at the University of Jyväskylä, Finland. Her work focuses on the social uses of different media in the lives of children and young people and the role of media in civic participation among youth. She has taken part in several national and international research projects on children, young people and the media.

Liza Tsaliki is assistant professor in the Faculty of Communication and Media Studies, at National and Kapodistrian University of Athens, and a visiting senior fellow at the London School of Economics and Political Science. Her areas of interest are children and new technologies, the porn industry, celebrity culture and online activism.

Laura Ustinavičiūtė is a doctoral student and lecturer in the Department of Psychology at Mykolas Romeris University, Lithuania. Her research interests lay in legal psychology. Her work focuses and concentrates on risk factors of criminal behaviour, recidivism, cyberbullying and its effects on children and young people's emotional well-being.

Sofie Vandoninck is a junior researcher in the Centre for Media Culture and Communication Technology at Catholic University of Leuven, Belgium. She is currently preparing a PhD on vulnerable children online.

Anca Velicu is senior researcher in the Institute of Sociology at The Romanian Academy, and researcher at the Media and New Technologies Studies Center, University of Bucharest, Romania. Her main interests include the sociology of the media, uses of information and communications technology (ICT), children and the media.

Cecilia von Feilitzen is scientific coordinator of The International Clearinghouse on Children, Youth and Media at Nordicom, University of Gothenburg, Sweden. She is professor in media and communication studies at the University of Södertörn, Sweden. She has published about 250 research reports, articles and books, many of which focus on children and the media.

Rita Žukauskienė is professor of psychology in the Department of Psychology at Mykolas Romeris University, Lithuania. She is author or editor of four books and many academic articles and chapters, including *Developmental psychology* (1996), *Psychology of criminal behavior* (2006), *Interpersonal development* (edited, with Brett Laursen, Ashgate, 2007) and *Bridging the gap between psychology and law: International perspectives* (edited, with David Canter, 2008, Ashgate).

ONE

Theoretical framework for children's internet use

Sonia Livingstone and Leslie Haddon

Introduction

Childhood is rarely viewed neutrally. Although strongly shaped by the past, childhood in the early 21st century is very different from the one that adults today remember. Looking into the face of a child seems to enable a 'gaze into the future'. It is no wonder, then, that ideas about childhood, including those expressed in academic contexts, are framed by hopes and anxieties, and by the tension between perceptions of continuity and change. Many features of social, political and economic life have altered, even transformed, childhood in recent decades, and each of these changes has been tracked by academic research, influenced by policy making and reflected on by the public. However, one recent change has grabbed the headlines, setting the agenda for debate about society's hopes and anxieties as well its many uncertainties regarding the degree and nature of change.

The 'digital revolution' – widespread access to personalised, interactive, convergent, ubiquitous technologies for networking information and communication processes – is accompanied by anxious speculation regarding the so-called digital generation, digital youth, digital natives, digital childhood. Notwithstanding the excessive hyperbole of the media coverage, the sense of being 'on the cusp of a new sociality' (Golding, 2000, p 166) is palpable. However, much of this speculation is not as naively technologically determinist as it is often made out to be, as it is generally understood that fundamental social, political and economic changes have shaped and made possible the particular 'digital' environment in which children now grow up. Where early commentators appeared to regard technological developments as not only influential but also inevitable, it is now understood that particular economic, political and cultural processes drive innovation in technology and marketing, and that these processes are in turn subject to influence and intervention. Commenting on global changes in late modernity, Beck (1986/2005, p 15) observes that 'a new twilight of opportunities and hazards [is coming] into existence – the contours of the risk society'. In the risk society, he argues, we are:

> ... concerned no longer exclusively with making nature useful, or with releasing mankind from traditional constraints, but also and essentially with problems resulting from techno-economic development itself....Questions of the development and employment of technologies ... are being eclipsed by questions of the political and economic "management" of the risks of actually or potentially utilized technologies. (p 19)

Moreover, these questions are experienced as pressing at all levels of society – from the state and also the growing array of supra-state organisations, down to the level of individuals. The downside of promoting individual empowerment, rights and autonomy, Beck argues, is that the adverse consequences of making poor choices (often in circumstances of insufficient or misleading information) fall increasingly on individuals, resulting in a disproportionate burden on those least resourced to cope. The internet, we suggest, represents a prime case in point. It is, crucially, a product of society, invented, shaped, monetised and promoted by major media conglomerates in order to bring a rich information and communication environment to many. But the consequences, albeit often unintended, of its thorough embedding in everyday life pose a source of considerable worry and fear among the many ordinary people who cannot exactly understand it, judge the quality of what it offers or anticipate the outcomes of their practices of use. What, then, do we know about the positive or negative experiences of families as they embrace the diverse modes of communication and interaction enabled by mass adoption of the internet?

This volume

As signalled by its title, this book examines the fascinating, but often fraught, relation between children, risk and the internet. Distinctively, it integrates multidisciplinary approaches to theory with a substantial body of new evidence and a considered effort to draw out nuanced policy implications. These policy implications are nuanced insofar as we are careful to avoid grandly universalistic assumptions about childhood or the digital because cultures and contexts matter, as amply revealed by the evidence base that grounds our work. The implications are also nuanced insofar as we hold that 'safety' is an important but not predominant concern: we argue that protection must be balanced against enabling children's rights, pleasures and opportunities, including the opportunities for risk-taking.

Our analysis is based on a unique in–depth survey conducted in 25 countries. It complements what has been, until now, a largely US body of work leading worldwide discussions regarding children and online risks.[1] The EU Kids Online survey was conducted by a network of over 100 researchers from diverse academic disciplines, with diverse methodological and professional expertise. The members of the network worked together first to scope the contours of the field, its strengths and gaps, and its methodological challenges and policy priorities (Hasebrink et al, 2009; Livingstone and Haddon, 2009; Staksrud et al, 2009), on which basis we designed and conducted a survey of 25,000 internet-using children (in 25 countries and as many languages) aged 9-16, who were interviewed at home, face-to-face. The collaborative effort required gives coherence to the project and to this book. However, the network members are not represented by a single voice, and the chapters in this volume testify to the debates over approach and focus that serve to illuminate the analysis of children and youth as they embrace the internet within their everyday lives, to a greater or lesser degree, for better or for worse.

The chapters in this book reveal the similarities and differences in the findings for children, contexts and countries, and in the policy responses; similarities enable the sharing of best practice while differences caution against the wholesale import of solutions from one context to another. We locate our project within three core debates emerging in the digital age regarding, first, childhood as crystallised in the debate over 'digital natives'; second, risk (too often framed in terms of moral panics rather than sober analyses of harm); and, third, responsibility (with 'multi-stakeholder' alliances claiming rather more than they deliver). This chapter concludes by proposing a working model to integrate theory, findings and policy and, thus, to guide future research.

Digital transformations: all change in the lives of children?

It is important first to address the broader discussions surrounding contemporary childhood that form the backdrop to the chapters that follow. Claims about the emergence of a 'digital generation' (Buckingham, 2006) or about children being 'digital natives' (Prensky,

2001; cf Helsper and Eynon, 2010) suggest that a revolutionary change of some kind is afoot. Undoubtedly the current generation of children has to deal with – often with relish – 'new' situations consequent on technological change. Social networking sites pose new questions about the social norms to be considered in relation to 'friends', 'best friends' and 'deletion' of friends as children learn to manage the amplified social dramas that occur online (boyd and Hargittai, 2010). Learning no longer requires a trip to the library, but rather, searching, navigating and evaluating on the internet, skills that are unfamiliar to many parents. Photo albums, birthday wishes, diaries, records of conversations and more are put online – nothing is lost, although it may be regretted.

Yet, fascinating as networked digital technologies may be, especially as they become ever more convergent, mobile and individualised, a sober assessment of the magnitude, nature and significance of changes in childhood generally points less to technology and more to sociohistorical shifts (Livingstone, 2009). In the 1950s, a youth culture emerged out of the coincidence of the smaller nuclear family, the growth of consumer culture, extended years of education and the human rights movement (Coontz, 1997; Cunningham, 2006). The importance of children's rights, to freedom to play and to explore, and the challenge to adult authority have shaped our present-day understanding of children's internet use. This has sometimes resulted in an over-celebratory tone, but has also mobilised the societal resources to support children's educational and participatory prospects in a digital age (Jenkins, 2006).

It seems that some things are, indeed, changing in young people's styles of learning and acting, and that the ways in which knowledge is represented or how pupils prefer to learn are being reshaped by the affordances of the technologies that they engage with and the pedagogic, commercial and peer cultures that contextualise their daily activities. These and other changes shape the appropriation of new technologies, contextualising their meanings and accounting for much of the diversity in their use. However, it is important to remember that the timescale of these changes is longer and far more variable and uneven than claims of a wholesale transformation might suggest. Moreover, continuities in the experiences of children are easily overlooked. In socialisation processes the roles of parents and teachers, and neighbourhoods, friends and cultural values, remain important. Hence, while the digital world may change the manner and expression of these traditional influences, the latter nevertheless continue to be decisive in structuring the conditions under which children act.

In sum, a critical lens is required to address questions about the supposedly radical historical break instituted by the internet. Are children really more digitally skilled than their parents, and does this vary by sociodemographic factors or by country? Just how innovative and creative is this generation of children, and how are their creative activities sometimes constrained by circumstances? It still seems that, for some, the internet is a rich, engaging and stimulating resource, while for others, it remains a narrow, sporadically used one. While some of these issues are addressed in the chapters of this book, the more important point is that this critical perspective on claims about contemporary childhood informs the volume as a whole.

Beyond moral panics: from risk to harm

The second debate that frames our project concerns the conceptualisation of risk and harm. Children's safety gives rise to considerable public anxiety, even moral panic, over childhood freedom and innocence, an anxiety compounded by uncertainty about the power of new and complex technologies and the mass media's tendency to generalise from individual instances of harm. The result is a context fraught with public and policy debate polarised by highly protectionist versus libertarian positions, which, it often seems, impede both analysis and proportionate decision-making. In relation to risk, there is a complex relation between evidence and policy. This is partly because in our previous research we have demonstrated how the evidence base is at best patchy in terms of revealing the incidence and nature of the harms that children can incur online and the benefits of particular policy actions (whether state intervention, industry self-regulation, education initiatives or awareness-raising). While the chapters in this volume aim to help fill this gap through looking at evidence about harm, it is first vital to consider the very nature of risk and harm.

To provide some initial idea of the topics being considered, EU Kids Online classifies the risks of harm to children from their online activities, again adopting a child-centred focus. In other words, as well as recognising the range of risks high on the public agenda, we also consider the potential role of the child and the child's activities in encountering these risks. Starting with the child's perspective permits us to ask questions not only about what the risks are, where they come from or what consequences they have, but also about what in the child's life (in terms of circumstances, motivations or interests) led them to encounter particular risks and how they respond once risks have been encountered (as individuals but also in relation to

5

their peers and family). Thus we distinguish content risks, where the child is positioned as the recipient of, usually, mass-produced images or text (although user-generated content is of growing significance), from contact risks, in which the child participates in some way, albeit possibly unwillingly or unwittingly, and both differ from conduct risks, in which the child is an actor in a peer-to-peer context, again, more or less knowingly (Hasebrink et al, 2009) (see Table 1.1).

Each of these risks has been discussed, to a greater or lesser degree, in policy circles, and some have been the focus of considerable multi-stakeholder initiatives. Crucially, however, while consensus is building about the range of risks, the nature of the harm at stake is not always clear. This may seem surprising, yet it remains the case that the harm associated with any particular risk tends to remain implicit, unstated even in the policy circles designed to address or reduce it. For example, although society tends to be anxious about children's exposure to pornography or racism or the circulation of sexual messages, the nature of the harm they cause, which, presumably, motivates the anxiety, is often ill defined. Does society worry about children's exposure to pornography, for example, because it will upset them in the here-and-now, or because it will damage their sexual development in the future, or because it undermines their childhood innocence, or for some other reason? Not only is the nature of harm associated with certain online risks often unclear but, in addition, the measurement of harm is difficult empirically and also in theoretical terms. Although we draw on research that seeks to assess the consequences of exposure to certain risks, in keeping with our child-centred perspective, in this book our intention is to give children a voice by listening to what they say bothers or upsets them. This reveals an agenda of concerns that does not always mirror that of adults.

Table 1.1: Risks associated with children's internet use (exemplars)

	Content **Receiving mass-produced content**	*Contact* **Participating in (adult-initiated) online activity**	*Conduct* **Perpetrator or victim in peer-to-peer exchange**
Aggressive	Violent/gory content	Harassment, stalking	Bullying, hostile peer activity
Sexual	Pornographic content	'Grooming', sexual abuse or exploitation	Sexual harassment, 'sexting'
Values	Racist/hateful content	Ideological persuasion	Potentially harmful user-generated content
Commercial	Embedded marketing	Personal data misuse	Gambling, copyright infringement

In terms of theory, we recognise that although the word 'risk' can have different connotations, we conceive of it primarily as the probability of harm (Hansson, 2010). Drawing on the commonly used analogy with road safety, of all those children who cross roads, a small percentage will have an accident: the risk (or probability) of harm is calculable and is a function of the likelihood of an accident and its severity. However, this analogy runs into problems when considering the digital world. Among those children who meet new people online, the percentage abused by a stranger is unknown, notwithstanding the instances of criminal and clinical cases. Consequently it tends to be the risk – meeting new people online – rather than the harm, on which policy focuses, and not just to guide or protect (the equivalent of road safety training and traffic management systems), but also to prevent any meetings with online contacts. This stands in contrast to the claim that one of the potential benefits of the internet is that it allows us to expand our social world, including through new online friends.

Certainly, online as well as offline, harm does occur (although for some risks, such as exposure to pornography, it is less clear). But in a context where the harm remains unspecified or elusive, it is important to recognise the difficulty of balancing the harm caused to the few who become victims against the resilience gained by the majority of children who, for whatever reason, learn to manage risk precisely through such exposure. The research reported in the book shows that the probability of harm associated with particular risks online appears relatively low. One further consideration is that the same risk might result in new opportunities (learning about sex from pornography, or making new friends from online contacts). Given that risks do not inevitably result in harm and that risks must always be offset against benefits, research and policy actors clearly need to proceed with caution when intervening to manage the risk factors (which increase the probability or severity of harm) and/or the protective factors (that reduce harm) (Schoon, 2006) in relation to children's internet use.

Multi-stakeholder responsibility for empowering and protecting children online

A third debate framing our project concerns responsibility for online safety. Without gainsaying the power of either political or economic interests, researchers expect evidence to inform the apportioning of responsibility across government, educators, industry, the third sector, families and others, and to guide each category about how to empower and protect children online (Nutley et al, 2007). For complex reasons, different countries have different expectations about whether the primary responsibility lies with government, or with schools or parents. Many also see the industry that provides the content and services with which children engage as being responsible. As noted, the stakeholders face a difficult balancing act between promoting online opportunities, which, without careful attention to safety, may promote online risk, and measures to reduce risk, which may have the unintended consequence of reducing opportunities. Judgements about when and how to intervene will depend heavily on what children themselves choose to do online and, additionally, how they cope when faced with something online that they find problematic, especially with the facility for going online in private places or on mobile devices, beyond the immediate guidance or protection of parents, teachers or even peers. In other words, the more that children are equipped to work out solutions for themselves – through skills, greater resilience or access to online resources to support them – the less others will need to step in to guide or restrict their online activities. Equipping children to cope, however, includes contributions from both parents and all those involved in the internet industry.

Parents have the primary responsibility for meeting the needs of their children, but in relation to the internet, they seem to have been wrong-footed. In relation to familiarity with the new technologies, the generation gap is often significantly reversed, although the research in this volume suggests that this holds mainly in relation to older children. Sometimes, with little personal experience to draw on, parents are unsure about how to support their children's internet use beyond the provision of access. Many parents resort to a range of approaches, and part of the researcher's task is to identify which forms of parental mediation work better under which circumstances. Is talking to their child and taking an interest in what they do effective? Do protectionist measures – setting rules, installing parental controls or monitoring children's activities – actually prevent harm, or do these backfire by reducing opportunities and even inadvertently encouraging the child to be deceitful? Despite scepticism that children will evade parental authority, governments and industry have recommended the latter approach despite the fact that it clashes with many parents' inclinations to trust their child and to believe in his or her capacity to cope. This form of mediation also clashes with the growing tendency for children to assert their rights to privacy and to negotiate ever-earlier independence.

Thus, parents are faced with some complex dilemmas – guiding their children while encouraging their independence, recognising the necessity for risk-taking, but fearing its consequences, asserting their particular values, but expecting the state or industry to step in if things go wrong, hoping that schools will relieve them of the responsibility, but recognising that (many) children feel antipathy towards their teachers. It is increasingly recognised that parents cannot, on their own, undertake the task of empowering or protecting their child online. As we will see, many expect schools to teach digital, as well as other forms of, literacy, yet we need to remember that teachers establish and live out particular relationships with their pupils. Their roles are highly circumscribed – structurally (by school authorities, teacher training and education curricula), normatively (they must treat all children equally and maintain authority relations) and practically (based on lack of time or inadequate technology). In fact, the research in this volume documents the (limited) extent to which children will turn to their teachers in the face of negative experiences online. More generally, the important question then becomes: under what conditions can children, parents and teachers, as well as others who have dealings with children in everyday life, receive empowerment, support and, indeed, protection? At the societal level, empirical findings on the strengths and, especially, the limitations of these everyday actors to manage their circumstances surely points to the imperative for institutional actors (government, industry, civil society and others) to play a complementary and vital role.

A working model for children's internet use: relating opportunities and risks

To bring together the arguments developed earlier, we end this chapter by presenting a working model. This provides a coherent account – a set of hypotheses, in effect – that anticipates how the many factors that shape children's internet use and consequences may be interrelated. Specifically, the chapters in this book develop our previous work (Livingstone and Haddon, 2009) to explore a child-centred approach to children's experiences, perspectives and actions in relation to the internet, contextualising them within concentric circles of structuring social influences – family, community and culture (Bronfenbrenner, 1979). This approach acknowledges the complex interdependencies between the institutions and structures that enable or constrain children's opportunities and their agency in choosing how to act online while negotiating these possibilities and constraints (Bakardjieva, 2005). Only within this wider framework do we formulate research questions associated with the internet and internet use, eschewing the temptation, for reasons explained earlier, to treat the internet as the sole cause of change in children's lives (for example, asking, 'How does the internet affect…?' 'What is the impact of the internet on…?'). Following Bronfenbrenner, although noting that his model can seem somewhat static (rather than dynamic or focused on processes), our working model concerns processes that operate at three levels – that of the individual user, of social mediations (in particular, home, school and peer culture) and third, the national or cultural level (where macro factors such as socioeconomic inequality, educational policy or technological development intervene and shape both social and individual levels, and vice versa).

Thus, while always contextualised at these three levels, and treating both the child and the country as the unit of analysis, the focus of the hypothetical path examined in the chapters that follow is as depicted in Figure 1.1. The analysis begins with the everyday contexts of children's internet use followed by accounts of their online activities. The aim is to identify the risk factors that shape online experience, then – taking nothing for granted – to identify the possible outcomes in terms of either harm as defined by the children themselves, or how they cope with risk so as to obviate harm. Children are all different and thus the analysis foregrounds demographic factors such as the child's age, gender and socioeconomic status, as well as psychological factors such as emotional problems, self-efficacy and risk-taking. Similarly, the social factors that mediate children's online and offline

Figure 1.1: The *EU Kids Online* model

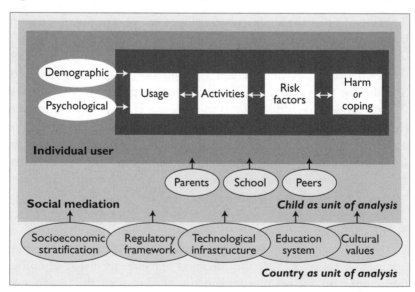

experiences, especially the activities of parents, teachers and friends, as well as an array of national-level factors, also serve to differentiate between children's online experiences, which necessarily complicates the findings reported in this volume.

The model in Figure 1.2 was operationalised in the design of the survey interviews with children, which began by scoping children's internet use (amount, device, location of use), followed by a mapping of their online activities (opportunities exploited, skills developed, risky practices engaged in) and online risks encountered. Children's actions cannot, on their own, be classified as 'beneficial' or 'harmful' – such judgements depend on the outcome of these actions rather than the activity itself. There are some activities that are likely to prove beneficial (for example, schoolwork) and others that seem rather negative (for example, bullying others). However, many are indeterminate (for example, making new friends online), and some involve a blurring of the boundary between risk and opportunity (for example, activities motivated by the desire to take risks, which enables young people to explore the confines of their social worlds, and to learn by transgressing as well as adhering to social norms thereby building resilience).

Children go online in a particular environment: they engage with certain services; the online interfaces they visit have specific characteristics; some content is more available or easier to access; and, crucially, many other people are online simultaneously. These

Figure 1.2: Operationalising the *EU Kids Online* model

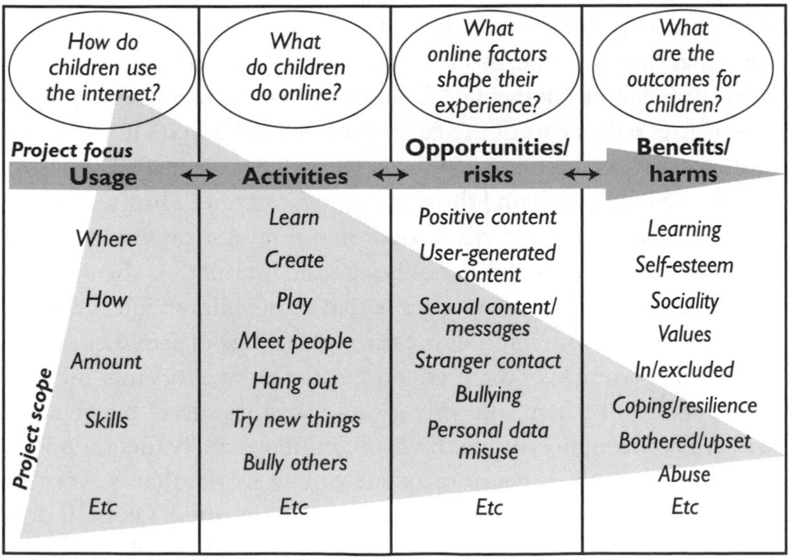

How do children use the internet?	What do children do online?	What online factors shape their experience?	What are the outcomes for children?
Project focus		**Opportunities/**	**Benefits/**
Usage ↔	**Activities** ↔	**risks** ↔	**harms**
Where	Learn	Positive content	Learning
	Create	User-generated content	Self-esteem
How	Play	Sexual content/ messages	Sociality
	Meet people		Values
Amount	Hang out	Stranger contact	In/excluded
		Bullying	Coping/resilience
Skills	Try new things	Personal data misuse	Bothered/upset
	Bully others		Abuse
Etc	Etc	Etc	Etc

Project scope

'environmental factors' interact with the children's activities to shape their online experiences. Some factors, labelled 'opportunities', may enhance the benefits of going online: for example, the provision of own-language creative or playful content, or a lively community of people with the same hobby. Others, labelled 'risks', may increase the incidence or severity of harm: for example, the ready availability of explicit pornography or the activities and opinions of people who are aggressive, racist or manipulative. Some factors are ambiguous: for example, video hosting sites may be fun, creative and empowering, but may infringe copyright rules, exploit intimacy or facilitate hostile interactions.

In the EU Kids Online project it was impossible to tackle all areas in which there may be risks to children, and hence four main risks formed the focus of the study. These were selected both because they attract considerable public and policy interest and also because there is already academic theory and evidence on which to build: encountering pornography, bullying/being bullied, sending/receiving sexual messages (or 'sexting') and going to offline meetings with people originally met online. The project also examined the risks linked to negative user-generated content and personal data misuse, although these have been little studied thus far in relation to children and young people. However, as already noted, risks may not necessarily be problematic and so – as befits our child-centred approach – we allowed the claim of harm (or otherwise) to rest with the child. Finally, the children's online experience of risk, whether problematic or not, was pursued further to understand how children respond to and/or cope with such experiences. To the extent that they do not cope, the outcome may be harmful, but to the extent that they do cope, this is a sign of their resilience.

The shaded funnel in Figure 1.2 illustrates that the focus of the project encompasses only a part of the larger picture of children's internet use. It is important to remember that the latter includes the many benefits of internet use that are beyond the scope of this volume. Thus, the funnel indicates a narrowing analytical focus that does not capture precisely the experience of most children who use the internet. As the chapters in this book show, we can hypothesise that most children in Europe are treading the path from internet use through a range of activities online, but that only a subset of them encounter the risk factors that increase the likelihood of harm, and only a subset of that subset experiences harm as a consequence. While this book more generally focuses on the potentially negative dimensions of the online world, that is precisely because it is addressing policy concerns in the domain of safety; it does not seek to capture an overall picture of children's life online. Hence, the last message in framing this volume is that, in enquiring into the factors that lead a minority of children to experience harm, it should be remembered that for most children, the consequences of using the internet are generally positive.

Note

[1] The 25 countries, which differ slightly from the EU25, are as follows: Austria (AT), Belgium (BE), Bulgaria (BG), Cyprus (CY), the Czech Republic (CZ), Denmark (DK), Estonia (EE), Finland (FI), France (FR), Germany (DE), Greece (EL), Hungary (HU), Ireland (IE), Italy (IT), Lithuania (LT), the Netherlands (NL), Norway (NO), Poland (PL), Portugal (PT), Romania (RO), Slovenia (SI), Spain (ES), Sweden (SE), Turkey (TR) and the UK. Unless countries are specified, findings reported throughout this volume are weighted averages across all countries.

References

Bakardjieva, M. (2005) *Internet society: The internet in everyday life*, London: Sage Publications.

Beck, U. (1986/2005) *Risk society: Towards a new modernity*, London: Sage Publications.

boyd, d. and Hargittai, E. (2010) 'Facebook privacy settings: who cares?', *First Monday*, vol 15, no 8 (http://firstmonday.org/htbin/cgiwrap/bin/ojs/index.php/fm/article/view/3086/2589).

Bronfenbrenner, U. (1979) *The ecology of human development*, Cambridge, MA: Harvard University Press.

Buckingham, D. (2006) 'Is there a digital generation?', in D. Buckingham and R. Willett (eds) *Digital generations*, Mahwah, NJ: Lawrence Erlbaum Associates, pp 1-13.

Coontz, S. (1997) *The way we really are: Coming to terms with America's changing families*, New York: Basic Books.

Cunningham, H. (2006) *The invention of childhood*, London: BBC Books.

Golding, P. (2000) 'Forthcoming features: information and communications technologies and the sociology of the future', *Sociology*, vol 34, no 1, pp 165-84.

Hansson, S.O. (2010) 'Risk: objective or subjective, facts or values', *Journal of Risk Research*, vol 13, no 2, pp 231-8.

Hasebrink, U., Livingstone, S., Haddon, L. and Olafsson, K. (2009) *Comparing children's online opportunities and risks across Europe: Cross-national comparisons for EU Kids Online*, London: London School of Economics and Political Science.

Helsper, E. and Eynon, R. (2010) 'Digital natives: where is the evidence?', *British Educational Research Journal*, vol 36, no 3, pp 502-20.

Jenkins, H. (2006) *An Occasional Paper on digital media and learning. Confronting the challenges of participatory culture: Media education for the 21st century*, Chicago, IL: The John D. and Catherine T. MacArthur Foundation.

Livingstone, S. (2009) *Children and the internet: Great expectations, challenging realities*, Cambridge: Polity Press.

Livingstone, S. and Haddon, L. (eds) (2009) *Kids Online: Opportunities and risks for children*, Bristol: The Policy Press.

Nutley, S.M., Walter, I. and Davies, H.T.O. (2007) *Using evidence: How research can inform public services*, Bristol: The Policy Press.

Prensky, M. (2001) 'Digital natives, digital immigrants', *On the Horizon*, vol 9, no 5, pp 1-2.

Schoon, I. (2006) *Risk and resilience: Adaptations in changing times*, New York: Cambridge University Press.

Staksrud, E., Livingstone, S. and Haddon, L. et al (2009) *What do we know about children's use of online technologies? A report on data availability and research gaps in Europe*, EU Kids Online, London: London School of Economics and Political Science.

TWO

Methodological framework:
the EU Kids Online project

Anke Görzig

A range of methodological challenges accompanies survey research, from specification of the research questions and associated measurements, to minimising coverage, sampling and response errors. Cross-national surveys need a balance to be struck between standardisation and use of culture-specific or appropriate techniques. In addition, all projects have practical and financial restrictions. This chapter offers an overview of the data set and methodological approaches adopted for the EU Kids Online project.

Questionnaire design includes content and response formats. The process of sampling and survey administration is described in this chapter, followed by fieldwork procedures and research ethics. The sampling, data entry and coding were conducted by a single agency to guarantee consistency of procedures across countries. To oversee national agencies and integrate feedback from national network members of EU Kids Online, nation-specific methods were employed (see Ipsos/EU Kids Online, 2011). The structure of the data set is described (see the Appendix at the end of the book for the key variables), including relations among country-level sampling and fieldwork variables. All methodological decisions imply some degree of error; there were also variations in the application of the research methodology across countries, thus, interpretation of pan-European or country differences should be made with caution.

Questionnaire development

Questionnaire development involves considerations of aspects such as wording of questions, response formats, comprehensibility and length. Designing a questionnaire to be administered to children in different age groups, from different cultural backgrounds, who speak different languages, is especially complex (cf Lobe et al, 2008). The questions must be age-appropriate, and should comply with ethical guidelines.

Comprehensibility for the range of different age and language groups is important for reliability and validity of responses. Those involved in the project – often members of a multinational and multidisciplinary network – need to be satisfied with the end product. The EU Kids Online II questionnaire took account of all these aspects and was developed within the overall theoretical framework outlined in Chapter 1. Children were interviewed face-to-face to obtain responses to questions in most sections of the questionnaire, and were then given the most sensitive questions in a questionnaire form for them to complete on their own. For each child, one parent/carer[1] was also given a questionnaire with a selection of questions that matched the questions in the child survey. The sections in the resulting three questionnaires are outlined below (asterisked items indicate the child–parent matched questions). An additional screening questionnaire was used to obtain sociodemographic information about the household and its internet use.

- Interviewer-administered child questionnaire (face-to-face), covering:
    - patterns of child's internet usage★ and activities online
    - digital skills
    - perceptions of parent's/carer's, teachers' and friends' mediation of online risks★.

- Self-completion child questionnaire (simple version for 9- to 10-year-olds, more complex version for 11- to 16-year-olds[2]), covering:
    - psychological factors
    - risky offline activities
    - experience of online risks★
    - coping with online risks
    - sources of education, advice and support.

- Interviewer-administered parent questionnaire (face-to-face), covering:
    - additional and repeated household demographics and internet access
    - parental patterns of internet usage★
    - perceptions of the child's internet usage and exposure to online risks★
    - parental mediation of the child's online risks★
    - sources of parental education, advice and support.

Most questions were multiple choice or used Likert-type response scales; some were open-ended. Assessment of risk and harm followed the child-centred approach outlined in Chapter 1, that is, they asked about the child's experience and perceptions. The questionnaire design applied a global approach but focused on online risks, four in particular – sexual images, bullying, sexual messages and new contacts – with matching questions for risk experiences to assess occurrence, frequency and types of risk experiences. Generally, pre-existing measures were adapted; in some cases new questions were designed. To keep the questionnaire to a length that children could cope with, some topics that are not the direct focus of this study were not investigated in depth, and some existing measures were reduced (for example, online opportunities, psychological measures). However, these reductions were kept to a minimum in order to maintain reliability and validity.

Cognitive testing is a valuable tool to ensure construct validity of survey measurement instruments (do they measure what they are intended to measure?) and compliance with ethical guidelines. Two phases of cognitive testing were applied to the survey (see Chapter 3 in this volume and Haddon and Ponte, 2010). Cognitive testing involved asking respondents about their understanding of the questions, the decision-making processes involved in selecting responses and whether or not certain questions made them feel uncomfortable in any way.

The first phase of testing was the English language master questionnaires that were administered to 14 children and 6 parents/carers across sociodemographic groups. After making several amendments the questionnaires were translated into the 24 languages.

The second phase of cognitive testing involved 113 interviews conducted in all the languages other than English. Nine- to ten-year-olds were over-sampled, because it was expected they would experience the greatest difficulties with responding to the questionnaire. Comprehensibility of questions and interpretation across languages and cultures was addressed in this phase of the testing. Several major changes were made to the questionnaires. Some questions were eliminated to reduce the length; routing was changed to reduce complexity; and the wording was changed in some languages to ensure greater comparability.

One of the difficulties in cross-national survey research relates to questions asking for subjective responses, such as attitudes and emotions (see Jowell et al, 2007). In the EU Kids Online survey this difficulty was mainly the assessment of *harm* for which the final English language version introduced feelings related to harm through phrases such as 'bothered', 'upset', 'worried' and 'uncomfortable'. The word 'upset' was used in the rating scales. However, translations of these terms are associated with different meanings and different emotional intensity in other languages. To keep cross-national differences in interpretation of the measures to a minimum, a list of concepts where correct translation was crucial was compiled, with input from network members to ensure the most comparable terms and most relevant national examples were used. However, the existence of country differences in conceptions of harm should be borne in mind.

The final questionnaire was piloted in 102 interviews involving five countries, to test final questionnaire length, respondent cooperation and intended fieldwork implementation methods. A few amendments were made.

Selecting a representative sample of children who use the internet

Several decisions have to be faced when creating a cross-national sample with the aim of being representative as a whole but also for each country that is included. On the one hand, the sample distribution should be proportionate to the actual distribution in the population; on the other hand, the sampling of smaller countries, regions and minority groups needs to ensure precision of estimates when compared to other groups. Should, then, sample sizes be the same across countries, or proportionate to the countries' populations? Should the sampling methods be the same in each country at the expense of national response rates, or be adapted to national customs but enhance sources for cross-national differences, at the expense of comparability? There is always a trade-off between the national optimum and cross-national comparability. The EU Kids Online methods aimed at striking a balance between these two aspects, by adopting procedures intended to maintain, as much as possible, a precise estimation of the differences between countries and to allow statistical analyses of under-represented groups, while ensuring representative estimates.

Sampling

A representative sample of about 1,000 internet-using children aged 9-16 and one of their parents or carers, from each of the 25 European countries, was selected. The overall sample size was 25,142. A three-stage (sampling points, addresses, individuals) random probability clustered sample was achieved. Details of the sampling process are outlined below.

Given that the target population of children *who use the internet* was unknown, the *sampling frame* started with a known population base taken from national registers, that is, the general population in most countries, and the population of children aged 9-16 in some. Using complete and official registers of geographical units, country regions were stratified to ensure that smaller geographical and rural areas were included. From each stratum (that is, area identified in the stratification process), random *sampling points* were selected with a selection probability proportionate to the number of children aged 9-16 living in the area. Different address selection methods imply different degrees of sample representativeness. Alternate address selection methods were chosen for some countries (see the next section), hence the number of sampling points differs by country, ranging from 16 in Norway to 350 in Slovenia.

A random probability sampling approach was employed to select addresses to be contacted. In most cases the *random walk technique* was used which results in random selection of a *seed address* from each sampling point. Interviewers were instructed to make contact at the seed address and the four neighbouring addresses, and to follow a pre-defined route before selecting the next five neighbouring addresses, and so on. In order to exploit best practice of address selection in each country, in some countries random walk was complemented by pre-selecting households from national registers and/or using telephone rather than face-to-face recruitment. Contact was made using the means deemed most appropriate for the particular cultural context and bearing in mind the topic and the need for a good response rate.

On first contact the interviewer *screened* the selected address to establish whether the household was *eligible*, that is, whether it included a child aged 9-16 who used the internet. The interviewer had to rely on the responses obtained from the person answering the door or the telephone. Therefore, a very inclusive definition of internet use was employed in the screening questionnaire: 'Could you please tell me if they [each of the children aged 9-16 living in your household] use the internet or not, whether at home, or elsewhere?'. If there was more than one eligible child, the interviewee was selected randomly using the nearest birthday method. The parent/carer interview was conducted with the parent/carer who knew most about that child's internet use; in about three quarters of cases, this was the mother, in a fifth it was the father, and in about one in 20 it was another household member.

Response rates

The interviewers needed to complete the following steps to achieve an interview: make contact at the selected address (up to four attempts), obtain consent for the screening questionnaire and establish whether at least one child aged 9-16 lived at the address and was using the internet, and then obtain consent for the child and parent/carer interviews (see Figure 2.1). These steps are part of the calculation of final response rates.

Contact, cooperation and response rates were calculated in accordance with standard definitions (AAPOR, 2008). It was estimated that in 53 per cent of interviewers' attempts to contact an eligible address (that is, a residential address with at least one child aged 9-16 who uses the internet), this was successful (*contact rate*). Contact rates ranged from 31 per cent in Germany to 89 per cent in Romania. In 79 per cent of the estimated eligible cases, when contact was made, the interviews were completed (*cooperation rate*), with a rate of 36 per cent in the Netherlands to 100 per cent in Poland[3] and Greece. The estimated overall *response rate* was 42 per cent of all potentially eligible cases (regardless of successful contact). Response rates ranged from 17 per cent in the Netherlands to 83 per cent in Romania.

Differences in response rates may be related to differences in sampling methodology and unexplained or unmeasured cultural differences. In Sweden, for example, respondents were pre-selected and recruited via the telephone, possibly explaining the high contact rate in that country (80 per cent). However, the same methodology was used in Norway, and this had one of the lowest contact rates (34 per cent). The low cooperation rate in Cyprus might be due to a lack of respondent incentives, but, on the other hand, the average incentive of €10.50 per respondent, among the highest in the sample, resulted in a low rate of cooperation in the Netherlands, a finding that is in line with past research (see de Heer, 1999; de Leeuw and de Heer, 2002). Note that incentives were offered in 13 countries, in the course of all or part of the fieldwork. The monetary value of these incentives ranged from an average of €1 (Turkey) to €38 (Norway) per household, with a range of €3 to €12 in those countries within the two centre quartiles (middle 50 per cent). Methodological issues mostly explain cross-country differences in response rates, but not in all cases, which suggests unmeasured cultural differences played a role.

Weighting

If the characteristics of those not selected for participation or who did not consent to an interview differed systematically from the characteristics of those who were interviewed, the sample could not be said to be representative. To obtain representativeness, sample composition was compared to an estimate of the composition of the population (all children aged 9-16 who use the internet in the selected

Figure 2.1: Fieldwork steps and respondent mortality

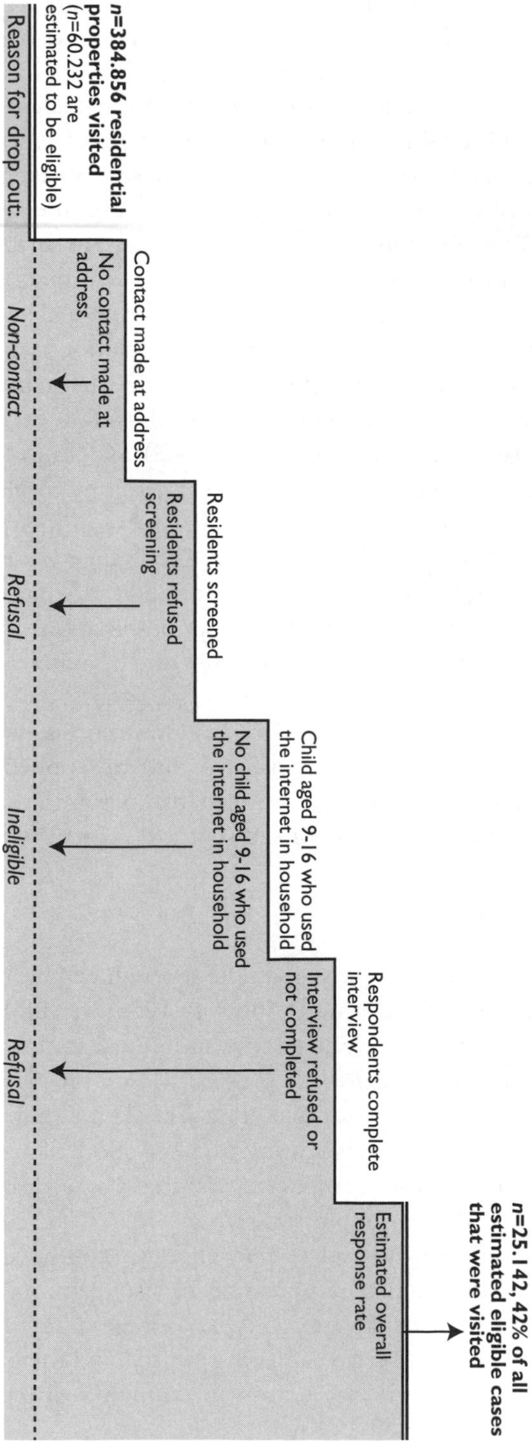

n=384.856 residential properties visited (*n*=60.232 are estimated to be eligible)

Reason for drop out:

Contact made at address

No contact made at address → *Non-contact*

Residents screening

Residents refused → *Refusal*

Residents screened

Child aged 9-16 who used the internet in household

No child aged 9-16 who used the internet in household → *Ineligible*

Respondents complete interview

Interview refused or not completed → *Refusal*

Estimated overall response rate

n=25.142, 42% of all estimated eligible cases that were visited

25 European countries). Those with under-represented traits were given a higher weight and those with over-represented traits were given a lower weight in the data set.

Within each country *design weights* correct for respondents' unequal selection probabilities due to the design of the data collection process, and *non-response weights* correct for varying response probabilities among different types of respondents. Design and non-response weights are combined into a single country-specific weight in the data set, which is used for the analyses of single countries or to compare countries. *European-level weights* correct for the selection of equal numbers of respondents in each country despite differences in country population sizes. The values of European weights are proportionate to the estimated population size of internet-using children aged 9–16 in each country, estimated on data from Eurobarometer (2008) and Eurostat (2002–10). The estimates range from 65 per cent in Turkey to 98 per cent in Sweden, the UK, Finland and Norway. In line with their estimated population sizes Turkey, the UK, Germany and France were given the highest weights and Cyprus, Slovenia, Estonia and Lithuania the lowest weights. The data are then weighted by a combination of country-specific and European weights for analyses on the whole sample of European children.

The EU Kids Online network generally follows a consistent approach to weighting: for descriptive statistics weights are applied to make them representative of the population; for statistical significance testing weights are not applied to avoid biased standard errors.

Effective sample sizes

The *effective sample size* is the actual sample size reduced by an amount that respondents and their answers show to be more similar to one another than they would have been in a simple random sample. The *design effect* indicates the degree of precision lost in a representative relative to a simple random sample. The EU Kids Online data set lost precision as a result of weighting and selection of respondents in clustered geographical areas. Every variable has a design effect; to estimate the effective sample size, design effects were calculated and averaged across key variables. The effective sample size of the approximately 1,000 actual sample size in each country[4] ranged from 473 in Turkey to 784 in Ireland. Due to large differences in the estimated sample population sizes in each country[5] and their associated weights, the actual sample size across all countries dropped to an effective sample size of 8,509.

Fieldwork and ethics

Interviewers and survey implementation

Interviewers were recruited based on their prior experience with interviewing children and the procedures applied. On average about 100 interviewers were employed per country. However, in the two centre quartiles (middle 50 per cent) of the countries the number of interviewers was between 52 and 105. This uneven distribution is due to the unusually high numbers of interviewers employed in a few countries such as Germany (400) and Slovenia (200).

Interviewers were trained locally, and received information about the EU Kids Online research along with detailed instruction books. They were briefed about the questionnaire, its terminology and routing procedures, and the sensitive nature of the questionnaire was emphasised. Interviewers were given a review of ethical protocols associated with child protection, and the need for informed respondent consent was stressed (ESOMAR, 2009). Interviewers were security checked and appropriately trained.

Fieldwork started in April 2010 and was completed by October 2010 (week 26); however, more than half of the countries completed by early July (week 11). Fieldwork was shortest in Romania and Hungary (6 weeks) and longest in Norway (23 weeks). Questionnaires were administered using computers (computer-administered personal interviewing, CAPI) in 11 countries, and were paper-based (PAPI) in 14 countries. The questionnaire sections were presented mostly to the child and parent/carer by the interviewer face-to-face, with the exception of the child's self-completion questionnaire, which contained sections with sensitive questions about experience of online risks. In the CAPI version of this questionnaire routing questions automatically pointed children to the next question/section; the PAPI version required children to follow the instructions in the questionnaire booklet. In both cases the interviewer was on hand to assist the child if necessary. Completion of the child and parent questionnaires took an average time per household of 56 minutes, ranging from 42 minutes in Cyprus to 68 minutes in Estonia.

Research ethics

Research ethics guidelines try to protect individuals' well-being. It is essential that research participants consent to and are informed about the research and its potential risks and the tools available to handle them.

Participants' privacy must be ensured and discrimination or exclusion avoided. The EU Kids Online had to cope with differences in national ethical guidelines, a sensitive survey topic and participants who were mainly minors. Sensitive questions directed to children required clearance from the London School of Economics and Political Science (LSE) Research Ethics Committee; all aspects of the research were in accordance with international ethical research guidelines (ESOMAR, 2009). The following steps were taken to ensure respondents' well-being.

The most sensitive questions were grouped in a child self-completion questionnaire that was not administered to the youngest children (9-10 years). All sensitive questions had a response option of 'prefer not to say' (as well as 'don't know') to allow the child to avoid answering questions that made him or her uneasy. Question routing ensured that no child was introduced to the details of sensitive issues for the first time. Requests for informed consent were given, in writing and verbally, and were worded in age-appropriate language. Respondents were told about the nature of the study and given contact details of the study's representatives (that is, the research and fieldwork company's directors), to consult if necessary. Children and parents/carers were guaranteed confidentiality and anonymity. Child interviews were only conducted after obtaining the consent of the parent/carer and the child.

Interviewers ensured that parents/carers were in proximity while the child was being interviewed, although they were asked to be in a different room from the child being interviewed in order not to influence the child's responses and also to ensure the child's privacy. Some parents/carers refused to cooperate on this latter requirement – interviewers are not permitted, ethically or legally, to insist on the parent's/carer's absence from the room. In 62 per cent of the interviews the parent/carer was present during the child's face-to-face interview (ranging from 15 per cent in Norway to 85 per cent in Turkey). Parents'/carers' presence during the child's self-completion questionnaire dropped to 51 per cent (ranging from 15 per cent in Norway to 72 per cent in Spain).

It was possible that the interview process would reveal a child at serious risk or experiencing harm. If this occurred, the national fieldwork companies had a protocol to follow to determine what action should be taken, in accordance with national law. However, since the most sensitive questions were in the child self-completion section, interviewers did not see the responses before leaving the child's home. However, having the procedure in place was important; had children or parents/carers told interviewers about problems, especially ongoing difficulties, the procedure could have been implemented. To benefit all children, a national language information leaflet, prepared for children and produced by EU Kids Online in association with Insafe, the European Commission's safety awareness-raising network, was provided to children, giving internet safety tips and information on local helplines. The aim was to give children appropriate information and contacts where they could get help if necessary.

To ensure the inclusion of certain minority group members in the study, respondents with language difficulties received support from a household member, the interviewer or, if the child insisted, the parent/carer. Support was provided by another household member in 7 per cent of the child interviews and 3 per cent of parent/carer interviews and in only 0.4 per cent (96 cases) to both child *and* parent/carer, that is, in an average of 10 per cent of cases one or both interviewees received support. In countries with more than one main language, such as Belgium and Cyprus, participants required more support, and the respective numbers were 36 and 25 per cent on average.

Data description

One of the main objectives of the EU Kids Online project was to make data available – to the EU Kids Online network and to the wider research community. Attention was paid to ensuring that the variables in the data set were consistently labelled and coded. The main types of variables are screening, core and derived variables. Screening variables contain selected sociodemographic information about the household and its members; core variables provide data on the survey questions; and derived variables are created or computed from the information derived from the other variables.

The sociodemographic composition of the weighted European-level data set shows an even distribution of boys and girls, with an average age of 12.6 years (SD=2.25). Parent/carer respondents were 80 per cent female, and the average age was 40.7 years (SD=6.53). Socioeconomic status of households was 28 per cent low, 41 per cent medium and 31 per cent high. Household educational status (parent/carer with the highest level of education[6]) was 14 per cent primary level or less, 24 per cent lower secondary, 38 per cent upper and post-secondary and 23 per cent tertiary. Urbanisation (or *rurality*) level was 27 per cent from small, mostly rural areas, 33 per cent lived in areas of medium and 42 per cent of larger size.

Education and occupation of the household's main wage earner were obtained from the screening questionnaire. Country-specific codes were standardised to obtain comparable variables across countries.

Socioeconomic status indicators were derived based on a combination of the occupation and education variables. Socioeconomic status was not evenly distributed across countries – the proportion of respondents with a high socioeconomic background ranged from 12 per cent in Turkey to 82 per cent in Norway, for medium socioeconomic background the range was 16 per cent in Norway to 67 per cent in Italy, and low socioeconomic background ranged from 2 per cent in Norway to 54 per cent in Portugal and Turkey. Hence, any findings related to socioeconomic status could be an indicator of between-country differences and vice versa. Rurality was derived from information about area size or population density at the sample-point level; it was transformed into the classification for degree of urbanisation.

Psychological differences were measured on scales derived or adapted[7] from existing measures for self-efficacy (Schwarzer and Jerusalem, 1995), the Strengths and Difficulties Questionnaire (SDQ) (Goodman, 1997; Goodman et al, 2003), sensation-seeking (Stephenson et al, 2003) and internet addiction (Šmahel et al, 2009).

The data set also contains *paradata, metadata* and *auxiliary data* (cf Nicolaas, 2011). Paradata give information on data collection processes, in this case variables for interview mode (CAPI, PAPI), screening outcome, interview completion, property type, interviewer observations and identifiers for each respondent, household, sample point and country. The technical report accompanying the data set provides information on questionnaire duration times and incentives per country. Metadata are data on the data, such as sample design and question coding, which are contained in the data set variables on sample points, in the questionnaires and in the interviewer briefing documents which contain introductory texts, coding instructions and definitions of complex terms; they are also provided in the technical report which provides information on actual numbers of interviewers per country. In addition, socioeconomic status and education packs provide information on national coding and recoding procedures concerning educational levels and occupational status into cross-national variables. Auxiliary data are data from external sources and include variables for information such as the Nomenclature of Territorial Units for Statistics (NUTS) (see Eurostat, 2010), population density and area size.

Patterns of sampling and fieldwork procedures

In cross-national research projects the methods and procedures used are often chosen to try to achieve a balance between national best practice and optimal cross-national comparability. If procedural differences between countries cause non-random or systematic variations in the data, this is problematic for the interpretation of cross-national differences. In checking for patterns in sampling and fieldwork procedures we found only a few significant relations (see Table 2.1).

To cope with low response rates, more interviewers were employed and pre-selected addresses were used. As expected, the number of interviewers is higher where more sample points were selected. Incentives were higher in those countries where fieldwork took longer; alternatively, when fieldwork seemed to be progressing slowly, the level of incentives was raised. We found also that incentives were lower when there were more sampling points. An unexpected finding was that interview time was longer when incentives were higher. However, this is possibly because in those countries where addresses were pre-selected, (higher) incentives were more likely and interview times were longer.

To further explain these findings, we ran three regression analyses with response rates, incentives, and fieldwork length as the dependent variables and all other sampling and fieldwork variables as well as country size area and number of 9-16 year olds per country as predictors. None of the predictors reached statistical significance, suggesting that the relations become meaningless when other variables are held constant. Figure 2.2 depicts the mostly unsystematic relations between response rate and fieldwork length when using the address selection method. There is a slight tendency for lower response rates to be associated with a longer fieldwork period; however, there are too many exceptions to this association for it to be significant. Similarly, although the random walk method is significantly associated with a higher response rate, there are exceptions of high response rates for pre-selected addresses (for example, Sweden and Turkey).

Since the EU Kids Online II data do not show systematic variation in the relation between sampling and fieldwork procedures, this suggests that any country differences in the data due to cross-national differences in the methodology will be minimal.

It can be said that EU Kids Online data are a unique and representative data set of internet-using children from 25 European countries. These are the first data focusing on children's internet use, and based on sensitive questions about the risks they face online. The data offer the possibility to match each child's responses to the responses of parent/carer, and provide information on different major online and offline risks. Survey quality was ensured through cognitive testing and piloting.

Obtaining the data involved many problems related to cross-national research and ethical issues related to surveying children. Data collection methods were adapted to national best practice; questionnaires were

Table 2.1: Correlations among sampling indicators and fieldwork procedures

	Range	M	95% CI		Correlations						
			Lower bound	Upper bound	1	2	3	4	5	6	7
1. Response rate (%)	17-83	50ª	42	59	1.00						
2. Fieldwork length (days)	43-158	79	67	92	-0.37	1.00					
3. Number of sampling points	16-350	143	114	171	-0.11	-0.26	1.00				
4. Number of interviewers	27-400	99	67	131	-0.41*	-0.17	0.57**	1.00			
5. Incentives (€/household)	0-37.5	4.9	1.5	8.4	-0.33	0.45*	-0.44*	-0.02	1.00		
6. Interview time (min/household)	42-68	56	53	58	0.02	0.03	-0.26	-0.09	0.49*	1.00	
7. Interview mode	0 = CAPI, 1 = PAPI	–	–	–	0.18	-0.19	0.04	-0.21	-0.19	-0.20	1.00
8. Address selection method	0 = random walk, 1 = pre-selected	–	–	–	-0.45*	0.30	0.07	0.27	0.51**	0.52**	-0.08

Notes: * Correlation significant at 0.05 level (two-tailed).
** Correlation significant at 0.01 level (two-tailed).
ª This number differs from the overall mean across the European sample (*M*=42; *n*=25,142) because it is the mean across countries (*n*=25).
Analyses performed at country level (*n*=25); 95% CI: 95% confidence interval.

Figure 2.2: Response rates and fieldwork length by address selection method

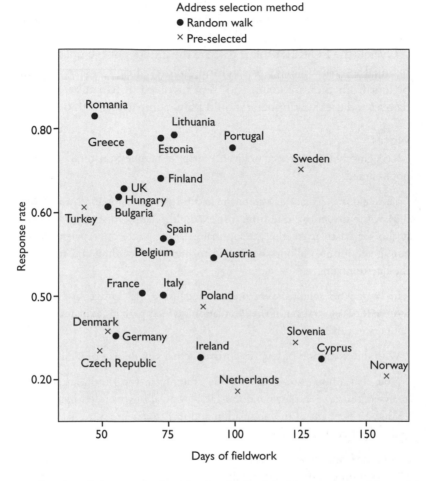

translated and rigorously double-checked; ethical issues were addressed within each nation's child safety framework; questionnaire content and length were balanced without sacrificing reliability and validity of measures; and estimates for a yet still unknown population (that is, children aged 9–16 who use the internet) have been calculated and much more.

Naturally, a cutting-edge research project of such cross-national reach also has some limitations. Reducing the length of the questionnaire meant that less central measures were shortened, and cognitive testing resulted in some of the original questions being excluded. Cross-national equivalence in meaning related to attitudinal and emotional measures cannot be guaranteed and a social desirability bias, particularly in relation to sensitive questions, is difficult to avoid. However, efforts were made to keep any possible biases to a minimum (for example, particular care was taken over translation of attitudinal measures, which were supported by examples, and comprehensibility was thoroughly pre-tested).

Overall, the EU Kids Online data are the product of exemplary cross-national interdisciplinary research on children; future research should benefit from the care taken and steps involved in its realisation. The data set and the questionnaire should allow comparison with other data.

Notes

[1] Recognising the existence of diverse forms of families, a natural parent was not assumed.

[2] The child face-to-face questionnaire had a separate version for 9- to 10-year-olds, without sensitive questions (for example, relating to sex and violence); it also served to make the questionnaire length more appropriate for this young age group. Colours were used to highlight wording and routing in the questionnaire.

[3] In Poland households were pre-selected using the 'Universal Electronic System for Registration of the Population', which perhaps explains the high cooperation rate.

[4] With the exception of Cyprus with an actual sample size of 806.

[5] Note that among the internet-using children in the European countries analysed, those in Turkey's and the UK's populations were estimated to be 15 and 13 per cent of the population and in Estonia and Slovenia were 0.2 and 0.3 per cent respectively.

[6] Education was classified according to ISCED-97 (International Standard Classification of Education) (UNESCO, 2006) and categorised in line with recommendations by the International Telecommunication Union (2010, p 30).

[7] See the Appendix at the end of the book for item selection for the adapted scales.

References

AAPOR (American Association for Public Opinion Research) (2008) *Standard definitions: Final dispositions of case codes and outcome rates for surveys* (5th edn), Lenexa, KA: AAPOR (www.aapor.org/AM/ Template.cfm?Section=Standard_Definitions&Template=/CM/ ContentDisplay.cfm&ContentID=1273).

de Heer, W. (1999) 'International response trends, results of an international survey', *Journal of Official Statistics*, vol 15, no 2, pp 129-42.

de Leeuw, E. and de Heer, W. (2002) 'Trends in household survey non-response: a longitudinal and international comparison', in R.M. Groves, D.A. Dillman, J.L. Eltinge and R.J.A. Little (eds) *Survey nonresponse*, New York: Wiley, pp 41-54.

ESOMAR (European Society for Opinion and Marketing Research) (2009) 'Interviewing children and young people' (www.esomar.org/ uploads/pdf/ESOMAR_Codes&Guidelines_InterviewingChildren. pdf).

Eurobarometer (2008) 'Towards a safer use of the internet for children in the EU – a parents' perspective' (http://ec.europa.eu/information_ society/activities/sip/surveys/index_en.htm).

Eurostat (2002-10) 'Individuals – internet use' (http://appsso.eurostat. ec.europa.eu/nui/show.do?dataset=isoc_ci_ifp_iu&lang=en).

Eurostat (2010) 'Introduction', in NUTS (Nomenclature of Territorial Units for Statistics) (http://epp.eurostat.ec.europa.eu/portal/page/ portal/nuts_nomenclature/introduction).

Goodman, R. (1997) 'The Strengths and Difficulties Questionnaire: a research note', *Journal of Child Psychology and Psychiatry*, vol 38, pp 581-6.

Goodman, R.R., Ford, T.T., Simmons, H.H., Gatward, R.R. and Meltzer, H.H. (2003) 'Using the Strengths and Difficulties Questionnaire (SDQ) to screen for child psychiatric disorders in a community sample', *International Review of Psychiatry*, vol 15, nos 1–2, pp 166-72.

Haddon, L. and Ponte, C. (2010) 'A pan-European study on children's online experiences: contributions from the cognitive testing', Paper presented at the International Association for Media and Communication Research (IAMCR) conference, Braga, Portugal, 18-22 July.

Ipsos/EU Kids Online (2011) *EU Kids Online II: Technical report*, London: EU Kids Online, London School of Economics and Political Science (www2.lse.ac.uk/media@lse/research/EUKidsOnline/ EUKidsII%20(2009–11)/Survey/Technical%20report.PDF).

ITU (International Telecommunication Union) (2010) *Partnership on measuring ICT for development, Core ICT indicators, 2010*, Geneva, Switzerland: ITU (www.itu.int/dms_pub/itu-d/opb/ind/D-IND-ICT_CORE-2010-PDF-E.pdf).

Jowell, R., Roberts, C., Fitzgerald, R. and Eva, G. (eds) (2007) *Measuring attitudes cross-nationally: Lessons from the European social survey*, Los Angeles, CA: Sage Publications.

Lobe, B., Livingstone, S., Ólafsson, K. and Simões, J.A. (eds) (2008) *Best practice research guide: How to research children and online technologies in comparative perspective*, London: EU Kids Online, London School of Economics and Political Science (http://eprints.lse.ac.uk/21658/).

Nicolaas, G. (2011) *Survey paradata: A review*, ESRC National Centre for Research Methods Review Paper, London: National Centre for Research Methods (http://eprints.ncrm.ac.uk/1719/1/Nicolaas_review_paper_jan11.pdf).

Schwarzer, R. and Jerusalem, M. (1995) 'Generalized self-efficacy scale', in J. Weinman, S. Wright and M. Johnston (eds) *Measures in health psychology: A user's portfolio. Causal and control beliefs*, Windsor: NFER-Nelson, pp 35-7.

Šmahel, D., Vondráčková, P., Blinka, L. and Godoy-Etcheverry, S. (2009) 'Comparing addictive behavior on the internet in the Czech Republic, Chile and Sweden', in G. Cardosso, A. Cheong and J. Cole (eds) *World wide internet: Changing societies, economies and cultures*, Macau, China: University of Macau, pp 544-82.

Stephenson, M.T., Hoyle, R.H., Palmgreen, P. and Slater, M.D. (2003) 'Brief measures of sensation seeking for screening and large-scale surveys', *Drug and Alcohol Dependence*, vol 72, no 3, 279-86.

UNESCO (2006) *International Standard Classification of Education 1997* (re-edition) (www.uis.unesco.org/Library/Pages/DocumentMorePage.aspx?docIdValue=144&docIdFld=ID).

THREE

Cognitive interviewing and responses to EU Kids Online survey questions

Christine Ogan, Türkan Karakuş, Engin Kurşun,
Kürşat Çağiltay and Duygu Kaşikçi

Children have only been used as survey respondents since about 1990 (Bell, 2007); before this, it was considered that their responses to questions would not be reliable or valid. More recently, cognitive interviewing has been used to determine what kinds of questions and their phraseology, and with what levels of complexity produce the best possible data quality in surveys of children. Geiselman and Padilla (1988) studied 7- to 12-year-old children and found that cognitive interviews elicited 21 per cent more information than standard interviewing methods (cited in Jaśkiewicz–Obydzińska and Wach, 1995).

   While piloting is common in the methodological development of survey questionnaires, few studies include a cognitive interview component. This chapter explains its application in the EU Kids Online study and provides a content analysis of some of the cognitive interview data. Additional analysis of the responses from the final version of the survey illustrates that interviewing children on sensitive subjects is problematic.

Cognitive development

Although Piaget's (1929) work has been criticised on various grounds, its contribution to a general understanding of children's cognitive development continues to be acknowledged. For example, 7- to 11-year-olds are described as being in the 'concrete operations' phase, in which many experience difficulty with logic (for example, negations), take literal meanings from what they read, and deal better with the concrete than the abstract (Flavell et al, 1993). Applying Piaget's theory to administering surveys, children in this age bracket may find it difficult to understand vague quantifiers, for instance, in questions asking for information about the frequency of their behaviours: they require clear definitions. Partially labelled options should be avoided because children need to interpret and translate options without hints (Borgers and Hox, 2000). Riley (2004, p 374) found that 6- to 11-year-olds found it difficult to recall events that occurred several months earlier, and that short recall periods were subject to a '*telescoping* bias, in which highly salient events and trauma are reported as occurring during the recall period, even when they may have happened much further back in time'.

Piaget (1929) labelled the next development stage 'formal thought'; in this stage children aged 11-15 are able to use formal thinking and manage negations and logic (Borgers et al, 2003). This age group is also able to manipulate hypothetical situations (Conger and Galambos, 1996), hence they find it easier (although cannot be completely relied on) to answer questions accurately. To put this into perspective, many adult respondents provide unreliable responses, especially when they are older or have less education (Alwin and Krosnick, 1991).

Fuchs' (2007, p 2687) study shows that, in general, most of the problems children have with questions are implicit, and they did not tend to use the 'don't know' option. Fuchs (2007, p 2689) concludes that implicit problems are a 'greater danger to the quality of the responses obtained compared to explicit problems', since these problems might go undetected by the interviewer. He also argues that despite attempts to tailor standardised survey questions to children, these questions may not elicit reliable data from both very young children and even 13- and 14-year-olds. Fuchs believes that research into the problems related to children responding accurately to survey questions is in its infancy. Therefore, the EU Kids Online research into children's attitudes and behaviours across so many cultures and languages can be seen as ground-breaking in terms of the scale of its aims and its finding related to cognitive interviewing.

Aims of the chapter

As they were aware of the difficulties related to conducting surveys of children, the EU Kids Online survey designers discussed, in depth, the influence of children's cognitive development before producing the first draft of the questionnaire. This draft version was tested in the UK, using cognitive interviewing, by the market research firm Ipsos MORI, and revised by the designers in the light of feedback. A second round of testing, using 95 of the interview questions, conducted in the other 24 countries in the study, resulted in further revisions.

This chapter presents a content analysis of the results of the cognitive interviews.

RQ1: Does cognitive testing for this study support the results of previous cognitive interviewing research on children and adolescents? Specifically, do younger children have more trouble with abstract questions or those where context is needed?
Do children of all ages have some difficulty in understanding the meaning of questions?

A content analysis was also conducted of some of the answers to questions in the final version of the questionnaire administered in the 24 countries provided by the 9- to 16-year-olds to answer the second research question:

RQ2: Are there differences between younger and older children's perceptions of their peers' internet risk-taking concerns that might be based on their level of cognitive development?

Cognitive interviewing process

Willis (2005) says that several different professionals use mostly cognitive interviewing to evaluate the transfer of information. More specifically, Willis (2005, p 3) describes the technique as being used 'to study the manner in which targeted audiences understand, mentally process, and respond to the materials we present – with a special emphasis on potential breakdowns in this process'. The aim of the EU Kids Online research was to understand cognitive processing, such as comprehension, retrieval of information, judgement and estimation, and decisions related to answering questions. This provides general information about 'how comfortable respondents feel discussing the subject matter, how long the survey is likely to take to complete, and whether the format of the questionnaire is suitable (for example the use of routing and showcards)' (Ipsos MORI, 2009, p 2).

A first draft of the questionnaire was developed by the project coordinators assisted by the EU Kids Online network and an international advisory panel. As reported by Haddon and Ponte (2010, p 5), 'this entailed deciding priorities, working out efficient structures and routing (and avoiding repetition), anticipating problems with answers, etc. At one point the network even participated, as pairs, in a role-play of the interview to discover some of the difficulties that might arise'. As already mentioned, the initial questionnaire was only tested in the UK (with 14 children aged 9-16) and six parents (with a gender and socioeconomic balance). The questions were modified based on general and specific understandings, ambiguity in phrasing and use of technical terms or terms that did not translate across cultures. Explanations were added for some of the critical concepts in the study (such as 'bothered' or 'worried') (Haddon and Ponte, 2010, p 9).

The next set of cognitive interviews was conducted with four respondents from each of the other 24 countries in the study. In 15 countries, only children aged 10 and younger were interviewed; in the other nine countries the samples included all age groups. The outcome yielded five problems: the questionnaire was too long; the children were unfamiliar with certain words – especially those related to the internet; children were embarrassed when asked questions on sensitive topics; there were translation problems with strategic filter questions; and routing was also a problem (Haddon and Ponte, 2010, p 9).

As a result of this feedback, some questions were dropped from the sections of the questionnaire addressed to 9- to 10-year-olds, some for reasons of complexity, and others because parents considered them unsuitable for that age group. Other questions were simplified to make them more comprehensible (Haddon and Ponte, 2010, p 11). The pilot survey was administered to 100 respondents in each of five countries — Germany, Ireland, Portugal, Slovenia and the UK. After some final adjustments, the questionnaire went to the field (Haddon and Ponte, 2010, pp 5-6). The iterative process of revising the questionnaire was tedious, but was critical for producing a final questionnaire that would, as accurately as possible, tap into children's attitudes and behaviours.

Children's understandings of the survey questions

To answer our own first research question, we re-examined the 96 interviews constituting the second trial involving respondents in 24 countries. This involved 95 of the survey questions from which 694 separate comments were elicited – either in the form of quotes from the children's responses, or interviewers' observations of the problems children encountered in trying to respond. These comments were analysed by three researchers. Inter-coder reliability for the cognitive interview data was 0.75, using Miles and Huberman's (1994) formula (total agreements/total codes). This agreement score was calculated by coding the *child's general reaction* because the three researchers had previously determined the types of questions. Miles and Huberman maintain that an agreement score of 0.70 is sufficient. A second reliability score calculated for the open-ended data was 0.81. Although the comments were not classified by respondent age, 16 per cent of the interviewer observations referred to younger children.

Second, content analysis was conducted of the responses to the only open-ended question in the survey. All the respondents were asked if they thought there were 'things on the internet that are risky or harmful for people about your age'. The child was asked to list them on paper and put the paper in an envelope and seal it to reassure the child that his or her list would be confidential. Although this was not part of the cognitive interviewing process, we thought it might reveal problems related to cognitive development, especially to age, and particularly because the question came towards the end of the survey when it would be expected that younger children would be more tired.

RQ1: Respondent age and difficulty in answering questions.

The interviewer was asked to make a general assessment of how well each child had understood the questions in the final version of the survey according to a ranking of: 'very well', 'fairly well', 'not very well' or 'not at all well'. Over half of the respondents were in the ranking 'very well' (52 per cent) or 'fairly well' (40 per cent). When these rankings were examined in relation to the age of the respondents, we found that the level of the child's understanding was positively correlated with age (r=0.34; p<0.001).

More detailed and more direct assessment of how well children understood and processed questions was gleaned from the cognitive interviews conducted in the 24 countries using an early version of the questionnaire. Some of these problems were explicit (see Fuchs, 2007, 2008); for instance, when children stated that they were confused or asked for an explanation or example in relation to particular questions. Other comments were based on the interviewer's observations about embarrassment or unwillingness to answer, or inability to focus and to follow a question that contained filters. Table 3.1 shows that while younger children had the most difficulty in remembering question content and being able to respond to questions, all children had some trouble with understanding the meaning of certain questions, which corroborates the findings from previous research.

Some of the confusions were related to item similarity. For example, one question asked about the devices children used to access the internet. The options included 'Your own PC (desktop computer)' and 'A PC shared with other members of your family'. Children were confused because a shared PC might be the child's own PC, and they could not easily determine which of the answers to select.

Table 3.1: Effects of the questions asked in cognitive interviews by age

	Age group	
	Reported for age 9-10 (%)	Reported for all age groups (%)
Difficulty in understanding	55	63
Loss of focus	6	4
Bothered, unmotivated, not willing to answer	5	2
Embarrassment, silence, parrying	4	11
Difficulty in response	27	16
Needs more explanation or example	3	5

All age levels experienced difficulties with understanding some of the questions (about 63 per cent of children in all age groups). This entailed interviewers re-reading questions and explaining the meaning of the words in more detail. Maintaining attention was harder for younger children, who were more likely to lose focus or motivation, or be unwilling to answer the questions. This is demonstrated by the high percentage of 9- to 10-year-olds who had difficulty remembering the questions (27 versus 16 per cent when all respondents were included). Remembering the frequency of an experience or when it had occurred appeared to present the most difficulty.

As the previous research shows, certain types of questions were a problem for respondents of all ages. Questions related to sexual issues, and questions requiring respondents to be self-critical that asked about experiences of cyberbullying or behaving badly towards someone on the internet, caused embarrassment and silence. The reaction to sexual questions was embarrassment in 56 per cent of the cases where the question caused problems, and 31 per cent in relation to questions calling for self-critical responses. Because, in this early phase, parents were frequently present when their children were being interviewed, they sometimes intervened and objected to questions, and particularly those about sexual subjects. Interviewers were told to ask parents to refrain from expressing any opinions or objections in front of the child.

Children's distress was apparent in relation to sexual questions. For example, some children in Austria were reluctant to answer any such questions. The children were embarrassed by the introductory text. They didn't say it directly – but they rolled their eyes, blushed, etc. One mother didn't want her child to read the questions in this section and felt this topic was not relevant for a young child. The section itself was easy to answer for the children and no major problems occurred. For the younger children it was too much to read and the sentences/ introduction was too long.

Routing or filtering questions were especially confusing for younger children. Questions that directed the respondent to another question if they gave a particular answer were perplexing – the children lost focus or skipped the question because they did not understand what was required. In particular, where there were several questions in a series, younger children tended to skip the whole section. Also, if the instruction was to skip the next question, many children skipped the entire section. The survey included sets of questions examining a particular experience in detail. Sometimes children lost focus and forgot what they were talking about. For example, in response to a sequence of questions related to an experience on the internet, some children had forgotten that the question originally related to online experiences and included offline experience in relation to later questions in the series.

In what follows, we analyse the types of questions and the related problems respondents encountered with each type. Note first that, of the 2,800 comments made overall, 70 per cent did not indicate problems – comments included 'OK', 'no problem with the question', or they left a blank which was assumed to indicate 'no problem with the question'. For the 694 comments (out of 2,800 overall) made in the cognitive interviews, we examined those that indicated problems (see Table 3.2).

Some children had trouble differentiating between the meanings of some words or terms such as 'encouraging', 'worrying' or 'upsetting'. In some languages, direct translations convey different meanings, and some children were confused about what kind of feeling they were being asked about. In 62 per cent of the cases where the words were ambiguous, the reaction was one of bewilderment. Some questions asked the respondents to recall incidents such as: 'I have caught myself surfing when I'm not really interested' and 'I have felt uncomfortable when I cannot be on the internet'. These questions were baffling for many children because they required some advance consideration of their feelings and experience.

Technical terms, such as 'uploading', 'downloading' and 'software', and internet language such as 'social networks', 'instant messaging' or the names of well-known websites, were difficult for some to understand. One example is the use in the draft questionnaire of the word 'avatar' to describe a virtual character; one child understood this as referring to the popular film of the same name. This might indicate that the child did not understand the meaning of avatar in the generic sense. Questions that used technical terms, such as 'download music', called for an understanding of the term and also an understanding of the process of downloading. When children had difficulties with these

Table 3.2: Types of question by child's reaction in cognitive interviews where problems occurred

		Effect of question (%)				
	Difficult to understand – confusing	Loss of focus	Bothering	Embarrassment	Difficulty in response	Needs more explanation or example
Unfamiliar terms (technical or social)	75	1	1	3	13	7
Time, frequency scales	63	1	4	7	21	4
Long intro, long statements, long items	70	6	6	0	14	4
Sexual content	19	5	4	57	13	3
Routing question	48	21	2	7	20	3
Recall question	60	3	2	13	17	5
Ambiguous words or meanings	62	5	4	v4	22	4
Abstract questions	75	0	3	0	13	9
Self-critical	33	8	10	31	19	0
Measuring knowledge	85	0	0	5	15	2
About bad experiences	53	5	3	6	32	1
Expressing feelings	78	0	0	5	15	2

understandings in the cognitive interviews, we referred to this as 'measuring knowledge'.

Every effort was made by the coordinators and the management team in London to address these problems through revisions to the wording of questions and better explanations before the full questionnaire went into the field.

RQ2: Respondent age and perception of risk.

The response rate for younger children was lower than that for older ones, perhaps due to a lack of understanding of the open-ended question, or fatigue given that it occurred near the end of the survey. From the answers provided, 89 per cent identified some kind of content that would pose risk or harm. The remaining answers were excluded from the content analysis. Many answered negatively: 'no' mostly from older children refusing the idea that things on the internet bothered anyone in their age group or 'don't know', or gave an answer not related to anything that could be seen as bothering anyone. The largest proportion of 'don't know' or 'no' answers came from the youngest children (71 per cent). Since we, the authors of this chapter, speak only Turkish and English, we were only able to analyse those responses from Ireland, the UK, Turkey and Portugal (these last were translated into English by the market research company). About 48 per cent of the children responded to the open-ended question. If we take age into consideration, fewer younger children responded. About 11 per cent of their answers did not address risk, and the rest showed that the youngest children (30 per cent of 9-year-olds and 35 per cent of 10-year-olds) responded to the question. Older children showed higher response rates – 60 per cent of 14-year-olds and 59 per cent of 16-year-olds. This is consistent with the cognitive development levels of these age groups.

For each age group, the most frequently listed risks in the open-ended question were similar, although the percentages were higher than for the closed response questions related to risk. Responses were: cyberbullying or insulting someone on the internet (25 per cent), pornographic material presented in visual format or bullying or insulting someone on the internet (25 per cent), meeting with strangers (13 per cent) and seeing or watching something violent (13 per cent). It is not likely to be coincidental that the most frequent items were similar across age categories – the children had been primed through previous questions about these risks in an earlier phase of the project. Child abuse, paedophilia, 'fake things' and drug-based websites were the only items mentioned that were additional to those included in the survey fixed-response questions.

Of interest to the researchers, but somewhat indirectly related to cognitive development, was the influence of social networks on the responses to this question: children who mentioned cyber- or online bullying frequently referred to a social network or messaging services. Several of these references were from children too young for legal participation in these social network sites on which personal information is disclosed. The minimum age of 13 established for Facebook and other social networks is based, at least partially, on a child's cognitive development and skills level. Yet one girl mentioned MSN, 'because my friend at school got upset at a message one of her friends sent her' (UK, female, 11). Another child referred to a social network causing online bullying: 'I think people will get upset by people writing statuses about them. And people could be upset because if you write anything nasty there isn't anything to remove it' (UK, female, 11).

Conclusion

Cognitive interviewing is a valuable tool for improving the quality of survey responses when the respondents are children. In a multi-country study of children exposed to different education systems, different parental styles and different internet educational environments, the researchers in this study are of the view that the time and effort spent on the cognitive interview process resulted in a more accurate assessment of children's attitudes and behaviours. Nevertheless, there are likely to be problems if researchers want to solicit children's attitudes to sensitive topics. It is important for any survey to identify potential underlying problems related to question construction. We would agree with those who call for more study of the nature of children's cognitive development to ensure more accurate results from surveys of this population. This chapter reflects how the *UK Kids Online* survey questionnaire was continuously improved based on the cognitive interview data and the findings in the literature on surveying children.

References

Alwin, D. and Krosnick, J. (1991) 'The reliability of survey attitude response', *Sociological Methods Research*, vol 20, no 1, pp 139-81.

Bell, A. (2007) 'Designing and testing questionnaires for children', *Journal of Research in Nursing*, vol 12, no 5, pp 461-9.

Borgers, N. and Hox, J. (2000) 'Item non-response in questionnaire research with children', *Journal of Official Statistics*, vol 17, pp 321-35.

Borgers, N., Hox, J. and Sikkel, D. (2003) 'Response quality in survey research with children and adolescents: the effect of labelled response options and vague quantifiers', *International Journal of Public Opinion Research*, vol 15, no 1, pp 83–94.

Conger, J. and Galambos, N. (1996) *Adolescence and youth: Psychological development in a changing world*, New York: Longman.

Flavell, J.H., Miller, P.H. and Miller, S.A. (1993) *Cognitive development* (2nd edn), Englewood Cliffs, NJ: Prentice Hall International Inc.

Fuchs, M. (2007) 'Face-to-face interviews with children. Question difficulty and the impact of cognitive resources on response quality', Section on Survey Research Methods, American Statistics Association, Joint Statistical Meetings, Salt Lake City, Utah.

Fuchs, M. (2008) 'The reliability of children's survey responses: the impact of cognitive functioning on respondent behavior', Proceedings of Statistics Canada's International Symposium Series, Symposium 2008: 'Data Collection, Challenges, Achievements and New Directions' (available online http://www.statcan.gc.ca/pub/11-522-x/2008000/article/10961-eng.pdf).

Geiselman, R.E. and Padilla, J. (1988) 'Cognitive interviewing with child witnesses', *Journal of Police Science & Administration*, vol 16, no 4, pp 236–42.

Haddon, L. and Ponte, C. (2010) 'A pan-European study on children's online experiences: contributions from cognitive testing', Paper presented at the International Association for Media and Communication Research (IAMCR), Braga, Portugal.

Ipsos MORI (2009) 'EU Kids Online II: UK cognitive testing report', Unpublished report, 30 November.

Jaśkiewicz-Obydzińska, T. and Wach, E. (1995) *The cognitive interview of children*, Krakow, Poland: Institute of Forensic Expert Opinions (www.canee.net/files/The%20Cognitive%20Interview%20of%20Children.pdf).

Miles, M.B. and Huberman, A.M. (1994) *Qualitative data analysis: An expanded sourcebook* (2nd edn), Thousand Oaks, CA: Sage Publications.

Piaget, J. (1929) *The child's conception of the world*, Totowa, NJ: Littlefield, Adams.

Riley, A.W. (2004) 'Evidence that school-age children can self-report on their health', *Ambulatory Pediatrics*, vol 4, no 4, pp 371-6.

Willis, G.B. (2005) *Cognitive interviewing: A tool for improving questionnaire design*, Thousand Oaks, CA: Sage Publications.

FOUR

Which children are fully online?

Ellen Helsper

Research shows that adults who are disadvantaged in traditional, offline ways tend also to be disadvantaged when it comes to engagement with information and communications technology (ICT) (Warschauer, 2004; van Dijk, 2005; Helsper, 2008). Some argue that this is not an issue for younger generations because they are growing up in technology-rich environments. Tapscott's (1998) distinction between digital natives and digital immigrants reflects this type of reasoning. The belief that all children are fully online is strong, but runs counter to the evidence (Facer and Furlong, 2001; Bennett et al, 2008; Helsper and Eynon, 2010). Work on understanding the differences between young people is scarce since there is hardly any generalisable, cross-national data on the youngest age groups (Cleary et al, 2006). This chapter uses EU Kids Online data to examine the extent to which patterns of inequalities in access are observable among young people. It explores whether differences in access to the internet are related to individual-level factors and if the national context is related to differences in access among different groups of children.

Digital exclusion research

Digital exclusion research has moved from the distinction between access and no access to more nuanced discussions around gradations of inclusion (Warschauer, 2004; Livingstone and Helsper, 2007). For populations where some form of internet access is widespread this is a useful approach. European children tend to have access somewhere; it is therefore likely to be type of access that differs between groups of children. Research shows that the type of access is important for determining how people engage with ICTs such as the internet (Helsper, 2007; Kuhlemeier and Hemker, 2007). Private, playful access is more likely to lead to learning and skills development than supervised and restricted access (Mumtaz, 2001; Ba et al, 2002; Livingstone, 2003). The ubiquity of internet access determines how embedded interaction with this technology is in people's everyday lives (Haddon, 2011). The differences between mobile and fixed platform use is also part of this debate (Ishi, 2004; Anderson, 2005; Smith, 2010). The EU Kids Online survey shows that half (49 per cent) of children access the internet from their bedroom, a private location, and a third (34 per cent) of European children access it through mobile devices. However, there are differences in access privacy and mobility related to gender, age and socioeconomic status (Livingstone et al, 2011).

Digital exclusion research with adults focuses on linking socioeconomic inequalities based on education and income to inequalities in access to ICTs. However, socioeconomic factors are not the only predictors of digital inequalities between adults – gender and age are also shown to be related to digital differences (McCreadie and Rice, 1999a, 1999b; van Dijk, 2005; Halford and Savage, 2010; Helsper, 2010).

National differences in inclusion

This chapter aims first to examine whether the links observed among adults between sociodemographic background and digital inclusion also apply to children in Europe. In Northern European countries, internet use among young people is approaching 100 per cent. The 2008 Eurobarometer study (European Commission, 2008) shows that in countries where internet diffusion in the general population is low, children are also less likely to be online. The Eurobarometer study is not sufficiently detailed to explain country differences and, unlike EU Kids Online II, it did not ask children directly about their access. It is therefore unclear to what extent societal factors influence the relationship between social and digital inequalities within Europe. Norris' (2001) argument is that inequalities in national resources lead to inequalities in internet diffusion, but problems in existing research prevent this from being tested. Data collection is often limited to one or only a few countries, and even when research is cross-national there is often not enough variation in national-level characteristics to study their effects on the relationship between individual background and digital inequalities. Thus this chapter also aims to understand whether the link between young people's sociodemographic backgrounds and internet access is similar across countries, and whether differences map onto differences in national socioeconomic and ICT characteristics.

Measuring access

In the EU Kids Online survey, one set of questions focused on access platforms ('Which of these devices do you use for the internet these days?') and the other on access locations ('Please tell me where you use the internet these days'). Ubiquity of access was measured by summing the locations and, separately, the platforms used. Besides access ubiquity, the extent to which access was supervised (or private) and mobile (or fixed) is important. Two additional measures were constructed to examine the level of privacy in home access (0 = 'no home access', 1 = 'access in a shared space at home', 2 = 'access in the bedroom') and the sophistication of mobile access (0 = 'no mobile access', 1 = 'access on a simple mobile phone', 2 = 'access on a smart phone').

National-level characteristics corresponding to the most frequently identified factors related to digital inequality among individual adults (that is, education, age, income and gender) were selected from United Nations (UN) statistics (UNDP, 2009) as indicators of country resources and inequalities. Resource indicators related to education (average years of schooling), age (proportion of the population below the age of 14) and income (GDP).[1] National-level inequality indicators are related to gender (gender gap index) and income (Gini index). Diffusion of internet use in each country (Eurostat, 2010) was incorporated as a national-level digital resource indicator. Using these indicators the following questions will be answered:

RQ1: Is there a pattern in the relationship between age, gender and household education level, and access in Europe?

RQ2: Do differences in the relationships between individual-level sociodemographic characteristics and access map onto national-level characteristics?

The hypothesis is that individual-level differences are most strongly related to corresponding national-level sociodemographic inequalities. That is, national differences in access between boys and girls are hypothesised to be most strongly related to national-level gender inequalities. Similarly, differences between children from households with highly and less highly educated parents should be largest in countries with fewer educational resources and higher income inequalities; also, more tentatively, differences between younger and older children might be most strongly related to national population distributions.

Findings

To answer the first question, we conducted linear regressions using ubiquity, privacy and mobility of access indicators as the outcome variables.

Table 4.1 shows that, in Europe, education, age and gender have a significant impact on all the access indicators: children from better-educated households, boys and older children have access to more locations and platforms, have more private access at home and more sophisticated mobile access. For all types of access, age is the strongest predictor, followed by education and gender.[2]

Figure 4.1 shows that the effect of education on private and mobile access among young people varies considerably in Europe. In eastern Europe (Estonia, Bulgaria, Romania and Hungary) and Turkey, the relationship between education and level of privacy of home access is stronger than in the rest of Europe. Children from better-educated households are more likely to have private access (in their bedrooms). In Estonia and Bulgaria the link with mobility is also strong. In most countries in northern Europe the relationship between education and mobile access is also strong: children whose parents have higher education have access to more sophisticated mobile platforms.

Other clusters of countries are less easily geographically defined. In some southern (Spain, Greece and Portugal) and eastern (Slovenia and the Czech Republic) European countries, and Ireland, the relationships between education and access are relatively weak, although children with higher educated parents tend to have more private access. In Finland, Italy and Belgium – countries with little in common geographically or otherwise – children with lower-educated parents have more sophisticated mobile access. The same trend for mobility is observed for Denmark, Cyprus and Poland, although in these countries children from higher educational backgrounds have more rather than less private access.

Table 4.1: Linear regressions of different access scales for all European countries

	Locations		Platforms		Privacy of home access		Sophistication of mobile access	
	b	β	b	β	b	β	b	β
(Constant)	0.41**		0.41**		0.09**		−0.55**	
Education[a]	0.23**	0.15	0.26**	0.15	0.16**	0.22	0.06**	0.09
Gender[b] (boys)	0.07**	0.02	0.20**	0.06	0.05**	0.04	0.04**	0.03
Age	0.16**	0.24	0.13**	0.17	0.07**	0.23	0.07**	0.23

Base: All children (*n*=25,142) weighted by European weight. ** b sign at *p*<0.001.
Notes: [a] ISCED (International Standard Classification of Education) categories (for parents' level of education) was used: 1 'primary or less', 2 'lower secondary', 3 'upper and post-secondary' and 4 'tertiary education'.
[b] Gender and age of the child were given by the parent.

Figure 4.1: Individual country coefficients for education in relation to mobility and privacy of access

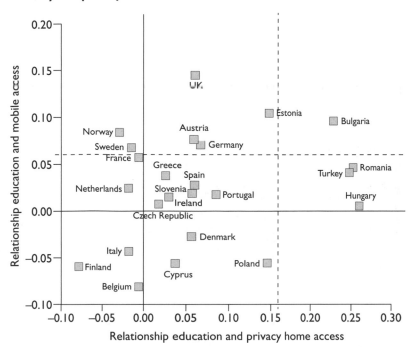

Base: All children (n=25,142) weighted by country weight.*
Note: Interrupted line indicates European average; continuous line indicates no differences in access between different education levels.
* Figures 4.1 and 4.2 depict the coefficients from regressions that control for the other two socio-demographic variables.

Figure 4.2 confirms that in most countries boys have more private home access than girls. The results for mobility are less clear-cut, with most countries close to the 'no relationship' line and clusters are less obvious. Ireland and the Czech Republic stand out for girls having more private and more mobile access than boys. In the Nordic countries (Denmark, Norway and Finland) and Austria girls have less mobile access than boys. Turkey is notable for disparity in private home access: girls are far less likely than boys to have private access at home although there are almost no differences for mobile access. The remaining countries are clustered around the European Union (EU) average, which tends towards no differences in mobile access and boys having more private access at home than girls. The latter is strongest in Germany, Lithuania, Poland and Romania and weakest in Belgium, Spain, Slovenia and the UK.

Figure 4.2: Individual country coefficients for gender in relation to privacy and mobility of access

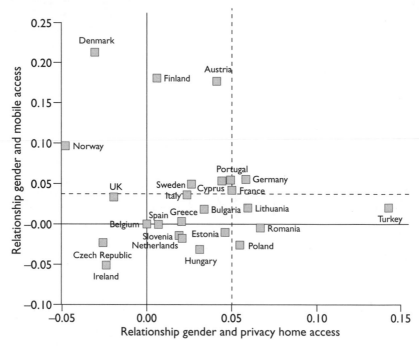

Base: All children (*n*=25,142) weighted by country weight.
Note: Interrupted line indicates European average; continuous line indicates boys and girls have equal access.

Figure 4.3 confirms that older children in Europe have more private home access and more mobile access to the internet. Those countries that show the strongest relationship between age and private home access also show a stronger relationship between age and sophistication of mobile access. Countries where age and access are strongly related include the UK and Norway; relationships in Bulgaria, the Czech Republic, Hungary, Poland, Spain and Italy are weaker.

So far we have seen that there are significant differences in access between different groups of children in Europe, but patterns of digital inclusion are inconsistent across countries. A classification based on country-level characteristics could explain why some countries show larger differences than others for access related to age, gender and parental education.

Figure 4.3: Individual country coefficients for age in relation to privacy and mobility of access

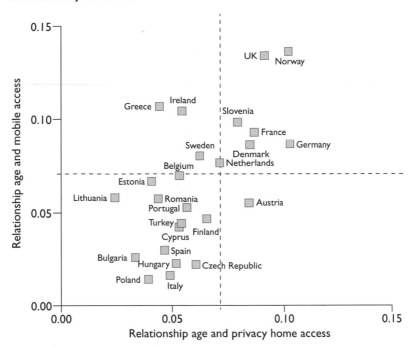

Base: All children (*n*=25,142) weighted by country weight.
Note: Interrupted line indicates European average; the axes indicate 'no relationship' between age and access.

Linking national and individual-level characteristics

This section maps the differences among countries in terms of the relationship between education, gender and age, and private and mobile access, based on national-level characteristics.

The relationship between national-level characteristics and differences among groups at the individual level can be studied by correlating national characteristics with the coefficients in Figures 4.1-4.3. These correlations show that socioeconomic resources and national-level inequalities are variously related to the differences in private access at home and mobile access. Education influences private access less in well-off and more equal countries. Countries with higher GDP, more years of schooling, higher levels of internet diffusion, smaller gender gaps and/or lower income inequalities have smaller differences in private access between children from high and low education households. Gender influences private access less but mobile access more in well-off and more equal countries. Differences between boys and girls in private access are smaller and differences in mobile access are larger in countries with more resources and lower levels of inequalities than in countries with less resources and higher levels of inequalities. Within-country age differences in access mobility and privacy are consistently larger in well-off and more equal countries.

These are general European trends and these relationships might not be valid across Europe. Table 4.2 examines country differences for private home access.

Most of the countries in Table 4.2 appear in those cells that suggest that national-level resources and inequalities are related to corresponding individual-level inequalities. For example, northern European countries (Belgium, Denmark, Finland, the Netherlands, Norway and the UK) have more educational resources and greater gender equality combined with smaller access differences for education and gender groups within the country. At the other end of the spectrum, the southern (Cyprus and Portugal) and eastern (Bulgaria, Poland and Romania) European countries and Turkey have less educational resources and higher gender inequalities combined with larger education and gender differences in access. Countries with more digital resources show smaller education and gender differences and larger age differences in access.

The outliers are interesting. A repeated outlier is Germany that as a country is low on gender inequality and high on internet resources, but shows larger access differences between children with different education and gender backgrounds. The Czech Republic, as a country high in gender inequality and lower in educational resources, shows smaller access differences between children's gender and education groups, while Italy and Greece are exceptional for low levels of diffusion combined with smaller educational differences in access.

Conclusion

This chapter has examined whether some European children are at risk of being excluded from ubiquitous, private and mobile access to the internet and to what extent these inequalities are linked to their home countries' national characteristics. Among European children, there are clear inequalities in access, similar to those found in research on adults (McCreadie and Rice, 1999a, 1999b; Selwyn, 2006; Hargittai and Hinnant, 2008; Helsper, 2010) and research on children within national boundaries (Facer and Furlong, 2001; Livingstone and Helsper, 2007). In most European countries there is a positive relationship between parental level of education and a child's private home access

Table 4.2: Map of country-level characteristics and individual-level education, gender and age relationships with private home access[a,b]

Within-country differences		Average years of education			Gender inequality			Internet diffusion		
		High	Medium	Low	Low	Medium	High	High	Medium	Low
Education differences in access	Largest	DK, ES, IE, SI	EE, LT, PT,	BG, HU, PL, RO, TR				DE, DK, UK	EE, HU, LT	BG, PL, PT, RO, TR
	Medium	DE, UK	AT, CY,					AT, ES, IE, SI	CZ, FR,	CY
	Smallest	EL, FI, NL, NO; BE, FR, IT, SE	CZ					BE, FI, NL, NO, SE	CZ, ES, IE	BG, EL, IT
Gender differences in access	Largest				DE	AT, EE, FR, LT, PT	CY, PL, RO, TR	DE	AT, EE, FR, LT,	CY, PL, PT, RO, TR
	Medium				SE	BG	EL, HU, IT, SI		HU, SI,	EL, IT
	Smallest				DK, FI, IE, NL, NO, UK	BE, ES	CZ	DE, DK, FI, NL, NO, UK	CZ, HU, IE	
Age differences in access	Largest							AT, FR, SI		BG, EL, IT
	Medium							BE, FI, SE	EE, ES, LT	BG, EL, IT, PL, RO
	Smallest									CY, PT, TR

Note: Shaded areas are where countries are expected to be if national-level inequalities and resources predict (similar) differences between sociodemographic groups within the country. Outliers in bold.

a For clarity, this table contains only information on national and individual characteristics that address similar differences. E.g., there is no theoretical reason to expect that gender inequalities at national level predict differences between educational groups in access. These data, therefore, are not reported.

b The table was constructed using tercile grouping. European countries were classified as being high, medium or low for the individual-level coefficients of age, gender and education for access. Terciles were also computed for national-level characteristics related to education resources, gender inequalities and internet diffusion. The 'ranking' of countries in Table 4.2 is relative to the European context, that is, a country that falls within the highest or lowest EU tercile of resources or inequality is likely to be in the middle tercile in a worldwide context.

and quality of mobile access. While gender is less predictive of private access, it is related to mobile access in most European countries. Boys are more likely to have high quality mobile connections than girls. Older children in Europe have more private and more mobile access than younger children. Thus, the answer to the first question posed in this chapter (namely, whether there are inequalities in access among groups of young people at a European level) is yes, not all European children are equally connected. There are differences not only between countries, but also among children within countries. Education and age are important differentiating factors in all European countries. Gender is important in some, but not others. While age differences in access might not be problematic, differences between children from different educational backgrounds or different genders are inequalities that require resolution. The pattern is not consistent across Europe. In general, southern and eastern European countries have larger educational and gender differences but smaller age differences related to internet use than northern European countries.

The second question posed in this chapter (whether these differences among children can be linked to national characteristics) is also confirmed. That is, in general, if a country has more resources (in terms of wealth, education or internet diffusion), or is more equal (in terms of gender or income), then the inequalities in access within the country are smaller. This supports the theory that social inequalities are reflected online (Norris, 2001; van Dijk, 2005; Helsper, 2008; Helsper and Galacz, 2009). This is particularly true for privacy of access. For example, in countries where people have, on average, more years of education, children from less educated households are more equal to their more educated peers in terms of private home access. Similarly, in countries with larger gender inequalities, boys and girls have less equal home access. Surprisingly, within-country gender differences in mobile access are larger in more gender-equal countries. Age also has a different effect: countries with more resources and greater equality show larger differences between younger and older children in both private and mobile access.

The EU Kids Online data do not allow for causal conclusions; this would require longitudinal research that tracked changes in diffusion and online inequalities in parallel with changes in offline inequalities and national-level diffusion policies. Also, internet diffusion and national socioeconomic characteristics tend to be too strongly connected. Therefore, it is difficult to disentangle the effects of internet diffusion initiatives and national socioeconomic circumstances.

The exceptions to the general correspondence between national characteristics and within-country inequalities might signpost the future of countries with low levels of diffusion. The Czech Republic, which has low levels of internet diffusion and high gender inequality, has a *more* equal online world. Since countries with higher diffusion tend to be more equal online as well as offline, it follows that their online equality will not disappear if higher levels of diffusion are forced through policy, as long as offline inequalities decrease in parallel. There was only one country, Germany, where a negative trend (of more inequalities online than offline) was present and the circumstances that lead to this need to be understood to prevent diffusion creating new inequalities in other countries.

Thus, to achieve greater digital equality, diffusion policies must be connected to and interwoven with social and economic policies. Further longitudinal and case study research is needed to establish whether changes to the digital environment can lead to changes in inequalities and resources at the cross-national and within-country level.

Notes

[1] EU Kids Online does not include a household income indicator, only a national-level indicator.

[2] Determined by looking at standardised coefficients.

References

Anderson, B. (2005) 'The value of mixed-method longitudinal panel studies in ICT research transitions in and out of "ICT poverty" as a case in point', *Information, Communication & Society*, vol 8, no 3, pp 343-67.

Ba, H., Tally, W. and Tsikalas, K. (2002) 'Investigating children's emerging digital literacies', *Journal of Technology, Learning, and Assessment*, vol 1, no 4, pp 1-49.

Bennett, S., Maton, K. and Kervin, L. (2008) 'The "digital natives" debate: a critical review of the evidence', *British Journal of Educational Technology*, vol 39, no 5, pp 775-86.

Cleary, P.F., Pierce, G. and Trauth, E.M. (2006) 'Closing the digital divide: understanding racial, ethnic, social class, gender and geographic disparities in internet use among school age children in the United States', *Information Society*, vol 4, pp 354-73.

European Commission (2008) *Towards a safer use of the internet for children in the EU – A parents' perspective* (Flash Eurobarometer 2008), Brussels: European Commission.

Eurostat (2010) *Individuals regularly using the internet*, Brussels: European Union.

Facer, K. and Furlong, R. (2001) 'Beyond the myth of the "cyberkid": young people at the margins of the information revolution', *Journal of Youth Studies*, vol 4, no 4, pp 451-69.

Haddon, L. (ed) (2011) *The contemporary internet*, Brussels: Peter Lang.

Halford, S. and Savage, M. (2010) 'Reconceptualizing digital social inequality', *Information, Communication & Society*, vol 13, no 7, pp 937-55.

Hargittai, E. and Hinnant, A. (2008) 'Digital inequality: differences in young adults' use of the internet', *Communication Research*, vol 35, no 5, pp 602-21.

Helsper, E.J. (2007) 'Internet use by vulnerable teenagers: social inclusion, self-confidence and group identity', Unpublished PhD thesis, London: London School of Economics and Political Science.

Helsper, E.J. (2008) *Digital inclusion: An analysis of social disadvantage and the information society*, London: Department for Communities and Local Government.

Helsper, E.J. (2010) 'Gendered internet use across generations and life stages', *Communication Research*, vol 37, no 3, pp 352-74.

Helsper, E.J. and Eynon, R. (2010) 'Digital natives: where is the evidence?', *British Educational Research Journal*, vol 36, no 3, pp 503-20.

Helsper, E.J. and Galacz, A. (2009) 'Understanding the links between social and digital inclusion in Europe', in A. Cheong and G. Cardoso (eds) *World wide internet: Changing societies, economies and cultures*, Macau: Macao University Printing House, pp 144-75.

Ishi, K. (2004) 'Internet use via mobile phone in Japan', *Telecommunications Policy*, vol 28, no 1, pp 43-58.

Kuhlemeier, H. and Hemker, B. (2007) 'The impact of computer use at home on students' internet skills', *Computers & Education*, vol 49, no 2, pp 460-80.

Livingstone, S. (2003) 'Children's use of the internet: reflections on the emerging research agenda', *New Media & Society*, vol 5, no 2, pp 147-66.

Livingstone, S. and Helsper, E. (2007) 'Gradations in digital inclusion: children, young people and the digital divide', *New Media & Society*, vol 9, no 4, pp 671-96.

Livingstone, S., Haddon, L., Görzig, A. and Ólafsson, K. (2011) *Risks and safety on the internet: The perspective of European children – Full findings*, London: London School of Economics and Political Science.

McCreadie, M. and Rice, R.E. (1999a) 'Trends in analyzing access to information. Part I: Cross-disciplinary conceptualizations of access', *Information Processing and Management*, vol 35, no 1, pp 45-76.

McCreadie, M. and Rice, R.E. (1999b) 'Trends in analyzing access to information. Part II: Unique and integrating conceptualizations', *Information Processing and Management*, vol 35, no 1, pp 77-99.

Mumtaz, S. (2001) 'Children's enjoyment and perception of computer use in the home and the school', *Computers & Education*, vol 36, no 4, pp 347-62.

Norris, P. (2001) *Digital divide: Civic engagement, information poverty, and the internet worldwide*, Cambridge, MA: Cambridge University Press.

Selwyn, N. (2006) 'Dealing with digital inequality: rethinking young people, technology and social inclusion', Paper presented at the Cyberworld Unlimited? Conference, Bielefeld, Germany, 9–11 February.

Smith, A. (2010) *Mobile access 2010*, Washington, DC: Pew Internet and American Life.

Tapscott, D. (1998) *Growing up digital: The rise of net generation*, New York: McGraw-Hill.

UNDP (United Nations Development Programme) (2009) *Human Development Report 2009. Overcoming barriers: Human mobility and development* (http://hdr.undp.org/en/media/HDR_2009_EN_Complete.pdf).

van Dijk, J.A.G.M. (2005) *The deepening divide: Inequality in the information society*, Thousand Oaks, CA: Sage Publications.

Warschauer, M. (2004) *Technology and social inclusion: Rethinking the digital divide*, Cambridge, MA: The MIT Press.

FIVE

Varieties of access and use

Giovanna Mascheroni, Maria Francesca Murru and Anke Görzig[1]

Introduction

The vast array of risks and opportunities that confront children in their daily media practices cannot be analysed in isolation from the broader context in which these practices emerge and become meaningful. Previous research (Livingstone and Helsper, 2007, 2009) indicates that the patterns and social contexts of general internet use are key factors shaping children's online activities and their exposure to risks.

In the EU Kids Online project, the institutional, social and cultural environment co-determining the quality of online experience has been analysed from the perspective of children's everyday lives (Livingstone et al, 2011). Online experience is defined as a pathway composed of the online activities engaged in by children, the online and offline factors that shape the safety of online environments and their harmful and beneficial outcomes.

This chapter focuses on the first step along this path, and analyses the increasing variety of internet access and use experienced by children in Europe. Locations, platforms, experience and the embeddedness of the internet in everyday life are accounted for in order to provide a full picture of the first and the most immediate sociocultural layer in which children's agency is exercised. Insofar as individuals' use of technologies is socially shaped within family and peer relations (Haddon, 2004), this chapter investigates the relationship between place of access, online experience and frequency of use of the internet, within the family's wider technological culture. It examines cross-national variations in patterns of usage and provides a classification of countries.

Emerging trends and cross-national variations

'Thinking holistically' (Haddon, 2003) seems to be one of the most noticeable trends in recent research on media practices. Media are no longer investigated in their individual textuality or as clusters of isolated material practices, but rather as the constituents in an 'ecology' (Ito et al, 2009), that is, as 'an overall technical, social, cultural and place-based system, in which the components are not decomposable or separable' (Ito et al, 2009, p 31).

'Media ecologies' are place- and time-based systems that can be studied from the viewpoint of the temporal and spatial coordinates in which they are rooted. This point is developed thoroughly in the domestication approach (Silverstone and Hirsch, 1992), whose theoretical and empirical insights constitute the framework for the analysis in this chapter. Consistent with the increasing pervasiveness of mobile media, the concept of domestication has been extended beyond the home (Haddon, 2004), to encompass the variety of spatio-temporal settings in which digital media are located. Bearing in mind that each context entails specific cultural and relational dynamics, patterns of use are taken into account as the preliminary, although not exhaustive, markers of the diverse media ecologies that shape children's online experiences.

The most notable trend in the process of domestication of the internet in Europe is the increasing privatisation of access – that is, children's unrestricted and unsupervised access through personal and/or mobile devices – and the growing incorporation of the internet into daily routines. In the EU Kids Online survey children were asked whether they used the internet in their 'own bedroom or any other private room' (private access) and 'How often do you use the internet?'. Figure 5.1 shows the positions of countries according to the percentages of children who accessed the internet from their bedrooms or another private room in the home, and the percentage of children who use the internet daily. Groups of countries with similar internet use can be identified.

The largest group of countries (Denmark, Sweden, Norway, the Czech Republic, Poland, Bulgaria, Finland, Slovenia, Lithuania, the Netherlands, the UK and Estonia) is characterised by higher levels of daily internet use and private access than the European average, and can be labelled 'highly private/highly embedded use'. A second group includes those countries (Austria, Germany, Italy, Greece and Portugal) where private access is above the European average, but where the internet is less embedded in children's everyday lives, labelled 'private access/low use'. The third group includes Ireland, France, Hungary, Spain and Turkey, with low levels of both privatisation and frequency of internet use, labelled 'shared use/low use' countries. The fourth group includes only Romania and Belgium, which show the characteristics of lower access from a private room at home, but heavy incorporation of the internet into children's everyday lives.

Figure 5.1: Children's internet access in bedrooms or private rooms at home, by daily internet use and country

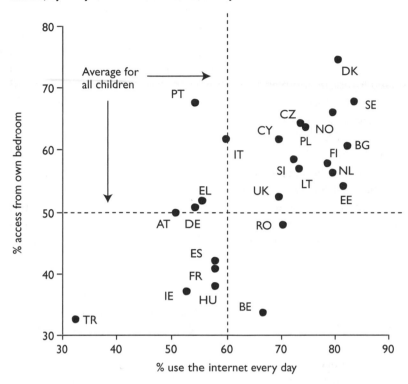

Base: All children who use the internet.
Note: See page 13 for explanation of country codes.

In the following sections we investigate the factors that shape the different contexts of internet use and contribute to the varying degrees of domestication of information and communications technology (ICT).

Access: private, public and shared

In the last two decades, there has been an evident trend towards increasing privatisation of media practices at home (media-rich bedrooms increasingly acting as the setting for children's practices related to identity and privacy) and significant diffusion of portable personal devices enabling internet access (Bovill and Livingstone, 2001). The 'bedroom culture' was observed in the first European cross-national research *Children and their changing media environment* (Bovill and Livingstone, 2001), and its persistence is confirmed by the findings from the EU Kids Online survey. Use of the internet among children in Europe is more frequent in their own bedrooms than in any other room in the home (see Figure 5.2).[2]

We can suppose that, thanks to 'ubiquitous internetting' (Peter and Valkenburg, 2006), children's use is on a continuum of private use in their daily lives, from totally individualised use to fully public and shared locations and platforms; they go online in several contexts and on several platforms, their different types of usage influenced by specific rules and social conventions.

Results from the EU Kids Online survey (Livingstone et al, 2011) show that home is the most frequent location of internet use. Based on children who access the internet in a shared room (38 per cent) and those who have access in their own bedrooms (49 per cent), the domestic context represents the main setting for internet activities (87 per cent) for European youth who use the internet. The second most common location is school or college (63 per cent of European children).[3]

However, the increasing privatisation of internet use, driven by availability of locations and platforms, does not exclude access from elsewhere in the home, nor does it automatically mean individualisation. Children who use the internet in their bedrooms may also access it elsewhere in the home. Some households in some countries have multiple points of access and their domestic social geography looks like the 'transitional homes' described by Roe (2000), which are characterised by an absence of single-purpose rooms and a predominance of open and community-oriented spaces. Friends' homes are also frequently identified as locations for internet use (about half of the sample, 53 per cent), showing that online activities are becoming a relevant part of the play time that children spend with peers. The internet is a significant resource for socialising among peers: on the one hand, it supports forms of 'perpetual contact' that extends face-to-face encounters beyond physical proximity; on the other hand, it is a resource for co-present interaction, and shared use in face-to-face meetings.

Although not absolute, the privatisation of internet usage in domestic space makes any sort of parental monitoring or sharing of media practices more difficult. However, the peer-oriented culture developing around the internet suggests that safety policies should target other social contexts in addition to the domestic, such as friends' homes and, more practical to access, the school context.

Figure 5.2: Children's use of the internet at home, by country (%)

Looking at this card, please tell me how you use the internet these days

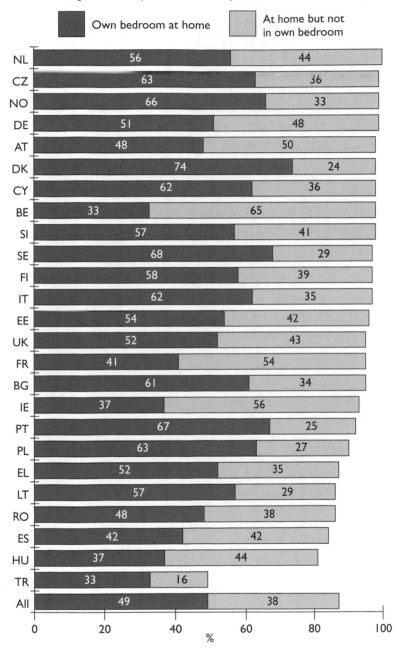

Base: All children who use the internet.
Source: Livingstone et al (2011)

Usage: experience and embeddedness

The process of incorporating ICTs into everyday life entails involving their accommodation in existing temporal routines and the emergence of new routines. Time is another dimension related to an analysis of children's experience of the internet, and two measures in particular: number of years the child has been using the internet, and frequency of use (daily or less). If the number of years spent online is a significant measure of an individual's experience, greater frequency of use and time spent online on a daily basis suggests a deeper incorporation of the internet into everyday life practices. An increasing number of daily activities is being mediated and takes place online. Prior research indicates that both experience and embeddedness are associated with a greater variety of online activities and, therefore, are positively correlated to the take-up of opportunities and exposure to risks (Livingstone and Helsper, 2007, 2009). This literature also shows also that internet use and online opportunities are positively associated with internet literacy and skills related to ensuring safety.

The EU Kids Online data (Livingstone et al, 2011) show that the age of first internet use in Europe is falling. On average, children aged 9–16 first used the internet when they were 9. Younger children tend to go online earlier, with those aged 9 and 10 saying that they first used the internet at age 7, while the average age of first use among older teenagers is 11. There are also cross-national variations: age at first use is significantly lower in northern Europe and highest in Greece, with Austria, Italy, Portugal, Romania and Turkey also above the average.

A further measure of how thoroughly the internet is incorporated into children's lives is frequency of use: the majority of children (60 per cent) use the internet daily or almost daily, and over one third (33 per cent) use it once or twice a week. This means that 93 per cent of all children go online at least once a week. Again, cross-national variations are relevant: in Bulgaria, Estonia, the Netherlands and Sweden, four out of five children aged 9–16 use the internet daily, while this number drops to only a third of Turkish children. Consistent with prior research (Livingstone and Helsper, 2007), there are age differences related to the amount of use (only a third of 9- to 10-year-olds go online every day compared to 80 per cent of older teenagers), while a gender gap in frequency of use is not apparent.

Insofar as age and frequency of use are associated with a greater variety of online opportunities and the development of safety and information skills, younger children may be less likely to encounter risks than older ones, but they are less well equipped to cope with them.

A further indicator of the process of incorporation is the amount of time spent online daily.[4] Children aged 9-16 spend on average 88 minutes per day online. The largest differences in the amount of daily use relates to age: younger children spend nearly an hour (58 minutes) online; older teenagers spend nearly two hours (118 minutes) online. Cross-national variations are significant ($LR(1)=1,761.71$, $p<0.001$) ranging from an average of 61 to 120 minutes with Ireland, Spain, Turkey, Portugal, Germany, France and Austria in the lower quartile and Bulgaria, Romania, Norway, Estonia, Sweden and Denmark in the upper quartile. In sum, the data show that while gender gaps are closing, age and cross-national disparities in online experience, frequency of use and amount of time online persist. At the same time, deeper incorporation of the internet in daily practices is increasing online opportunities and digital literacy and promoting safer and more skilled use.

Explaining access and usage

The literature on the digital divide tends to focus on social inequalities to explain variations in access and use. However, the domestication perspective points to how technologies are variously negotiated and used in different social contexts. In order to untangle the process of domestication, we explore the correlations between different factors that shape the social context of internet use:

- parents' domestic access (yes/no), and parents' daily use (yes/no);
- children's quality of access – access from own bedroom (yes/no) as an indicator of the process of privatisation and children's incorporation of the internet into their lives as expressed by age of first online experience;
- children's frequency and quality of use: children's daily use of the internet (yes/no) and average number of online activities (total 17).[5]

Figure 5.3 displays the correlations for European children's daily internet use to investigate this theoretical model further.

Parents' domestic and daily internet usage is positively associated with children's access from their bedrooms. The associations are very small, but statistically significant ($r=0.07$ and 0.04). Daily internet use by the parent also shows a small and significant association with the child's bedroom access ($r=0.07$) and a more reasonable association with number of years since the child went online ($r=0.19$). These outcomes suggest that parents' domestic use and, especially, frequency of use, are

Figure 5.3: Correlations between indicators of domestication, access and usage

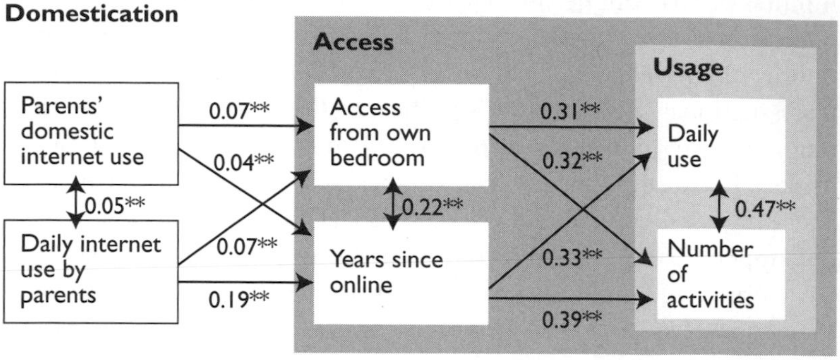

Note: ** p<0.01, 2-tailed tests.

related to children's access. However, given that associations are small, other indicators must also be considered relevant.

Children's daily use is interrelated with their online experience (r=0.33), private access (r=0.31), and by proxy with parents' frequency of use: children with longer online experience, who benefit from unrestricted access and whose parents are regular users themselves, use the internet on a daily basis.

Indicators of children's private access are correlated with the number of activities performed online (r=0.32), which is also positively associated with number of years the child has been using the internet (r=0.39). Accessing the internet from the bedroom, and longer experience of using the internet encourages its more thorough incorporation into daily lives, measured here in terms of the online opportunities exploited.

Overall, the quality of access and longer use are strongly correlated to the degree of mediatisation of children's lives: the more unrestricted domestic access (as in the 'bedroom culture' pattern), or the possibility to go online from various locations and throughout the day, and the more years of experience of the internet, the more activities they will perform online. Thus, quality of access and age at first use are strongly connected to the opportunities encountered online, and, consequently, also to children's exposure to risks.

Consistently, within the domestication framework, correlations show that parents' domestic use of the internet is associated with the 'technological culture' in the household, which, in turn, shapes children's use. More specifically, parental domestication of the internet is positively associated with private access and years of online experience, both of which shape the context of use. At another level, these aspects might indirectly mediate frequency of use and time, since access to and experience with the internet are correlated to higher embeddedness of the internet in children's daily lives.

We also performed two stepwise logistic regression analyses to include sociodemographic background variables and to test for the relations between domestication, access and usage. The first analysis (see Table 5.1) focused on the factors that predict children's access from their bedrooms. In the first step we examined the sociodemographic variables (that is, child's age, child's gender and parents' level of education) as indicators of the household's cultural and economic capital.[6] The second step adds indicators of domestication (that is, parents' domestic and daily use). The results show that older children, boys and the children of more highly educated parents are more likely to have private access from their own bedrooms. The odds of a child having access from his or her bedroom increase by 31 per cent for each year of age, are 10 per cent higher for boys than for girls, and increase by 8 per cent with a one-point (out of seven) increase in parents' education. Parents' domestic internet use appears to be the most influential predictor of children's internet access in the bedroom. For children of the same age and gender, from families where parents have similar educational backgrounds, the odds of having internet access in their bedrooms are 122 per cent higher if the parents use the internet at home.[7] However, parents' daily use does not seem to play a role for children's bedroom access when the other predictors are considered simultaneously.

The second analysis (see Table 5.2) focused on the factors that predict children's daily internet use, first, by considering sociodemographic variables (that is, child's age, child's gender, parents' level of education), and second, by adding indicators of domestication (that is, parents' domestic and daily use). In a third step we included indicators of children's internet access (that is, from the bedroom, number of years since going online). We see that older children, boys and children whose parents have better educational qualifications are more likely to use

Table 5.1: Access: logistic regression predicting children's access from own bedroom

	Model 1 – OR	Model 2 – OR
Child age	1.31**	1.31**
Child gender (female = 0)	1.10**	1.10**
Parent's highest education	1.08**	1.08**
Parent's domestic internet use		2.22**
Daily internet use by parents		1.01

Notes: ** $p<0.01$; OR=Odds Ratio.

Table 5.2: Usage: logistic regression predicting children's daily use

	Model 1 – OR	Model 2 – OR	Model 3 – OR
Child age	1.49**	1.50**	1.30**
Child gender (female = 0)	1.12**	1.12**	1.05**
Parent's highest education	1.14**	1.14**	1.06**
Parent's domestic internet use		2.95**	2.40**
Daily internet use by parents		1.01	1.01
Bedroom access			2.35**
Years online			1.28**

Notes: ** *p*<0.01; OR=Odds Ratio.

the internet daily. The odds of a child using the internet daily increase by 49 per cent for each year of age, are 12 per cent higher for boys than for girls, and increase by 14 per cent for every one-point (out of seven) increase in parents' level of education. Also, parents' domestic internet use, children's access from their bedrooms and years that the child has been online appear to promote daily use by children. For children of the same age and gender and from families with similar levels of education, the odds of using the internet daily are 195 per cent higher for children whose parents use the internet at home. For children with parents with similar domestic and daily use of the internet and for children of the same age and gender whose parents have similar levels of education, the odds of using the internet daily are 135 per cent higher if the children can access the internet from their bedrooms. Last, a child's odds of using the internet daily increase by 28 per cent for each additional year that the child has been online. As with bedroom access parents' daily use did not play a role when considering other predictors.

Conclusion

In this chapter we examined the social context of internet use. One main finding is that among European children access is no longer a simple, unitary phenomenon: it is diversifying in terms of locations and platforms. The ubiquity of the internet in the everyday lives of European youth is leading to its deeper incorporation in their daily routines and practices. This changing media environment is characterised by two major trends that shape young people's online experiences. On the one hand, access tends to be increasingly private, unrestricted and unsupervised, with media-rich bedrooms among the most important social contexts for internet use. On the other hand, the internet is more and more embedded in children's lives, with the majority of children using it on a daily basis and for a variety of online activities. Both processes seem to be positively associated to parents' domestication of the internet, that is, their domestic access and, to a smaller degree, daily use of the internet. More specifically, children of the same age, gender and educational background are much more likely to use the internet daily and from their own bedroom if their parents are domestic users, but taking these sociodemographic factors into account, parents' daily use does not play a role. At the same time, if the sociodemographic characteristics and patterns of parental domestication are the same, daily use by children is shaped primarily by private access and years of online experience.

Cross-national variations persist: while divides in access are reducing, the process of domestication of the internet is far from homogeneous across countries, leading to different social contexts in which children's online experiences are embedded. These differences are relevant for policy insofar as access shapes use, which, in turn, is associated with the take-up of online opportunities, the development of digital skills to enable secure use and exposure to risks.

Notes

[1] The authors contributed equally to this chapter.

[2] This finding relates to the European countries as a whole. However, some countries are notable exceptions with either equal amounts of access from bedrooms and other rooms at home (Germany and Austria) or a higher amount of access from other rooms at home than the bedroom (Belgium, France and Ireland).

[3] Other locations: friend's home (53 per cent), relative's home (42 per cent), internet café (12 per cent), public library (12 per cent) or when 'out and about' (9 per cent) (Livingstone et al, 2011)

[4] Average time spent online each day calculated combining two separate measures: average time spent online on a school day, and time spent online on a non-school day.

[5] The online activities included in the questionnaire were: play internet games on your own or against the computer; use the internet for schoolwork; watch video clips; visit a social networking profile; use instant messaging; send/receive email; read/watch the news online; play games with other people on the internet; download music or films; post photos, videos or music to share with others; use a webcam, put (or post) a message on a website; visit a chatroom; use file-sharing sites; create a character, pet or avatar; spend time in a virtual world; and write a blog or online diary.

[6] This variable was measured on a different scale for each country, according to its education system, then standardised according to a single European country scale of: 1 = Not completed primary education, 2 = Primary or first stage of basic, 3 = Lower secondary or second stage of basic, 4 = Upper secondary, 5 = Post-secondary, non-tertiary, 6 = First stage of tertiary, 7 = Second stage of tertiary. This education variable is not strictly continuous and is also confounded by country; these correlations should be considered with caution.

[7] It should be noted that even though the exploration of the overall model showed a very small correlation between parents' domestic use and bedroom access, when controlling for other variables, parents' domestic use appears to be one of the strongest predictors. This suggests that the variation across the other sociodemographic predictors must have obscured the size of this relation within the correlation analysis.

References

Bovill, M. and Livingstone, S. (2001) 'Bedroom culture and the privatization of media use', in S. Livingstone and M. Bovill (eds) *Children and their changing media environment: A European comparative study*, Mahwah, NJ: Lawrence Erlbaum, pp 179-200.

Haddon, L. (2003) 'Research question for the evolving communications landscape', in R. Ling and P.E. Pedersen (eds) *Mobile communications. Re-negotiation of the social sphere*, London: Springer, pp 7-22.

Haddon, L. (2004) *Information and communication technologies in everyday life: A concise introduction and research guide*, Oxford: Berg.

Ito, M., Baumer, S., Bittanti, M., boyd, d., Cody, R., Herr-Stephenson, B., Horst H.A., Lange, P., Mahendran, D., Martìnez, K.Z., Pascoe, C., Perkel D., Robinson, L., Sims, C. and Tripp, L. (2009) *Hanging out, messing around, and geeking out. Kids living and learning with new media*, Cambridge, MA: The MIT Press.

Livingstone, S. and Helsper, E. (2007) 'Gradations in digital inclusion: children, young people and the digital divide', *New Media & Society*, vol 9, no 4, pp 671-96.

Livingstone, S. and Helsper, E. (2009) 'Balancing opportunities and risks in teenagers' use of the internet: the role of online skills and internet self-efficacy', *New Media & Society*, vol 11, no 8, pp 1-25.

Livingstone, S., Haddon, L., Görzig, A. and Ólafsson, K. (2011) *Risks and safety on the internet: The perspective of European children. Full findings*, London: London School of Economics and Political Science.

Peter, J. and Valkenburg, P. (2006) 'Adolescents' internet use: testing the "disappearing digital divide" versus the "emerging digital differentiation approach"', *Poetics*, vol 34, pp 293-305.

Roe, K. (2000) 'Adolescents' media use: a European view', *Journal of Adolescent Health*, vol 27, no 2, pp 15-21.

Silverstone, R. and Hirsch, E. (1992) (eds) *Consuming technologies: Media and information in domestic space*, London: Routledge.

SIX

Online opportunities

Pille Pruulmann-Vengerfeldt and Pille Runnel

This chapter analyses children's take-up of online opportunities and their outcomes, based on an analysis of the range and types of children's online activities. There are certain continuities between children's online and offline worlds – searching for information, entertainment and gaming and social networking online are, to a large extent, extensions or modifications of practices that are located in everyday life, that is, they are not particularly on one side or the other of the 'real'/'virtual' divide. But there is little question that the internet has not added to the breadth and depth of children's everyday opportunities.

The EU Kids Online research has shown that the internet usage of children in Europe involves constant negotiation of opportunities and risks which, if well balanced, will contribute to a meaningful life, a valued identity and satisfactory relations with others (Livingstone and Haddon, 2009a, p 4). Analysing internet usage in terms of opportunities and risks requires its examination through the conceptual lenses of structure and agency. Agency refers to freedom, choice, control and motivation; structure is the set of rules and resources. The starting point of this chapter is children's agency. Identifying children's online activities allows reflection on their knowledge, interests and motivations. Internet usage practices connect the agency side and its social context, within the structure of offline and online activity, which enables certain factors and restricts others.

Research on children's online activities employs the concept of a 'ladder of opportunities' (Livingstone and Helsper, 2007; Kalmus et al, 2009) in order to structure the types of activities in which children engage, in a systematic way. It suggests a progression through stages of use. According to this approach, progress is related to increasing skills and more complex internet usage. The 'ladder of opportunities' approach is based on the notion that children fall into groups based on the range of the opportunities they use, from information-related sources to communication, to more advanced uses, such as online content creation, practised by only a few.

While this framework has some merits, it should be noted that the analysis of EU Kids Online data in this chapter suggests that some of these activities should be grouped rather than considered in terms of a step-by-step advancement, and also, some activities might fit into more than one group, depending on the backgrounds of the children involved. This may be a reflection of how the internet's affordances have changed over time alongside shifts in the ways that children use the internet. However, the national variations presented below also suggest that we should perhaps seek a more nuanced picture, which might include multiple 'ladders of opportunities' rather than only one.

This chapter looks specifically at children's online activities in relation to the 17 activities asked about in the EU Kids Online survey, and analyses the average number of activities in which young people engage. It extends this examination by comparing and discussing the findings in Livingstone and Helsper's (2007) and Kalmus and colleagues' (2009) studies of the ladder of opportunities. Groups of activities in Europe and among different countries within the EU Kids Online project are examined in order to identify similarities and differences across countries. Opportunities are measured by listed activities. We acknowledge that it is not a complete list and this kind of activity-centred approach misses many nuances regarding different uses. However, these are sacrificed in favour of cross-national comparisons. Further research should investigate these differences in more detail.

Average number of activities

Overall, children undertake nearly half (7.2) of the 17 activities in the survey (see Table 6.1). The number of activities young people engage in increases with age and with years of internet use. There are gender differences in terms of both older and younger boys being involved in a wider variety of activities than girls of the same ages. Differences in the averages, while always statistically significant, are smaller for younger children and become more pronounced over time.

While in most cases, older age increases the likelihood of the child using a particular application, there are a few differences. For example, fewer of the older girls play games against the computer, and fewer older girls had created a pet, character or avatar in the month before the survey.

Table 6.1, column 1 (content, contact and conduct, based on earlier work by EU Kids Online; see Livingstone and Haddon, 2009b) shows that among the three types of online opportunity, content-based activities are by far the most popular. Contact-based activities, using

Table 6.1: Children's engagement in different online activities in the past month

% of children who have done following activities in past month		Age 9-12		Age 13-16		
		Boys	**Girls**	**Boys**	**Girls**	**Total**
Average number of activities engaged in monthly (of all 17)		5.7	5.5	9.1	8.2	7.2
Content-based activities	Used the internet for schoolwork	78	81	87	90	84
	Played games on your own or against the computer	84	81	86	68	80
	Watched video clips	65	64	87	84	76
	Read, watched the news on the internet	37	35	59	57	48
	Downloaded music or films	27	25	61	55	43
Contact/ communication-based activities	Used instant messaging	42	46	75	76	61
	Visited social networking profile	39	41	80	80	61
	Sent/received email	42	46	73	74	60
	Played games with other people online	46	32	62	32	43
	Used a webcam	23	25	36	37	31
	Visited a chatroom	14	13	34	28	23
Conduct/peer participation activities	Put or posted photos, videos or music to share with others	21	23	53	54	39
	Put or posted a message on a website	17	18	43	39	30
	Created a character, pet or avatar	19	17	20	12	17
	Used file-sharing sites	10	8	29	21	17
	Spent time in the virtual world	15	13	21	11	15
	Written a blog or online diary	4	6	14	17	11

Note: All row differences for gender and age are statistically significant, $p<0.001$ (Chi-square tests).

the internet for communication, come second; conduct–based activities, requiring the initiative to generate own content, are the least frequent activities. There are significant differences regarding activities that demand more skill (either technical skills, for example, downloading music or films in the content category, or content–based skills, for example, reading/watching news). These activities are exploited by fewer, and taken up only when children get older.

The average number of activities young people engage in differs according to socioeconomic status. The highest socioeconomic status group engaged in 7.6 activities, the medium socioeconomic status group 7.3 activities, and children from the low socioeconomic status group engage in 6.7 activities on average ($p<0.001$). This indicates the relevance of the context of use in relation to the wider social structure.

We investigate the role of social context further when analysing country variations in the take-up of opportunities. The number of activities engaged in also corresponds to the length of time young people spend online. If more hours are spent online, then the range of activities increases. Young people who spend 30 minutes or less per day using the internet average 4.4 online activities; those who spend 3 hours or more per day online average 10.2 activities ($p<0.001$).

Communication activities are key to understanding the time children spend online – using the internet for communication is very common, especially among older children. The frequent popular debate about whether email is being replaced by social networking or instant messaging (see, for example, www.emailisnotdead.com/) seems to be irrelevant in relation to European children: all three communicative activities are used almost equally. Sixty per cent of young people use email, 61 per cent use instant messaging, and 61 per cent use social networking sites. There are indications that use of social networking sites is the most age-dependent since the differences are greatest for younger and older children's use of this communication tool. However, the actual usage behind the figures needs further investigation.

As expected, the average number of internet activities and the average number of skills are strongly related (Pearson's correlation 0.231, $p<0.001$). Those children who report knowledge of the eight skills listed in the survey also engage regularly in an average of 10.9 activities online; children reporting no skills engage in an average of 4.7 activities. The correlation is even stronger for number of years online and number of online activities (Pearson's correlation 0.384, $p<0.001$). Young people who have been using the internet for five years or more show average take-up of 9.3 activities; young people who have used the internet for less than a year engage in only 4.8 activities.

The analysis in the next section shows that if the number of online activities is smaller, these activities are likely to be related to content and to contact/communication opportunities, in that order. Activities related to online conduct, where the child becomes an active agent shaping the online environment by contributing content, is in most cases taken up only if the more straightforward activities are well established.

Average number of activities across countries

Figure 6.1 shows that there are some quite large differences across countries. Countries can be grouped according to the number of activities in which children engage. The most active group is Lithuania,

Figure 6.1: Average number of online activities in the past month and in the past week, by country

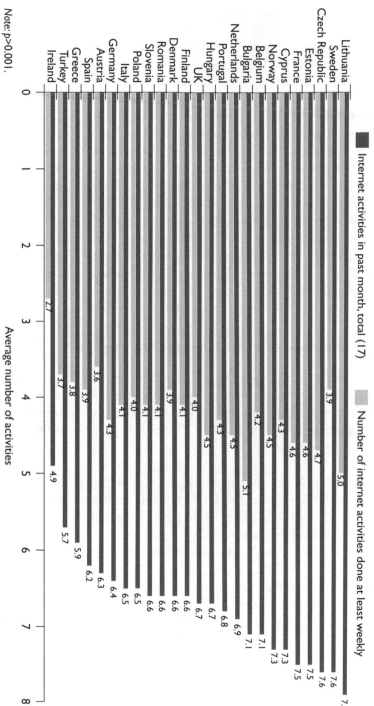

■ Internet activities in past month, total (17)   ▨ Number of internet activities done at least weekly

Average number of activities

Lithuania 5.0 / 7.9
Sweden 7.6
Czech Republic 3.9 / 7.6
Estonia 4.7 / 7.5
France 4.6 / 7.5
Cyprus 4.3 / 7.3
Norway 4.5 / 7.3
Belgium 4.5 / 7.1
Bulgaria 4.2 / 7.1
Netherlands 5.1 / 6.9
Portugal 4.5 / 6.8
Hungary 4.5 / 6.7
UK 4.3 / 6.7
Finland 4.0 / 6.6
Denmark 4.1 / 6.6
Romania 3.9 / 6.6
Slovenia 4.1 / 6.6
Poland 4.1 / 6.5
Italy 4.0 / 6.5
Germany 4.1 / 6.4
Austria 4.3 / 6.3
Spain 3.6 / 6.2
Greece 3.9 / 5.9
Turkey 3.8 / 5.7
Ireland 3.7 / 4.9

Note: *p*>0.001.

Sweden, the Czech Republic, Estonia, France, Cyprus and Norway. The second group, which also is closest to the European Union (EU) average, is Belgium, Bulgaria, the Netherlands, Portugal, Hungary, the UK, Finland, Denmark, Romania and Slovenia. The third group comprises Poland, Italy, Germany, Austria, Spain, Greece, Turkey and Ireland.

If we consider weekly activities, the differences are smaller, but follow a different country hierarchy. For instance, if we consider the activities of young people in Bulgaria, per month, the range is close to the EU average; if we look at Bulgarian children's activities per week, then this country is ranked first. For Sweden, for range of activities per month it is ranked second, but it is ranked very low if weekly activities are measured. Weekly use refers to the most popular (frequent) activities while monthly activities include ones that may have been tried, but are possibly not in the young person's regular repertoire of activities. The differences in these numbers are difficult to encompass in a single hypothesis that covers the whole of Europe; context and country-specific reasons should be investigated in future studies.

Types of activities in which children engage

In order to clarify the argument in this section, and to follow the stages of online use, we grouped the young respondents according to the number of online opportunities they engaged in, forming sum indices. The five groups roughly follow the distribution of the take-up of the 17 online opportunities:

- 0-2 opportunities, taken up by 12 per cent of respondents;
- 3-5 opportunities, taken up by 23 per cent of respondents;
- 6-9 opportunities, taken up by 36 per cent of respondents;
- 10-12 opportunities; taken up by 19 per cent of respondents;
- 13-17 opportunities; taken up by 9 per cent of respondents.

Figure 6.2 shows the distribution of these groups according to respondents' age and gender. Among younger children, gender differences are much smaller. Among older children, boys' usage is broader and more versatile: they engage in more than 13 activities.

The grouping of online opportunities follows Livingstone and Helsper (2007) and Kalmus et al (2009). Activities were ordered first according to the percentage of users for each activity. Then activities were grouped into stages, where stage 1 is the activities taken up by most young internet users, and stage 5 represents the least frequent activities,

Figure 6.2: Range of opportunities taken up according to age and gender

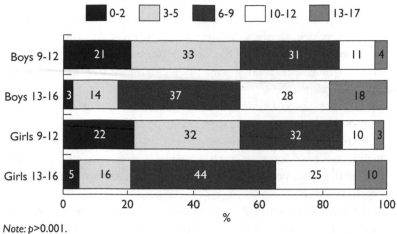

Note: p>0.001.

taken up only by the users engaging in more than 13 activities. If we compare these activities according to children's take-up with the results from other studies, we see that many uses have stabilised at specific stages, but also that there are fluctuations in the online environment.

Comparison of different stages is subject to methodological limitations: they differ in relation to the types of use surveyed in each study. However, it is clear that in the five or six years previous to the current survey, the structure of the young people's online environment has become increasingly multi-media based. Many of the activities recorded in earlier studies were regarded as highly resource bound (for example, demanding high-speed internet access). As these resources have become more available, the nature of practices has shifted. For example, we see that watching video clips online, not frequent or particularly relevant in 2004 (Livingstone and Helsper, 2007), and clearly resource-sensitive in 2005 (Kalmus et al, 2009), has become one of the most popular online experiences. The current study also indicates that playing games is fast becoming an important and relevant activity for stage 1 users, competing with or replacing school-related use.

Table 6.2 provides an overview of the composition of the stage activities and how they are used by different groups of young people. The stages include:

- Stage 1, the most frequent activities, which include users that engage in only 1-2 activities – use of the internet for schoolwork and playing solo games against the computer.

- Stage 2, watching video clips, which applies to more than half of those who engage in 3-5 activities.
- Stage 3, communicative and news-related activities, mainly visiting social networking sites, using instant messaging and sending/ receiving email. Watching the news online is also included in this group, which applies to young people who engage in 6 or more activities online.
- Stage 4 applies to children who engage in 10 or more activities, including playing games against other people, downloading music or films, posting photos, using a webcam or posting messages on websites. These activities include some conduct-related practices rendering the young people active contributors to online environments.
- Stage 5, activities regularly practised only by children who engage in 13 or more online activities. Although visiting chatrooms, using file-sharing sites, creating characters, spending time in virtual worlds

Table 6.2: Opportunities taken up, by frequency with which children do the activity (%)

Stage		No of opportunities taken up (%)					
		0-2	3-5	6-9	10-12	13-17	Average
1	Used the internet for schoolwork	68	78	87	92	95	84
	Played games on their own or against the computer	61	77	78	86	93	80
2	Watched video clips	19	61	87	97	99	76
3	Visited social networking profile	3	31	73	94	99	61
	Used instant messaging	3	29	73	94	98	61
	Sent/received email	5	31	71	90	97	60
	Read/watched the news on the internet	8	30	52	70	84	48
4	Played games with other people online	6	29	42	65	92	43
	Downloaded music or films	2	17	45	75	90	43
	Put or posted photos, videos or music to share with others	1	8	39	73	92	39
	Used a webcam	1	11	29	55	77	31
	Put or posted a message on a website	0	5	27	57	89	30
5	Visited chatroom	1	3	19	42	80	23
	Used file-sharing sites	1	2	12	34	68	17
	Created a character, pet or avatar	1	6	14	27	58	17
	Spent time in the virtual world	1	5	12	24	57	15
	Wrote a blog or online diary	0	1	5	20	52	11

Note: Shading indicates those opportunities taken up by more than 50% in the relevant column; $p>0.001$.

and writing blogs or a diary are generally practised by only a small percentage of the overall population, more than half of those who engage in 13-17 activities also engage in these activities.

Country comparisons

It is interesting that while this grouping of stages is appropriate for EU-level analysis, each of the countries in our sample has a slightly different ladder of opportunities. These differ in relation to the order of take-up of opportunities and the percentage of users in each stage (see Table 6.3). It seems that contextual factors, for example, social

Table 6.3: First two stages of all surveyed countries (% of total users in brackets)

	Stage 1 (%)	Stage 2 (%)
Austria	Games against computer (79)	Video (79) Schoolwork (67)
Belgium	Games against computer (80)	Video (84) Schoolwork (76)
Bulgaria	Games against computer (91)	Schoolwork (74) Instant messaging (89)
Cyprus	Games against computer (87)	Video (86) Schoolwork (80)
Czech Republic	Games against computer (82)	Schoolwork (86)
Denmark	Games against computer (88)	Video (88) Schoolwork (83)
Estonia	Games against computer (78)	Video (91) Schoolwork (81)
Finland	Games against computer (80)	Video (80) Schoolwork (71)
France	Games against computer (77)	Read-watched news online (88) Video (81) Schoolwork (81)
Germany	Schoolwork (85)	Video (80 Games against computer (76)
Greece	Games against computer (94)	Video (84) Schoolwork (76)
Hungary	Games against computer (80)	Video (75) Schoolwork (72)
Ireland	*None of the activities is taken up by more than 50% of young people who engage in 0-2 activities*	Video (76) Games against computer (74) Schoolwork (58)
Italy	Schoolwork (83) Games against computer (78)	Video (77)

(continued)

81

Table 6.3: First two stages of all surveyed countries (% of total users in brackets) (continued)

	Stage 1 (%)	Stage 2 (%)
Lithuania	Games against computer (84)	Instant messaging (80)
Netherlands	Games against computer (78)	Video (88) Schoolwork (77)
Norway	*None of the activities is taken up by more than 50% of young people who engage in 0-2 activities*	Video (89) Schoolwork (75)
Poland	Schoolwork (91) Games against computer (78)	*Stage 2 cannot be separated from stage 3* Video (71) Visited social networking site profile (58) Instant messaging (68) Sent/received email (58) Read/watched news (61) Played games with people (51) Download music, films (49)
Portugal	Schoolwork (90)	Games against computer (79) Video (77)
Romania	Schoolwork (87) Games against computer (81)	Instant messaging (82) Video (77)
Slovenia	Games against computer (78)	Video (86)
Spain	Schoolwork (83) Games against computer (78)	Video (78)
Sweden	Games against computer (69)	Video (90)
Turkey	Schoolwork (91) Games against computer (88)	*Stage 2 cannot be separated from stage 3* Video (59) Visited social networking site profile (44) Instant messaging (45) Sent/received email (44) Played games with people (47) Download music, films (40) Put (or posted) photos, videos or music to share with others (40)
UK	Schoolwork (92) Games against computer (80)	Video (75)

Note: p>0.001.

structure differences, have a strong influence on what is popular, what is permitted and what is encouraged and supported in a particular country.

In most of the countries surveyed, stages 1 and 2 include games, videos and schoolwork (in different orders); however, in Bulgaria, France, Poland, Romania and Turkey, stage 2 includes other important activities. The most popular activities are social networking, instant messaging and watching news, showing that although content-related activities lead the ladder of opportunities on average in EU countries, communication-related activities are becoming increasingly important in some countries in the early stages of internet use.

Table 6.3 illustrates that although in many countries, stage 1 consists of gaming, the eventual take-up of other services may outnumber the total number of players. In Lithuania, Sweden and Slovenia, schoolwork does not figure in stages 1 and 2; the figures suggest that school-related use will continue to be slow in these countries.

The stage activities in different countries also vary in other ways, indicating that in some countries differences among uses are bigger, but this depends on the overall distribution of stages in each country. Figure 6.3 provides an overview of the differences, showing that distribution varies widely across countries. Those countries most different from the norm are Ireland, where very few children engage in a broad range of activities, and Lithuania, where 16 per cent of young people engage in 13 or more activities. In France, Bulgaria, the Czech Republic and Sweden there are also high percentages of children using 13 or more activities. Denmark stands out for the largest average group, with 49 per cent use of 6-9 activities. The Czech Republic, Cyprus, Estonia, the Netherlands and Sweden have the smallest percentage of internet users, engaging in only 0-2 activities.

Conclusion

This examination of children's internet practices shows that they are related to many real-life activities, ranging from schoolwork to discussing the health of a pet with peers. It is claimed that any kind of internet usage subtly alters rather than replaces existing practices (Runnel, 2009); therefore, understanding the various wider contexts of such use is increasingly relevant.

This chapter is a first step towards understanding these contexts. The different internet uses of boys and girls, and younger and older children, show that the number of internet-related practices they engage in increases over time. However, we also see that there is no clear hierarchy of uses, but rather alternate paths in terms of stages of online opportunities. These choices are supported and influenced by numerous mediators – peers, parents, the school system, and also cultural background, social fashions and public acceptance of different activities.

The choices about online opportunities differ most by country. Schoolwork-related use, a clear trigger of internet use in earlier years, is being paralleled by activities such as watching videos and playing games. Internet use among children may vary in different countries because of particular national contexts, including available resources (for example, the quality of the internet provision) and existing rules (different restrictions on children, peer norms, common understandings of what

Figure 6.3: Countries compared according to the range of opportunities taken up

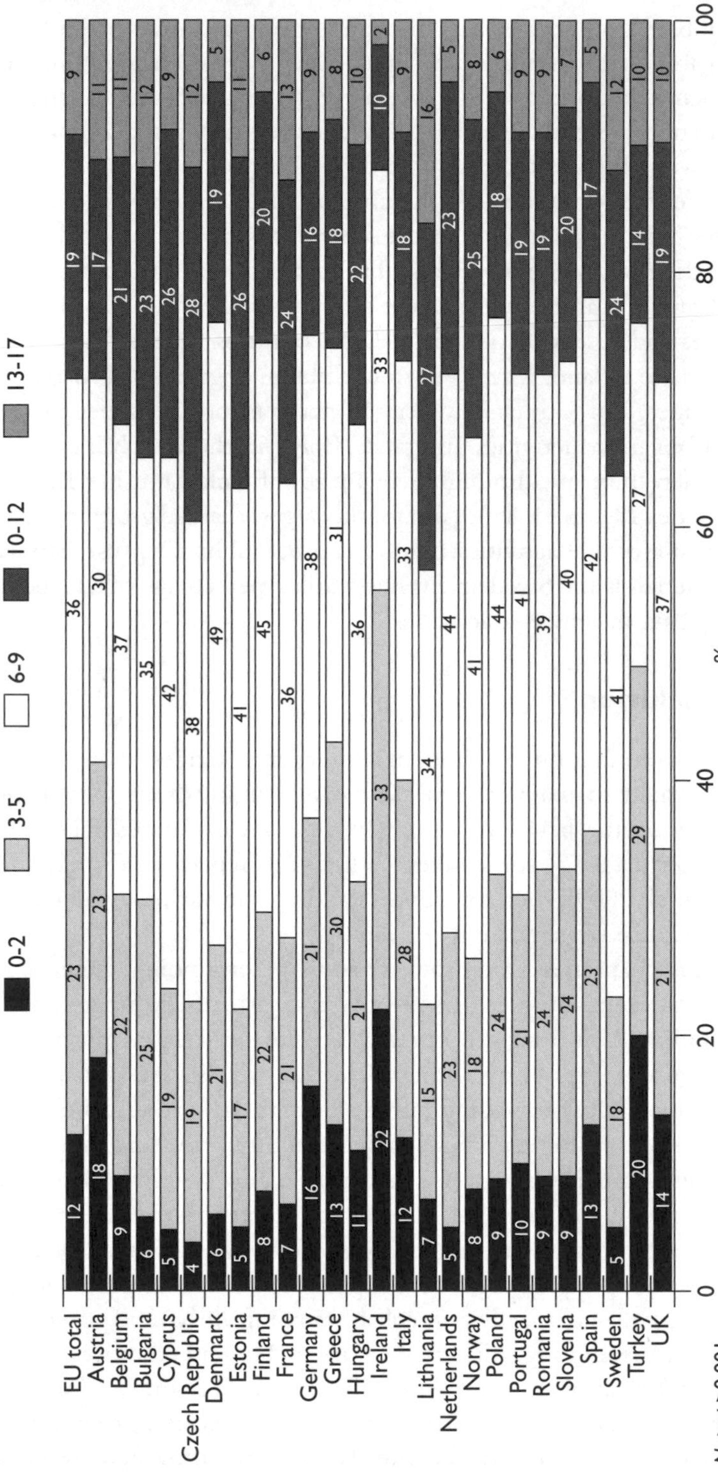

Note: p>0.001.

is popular, etc). However, the analysis in this chapter highlights many unanswered questions regarding context, variations and implications about future use. A more detailed examination is needed to analyse how internet practices are not isolated within the online environment.

Acknowledgements

The preparation of this chapter was supported by Research Grant No ETF8527 financed by the Estonian Science Foundation and Project Nos SF0180002s07 and SF0180017s07 financed by the Estonian Governmental Scientific Research Support Scheme.

References

Kalmus, V., Runnel, P. and Siibak, A. (2009) 'Opportunities and benefits online', in S. Livingstone and L. Haddon (eds) *Kids online*, Bristol: The Policy Press, pp 71–82.

Livingstone, S. and Haddon, L. (2009a) 'Introduction', in S. Livingstone and L. Haddon (eds) *Kids online*, Bristol: The Policy Press, pp 1-15.

Livingstone, S. and Haddon, L. (2009b) *EU Kids Online: Final report*, London: London School of Economics and Political Science (http://eprints.lse.ac.uk/24372/).

Livingstone, S. and Helsper, E.J. (2007) 'Gradations in digital inclusion: children, young people and the digital divide', *New Media & Society*, vol 9, no 4, pp 671-96.

Runnel, P. (2009) *The transformation of the internet: Usage practices in Estonia*, Tartu, Estonia: University of Tartu Press.

SEVEN

Digital skills in the context of media literacy

Nathalie Sonck, Els Kuiper and Jos de Haan

Digitally literate children?

New names are continuously being invented for new internet generations. In 1998, Don Tapscott talked about the 'Net Generation', in 2001 Marc Prensky coined the term 'digital natives', and in 2006 Wim Veen and Ben Vrakking made reference to 'homo zappiens'. All these authors are highlighting a discrepancy between older and younger generations, emphasising the seemingly natural capability of the latter to use and cope with an increasingly digitised world. These authors suggest that computers hold no secrets for the children of our era, who seem to master quite naturally the necessary digital skills. Although many parents and teachers share their opinion, they also worry about their children's lack of the skills that enable these opportunities to be exploited in a way that is not harmful to the child.

To an extent, their anxieties are justified: research into children's internet information skills, for example, shows that they often lack evaluative and strategic skills, that is, they do not know how to evaluate the utility or reliability of internet information (see, for example, Kuiper et al, 2008; Walraven et al, 2009). It could be argued that children's length of experience with the internet and their participation in a wide range of internet activities is contributing to their digital skills, but most research does not relate the amount and range of children's internet activities to the skills they possess. This chapter addresses both of these issues. The findings are compared to children's own accounts of their capabilities, which reflect their beliefs in their abilities. Although self-reports are less valid than performance tests for evaluating digital literacy (van Deursen and van Dijk, 2010), they are an obvious measure for investigating a large sample. However, whether the three self-reported measures can be used as a proxy for digital literacy is another question. There are many definitions of digital and media literacy, but most refer to a combination of skills, knowledge and attitudes (see, for example, Hargittai, 2007; Snyder, 2007; Rosenbaum et al, 2008; Livingstone, 2009; Merchant, 2009). We take a critical look at the meanings of our measurements of digital literacy in relation to which component of digital literacy is being measured and what it means for future research.

Three ways of measuring digital literacy

The EU Kids Online survey includes three measures of digital literacy: specific digital skills, range of online activities and children's beliefs about their internet abilities. Table 7.1 shows how these measures differ. While one method gives children a list of actual skills about internet safety, navigation and website evaluation, another method asks more implicitly about children's skills, based on the diversity of internet activities they do. We are interested in whether these methods are related and measure the same underlying concept of digital literacy. Since the skills questions are addressed only to 11- to 16-year-olds, the analysis in this chapter is based on this age group. For comparability, all scales are transformed into scales ranging between 0 and 10.

In relation to *specific digital skills*, children were asked which they possessed from a list of eight skills, including instrumental (mainly safety-related) and informational skills. Table 7.1 shows that children aged 11-16 most frequently claimed mastery of the skills required for bookmarking a website, blocking messages from people and finding safety information. They least often mentioned the ability to change filter preferences. On a 0-10 scale, European children, on average, have mastered about half (5.2) of the skills surveyed. The reliability of this scale is quite high (KR-20=0.84).[1]

For *range of online activities* children reported undertaking in the month previous to the survey, the underlying idea is that the more diverse the children's online activities, the more experienced they could be expected to be in their performance, and the more skilled they might be in internet usage. Table 7.1 displays the 17 online activities surveyed. Most children reported using the internet in the past month for schoolwork, playing games and watching video clips, and for communication-based activities such as social networking, instant messaging and email. The least common activities were using the internet to write a blog, spending time in a virtual world and creating a character. On a scale of 0-10, children on average engaged in almost half (4.7) of the online activities listed. The reliability of the scale is reasonably high (KR-20=0.76).

Table 7.1: Three methods of measuring digital literacy: specific digital skills, range of online activities and beliefs in internet abilities

Method 1 – Self-reported digital skills	
Ability to perform specific tasks:	**%**
Bookmark a website	64
Block messages from someone you don't want to hear from	64
Find information on how to use the internet safely	63
Change privacy settings on a social networking profile	56
Compare different websites to decide if information is true	56
Delete the record of which sites you have visited	52
Block unwanted adverts or junk mail/spam	51
Change filter preferences	28
Average number of skills (on a scale from 0-10)	*5.19*

Method 2 – Range of online activities	
Activities done in the past month:	**%**
Used the internet for schoolwork	88
Played internet games on your own or against the computer	82
Watched video clips	81
Visited a social networking profile	71
Used instant messaging	70
Sent/received email	69
Read/watched the news on the internet	54
Downloaded music or films	51
Put or posted photos, videos or music to share with others	47
Played games with other people online	46
Put or posted a message on a website	36
Used a webcam	34
Visited a chatroom	27
Used file-sharing sites	22
Created a character, pet or avatar	18
Spent time in a virtual world	16
Written a blog or online diary	13
Average number of activities (on a scale from 0-10)	*4.67*

Method 3 – Beliefs in internet abilities	%	%	%
Statements about knowledge:	**Not true**	**A bit true**	**Very true**
I know more about the internet than my parents	24	33	43
I know lots of things about using the internet	12	49	39
Average knowledge about the internet (2nd item; on a scale from 0-10)	*6.35*		

Note: The averages are based on the individual-level mean scores of the items for each scale (for specific digital skills 8 items; online activities 17 items; belief in internet abilities 1 item). The scales are standardised to range from 0-10.

The survey asked children to estimate whether they knew more than their parents about the internet, and also enquired specifically about the child's knowledge of the internet. Table 7.1 shows that about three quarters of the group claimed to know more than their parents about the internet (76 per cent), and 88 per cent claimed to know a lot about using the internet. Note that these items do not measure the same things: *belief about internet abilities* relates to the second item only. This corresponds most closely to the concepts of self–confidence, self–assessment or ability self–perception (Eccles et al, 1993, 2005; Kruger and Dunning, 1999). On a scale of 0–10, children report a fairly high belief on average in their own internet abilities (6.35). Although it contains only one item and is, therefore, a rather crude measure compared to indicators that include 8 or 17 items, it gives some idea of children's beliefs about their skills.

The three self–reports indicate that European children aged between 11 and 16 report a reasonable level of (safety–related) internet skills, a variety of internet activities and a fairly high degree of belief in their own internet abilities. However, the range of activities that children undertake online could be broader, and performance of particular tasks on the internet could be increased. These measures are positively associated, and these associations are statistically significant (all p-values are <0.001), indicating that a higher level of self–reported skills is accompanied by a more diverse range of online activities and a higher level of self–reported knowledge about the internet. The correlations point to a mutual relationship between the indicators, but do not tell us about their causal direction. Hence, while children are acquiring certain skills by participating in diverse online activities, they may also be acquiring abilities related to internet safety. Also, the opposite might be true: children with good internet skills may use the internet for more activities than less–skilled children. Specific digital skills and the range of online activities show a correlation (r=0.55) with a large size effect (cf Cohen, 1992); the correlation of beliefs in internet abilities with either skills (r=0.43) or activities (r=0.36) show a medium to large size effect.[2]

Differences in children's digital literacy

Studying the influence of children's background characteristics is relevant to discussions on new forms of digital divide and children's capability to cope with the demands of a digitalised society (see, for example, Peter and Valkenburg, 2006; Livingstone and Helsper, 2007). Differences among children might indicate a 'second–level digital divide', which Hargittai (2002) claims is less about having or not having access to the internet, and more about the degree of internet skills required to participate in society. To study this, we examined the effects of children's gender and age and parents' level of education. (Chapter 4 shows that these characteristics are related to differences in internet access.)

Table 7.2 shows that boys reporting slightly higher skills undertake a wider range of online activities and are more confident than girls about their online behaviour. This is consistent with research on gender differences with regard to self-reported digital skills (Hargittai and Shafer, 2006). We find large differences among age groups. Older children are of the opinion that they master more skills, use more online applications and report a higher degree of belief in internet abilities compared to younger children. In relation to family socioeconomic background, it seems that better (higher) educated parents are associated with higher levels of the specific digital skills and the more diverse online activities among children. The relationship with belief in internet abilities is less clear. Children whose parents were educated to primary level or less report the lowest level of belief in internet abilities. However, children with lower secondary educated parents have a stronger belief in their internet abilities than children of parents educated to higher levels. There is some evidence in the literature that

Table 7.2: Self-reported digital literacy by gender, age and highest education of the parents

	Specific digital skills (0-10)	Range of online activities (0-10)	Belief in internet abilities (0-10)
Total	*5.19*	*4.67*	*6.35*
Gender of child			
Male	5.37	4.87	6.62
Female	5.02	4.48	6.08
Age of child			
11-12	3.52	3.80	5.32
13-14	5.41	4.79	6.43
15-16	6.55	5.37	7.24
Highest education of parents in household (ISCED9711)			
Primary or lower	4.11	4.00	6.06
Lower secondary	4.94	4.69	6.45
Upper or post-secondary	5.36	4.74	6.41
Tertiary	5.91	4.98	6.36

Note: The general differences in digital literacy, that is, main effects by gender, age and parental education are significant at ***p<0.001.

people with lower level skills lack the knowledge necessary to recognise their lack of skill (Ehrlinger et al, 2008).

Differences in digital literacy among countries

Country variations in specific digital skills, online activities and belief in internet abilities might be due to differences in technological infrastructures or education systems, which might focus on different skills. Table 7.3 shows that children in Finland, for example, report the highest level of specific digital skills in Europe, and have above-average levels of belief in their internet abilities; however, they undertake only an average range of activities online. Lithuanian children, on

Table 7.3: Self-reported digital literacy by European country

	Means			Correlations		
	Specific digital skills (0-10)	Range of online activities (0-10)	Belief in internet abilities (0-10)	Specific digital skills*Range of online activities	Specific digital skills*Belief in internet abilities	Range of online activities* Belief in internet abilities
Total	5.19	4.67	6.35	0.55	0.43	0.36
Finland	7.24	4.70	7.31	0.53	0.45	0.36
Slovenia	6.79	4.76	6.66	0.50	0.53	0.38
Netherlands	6.68	4.82	5.77	0.44	0.33	0.29
Estonia	6.40	5.29	6.57	0.49	0.42	0.34
Czech Republic	6.28	5.39	7.56	0.53	0.51	0.37
Sweden	6.26	5.23	7.34	0.45	0.39	0.31
Norway	6.22	5.06	5.54	0.56	0.41	0.35
Portugal	6.16	4.89	6.50	0.46	0.38	0.27
Lithuania	6.03	5.65	6.82	0.57	0.42	0.34
Austria	5.92	4.56	7.20	0.64	0.50	0.42
UK	5.87	4.91	7.50	0.54	0.42	0.35
Bulgaria	5.84	5.08	6.87	0.58	0.48	0.36
France	5.83	5.37	6.37	0.53	0.47	0.36
Denmark	5.72	4.64	7.16	0.51	0.41	0.30
Poland	5.64	4.46	7.16	0.51	0.38	0.26
Spain	5.57	4.46	5.73	0.54	0.42	0.32
Belgium	5.54	5.06	6.30	0.54	0.48	0.43
Germany	5.22	4.63	5.97	0.60	0.47	0.47
Ireland	5.00	3.48	6.34	0.53	0.50	0.45
Cyprus	4.76	5.10	6.48	0.47	0.40	0.33
Greece	4.64	4.51	6.88	0.62	0.46	0.42
Hungary	4.31	4.85	5.44	0.42	0.34	0.36
Romania	4.26	4.69	5.96	0.57	0.40	0.44
Italy	4.10	4.51	5.97	0.53	0.41	0.40
Turkey	3.28	3.94	5.46	0.54	0.33	0.30

the other hand, exploit the widest range of online applications, but score slightly above the European average for skills and belief in their internet abilities. Although children in Ireland show an average level of specific digital skills and belief in their internet abilities, their range of online applications is the smallest in Europe. In Turkey, all three measures of digital literacy are quite low. Thus, although generally countries whose children report a higher level of specific digital skills also show larger repertoires of online activities, the variation in the correlations presented in Table 7.3 indicates different relationships among European countries.[3]

Differences in digital literacy among children and countries

We conducted a multilevel analysis to study the factors that explain differences in digital skills. This analysis enables simultaneous study of individual-level (micro) and country-level (macro) differences in digital literacy. Table 7.4 displays the results. Children's age and gender and parents' education level are included in the analyses because they correlate with the self-reported skill measures. To investigate explicitly the influence of inequalities among countries, we also analyse country-level factors. We added to the model parents' average highest level of education, the Gini index (Eurostat, 2009a) and the percentage of internet use (Eurostat, 2009b). The average highest education of parents was calculated based on individual-level data (four-level variable based on ISCED 9711 [International Standard Classification of Education]), averaged by country. The Gini index is a measure of national social inequality, and ranges from between 0 per cent (total equality) and 100 per cent (total inequality). The inclusion of both these measures controls for differences in countries' social inequality as well as socioeconomic differences among children. Including the percentage of country-level internet usage[4] controls for differences in countries' internet experience.

We found that 6 per cent of the differences in children's specific digital skills were due to national differences (differences among countries), while 94 per cent were due to individual-level differences (differences among children). Thus, individual-level differences are more important than differences among countries. The inclusion of children's background characteristics and country-level factors explains 13 per cent of the differences in specific digital skills among children and 18 per cent of the skills differences among countries. The results

Table 7.4: Multilevel analyses with children's specific digital skills, online activities and belief in internet abilities as dependent variables, controlled for clustering between countries (standardised regression coefficients)

	Specific digital skills (0-10)		Range of online activities (0-10)		Belief in internet abilities (0-10)	
	Model 0	Model 1	Model 0	Model 1	Model 0	Model 1
Fixed part – individual level						
Intercept	0.03	–0.51***	0.02	–0.37***	0.01	–0.31***
Girl (ref = Boy)		–0.06***		–0.06***		–0.08***
Age						
11-12 (ref)						
13-14		0.62***		0.46***		0.36***
15-16		0.99***		0.70***		0.59***
Highest education of parents in household (1-4)		0.07***		0.05***		–0.03**
Fixed part – country level						
Gini index of social inequality		0.02		0.01		0.00
Percentage of internet usage		0.15*		0.01		0.02
Highest education of parents in household (1-4)		–0.00		0.05		0.04
Random part						
Variance between countries (SE)	0.06 (0.02)	0.05 (0.02)	0.05 (0.01)	0.05 (0.02)	0.04 (0.01)	0.04 (0.01)
Variance within countries (SE)	0.92 (0.01)	0.75 (0.01)	0.93 (0.01)	0.84 (0.01)	0.96 (0.01)	0.90 (0.01)
R^2 at children's level (%)		13		10		6
R^2 at country level (%)		18		9		7

Note: Model 0 refers to the intercept-only model (without any independent variables); Model 1 includes the children's background characteristics, gender, age and highest education of parents, as well as the average highest education of parents by country, the country-level Gini index and the percentage of internet usage. The analyses are based on 24 countries; Turkey was excluded from the analyses, due to the absence of country-level information.
Significance levels: * $p<0.05$; ** $p<0.01$; *** $p<0.001$.

are similar for range of online activities and children's belief in their internet abilities.[5]

Boys and older children reported significantly more digital skills than girls and younger children. As already noted, children with higher educated parents reported more skills and a wider repertoire of online activities, but less belief in their internet abilities. Based on the size of the standardised regression coefficients, the influences of gender and socioeconomic family background on specific digital skills are small compared to the influence of age.

Average education of parents at country level and the Gini index of social inequality showed no significant relationships with the three measures of digital literacy if we control for children's basic background characteristics. Percentage of internet usage at country-level is positively related to specific digital skills at the individual level. This supports the view that the larger the number of people using the internet in a country, the larger the number of children that claim to be digitally skilled.

Conclusion

Can specific digital skills, online activities and belief in internet abilities combined be used as a proxy for digital literacy? We found that children's levels of specific digital skills and diversity of online activities were highly correlated, and the results were similar for specific digital skills or range of activities. Children's belief in their internet abilities showed a different relationship, possibly indicating that this variable does not measure digital literacy in the same way. Since the survey measures might be subject to possible over- and/or under-estimation, further work is needed to compare the outcomes of performance tests with self-reports of skills in order to validate a set of questions for a survey to measure digital literacy (see van Deursen and van Dijk, 2010 or Hargittai, 2005).

How do these self-reports of digital skills relate to digital literacy, which is a component of the broader concept of media literacy? Although there are many definitions of digital (and media) literacy, most refer to the combination of skills, knowledge and attitudes. Therefore, only relating literacy to skills may be too shallow an approach. The study in this chapter focuses on a particular subset of the skills children might master, namely, safety-related skills; producer-oriented and information skills are only touched on in the questionnaire. Schols, Duimel and de Haan (2010) observe a positive influence of digital skills on creation of user-generated content. Thus, digital literacy refers not only to the ability to understand digital information, but also the ability to use digital information in a critical way, and for personal benefit as well as to participate and contribute to the digital society. Hence, children's digital skills can be seen as a necessary, but not sufficient, component of their digital literacy level. Future research should focus on children's knowledge of different types of internet use and their attitude to using different aspects of the internet. A closer look at children's production of digital content and participation in web-based communities would be useful.

The results of the analysis in this chapter have implications for policy and demonstrate the essential role of formal education in the acquisition of digital literacy, especially for children from lower socioeconomic backgrounds. Given the increasing importance of information technology in contemporary society, mastery of internet skills should be considered a form of essential human capital. While children can acquire basic skills through experimentation, more advanced skills need to be supported by other interventions, including education.

Notes

[1] This measure is the Kuder-Richardson Formula 20 (KR-20) that is analogous to Cronbach's alpha, but computes the reliability coefficient of a set of dichotomous items. It ranges between 0 and 1 – the higher the scores, the more reliable the index variable.

[2] Correlations are similar regardless of whether only the item knowledge of using the internet is used, or it is combined with the item comparing abilities to those of parents. The correlations show smaller effect sizes only if the item knowledge of the internet compared to parents' knowledge is included (respectively, $r=0.36$; $r=0.26$). However, all bivariate correlations are significant at $p<0.001$.

[3] The correlations for specific digital skills and online activities range between $r=0.42$ and $r=0.64$. The correlations for online activities and beliefs in internet abilities range from $r=0.26$ to $r=0.47$. The correlations for specific digital skills and beliefs in internet abilities vary between $r=0.33$ and $r=0.53$.

[4] The percentage of internet usage refers to individuals aged 16-74 who used the internet in the three months previous to the survey (Eurostat, 2009b). The results of the multilevel analysis are similar whether this overall measure of internet use or the percentage of individuals who use the internet at least once a week is included.

[5] Table 7.4 shows that 5 per cent of the difference in the range of online activities is due to national differences, while 95 per cent is due to individual differences. This is respectively 4 and 96 per cent for belief in internet abilities. The inclusion of individual and country-level characteristics explains 10 per cent of the difference in the range of online activities and 6 per cent of the difference in belief in internet abilities among children (at the individual level) and, respectively, 9 and 7 per cent of the difference in the range of online activities and belief in internet abilities among countries (at the national level).

References

Cohen, J. (1992) 'A power primer', *Psychological Bulletin*, vol 112, no 1, pp 155-9.

Eccles, J.S., O'Neill, S.A. and Wigfield, A. (2005) 'Ability self-perceptions and subjective task values in adolescents and children', in K. Moore and L.H. Lippman (eds) *What do children need to flourish? Conceptualizing and measuring indicators of positive development*, New York: Springer Science, pp 237-49.

Eccles, J., Wigfield, A., Harold, R.D. and Blumenfeld, P. (1993) 'Age and gender differences in children's self- and task perceptions during elementary school', *Child Development*, vol 64, no 3, pp 830-47.

Ehrlinger, J., Johnson, K., Banner, M., Dunning D. and Kruger, J. (2008) 'Why the unskilled are unaware: further explorations of (absent) self-insight among the incompetent', *Organizational Behavior and Human Decision Processes*, vol 105, pp 98-121.

Eurostat (2009a) 'Gini coefficient' (http://appsso.eurostat.ec.europa.eu/nui/show.do?dataset=ilc_di12&lang=en).

Eurostat (2009b) 'Internet usage in 2009: households and individuals' (http://epp.eurostat.ec.europa.eu/cache/ITY_OFFPUB/KS-QA-09-046/EN/KS-QA-09-046-EN.PDF).

Hargittai, E. (2002) 'Second level digital divide: differences in people's online skills', *First Monday*, vol 7, no 4, 1 April (http://firstmonday.org/htbin/cgiwrap/bin/ojs/index.php/fm/article/view/942/864).

Hargittai, E. (2005) 'Survey measures of web-oriented digital literacy', *Social Science Computer Review*, vol 23, no 3, pp 371-9.

Hargittai, E. (2007) 'A framework for studying differences in people's digital media uses', in N. Kutscher and H.-U. Otto (eds) *Cyberworld unlimited*, Wiesbaden: VS Verlag für Sozialwissenschaften/GWV Fachverlage GmbH, pp 121-37.

Hargittai, E. and Shafer, S. (2006) 'Differences in actual and perceived online skills: the role of gender', *Social Science Quarterly*, vol 87, vol 2, pp 432-48.

Kruger, J. and Dunning, D. (1999) 'Unskilled and unaware of it: how difficulties in recognizing one's own incompetence lead to inflated self-assessments', *Journal of Personality and Social Psychology*, vol 77, no 6, pp 1121-34.

Kuiper, E., Volman, M. and Terwel, J. (2008) 'Students' use of web literacy skills and strategies: searching, reading and evaluating web information', *Information Research*, vol 13, no 3, paper 351 (http://informationr.net/ir/13-3/paper351.html).

Livingstone, S. (2009) *Children and the internet. Great expectations, challenging realities*, Cambridge: Polity Press.

Livingstone, S. and Helsper, E. (2007) 'Gradations in digital inclusion: children, young people and the digital divide', *New Media & Society*, vol 9, no 4, pp 671-96.

Merchant, G. (2009) 'Literacy in virtual worlds', *Journal of Research in Reading*, vol 32, no 1, pp 38-56.

Peter, J. and Valkenburg, P. (2006) 'Adolescents' internet use: testing the "disappearing digital divide" versus the "emerging digital differentiation" approach', *Poetics*, vol 34, pp 293-305.

Prensky, M. (2001) 'Digital natives, digital immigrants', *On the Horizon – The Strategic Planning Resource for Education Professionals*, vol 9, no 5, pp 1-6.

Rosenbaum, J.E., Beentjes, J.W.J. and Konig, R.P. (2008) 'Mapping media literacy: key concepts and future directions', in C.S. Beck (ed) *Communication yearbook 32*, New York: Routledge, pp 312-53.

Schols, M., Duimel, M. and de Haan, J. (2011) *Hoe cultureel is de digitale generatie? Het internetgebruik voor culturele doeleinden onder schoolgaande tieners* [*How cultural is the digital generation? Use of the Internet for cultural purposes by school-age teenagers*], The Hague: The Netherlands Institute for Social Research.

Snyder, I. (2007) 'Literacy, learning and technology studies', in R. Andrews and C. Haythornthwaite (eds) *The SAGE handbook of e-learning research*, London: Sage Publications, pp 394-415.

Tapscott, R. (1998) *Growing up digital. The rise of the Net Generation*, New York: McGraw-Hill.

van Deursen, A.J.A.M. and van Dijk, J.A.G.M. (2010) 'Measuring internet skills', *International Journal of Human-Computer Interaction*, vol 26, no 10, pp 891-916.

Veen, W. and Vrakking, B (2006) *Homo zappiens. Growing up in a digital age*, London: Continuum International Publishing Group Ltd.

Walraven, A., Brand-Gruwel, S. and Boshuizen, H.P.A. (2009) 'How students evaluate sources and information when searching the world wide web for information', *Computers & Education*, vol 52, no 1, pp 234-46.

EIGHT

Between public and private: privacy in social networking sites

Reijo Kupiainen, Annikka Suoninen and Kaarina Nikunen

Introduction

Social networking has changed many people's everyday lives, and in an extraordinarily short time. Children and young people, especially, are adopting social networking as a part of their social relationships, learning, consumption and creative practices. What defines children and young people as social beings is happening more and more often in social networking sites (SNS), which are online spaces where people can communicate, play, watch video clips, look at photographs and share their feelings and thoughts with others. They are manifestations of 'public culture', the term that Appadurai and Breckenbridge (1995) suggest as an alternative to 'popular culture' or 'mass culture'. Public culture links engagement in popular culture to the practices of participation in the public sphere. Ito and colleagues (2010, p 19) understand public culture as indicating a change from audiences purely consuming media to the 'active participation of a distributed social network in the production and circulation of culture and knowledge'. They refer to 'networked publics', which facilitate the development of public identities and friendship-driven practices on the internet.

As previous research points out, SNS offer a range of possibilities for children to perform, express identity, create and communicate with others (boyd and Ellison, 2007; Green and Hannon, 2007; boyd, 2008; Notley, 2009; Sharples et al, 2009). Young people, in particular, are adapting easily to the new digital cultures, and are eagerly exploring online worlds that appear strange to many adults. However, SNS also involve risks, which are of concern to parents and educators (Livingstone and Helsper, 2007; Ybarra et al, 2007; Staksrud and Livingstone, 2009). Public profiles on SNS and open sharing of materials on the internet can lead to misuse of personal information.

Concerns have been expressed that children and young people do not have a sense of privacy, nor do they understand the dangers of personal data being misused or the risks involved in meeting strangers online. These concerns are illustrative of the blurring of the boundaries between public and private that occurs when SNS connect the private sphere of home to global media and youth culture (see Morley, 2000). It is argued that online worlds create media spaces that overlay the physical locations in which media users live, such as their homes or even their bedrooms (Scannel, 1996; Couldry, 2003). Media are shaping experience in those spaces, and reorganising social relations such as those between parents and children, or those between friends and strangers (see Moores, 2004).

Previous research shows that the offline and online worlds of young people are intertwined (boyd, 2008; Livingstone, 2009; Notley, 2009; Liu, 2011). Young people seem to use SNS predominantly to connect online with friends made offline (Valkenburg et al, 2005; Ellison et al, 2007; boyd, 2008; Peter et al, 2009). However, research also shows the way that SNS are facilitating social inclusion for teenagers that are marginalised in some way (Notley, 2009; Nikunen, 2010). While some argue that SNS have profoundly changed the way children interact and form social relations, others point to continuities (Livingstone and Brake, 2010), to the ways that the internet and SNS have provided social relations and identity construction with a new visibility rather than reconfiguring them completely (Notley, 2009; Nikunen, 2010; Robards and Bennett, 2011). However, the blurring of the boundaries between public and private poses new challenges and opens up space for various risks. Parents often find it difficult to monitor their children's online lives: children's online lives are often visible to their peers and the internet, but private as far as their parents are concerned (boyd, 2008, p 131).

This chapter explores the nature of and problems related to young people's networked publics. We focus on the issue of privacy and explore in particular how it relates to parents, friends and misuse of personal data. In what ways do parental attitudes towards SNS affect children's social networking? Are the profiles of children and teenagers private or public and, if private, is this privacy connected to the formation of friendships on SNS? How common is the misuse of children and young people's personal data – by themselves and others – and what makes them vulnerable to data misuse?

Popularity of social networking among the children

One of the reasons for the popularity of SNS among young people is that participation in them can enhance social relationships by providing individual spaces for the young to share their thoughts, feelings and content (see Livingstone, 2008). SNS are popular with teenagers across Europe. According to EU Kids Online data, 59 per cent of 9- to 16-year-old internet users have a social networking profile, and 23 per cent of these have more than one profile. Also, 77 per cent of 13- to 16-year-olds have a social networking profile, although the figures vary from slightly less than two thirds in Turkey and Romania, to over 90 per cent in Norway, Slovenia and the Czech Republic. Only 38 per cent of 9- to 12-year-old European children have social networking profiles, and country differences in their use of SNS are large. In France and Germany only slightly more than a quarter of 9- to 12-year-olds have SNS profiles, compared to over two thirds in the Netherlands.[1] In 15 of the 25 countries surveyed, Facebook was the main site for at least two thirds of site users, and in 17 countries it was the primary site for more than half social networkers.[2]

Figure 8.1 shows contrasting age patterns for users of SNS in a few selected countries. The UK is fairly typical of Europe in general: the percentage of SNS users is growing steadily, from 21 per cent among 9-year-olds to over 90 per cent among 16-year-olds. In the Netherlands and Denmark SNS are exploited at younger ages, and the percentage of

Figure 8.1: SNS use by age in five European countries (% of those with SNS profile of all internet users)

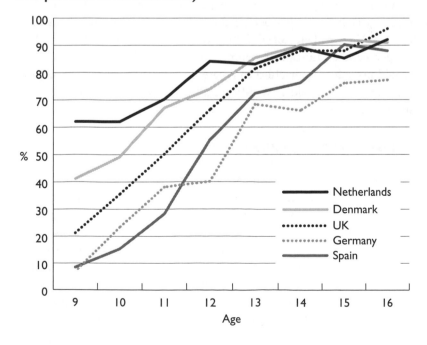

users is above the European average for 9- to 12-year-olds. In Germany and Spain, SNS are more popular with older age groups. In Germany use is below the European average, for all age groups; in Spain the pattern is of a steep rise following a slow start, with some 90 per cent of older Spanish teenagers having a SNS profile.

Media and the internet are often seen as partly replacing the role of traditional authorities or agents related to locality, community and family in young people's lives (Ziehe and Stubenrauch, 1982). However, since the offline and online worlds are intertwined, activity online is regulated and organised in accordance with the offline worlds of home, school and community. This is demonstrated by the way that parental approval affects children's use of SNS. For example 77 per cent of parents of 9- to 12-year-olds who do not have a social networking profile say that they do not allow their children to have one, and 14 per cent said that they would allow them to have one with permission or supervision. In those countries where younger children have the lowest percentages of social networking profiles, the activity is most often restricted by parents. In the five countries represented in Figure 8.1, 81 per cent of Spanish, 74 per cent of German and 67 per cent of British parents of 9- to 10-year-old children said that they would not allow their children to have a social networking profile while this applies to 43 per cent of parents in Denmark and 28 per cent of parents in the Netherlands.

When children become teenagers, country differences diminish (see Figure 8.1). It seems that parents are less concerned about adolescents' use of SNS (see Peter et al, 2009) and are less likely to ban it. Only 15 per cent of European parents of 13- to 16-year-olds said they would not allow their child to create a social networking profile, and only 18 per cent said it would be allowed only with permission or supervision.

Privacy of SNS profiles

Privacy on the internet and SNS is high on the agendas of public debates in many countries, but the research findings are contradictory. For example, Gross and Acquisti (2005) argue that SNS users give out personal information that exposes them to various online risks, while Livingstone (2008) maintains that there are no reasons to conclude that teenagers are not concerned about their privacy. Users of SNS have to make decisions about how much information about themselves they will provide. Looking for new friends on the internet requires the revelation of a certain amount of personal information, but profiles on SNS are more often social group place-markers than personal self-portrayals (Peter et al, 2009).

Fahey (1995, p 688; see also Livingstone 2008, p 406) argues that 'it may be more accurate to speak of more complex re-structuring in a series of zones of privacy' which does not fit with the standard public/private dichotomy. These 'zones of privacy' are now part of online life, allowing people to create spaces of intimacy with their closest friends, while 'zones of public' allow them to perform their identities before a larger online community.

boyd (2008, p 131) points out that networked publics make structurally enforced borders of intimacy almost impossible. In a global network it is not possible to move without leaving digital traces and, indeed, young people go online precisely to see and be seen by others. Also, SNS are designed to provide personal information, such as names or photographs (Livingstone and Brake, 2010). One structural tactic for controlling intimacy involves privacy settings that allow choices to be made about who can see content.

According to the EU Kids Online survey 44 per cent of 9- to 16-year-old SNS users keep their profiles private, 29 per cent keep them partially private and 27 per cent reported that their profiles were public. Public profiles are most common in Hungary, Turkey and Romania, where over 40 per cent of the profiles on the SNS are public; this applies to only 11 per cent of profiles in the UK and Ireland. In most countries public profiles are slightly more common among teenage boys than teenage girls.

Willingness to share personal data on SNS is understandable when the aim is to find new contacts on the internet, or to extend a friendship circle with the addition of global contacts. This is common, for example, in online gaming. The blurring of public and private domains has implications for negotiations with 'friends' and 'strangers'. In the online world, there is no simple distinction between friends and strangers; on SNS many strangers are actually friends of friends. Therefore, friendships are negotiated through complex networks of relationships (Notley, 2009) and, as members share personal information and spend time together online, it becomes increasingly difficult to differentiate friends from strangers. As SNS audiences multiply, with mixed groups of friends, friends of friends, parents and relatives, identity construction also becomes more complex (Robards and Bennett, 2011).

Finding new friends seems to be one of the basic functions of SNS and would seem to be quite clearly connected to teenagers' desires to explore the world and widen their familiar circles. The media industry supports this activity by providing tools that can be used to look for new 'friends'. The activity of looking for new friends on the internet is more common among 13- to 16-year-olds than among 9- to 12-year-olds, and is more common among young people with SNS profiles than among those without. Forty-two per cent of 9- to 12-year-olds with a SNS profile had looked for new friends using the internet in the 12 months previous to the survey, and 47 per cent of all 13- to 16-year-olds and 51 per cent of those 13- to 16-year-olds with a SNS profile had looked for new friends on the internet. Twenty-nine per cent of 13- to 16-year-olds with a SNS profile had looked for new friends at least once a month in the year preceding the survey. However, a private profile does not necessarily mean a focus only on current friends. While 61 per cent of European teenagers with public profiles had looked for new friends in the 12 months previous to the survey, 43 per cent of those with private profiles had also done so.

Figure 8.2 shows country averages for the different profile settings, and frequency of search for new friends on the internet. It shows that there are no clear connections between typical profile types within a country and frequency of searching for new friends on the internet ($r=0.16$, $p=0.44$).

The search for new friends on the internet among teenagers is most frequent in Bulgaria and Romania and least frequent in Spain and Finland. In Bulgaria public profiles are more common than generally in Europe; in Spain most SNS profiles are private. It would seem that profile settings do not affect how often teenagers search for new friends on the internet. Also, the correlation between searching for new friends and the teenager's number of contacts enabled by SNS is very low. Note, however, that searching for new friends can be enabled by other platforms than SNS.

Misuse of personal data

A public profile and open sharing of information on SNS can be seen as problematic if they lead to misuse of personal data. Every use of the internet leaves digital traces, which commercial companies, for example, find valuable. Users of the internet and SNS who share personal information or passwords are also vulnerable to stalking and grooming, sexual abuse and online bullying. However, general misuse of personal information seems to be a more frequent risk than attempts at grooming, for example (Livingstone and Brake, 2010). The most important group experiencing risks related to personal data-sharing is teenagers who have recently created a profile and want to recreate their identities and establish contacts with their peers in the online community.

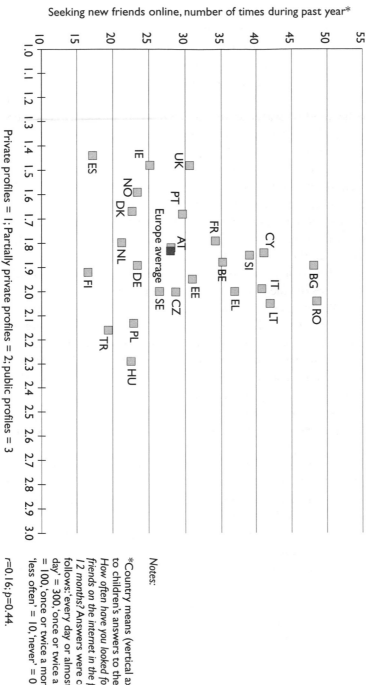

Figure 8.2: SNS profile settings and seeking new friends online (among 13- to 16-year-old SNS users)

Notes:

*Country means (vertical axis) refer to children's answers to the question, *How often have you looked for new friends on the internet in the past 12 months?* Answers were coded as follows: 'every day or almost every day' = 300, 'once or twice a week' = 100, 'once or twice a month' = 30, 'less often' = 10, 'never' = 0

r=0.16; p=0.44.

The EU Kids Online study asked respondents aged 11 or over whether during the 12 months before the survey they had experienced any kind of misuse of personal data: 9 per cent of 11- to 16-year-olds and 11 per cent of those with their own social networking profiles said that they had (see Figure 8.3). The most common type of data misuse related to misuse of passwords (experienced by 7 per cent of all those to whom the question was addressed, and 8 per cent of social networkers). Misuse of personal data was most common among teenage girls: 11 per cent of 13- to 16-year-old girls had experienced some type of personal data misuse and the percentage was 13 per cent for social networkers. However, in relation to the extensiveness of use of internet and SNS, the number experiencing misuse of data was quite low.

There are some types of behaviour that may increase vulnerability to misuse of young people's personal data. Data misuse is experienced more often by those who, at least once a month, had been in direct contact with people they had not met face to face. Contacts included sending photos or videos of themselves, providing personal information (for example, full name, address, telephone number) and adding the person to their 'friends' list or address book (see Figure 8.3). A quarter of young people who had sent personal information or photos or videos of themselves to people they had not met face to face had experienced misuse of personal data, and misuse was experienced by a fifth of those who added people they had not met in the physical world, to their friends lists or address books.

Twenty per cent of 11- to 16-year-olds who had experienced direct contact with people they had not met face to face had experienced some kind of misuse of their personal data. Only 8 per cent of those with fewer direct contacts with people they had not met experienced similar data misuse. There were no differences among age groups, between genders or in terms of the usage of SNS.

At the same time, 80 per cent of young people who had direct contacts with people only met online had not had their data misused. Therefore, sending photos and personal information to internet acquaintances and adding them to friends lists and address books did not generally lead to misuse of personal data; these reasons cannot be said to increase instances of data misuse.

Nevertheless, there is a clear connection between experiencing data misuse and behaviour, referred to in this study as 'risky online activity': 24 per cent of those who had indulged in all five types of risky online behaviour in the 12 months previous to the survey had experienced data misuse, while this applied to only 5 per cent of those whose behaviour online was 'good'.

Figure 8.3: Percentage of 11-16 year olds who have experienced misuse of personal data, by online behaviour

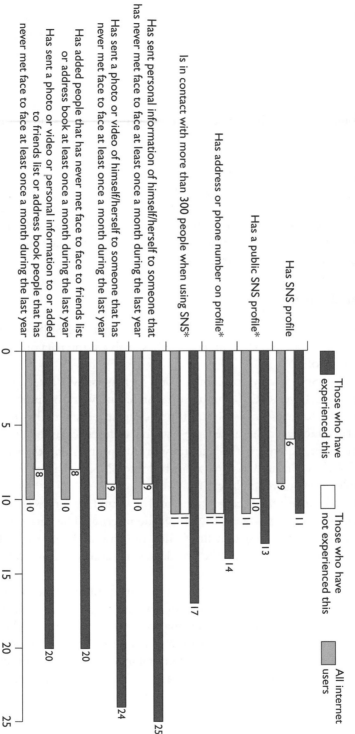

Note:*All SNS users.

The data do not suggest that data misuse is connected only with new contacts on the internet; personal data can be misused by existing contacts as a joke among friends. However, it may also be used for online bullying: 30 per cent of 11- to 16-year-olds who said that they had been bullied on the internet had experienced misuse of personal data, while only 7 per cent of those who had not been the victims of online bullying had experienced data misuse. The kind of online bullying that includes data misuse usually takes place on SNS or through instant messaging.

This finding is in line with research showing that disclosure of personal information may not in itself cause risk (Wolak et al, 2008). However, multiple online activities, such as interacting or including on friends lists people not known in the physical world, seeking out pornography and being rude to others, seem to increase the risk of online victimisation (Ybarra et al, 2007).

Conclusion

While sharing information is an essential aspect of SNS, there are concerns about privacy. This chapter has analysed the data on the risk potential of SNS.

Use of SNS is very common among teenagers: over three quarters in Europe have at least one personal social networking profile, and in most countries this is 80 to 90 per cent of teenagers that use the internet. However, there are large national differences in the numbers of younger children with social networking profiles and their use of SNS is closely related to parental attitudes to SNS, with many banning profiles for younger children.

It has been assumed that a private profile would be connected to less frequent searching for new friends on the internet. The data explored in this chapter suggest that this is not the case and that there is no clear connection between the profile setting and the search for new friends online.

We also found that use of SNS was not particularly risky for young people based on the data for misuse of children's personal details. Having a public profile that includes personal contact information, and being in contact with hundreds of people during activity on SNS, did not seem to make children especially vulnerable to data misuse. Some data misuse experienced by children was unconnected to contacts with strangers and could be construed as online bullying.

Notes

[1] In the Netherlands the most popular site among children and teenagers is Hyves, which is a national SNS aimed especially at young people, and may explain the popularity of social networking among younger children in the Netherlands.

[2] In five countries (the Netherlands, Poland, Spain, Germany and Hungary) one or two national SNS were the most important for at least two thirds of users. In three countries (Romania, Lithuania and Estonia) several sites (including Facebook) were identified as important.

References

Appadurai, A. and Breckenridge (1995) 'Public modernity in India', in C.A. Breckenridge (ed) *Consuming modernity: Public culture in a South Asian world*, Minneapolis, MN: University of Minnesota Press, pp 1–20.

boyd, d. (2008) 'Why youth [love] social network sites: the role of networked publics in teenage social life', in D. Buckingham (ed) *Youth, identity, and digital life*, The John D. and Catherine T. MacArthur Foundation Series on Digital Media and Learning, Cambridge, MA/London: The MIT Press, pp 119–42.

boyd, d. and Ellison, N. (2007) 'Social network sites: definition, history, and scholarship', *Journal of Computer-Mediated Communication*, vol 13, no 1, pp 210–30.

Couldry, N. (2003) 'Media, symbolic power and the limits of Bourdieu's field theory', Media@lse Electronic working papers, Department of Media and Communications, *LSE No 2* (http://eprints.lse.ac.uk/13451).

Ellison, N.P., Steinfield, C. and Lampe, C. (2007) 'The benefits of Facebook "friends": social capital and college students' use of online social network sites', *Journal of Computer-Mediated Communication*, vol 12, no 4, pp 1143–68.

Fahey, T. (1995) 'Privacy and the family', *Sociology*, vol 29, no 4, pp 687–703.

Green, H. and Hannon, C. (2007) *Their space: Education for a digital generation*, London: Demos.

Gross, R. and Acquisti, A. (2005) 'Information revelation and privacy in online and social networks (The Facebook case)' (www.heinz.cmu.edu/~acquisti/papers/privacy-facebook-gross-acquisti.pdf).

Ito, M., Horst, H., Bittanti, M., boyd, d., Herr-Stephenson, B., Lange, P. G., Pascoe, C. J. and Robinson, L. (2010) *Hanging out, messing around, and geeking out: Kids living and learning with new media*, Cambridge, MA/London: The MIT Press.

Liu, F. (2011) *Urban youth in China: Modernity, the internet and the self*, New York and London: Routledge.

Livingstone, S. (2008) 'Taking risky opportunities in youthful content creation: teenagers' use of social networking sites for intimacy, privacy and self-expression', *New Media & Society*, vol 10, no 3, pp 393-411.

Livingstone, S. (2009) *Children and the internet*, Cambridge: Polity Press.

Livingstone, S. and Brake, D. (2010) 'On the rapid rise of social networking sites: new findings and policy implications', *Children & Society*, vol 24, pp 75-83.

Livingstone, S. and Helsper E.J. (2007) 'Taking risks when communicating on the internet', *Information, Communication & Society*, vol 10, no 5, pp 619-44.

Moores, S. (2004) 'The doubling of place: electronic media, time-space arrangements and social relationships', in N. Couldry and A. McCarthy (eds) *Media space: Place, scale and culture in a media age*, London: Routledge, pp 21-36.

Morley, D. (2000) *Home territories: Media, mobility and identity*, London and New York: Routledge.

Nikunen, K. (2010) 'Online among us: experiences of virtuality in the everyday life', *Nordicom Review*, vol 32, no 2-3, pp 75-82.

Notley, T. (2009) 'Young people, online networks and social inclusion', *Journal of Computer-Mediated Communication*, vol 14, no 4, pp 1208-27.

Peter, J., Valkenburg, P.M. and Fluckiger, C. (2009) 'Adolescents and social network sites: identity, friendships and privacy', in S. Livingstone and L. Haddon (eds) *Kids online: Opportunities and risks for children*, Bristol: The Policy Press, pp 83-94.

Robards, B. and Bennett, A. (2011) 'My tribe: post-subcultural manifestations of belonging in social network sites', *Sociology*, vol 42, no 2, pp 303-17.

Scannell, P. (1996) *Radio, television and modern life*, Oxford: Blackwell.

Sharples, M., Graber, R., Harrison, C. and Logan, K. (2009) 'E-safety and web 2.0 for children aged 11–16', *Journal of Computer Assisted Learning*, vol 25, no 1, pp 70-84.

Staksrud, E. and Livingstone, S. (2009) 'Children and online risk', *Information, Communication & Society*, vol 12, no 3, pp 364-87.

Valkenburg, P.M., Schouten, A.P. and Peter, J. (2005) 'Adolescents' identity experiments on the internet', *New Media & Society*, vol 7, no 3, pp 383-402.

Wolak, J., Finkelhor, D., Mitchell, K.J. and Ybarra, M.L. (2008) 'Online "predators" and their victims: myths, realities and implications for prevention and treatment', *American Psychologist*, vol 63, no 2, pp 111-28.

Ybarra, M., Mitchell, K., Finkelhorn, D. and Wolak, J. (2007) 'Online victimization of youth: five years later', *Journal of Adolescent Health*, vol 40, no 2, pp 116-26.

Ziehe, T. and Stubenrauch, H. (1982) *Plädoyer für ungewöhnliches Lernen. Ideen zu Jugendsituation* [*Pleading for unusual learning*], Hamburg: Rowohlt.

NINE

Experimenting with the self online: a risky opportunity

Lucyna Kirwil and Yiannis Laouris[1]

Introduction

Developmental theories assume that at the beginning stages of adolescence, young people's developmental tasks and the instability of their 'selves' motivate them to experiment with their identities and self-presentation. There is growing evidence that adolescents use the internet to experiment in this way, especially on social networking sites (SNS) (Calvert et al, 2003; Valkenburg et al, 2005; Williams and Merten, 2008). This experimentation should gradually decrease as children get older and fulfil their developmental tasks, that is, younger children should experiment more than older ones (Valkenburg et al, 2005; Livingstone, 2008) – the closer to the goal, that is, being adult, an adolescent is, the stronger should be his/her motivation to complete a developmental task.

Experimenting with the self is considered here as experimenting with self-presentation online. It is defined as pretending to be someone else, of another gender, practised more often by boys than girls, or, more commonly, of a different age (Calvert et al, 2003; Valkenburg et al, 2005; Valkenburg and Peter, 2008; Williams and Merten, 2008). For example, some girls want to be perceived as younger and nicer while others want to present themselves as older or attractive (Calvert et al, 2003; Valkenburg et al, 2005). Of course, teenagers are working out who they really are. Experimentation is about necessary and constructive exploration and discovery rather than deceit. Motivations of experimentation include social compensation (i.e. to overcome shyness, communication difficulty or other weaknesses), self-exploration (i.e. taking various personality features or identities to investigate how others react on an adolescent), and social facilitation (to facilitate dating, making friends and relationship formation).

Research aims and methods

The first part of the chapter explores the hypothesis that this experimentation is common. We also hypothesise that age matters substantially, being less prevalent among older children. Our third hypothesis predicts that experimenting with self-presentation online is more common among boys for two reasons: boys are developmentally further from adulthood than girls of the same age (Allison and Shultz, 2001; Lerner and Steinberg, 2004; Sax, 2007), thus they feel more pressure to pass through consecutive developmental stages; and boys undertake more online activities measured in terms of variety, frequency and length of time (Jackson, 2008; Gui and Argentin, 2011), so they are also more likely to experiment online.

This chapter also examines whether 'wearing' a changed identity is associated with engaging in risky online activities. In mid-adolescence, according to Steinberg (2010), at ages 12-13 and 14-15 in particular, adolescents are especially vulnerable to reward-seeking. Teenagers show a very rapid increase of sensation-seeking. Their vulnerability itself may lead to more intensive experimentation in order to be attractive and rewarded socially by other people. At the same time, between 14 and 16 years of age, reward and sensation-seeking constitutes a predictor of risky activities (Slater, 2003; Romer et al, 2010; Steinberg, 2010). We hypothesised that experimentation also leads to more harm/negative experiences.

Finally, we examine whether this experimentation predicts undertaking risky online activities in the presence of other factors important during adolescence, such as self-efficacy and individual need for stimulation, that is, sensation-seeking (which is correlated with reward seeking; see Kirwil, 2011), as well as the developing child's age and gender.

In this chapter we consider two forms of presentational behaviour: (a) pretending to be a different kind of person online than child really is and (b) claiming to be different age on a SNS from the child's real age. We use the modified definition of risky online activities adopted from risky online activities in the UK Children of Go Online survey (Livingstone and Helsper, 2007), including only four (instead of five) risky online activities: (1) looking for new friends on the internet; (2) adding people to friends list or address book that the child has never met face to face; (3) sending personal information to someone that the child has never met face to face; (4) sending a photo or video of child him or herself to someone that the child has never met face to face. We define harm as being bothered by experiences on the internet that make a child feel uncomfortable or upset.

Findings

Prevalence of experimentation

We found that a similar number of children pretended to be a different person online (15 per cent of 21,281 responses) and assumed a different age (16 per cent of 15,722 responses). Two of three of the 11- to 16-year-old children (67 per cent of 2,703 responses) who agreed to have ever 'Pretended to be a different kind of person on the internet from who I really am' also said that they 'find it easier to be myself on the internet than when I am with people face to face', which was significantly more than those not presenting themselves online as a different kind of person (46 per cent of 14,029 responses) (chi^2(1)=398.7; p<0.001). Similar, although smaller, differences between those who did and did not give a false age in their SNS profile existed: 56 per cent (of 2,026 responses) versus 52 per cent (of 11,543 responses) said they 'find it easier to be myself on the internet than when I am with people face to face' (chi^2(1)=12.6; p<0.001). On average, one in five children (21 per cent of 15,091 children aged 11–16) reported one of the two indices of experimenting with self-presentation, implying it is not a very common behaviour.

The fact that in other studies the prevalence was substantially higher (Valkenburg et al, 2005; Williams and Merten, 2008) may be because researchers used a wider variety of measures of experimentation. But it may also be because the cited studies were conducted in one country. In fact, we observed substantial variations across European countries in pretending to be a different kind of person: from less than 12 per cent in Hungary, the UK, Cyprus, Spain, the Netherlands, Belgium, Greece and Denmark to 12 to 17 per cent in France, Ireland, Italy, Bulgaria, Portugal, Poland, Slovenia and Finland, to 19 to 27 per cent in the Czech Republic, Lithuania, Romania, Sweden, Austria, Norway, Turkey and Estonia. This national variation is significant (chi^2 (24)=409; p<0.001) but it seems to be associated with such factors as geographical location and culture.

Table 9.1 also shows how the two indices of experimentation compare across countries. Claiming to be a different age occurs for only 2 to 10 per cent of children from Hungary, Poland, the Netherlands, Germany, Lithuania and Bulgaria, but the figure is higher elsewhere.

Table 9.1: Prevalence of two forms of experimenting with self-presentation on the internet among European children

Country of interview	% of children experimenting with self-presentation		Rank of the country on prevalence of experimenting with self-presentation	
	Different kind of person[a]	Different age at SNS profile[b]	Different kind of person	Different age at SNS profile
Hungary	6	2	1	1
UK	7	21	2	20
Cyprus	8	23	3	21
Spain	9	27	4	25
Netherlands	10	6	5	3
Belgium	10	21	6	19
Greece	11	19	7	15
Denmark	11	24	8	23
France	12	18	9	12
Ireland	13	23	10	22
Italy	14	20	11	16
Bulgaria	15	10	12	6
Germany	16	8	13	4
Portugal	16	25	14	24
Poland	16	3	15	2
Slovenia	17	21	16	18
Finland	17	14	17	10
Czech Republic	19	13	18	8
Lithuania	19	7	19	5
Romania	19	12	20	7
Sweden	19	19	21	14
Austria	19	14	22	9
Norway	19	17	23	11
Turkey	21	18	24	13
Estonia	27	20	25	17
European mean	15	16		

Note: Countries in bold form the group of 14 countries with the positive relationship between two forms of experimenting with self-presentation online: the more children pretend to be a different person online, the more of them use another age in SNS (social networking site) profile. Those not in bold represent 11 countries with the negative relationship between two forms of experimenting with self-presentation online: the more children use another age in SNS profile, the less pretend to be a different person online.

[a] *Base:* 21,278 children aged 9-16, who replied to the question: 'Have you done any of the following things in the PAST 12 MONTHS? Pretended to be a different kind of person on the internet from who I really am'. Percentage weighted.

[b] *Base:* 15,723 children aged 11-16, who replied to the question: 'Which of the bits of information on this card does your [SNS] profile include about you? An age that is not your real age?' Percentage weighted.

The differences between the countries are significant (chi^2(24)=564; $p<0.001$), but the pattern is not easy to explain.

The countries form two groups, the first composed of 14 countries in which the relationship between the two forms of experimenting with self-presentation online is positive: Turkey, Bulgaria, Romania, Hungary, Austria, the Czech Republic, Poland, Lithuania, Estonia, Finland, Sweden, Norway, the Netherlands and Germany. The second group is the 11 countries where the relationship between two forms of experimentation is negative: Portugal, Spain, France, Ireland, the UK, Belgium, Denmark, Slovenia, Italy, Greece and Cyprus.

Comparing the average percentage of the two indices, in the first group of 14 countries (mainly Middle and Eastern Europe), the average percentage of children presenting themselves as a different kind of person (M=17.3; SD=4.9) is higher than the average percentage of children presenting a different age (M=11.6; SD=5.8; $t(13)$=5.8; $p<0.001$), and both forms of experimentation are positively correlated (r=0.79; p=0.001). The prevalence of experimentation in the 11 other countries (mainly Western Europe) forms a different pattern. The average percentage of children experimenting with their age (M=22.0; SD=2.7) is higher than that of children who pretend to be a different person (M=11.6; SD=3.2; $t(10)$=8.0; $p<0.001$), but the two forms of experimentation are not intercorrelated (r=−0.08; ns). In the 14 Middle and Eastern European countries children presenting themselves as a different kind of person is significantly more common ($F(1,23)$=18.9; p=0.003), and presenting their age falsely is significantly less common ($F(1,23)$=29.5; $p<0.001$) than in the 11 Western European countries.

We conclude that experimenting with the self-presentation is less common than expected and that the prevalence of this behaviour in Europe varies. National differences might be based on the ease of undertaking direct communication by children embedded in their cultures of communication or differences in a level of reward from online communication. It is possible that more children experiment with self online in some countries as an attempt to balance lower levels of expressiveness in their daily life (Pennebaker and Francis, 1996).

Age and gender differences in experimenting with self-presentation online

Younger children are more likely to falsify their age than pretend to be a different kind of person. When approaching adolescence, children become less interested in experimenting with their age on SNS, which may in part reflect that they have less need to since this is the legitimate threshold for joining many such sites (see Figure 9.1).

Figure 9.1: Developmental trends in experimenting with the self online, by age

—◆— 'An age that is not your real age' in the SNS profile: Boys

—■— 'An age that is not your real age' in the SNS profile: Girls

—△— 'Pretended to be a different kind of person on the internet from who I really am': Boys

—○— 'Pretended to be a different kind of person on the internet from who I really am': Girls

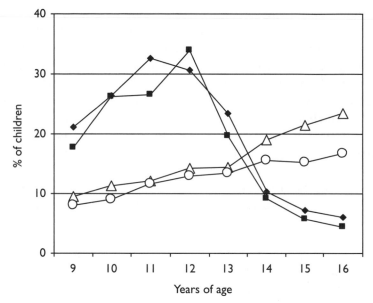

Base: All children replied the questions given in the legend.
Note: Boys and girls differ on all age trends significantly on the level *p*<0.001.

Pretending to be a different kind of person becomes gradually more common from the ages of 9-16, increasing from 9 to 20 per cent (chi^2(7)=220; *p*<0.001), that is, a fifth of 16-year-olds are still experimenting with their self-presentation online.

From age 9 (19 per cent) to 12 (32 per cent) there is a dynamically increasing prevalence of experimenting with age, but this decreases rapidly from 32 to 10 per cent between 12 and 14 years of age, and slowly from 10 to 5 per cent between 14 and 16 years of age. Age changes in prevalence of presenting another age on SNS are significant (chi^2(7)=1215; *p*<0.001), and the relationship is curvilinear with a highest activity at age 12, fitting Steinberg's (2010) claim that at age 12-13 reward-seeking is most intensive.

There is a more rapid increase in experimenting with age among girls aged 12 than among boys of the same age. In both the younger and older age groups, a slightly smaller percentage of girls (15 per cent on average) than boys (17 per cent on average) experiment with age online. It is only at age 12 that girls (34 per cent) are more active than boys (31 per cent). This might be confirmation that the developmental task of transition to the adult world is achieved more quickly by girls. More boys than girls experiment in pretending to be a different person ($chi^2(1)=38$; $p<0.001$), pretending to be another age ($chi^2(1)=8.8$; $p=0.003$), and experiment in both forms taken together ($chi^2(2)=32$; $p<0.001$) − and girls show an earlier reduction in this behaviour. The difference is systematic, but we have to show caution in interpretation because there were only two measures − other aspects of self-presentation, for instance, being nice or attractive, may show that girls experiment more with self-presentation.

Does experimenting with self-presentation online matter for negative online experience?

Among children who experiment with self-presentation online, we expected that there would be more children with at least one of seven tested negative experiences on the internet, that is, being bullied online, exposed to sexual images, receiving sexual messages, meeting new contacts online, meeting new online contacts offline, exposed to potentially harmful user-generated content (such as hate, pro-anorexia, self-harm drug-taking or suicide) and experiencing personal data misuse (together, the seven online risks analysed elsewhere in this book). Indices of 'harm from risks encountered online' included measures of intensity and duration of emotional negative states (that is, feeling upset) relating to four risks: being bullied online, receiving sexual messages, exposure to sexual images and meetings online contacts offline.

Table 9.2 shows that some negative online experiences are more prevalent among children who experiment with their self-presentation online. The findings reveal that children's experimenting through pretending to be a different kind of person online, more than their experimentation with age, is associated with a greater prevalence of experiencing risks on the internet (33 per cent more among the children who experimented this way than among those who did not). Encountering online risks was 5 per cent more prevalent among children who did not pretend to be an age that was not their real age than among those who did this. This is the opposite of what was expected, and may be because those who do not experiment with their

Table 9.2: Children who encountered at least one of seven risks online, by whether they experimented with self-presentation online

Group on experimenting with self-presentation online	Has child encountered any of the 7 risks	Did child suffer harm – harm index from:			
		being victim of bullying	seeing sexual images	meeting online contacts	sexual messages received
Pretended to be a different kind of person from who child really is	76% of 3,134	79% of 310	83% of 239	28% of 53	87% of 174
Not pretended to be a different kind of person from who child really is	43% of 18,044	77% of 721	83% of 509	14% of 49	91% of 257
Between-groups difference in prevalence	33%	2%	0%	14%	−4%
Chi² [a]	1,156***	<1	0	3.0⁺	2.3
N base	21,178	1,031	748	102	431
Pretended to be at age that is not child's real age	53% of 2,560	82% of 163	90% of 109	11% of 18	91% of 65
Not pretended to be at age that is not child's real age	58% of 12,713	78% of 786	83% of 513	25% of 79	88% of 321
Between-groups difference in prevalence	−5%	4%	7%	14%	3%
Chi² [a]	26***	1.7	3.2*¹	1.7	<1
N base	15,273	949	622	97	386

Note: *** $p<0.001$; ** $p<0.01$;* $p<0.05$; ⁺ $p<0.10$.

[a] One-tail test.

The base in each cell is all children who replied to the questions on experimenting with self-presentation, experienced any of the seven risks (the second column from the left) or encountered one of the seven risks and suffered one of four harms (four columns on the right).

age tended to be older (*M*=13.5; *SD*=2.0; *N*=12,713) than those who do (*M*=12.2; *SD*=1.8; *N*=2,560; *t*(4080)=31; *p*<0.001).

As regards harm, more children who experimented with their 'selves' pretending to be a different kind of person online (28 per cent) than children who did not experiment this way (14 per cent) suffered harm after meeting their online contacts offline (chi^2(1)=3; *p*=0.07, one-tail test). Harm experienced as a result of exposure to sexual images is more prevalent among children who pretended to be another age on SNS (90 per cent) than among those who did not (83 per cent; chi^2(1)=3.2; *p*=0.05, one-tail test).

In Table 9.3 the first two rows show that the more often children aged 9-16 pretend to be a different kind of person online than they are really are, the more often they undertake risky online activities. Paradoxically, children who experiment with age in their SNS profiles, probably because they are younger, undertake less often risky online activities. However, we do not see evidence that experimenting with

Table 9.3: Correlations between forms of experimenting with self-presentation on the internet and undertaking risky activities, encountered online risks and measures of harm from online risks

Indices of risky online activities, experienced risks and harm		Pretended to be a different kind of person on the internet from who I really am (frequency)[b]	On SNS profile an age that is not real age (yes/no)[c]
Mean frequency of four risky online activities	r	0.42***	−0.06***
	n	19,590	13,264
Experience of any of the seven risks (no, yes)	r	0.20***c	−0.04***
	n	21,178	15,273
Harm index – from being victim of bullying[a]	r	0.04	0.05
	n	1,031	949
Harm index – sexual images[a]	r	0.06	0.10*
	n	748	622
Harm index – meeting online contacts offline[a]	r	0.18*c	0.01
	n	161	152
Harm index – sexual messages[a]	r	−0.00	−0.04
	n	431	386
Harm index total – mean 4 risks[a] (sexual images, sexual messages, being bullied and meeting online contacts)	r	−0.02	0.06
	n	15	18

Base: All children who experienced harm of a given kind and replied to the questions about experimenting with self-presentation.

Notes: *** *p*<0.001; * *p*<0.05.
[a] Experienced harm index of: intensity of harm by duration of harm (0 = low, 12 = high).
[b] Pearson correlation coefficient (except indexed with [c]).
[c] Spearman rank correlation coefficient.
r = correlation coefficient; *n* = sample size.

self-presentation is associated with actually experiencing harm from online risks; except for harm from meeting face to face online contacts and harm from sexual images online is the latter being associated with experimenting with age. The other indices of harm suffered by children from online risks were not significantly associated with our measures of experimentation. This contrasts with another study, where we show that children who indulge more often in pretending to be a different kind of person online are more at risk of being victimised through cyberbullying (Kirwil, 2010; Laouris and Kirwil, 2010). It is worth adding that few children experienced intensive and long-lasting harm from online risks.

Thus moral anxiety about the negative impact of experimenting online with the self does not find strong confirmation, because only two among eight tested indices appeared to be interrelated to measures of experimenting with self-presentation online.

How much does experimenting with self-presentation online matter as a predictor of undertaking risky activities online?

Recent literature underlies that risk-taking reaches an extreme intensity and is more common behaviour during adolescence than in other stages of development, especially in boys (Romer et al, 2010; Steinberg, 2010). Higher sensation-seeking should be a strong predictor of undertaking risky online activities. Self-efficacy should be a protective factor against experiencing harm from countering unexpected online risks. However, higher self-efficacy should create more self-confidence in young internet users and as a consequence may lead them to undertake more risky activities online.

For this analysis we focus just on pretending to be a different person. Sensation-seeking is measured as the mean of two items ('I do dangerous things for fun' and 'I do exciting things, even if they are dangerous', Cronbach alpha=0.78) previously used by Slater (2003) and by Stephenson, Hoyle, Palmgreen and Slater (2003). Self-efficacy was the mean of four items (for example: 'It's easy for me to stick to my aims and achieve my goals', 'I can generally work out how to handle new situations') adopted from the scale used by Schwarzer and Jerusalem (1995) with a Cronbach alpha equal to 0.66. We use two criterion variables to test the hypothesis that experimenting with the self is a significant predictor for undertaking risky online activities even in the presence of other important contributing factors that emerge during adolescence, such as self-efficacy and sensation-seeking, as well as child's age and gender. The first variable is the frequency of undertaking risky online activities calculated as the mean of four items describing risky online activities: looking for new friends on the internet; sending personal information (for example, full name, address, telephone number) to someone not encountered face to face; adding people not met face to face, to friends lists or address books; and sending a personal photo or video to someone not met face to face (Cronbach alpha=0.77). The second criterion variable is the index of harm from being bullied online calculated as the product of the intensity and duration of harm experienced from being bullied online. We ran two separate regression analyses for these criterion variables.

The final step in the stepwise regression analysis shows that pretending to be a different kind of person is a significant predictor (R_{change}=0.184; F_{change}(1;19,429)=4,372; $p<0.001$) of other risky online activities undertaken in the previous 12 months (see Figure 9.2). It remains significant even when other two significant predictors – sensation-seeking and the child's age – are included into the model. Self-efficacy and the child's gender were not significant.

In the whole European sample the model explains 24.7 per cent of variance in undertaking risky activities online, by children aged 11-16: the more often they pretend to be another kind of person online, the more likely they will undertake the risky online activities noted above. Experimenting with self-presentation is a more powerful

Figure 9.2: Predicting children's risky activities online by experimenting with self-presentation[a] online and other factors

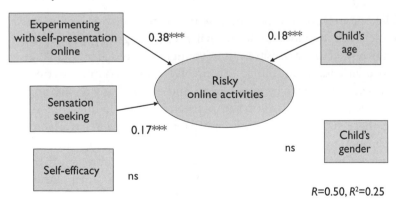

*** *p<0.001*

Base: European sample of children who replied the questions included into analysis. The figures shows standardised betas in stepwise regression analysis (European sample; *n*=19,361).
Note: [a] Frequency of 'pretending to be a different kind of person on the internet from who I really am'.

explanatory factor than age or sensation-seeking. Figure 9.2 shows that other predictors (but not gender and self-efficacy) are also important for children undertaking risky online activities. Nevertheless, experimenting with self-presentation online remains the most influential factor (explaining 18 per cent of variance) even when the child's age (explaining 4 per cent of variance) in the second step and sensation-seeking (explaining 3 per cent of variance) in the third step of analysis are included.

The analysis of suffering harm from being bullied revealed a model with only two significant predictors: the child's gender and pretending to be a different kind of person. Both were not strong predictors; the whole model explaining only 4.5 per cent of the variance ($R=0.211$, $R^2=0.045$); the child's age explains 3.9 per cent of variance ($R_{change}=0.039$; $F(1, 1074)=44$; $p<0.001$); and pretending to be a different kind of person online explains only 0.5 per cent of variance ($R_{change}=0.005$; $F(1, 1073)=6$; $p=0.014$). Another analysis, not presented here, showed that experimenting with age on SNS explains 2.8 per cent of variance in harm experienced by children from sexting ($F(1, 682)=19$; $p<0.001$).

In conclusion, it seems that experimenting with self-presentation online is a factor that increases the probability of undertaking online risky activities, but seems to have a low power in terms of predicting the harm children experience.

Conclusion

The opportunity to experiment with self-presentation online during adolescence provides an additional means to gratify developmental needs related to the transition from younger school age into adolescence and then adulthood. But it can involve online communication not fully controlled by the young person, and can lead to victimisation and bullying of and by others on the internet. Children in mid-adolescence are more likely to take risks, probably due to a relatively higher inclination towards reward-seeking, and still maturing capacities for self-control. Our findings suggest that boys may be at more risk than girls because they are greater risk-takers and this includes undertaking risky online activities; for instance, adolescents, especially boys, seek sensation, use a diversity of websites and interact easily with others. However, our findings also suggest that experimenting with self-presentation online, first, is less common at this stage of development than other studies showed. Second, it does not inevitably lead to experience of harm. Hence, although experimenting with self-presentation online, at least in two forms investigated in this study, seems to be a risky opportunity, our findings do not confirm moral panics about the negative effects of such experiences.

Note

[1] The authors are very grateful to Sonia Livingstone, Leslie Haddon and Anke Görzig for their helpful comments and suggestions that shaped the final content of the chapter.

References

Allison, B. and Schultz, J.B. (2001) 'Interpersonal identity formation during early adolescence', *Adolescence*, vol 36, no 143, pp 509-23.

Calvert, S., Mahler, B., Zehnder, S., Jenkins, A. and Lee, M. (2003) 'Gender differences in preadolescent children's online interactions: symbolic modes of self-presentation and self-expression', *Journal of Applied Developmental Psychology*, vol 24, no 6, pp 627-44.

Gui, M. and Argentin, G. (2011) 'Digital skills of internet natives: different forms of digital literacy in a random sample of northern Italian high school students', *New Media and Society* [first published on 8 March 2011].

Jackson, L.A. (2008) 'Adolescents and the internet', in D. Romer and P. Jamieson (eds) *The changing portrayal of American youth in popular media*, New York: Oxford University Press, pp 377-410.

Kirwil, L. (2010) 'EU Kids Online: what does the research say?', Paper presented at the International Conference on the Safer Internet, Warsaw, 27 September.

Kirwil, L. (2011) 'Zależności między agresją a Behawioralnym Systemem Hamującym (BIS) i Behawioralnym Systemem Aktywacyjnym (BAS)' ['Relationships between aggression and Behavioral Inhibition System (BIS) and Behavioral Activation System (BAS)'], in J. Strelau and M. Marszał-Wiśniewska (eds) *Temperament uwikłany* (*Entangled temperament*), Warsaw: Wydawnictwo Naukowe Scholar, pp 303-32.

Laouris, Y. and Kirwil, L. (2010) 'Kids experimenting with self online are at more risk of being bullied and bullying others on the internet. The findings from the EU Kids Online II', Insafe Conference, Berlin, 5 December.

Lerner, R.M. and Steinberg, L. (2004) *Handbook of adolescent psychology* (2nd edn), Habocken, NJ: John Wiley & Sons.

Livingstone, S. (2008) 'Taking risky opportunities in youthful content creation: teenagers' use of social networking sites for intimacy, privacy and self-expression', *New Media & Society*, vol 10, no 3, pp 393-411.

Livingstone, S. and Helsper, E.J. (2007) 'Taking risks when communicating on the internet: the role of offline social-psychological factors in young people's vulnerability to online risks', *Information, Communication & Society*, vol 10, no 5, pp 619-43.

Pennebaker, J. and Francis, M. (1996) 'Cognitive, emotional, and language processes in disclosure', *Cognition & Emotion*, vol 10, no 6, pp 601-26.

Romer, D., Duckworth, A.L., Sznitman, S. and Park, S. (2010) 'Can adolescents learn self-control? Delay of gratification in the development of control over risk taking', *Prevention Science*, vol 11, no 3, pp 319-30.

Sax, L. (2009) *Boys adrift: The five factors driving the growing epidemic of unmotivated boys and underachieving young men*, Philadelphia, PA: Basic Books.

Schwarzer, R. and Jerusalem, M. (1995) 'Generalized self-efficacy scale', in J. Weinman, S. Wrights and M. Johnston (eds) *Measures in health psychology: A user's portfolio. Casual and control beliefs*, Windsor: NFER-Nelson, pp 35-7.

Slater, M.D. (2003) 'Alienation, aggression, and sensation seeking as predictors of adolescent use of violent film, computer, and website content', *Journal of Communication*, vol 53, no 1, pp 105-21.

Steinberg, L. (2010) 'A dual system model of adolescent risk taking', *Developmental Psychobiology*, vol 52, pp 216-24.

Stephenson, M.T., Hoyle, R.H., Palmgreen, P. and Slater, M.D. (2003) 'Brief measures of sensation seeking for screening and large-scale surveys', *Drug and Alcohol Dependence*, vol 72, no 3, pp 279-86.

Valkenburg, P. and Peter, J. (2008) 'Adolescents' identity experiments on the internet: consequences for social competence and self-concept unity', *Communication Research*, vol 35, no 2, pp 208-31.

Valkenburg, P.M., Schoouten, A.P. and Peter, J. (2005) 'Adolescent's identity experiments on the internet', *New Media & Society*, vol 7, no 3, pp 383-402.

Williams, A. and Merten, M.J. (2008) 'A review of online social networking profiles by adolescents: implications for future research and intervention', *Adolescence*, vol 43, no 170, pp 253-74.

TEN

Young Europeans' online environments: a typology of user practices

Uwe Hasebrink

Introduction

The internet is sometimes discussed as something external, with a given set of characteristics that have positive or negative effects on children. However, 'the internet' cannot be a meaningful indicator of young people's everyday experiences. Online services are so heterogeneous that we can expect substantial inter-individual differences in how young people use the internet and the kinds of online environments they experience.

The EU Kids Online network tried to avoid the simple construction of 'the' internet in conceptualising opportunities and risks resulting from a transactional process between the set of available online services and their young potential users, within a given social and cultural context (see Chapter 1). Young people's online environments, or 'media ecologies' (see Chapter 5), are – at least partly – constructed by their own behaviours and practices. To satisfy the overall objective of the EU Kids Online network we need to analyse children's activities and practices, asking the question: what do children do with the internet?

We present some conceptual considerations and empirical evidence from existing studies followed by an operationalisation of the main indicators used in the analysis and their interrelations. Types of online usage are identified by means of cluster centre analyses and we investigate individual and country-related determinants of patterns of usage.

Conceptual and methodological considerations

The analyses follow the so-called repertoire-oriented approach to research on media use (see Hasebrink and Popp, 2006). The concept of media repertoires refers to how users combine different media to create comprehensive patterns of media use. Media repertoires are the result of multiple single situations of selective – particularly habitualised – behaviours, which represent the typical structure of an individual's everyday life. Media repertoires are composites of many media contacts, including a variety of different media and content.

The concept of media repertoires is related to the arguments in Chapter 5, which refer to a holistic approach to media use (Haddon, 2003), and develop the notion of media ecologies (Horst et al, 2009). A European study of children's changing media environments attempts to identify patterns of media use (Johnsson-Smaragdi, 2001), and Endestad et al (2011) study media user types and their relationship to social displacement.

All these approaches have a common starting point. The complexity of young people's media surroundings and the highly contextualised media-related practices they develop in the process of socialisation (see Chapter 20) makes it unlikely that online practices can be operationalised using one or even a few linear variables. We need to deal with 'patterns' of behaviours, with combinations of different aspects of media use. There is no agreement about how many and which kinds of indicators should be used to identify patterns, and the selection of indicators reflects the specific objectives and questionnaires used. Below, we discuss some indicators of children's media use based on their relevance for describing patterns of online usage.

Operationalisation

The indicators for children's online use assessed in the EU Kids Online survey (for methodology, see Chapter 2) include the following. The most prominent empirical indicators, *frequency* and *amount of use* of a specific medium, provide plausible information on the quantitative presence of the internet in young people's everyday lives. They reflect the temporal resources young people devote to online activities and define the time frame for more or less opportunities and risks. To an extent, these indicators reflect young people's interests and needs. Those who expect more gratification and more opportunities from using the internet will spend more time on it, making these indicators plausible predictors of online risk. Increased time spent online should increase the likelihood of negative experiences – and also opportunities. Frequency and amount of use are strongly correlated (r=0.44). Because frequency provides a very rough measure – 60 per cent say they use the internet (almost) daily, 33 per cent once or twice a week, 7 per cent less than that – we focus on duration of use.

Survey respondents were asked about their participation in 17 different online activities during the previous month (see Chapters 6 and 7). The second relevant indicator is *range of activities*, calculated as the number of activities in the previous month, seen also as indicating the level of online-related skills (see Chapter 7). Chapter 6, on the 'ladder of opportunities', shows that children differ in how many different services they use. Given the relation between opportunities and risks it is assumed that a broader range of activities is linked to more risks. Range of activities is also substantially correlated with duration of use (r=0.46). However, as shown in Chapter 6, range of activities is regarded as a strong indicator of patterns of online usage; therefore, we include it in the analysis.

We are also interested in the constellation of activities. It is plausible that specific online activities, for example, visiting chatrooms or social networking sites, are linked to specific risks. We show that all activities are positively correlated to duration of use and also range of activities. Factor analyses were performed to explore the dimensions of these activities: on the basis of *whether* they have done the activities within the last month, and among 11- to 16-year-olds, with what *frequency*. However, the respective factor solutions are not statistically clear; several activities had double loadings on several factors. Although this usually leads to the assumption of a clear dimensional structure being rejected, in our case the double loadings would seem to reflect the hybrid character of many online activities. For example, playing online games with others has both a strong communicative component and involves dealing with interactive content. Visiting a social networking profile might be for communicative or self-presentation reasons.

In line with the heuristic objectives of this project we follow a factor analytical approach to reduce analytical complexity. To the 17 indicators for online activities, we added two aspects of online behaviour that seemed particularly important. These indicators are meant to emphasise variance in possibly risky activities:

- *Having own profile on a social networking site* (or even more than one profile) is linked to a whole range of possible risks. We included a variable 0 = no profile, 1 = one profile, 2 = more than one profile.
- Some activities linked to social, web-related functionalities are investigated as *risky online activities* (looked for new friends on the internet; sent personal information, for example, full name, address or telephone number, to someone never met face to face; added people

to friends list or address book never met face to face; pretended to be a different kind of person on the internet from who I really am; sent a photo or video of myself to someone that I have never met face to face; see also the Appendix at the end of this book). These activities were assessed in the survey through the options 'never' (0) to 'almost every day' (4). We defined the frequency of these activities as an additional variable ranging from 0 (none of the activities are ever performed), to 1 (all five activities performed almost every day).

The 19 variables are factor analysed to identify the underlying dimensions of online activities; this provides[1] four factors (see Table 10.1).

• *Factor 1 ('Communication'):* visiting social networking profiles is the marker variable, thus, the factor includes several activities that are mainly communicative. The fact that watching video clips and downloading music or films have the highest loadings may be because these activities are closely related to peer-to-peer communication.

Table 10.1: Factor analysis of online activities

	Factor 1	Factor 2	Factor 3	Factor 4
Visited a social networking profile	**0.82**			
How many profiles on social networking site	**0.78**			
Used instant messaging	**0.62**			
Put photos, videos or music to share with others	**0.61**	0.34		
Sent/received email	**0.54**			0.31
Watched video clips	**0.49**			
Downloaded music or films	0.46			0.38
Frequency of risky online activities	0.41	0.37		
Written a blog or online diary		**0.69**		
Put a message on a website	0.37	**0.55**		
Visited a chatroom		0.46		
Used file-sharing sites		0.43		
Used a webcam		0.36		
How often played internet games			**0.72**	
Played games with other people on the internet			**0.70**	
Spent time in a virtual world		0.46	**0.53**	
Created a character, pet or avatar		0.47	**0.50**	
Used the internet for schoolwork				**0.75**
Read/watched the news on the internet				**0.59**

Base: All children who use the internet.

Note: Only loadings ≥0.30.

- *Factor 2 ('Creativity'):* although the loadings are rather moderate, all activities involve some degree of creativity or productivity.
- *Factor 3 ('Gaming'):* this factor clearly represents gaming and activities linked to it. Two items have highly plausible double loadings with 'Creativity'.
- *Factor 4 ('Learning'):* the main variable is using the internet for schoolwork, but also includes reading or watching news on the internet.

Note that 'risky online activities' cannot be attributed to any one of these factors. Risky online activities are moderately linked to communicative and creative activities, reflecting the link between these activities and use of social media.

Identifying patterns of online usage

Duration of use, range of activities and the above four factors were subjected to cluster centre analyses. Based on the criteria of interpretability, stability of cluster membership and the respective *F*-values of the variables included, a solution with six clusters was selected. Table 10.2 describes these clusters based on the original variables:

- *Cluster 1:* cluster members are characterised by a small amount of online use and a small range of activities. Risky activities are very unlikely; only a few have their own profiles on a social networking site. Except for schoolwork, activities are rare. After schoolwork and watching video clips, reading or watching news is the most frequent activity.
- *Cluster 2:* this cluster shows moderately higher values for all activities with the notable exceptions of schoolwork and watching/reading news. There is a high level of interest in visiting social networking profiles.
- *Cluster 3:* a wider range of activities than Cluster 2; some are more integrated into the group's everyday practices, particularly schoolwork and news. There is a smaller likelihood of social networking or posting photos/videos or text messages.
- *Cluster 4:* this group spends almost two hours per day on the internet and has the biggest range of activities and highest frequency of risky online activities. Its members are most likely to read/watch news, to download music or films, to send or receive emails, to play games with others and to use a webcam. The less popular, more

Table 10.2: Description of clusters representing patterns of young people's online use

	Cluster 1	Cluster 2	Cluster 3	Cluster 4	Cluster 5	Cluster 6
Number of cases	7,175	3,036	5,904	2,732	2,729	3,564
% of total sample	28.5	12.1	23.5	10.9	10.9	14.2
Average values (scales)						
Duration of online use (min/day)	50	72	71	118	180	108
No of online activities (0-17)	3.0	5.8	7.7	13.2	9.8	9.6
Frequency of risky online activities (0.0-1.0)	0.01	0.09	0.05	0.21	0.14	0.13
No of social networking site profiles (0-2)	0.1	1.1	0.6	1.2	1.2	1.2
% of children within each cluster who did the activity last month						
Content-based activities:						
Schoolwork	78	55	99	91	89	93
Played games alone (almost every day)	12	22	24	36	54	3
Video clips	41	76	91	96	97	92
News online	24	12	70	74	49	73
Download music or film	9	23	58	73	68	65
Contact/communication-based activities:						
Instant messaging	13	63	75	90	89	90
Visit social networking site	7	93	60	92	93	97
Email	18	55	76	91	82	87
Games with others online	23	31	55	90	80	18
Used webcam	9	12	31	66	41	54
Visit chatroom	2	15	16	72	35	36
Post photos or videos	3	41	30	79	62	76
Conduct/peer participation activities:						
Posted message	5	21	17	80	41	67
Create avatar	9	11	9	74	25	6
Uses file-sharing sites	2	9	10	59	26	33
Virtual world	7	10	8	73	21	3
Written blog or diary	1	1	1	50	2	33

creative activities are most frequent in this group: creating avatars, using file-sharing sites, spending time in virtual worlds and writing blogs or diaries.

- *Cluster 5:* this group has the longest duration of daily online use (three hours per day), a smaller range of activities than Cluster 4, but still above the overall average. Playing games on their own or against the computer and watching video clips show the highest values among all the clusters. Schoolwork, reading/watching the news and activities related to producing or publishing (writing blogs or diaries, posting messages) score low.
- *Cluster 6:* this group shows slightly above-average use and range of activities. The most obvious characteristic is an almost complete absence of gaming activities. Visiting social networking profiles is very frequent and some other activities are almost as frequent as in Cluster 4: reading/watching news, instant messaging, posting photos or music and writing blogs or diaries.

The order of the clusters reflects the average age of the cluster members (cluster 1 is the youngest and cluster 6 the oldest) (see Table 10.3). While the three younger clusters include almost equal numbers of boys and girls, clusters 4 and 5 include considerably more boys, and cluster 6 considerably more girls.

Figure 10.1 illustrates the cluster distribution within gender and age groups. Girls and boys differ with regard to the likelihood of belonging to clusters 4, 5 and 6. Almost 90 per cent of the youngest users are in the first three clusters, with an average duration of online use of less than 90 minutes.

The cluster descriptions show the general tendency of 'the more … the more' rule, according to which time spent online, range of activities and also most specific activities are positively correlated. This observation is in line with the 'ladder of opportunities', as presented in Chapter 6. However, the clusters show that patterns of use do not

Table 10.3: Distribution of age and gender groups within clusters (%)

	Cluster 1	Cluster 2	Cluster 3	Cluster 4	Cluster 5	Cluster 6
Girls	50	55	48	38	37	67
Boys	50	45	52	62	63	33
9-10 years	48	20	16	10	12	4
11-12 years	30	27	30	22	15	13
13-14 years	15	28	32	32	31	33
15-16 years	8	25	22	36	42	50
Average age	11.1	12.7	12.7	13.5	13.6	14.1

Figure 10.1: Distribution of user types within gender and age groups

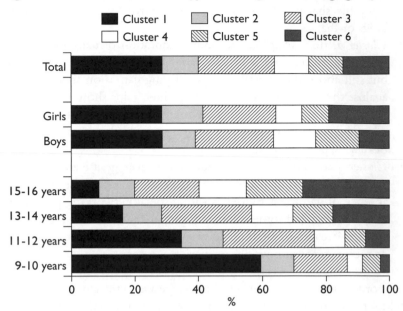

completely follow this rule. Cluster 5 members spend by far the longest time online, but engage in only a moderate range of activities; the reverse applies to cluster 4. Members of clusters 2 and 3 are the same age and show almost the same duration of use, but use the internet for different kinds of activities.

We propose the following labels for the six clusters:

Cluster 1: 'Low risk novices'
Cluster 2: 'Young networkers'
Cluster 3: 'Moderate users'
Cluster 4: 'Risky explorers'
Cluster 5: 'Intensive gamers'
Cluster 6: 'Experienced networkers'.

Individual determinants of patterns of online usage

In order to analyse the extent to which cluster membership can be explained by certain individual characteristics, a multinomial logistic regression analysis was calculated with cluster membership as the dependent variable and several independent variables: age, gender and parents' highest education as indicators for the children's social position, and sensation-seeking, psychological difficulties,[2] self-efficacy and digital skills[3] as indicators for personal characteristics.[4]

Table 10.4 shows the Exp(B) values of this analysis. The youngest age cluster ('Low risk novices') was used as the reference group; thus the values indicate the degree to which the likelihood of belonging to one of the other clusters increases with the variation of the independent variable.

Since the youngest age group is the reference group, all values for *age* are positive. The older the respondents, the more likely it is that they will belong to clusters 5 or 6.

Gender does not explain membership in cluster 3; being a boy increases the likelihood of belonging to clusters 4 and 5; being a girl increases the likelihood of belonging to clusters 2 and 6.

Parent's education has almost no effect on cluster membership; the children of better-educated parents are slightly more likely to belong to clusters 3 and 6.

For *sensation-seeking* it is clear that all the clusters are more interested in sensation-seeking than the reference group, and particularly the most active cluster 'Risky explorers'.

The findings for *psychological difficulties* indicate that the two boy-dominated groups have considerably more psychological difficulties, while 'Moderate users' and 'Experienced networkers' have the lowest values.

All the groups but one show lower values for *self-efficacy* than the reference group; however, the difference is significant only for cluster 2.

Table 10.4: Multinomial logistic regression: determinants of patterns of online use (Exp(B) values)

	Cluster 2: 'Young networkers'	Cluster 3: 'Moderate users'	Cluster 4: 'Risky explorers'	Cluster 5: 'Intensive gamers'	Cluster 6: 'Experienced networkers'
n	2,401	4,885	2,430	2,376	3,372
Age	*1.22	*1.17	*1.24	*1.46	*1.55
Gender (1 = girls, 2 = boys)	*0.77	1.08	*1.38	*1.54	*0.42
Parents' education	1.01	*1.03	1.03	1.03	*1.05
Sensation-seeking	*1.38	*1.17	*1.57	*1.40	*1.42
Psychological difficulties	0.84	*0.59	*1.88	1.35	0.75
Self-efficacy	*0.77	0.89	0.98	0.87	1.12
Online skills	*1.43	*1.46	*2.02	*1.82	*1.81

Note: The first cluster ('Low risk novices') has been used as the reference group. Exp(B) values indicate the increase/decrease of the likelihood to belong to the clusters shown.
* Significance=0.000; Nagelkerke R^2=0.36.

As expected, *online skills* are higher for all groups than in the reference group; cluster 4 shows the highest value, indicating that skills are not linked primarily to age (average age in clusters 5 and 6 is higher), but to the specific kind of online practices.

We can conclude that cluster 2, whose members are only slightly older than the reference group, is more interested in sensation-seeking. Although it is difficult to explain its low self-efficacy values, it is plausible that the slightly broader range of online activities is accompanied by greater online skills. The 'Moderate users' are characterised by very low levels of psychological difficulties and rather low interest in sensation-seeking. Due to the older age of this group, online skills are clearly higher than in the reference group. Cluster 4 stands out with the highest values for sensation-seeking, psychological difficulties and online skills. Clusters 5 and 6, the oldest age groups, are the most clearly separated by gender, with boys experiencing more psychological difficulties.

This analysis shows that the different patterns of online usage identified in the first step have positional and individual origins that influence the likelihood of belonging to the different groups.

Countries as determinants of patterns of online usage

The final step is to analyse how the 25 countries differ in the frequency of the six clusters. Table 10.5 shows that countries vary substantially with regard to the percentages of different patterns of online usage. The table is ordered along the frequency of cluster 1 ('Low risk novices'). The range between the highest (Turkey with 42.7 per cent) and the lowest (Lithuania with 13.0 per cent) values is notable. Ireland, Germany, Austria and France, as well as most of the southern European countries, also show high figures for this type, while the northern European countries, and the Netherlands, Cyprus and Slovenia, have particularly low numbers in this cluster. This confirms that this pattern of online usage represents a kind of base line, a starting level of use of the internet, with younger children and children from countries with a more recent tradition of internet use being most likely to follow this pattern.

Cluster 2 ('Young networkers') has very high values for Ireland and Slovenia. Children from France, Romania and Germany are least likely to belong to this cluster. Poland, Portugal and Romania have the highest values in cluster 3 ('Moderate users'), the lowest being for Sweden, Ireland and Slovenia.

The distribution in cluster 4 ('Risky explorers') is the most balanced. Differences among countries are relatively small, with Ireland and Spain at the lower end and Sweden and Lithuania at the upper end of the

Table 10.5: Patterns of online usage by country (%)

	Cluster 1: 'Low risk novices'	Cluster 2: 'Young networkers'	Cluster 3: 'Moderate users'	Cluster 4: 'Risky explorers'	Cluster 5: 'Intensive gamers'	Cluster 6: 'Experienced networkers'
Turkey	42.7	8.5	24.4	11.1	6.7	6.6
Ireland	39.5	37.4	7.1	5.3	3.4	7.3
Germany	33.6	8.1	24.4	9.7	7.7	16.4
Greece	32.5	14.7	26.5	8.1	12.6	5.7
Austria	30.2	19.8	12.3	14.8	6.7	16.2
Spain	29.0	16.4	28.4	5.2	6.8	14.2
Italy	28.8	13.3	24.4	9.8	10.0	13.7
UK	27.0	14.5	14.1	13.4	15.7	15.3
France	25.1	4.8	27.0	14.6	5.5	22.9
Hungary	24.8	21.7	17.9	13.1	13.0	9.5
Romania	24.5	5.6	31.7	10.0	20.2	8.0
Portugal	23.9	11.5	34.3	11.2	10.7	8.3
Finland	22.2	15.8	21.7	9.3	12.4	18.6
Bulgaria	21.7	12.8	21.1	11.1	22.4	10.9
Belgium	21.6	16.4	23.1	14.0	8.0	16.9
Norway	20.9	12.7	15.9	10.7	15.7	24.1
Poland	20.5	11.9	34.9	6.7	16.1	9.9
Denmark	19.1	21.2	15.4	8.0	22.3	13.9
Slovenia	18.8	33.8	9.9	11.1	11.5	14.9
Sweden	17.1	23.1	5.7	16.6	13.0	24.4
Cyprus	16.2	17.1	21.3	14.7	24.0	6.6
Netherlands	15.9	23.4	20.2	8.2	12.0	20.3
Czech Republic	15.7	9.4	25.4	13.1	23.1	13.3
Estonia	13.5	14.2	23.7	11.8	21.0	15.7
Lithuania	13.0	17.0	16.4	15.7	22.4	15.3
Total (weighted percentages)	**28.5**	**12.1**	**23.5**	**10.9**	**10.9**	**14.2**

scale. Cluster 5 ('Intensive gamers') shows high percentages for some central and eastern European countries, and Denmark and Cyprus. Children from Ireland, Spain, France, Austria and Turkey are the least likely to be risk-takers.

Country differences for cluster 6 ('Experienced networkers') are also comparatively small. The cluster is represented mostly by children from Norway and Sweden, with a few from Greece and Turkey.

In some countries the distribution across the six types is concentrated on one or two patterns of usage. Turkey is an outlier with regard to cluster 1, which, together with the 'Moderate users' cluster, accounts for some two thirds of the Turkish children surveyed. Similarly, clusters 1 and 2 account for 77 per cent of Irish children.

If we sum clusters 4 to 6, this accounts for more than half of Norwegian, Swedish and Lithuanian children, who can be regarded, therefore, as engaging in more 'advanced' forms of online usage. This applies to less than 30 per cent of children from Ireland, Turkey, Spain and Greece. This supports the overall finding that countries differ with regard to how much practices of using the internet are established within everyday routines.

However, it should be emphasised that the overall pattern represented by the percentages in Table 10.5 does not follow just a simple linear line, that is, from 'low use' to 'high use' countries; there are highly specific combinations of the six clusters, which warrant further examination. For example, why are so many children from central and eastern European countries 'Intensive gamers' (cluster 5)? What is the explanation for the complex patterns in the two youngest age clusters of internet use related to schoolwork and social networking?

Conclusion

This chapter set out to identify comprehensive patterns of online usage. Within the overall model of opportunities and risks related to children's internet use, how children make use of the internet is a crucial issue. It reflects children's agency (they decide what they will do on the internet) and shows indirect influences of their societal position (any behaviour is shaped by the child's position based on age, gender, parents' education and the child's personal characteristics – sensation-seeking, psychological difficulties, self-efficacy). The analyses described in this chapter show that children and young people differ substantially in how they use the internet, and that it is possible to identify meaningful patterns of usage, which represent different types of online experiences that are rooted in specific social and individual circumstances. We have also seen that these patterns of usage are uneven across Europe; the countries surveyed in this study differ substantially for relative frequency of different user types. It might be concluded, therefore, that country differences regarding experiences of risk and harm are due partly to differences in how different children use the internet. This is analysed in more detail later, in Chapter 25.

Notes
[1] Principal component analysis, varimax rotation, variance explained: 45.5 per cent.

² For this analysis the full scale was used; see the Appendix at the end of this book.

³ For a definition of digital skills, see Chapter 7.

⁴ The model only included the main effects of the seven factors; pseudo R^2 (Nagelkerke) = 0.36.

References

Endestad, T., Heim, J., Kaare, B., Torgersen, L. and Brandtzæg, P.B. (2011) 'Media user types among young children and social displacement', *Nordicom Review*, vol 32, no 1, pp 17-30.

Haddon, L. (2003) 'Research question for the evolving communications landscape', in R. Ling and P.E. Pedersen (eds) *Mobile communications. Re-negotiation of the social sphere*, London: Springer, pp 7-22.

Hasebrink, U. and Popp, J. (2006) 'Media repertoires as a result of selective media use. A conceptual approach to the analysis of patterns of exposure', *Communications*, vol 31, no 3, pp 369-87.

Horst, H.A., Herr-Stephenson, B. and Robinson, L. (2009) 'Media ecologies', in M. Ito et al (eds) *Hanging out, messing around, and geeking out. Kids living and learning with new media*, Cambridge, MA: The MIT Press, pp 29-78.

Johnsson-Smaragdi, U. (2001) 'Media use styles among the young', in S. Livingstone and M. Bovill (eds) *Children and their changing media environment: A European comparative study*, New York: Lawrence Erlbaum Associates, pp 113-39.

ELEVEN

Bullying

Claudia Lampert and Verónica Donoso

What is (not) cyberbullying?

Although the term 'cyberbullying' is being used more frequently in academic research, there is no standard definition of this phenomenon. Most descriptions consider that cyberbullying is 'a new form of aggression ... that occurs through modern technological devices, and specifically mobile phones or the internet' (Slonje and Smith, 2008, p 147), but also displays some characteristics typical of traditional bullying (Slonje and Smith, 2008), for example, aggressive and intentional actions undertaken by a group or an individual (repeatedly over time) against a victim (Whitney and Smith, 1993; Olweus, 1999). However, some aspects of traditional bullying (for example, repetition or imbalance of power between perpetrator and victim) may be less directly 'translatable' to online contexts, and less reliable for determining incidences of cyberbullying as opposed to offline bullying (Smith, 2011b).

Incidence of cyberbullying

The populations researched and the methodologies employed (for example, children's face-to-face, online and written surveys; teacher or parents' accounts, etc) vary considerably among studies of cyberbullying. Quantitative studies may use different types of measurement instruments (for example, several adaptations of the subscales of the 'Bully/Victim Questionnaire' developed by Olweus, 1999), and various operationalisations of cyberbullying. Samples vary in terms of respondents' sociodemographic characteristics and backgrounds. This methodological variety is reflected in the diverse and sometimes inconsistent results on the prevalence of cyberbullying.

Recent reviews of cyberbullying literature (see, for example, Kowalski et al, 2008; Schrock and Boyd, 2008; Tokunaga, 2010) find that results can vary between 4 and 46 per cent for the victims of cyberbullying, and from 11 to 33 per cent for its perpetrators. This wide disparity in results would seem to be a reflection of the range of approaches adopted towards researching the cyberbullying phenomenon and the influences of other factors such as cultural and technological differences (Mora-Merchán and Ortega-Ruiz, 2007, cited in Specht, 2010).

Sociodemographic and personal factors affecting cyberbullying

There is no clear consensus on how various sociodemographic and personal factors influence cyberbullying behaviour (Specht, 2010). For instance, Smith et al (2006) find no effect of age among 11- to 16-year-olds, whereas Ybarra and Mitchell (2004a) find that students aged over 15 are more often internet aggressors than children in the younger age group of 10-14. There is, however, some consistency in the finding of a curvilinear relation, with a peak in cyberbullying between the ages of 13 and 15 (Vandebosch et al, 2006; Wolak et al, 2006; Tokunaga, 2010).

Gender effects are less clear-cut (Smith, 2011a). Some studies report more girls being victims of cyberbullying and more boys being perpetrators (see, for example, Smith et al, 2006; Li, 2007; Slonje and Smith, 2008; Festl and Quandt, 2011), but this is not confirmed by Patchin and Hinduja (2006), Hinduja and Patchin (2008) or Smith et al (2008).

There is some evidence that the traditional roles of (offline) bully and victim are reproduced online (Hinduja and Patchin, 2008; Gradinger et al, 2009). However, while Ybarra and Mitchell (2004b) and Steffgen et al (2010) provide evidence to support this claim, Gradinger et al (2009) do not. Some studies consider both cyberbullies and cybervictims, and also *cyberbully/victims*, a group identified as taking both roles (see, for example, Ybarra and Mitchell, 2004a; Festl and Quandt 2011). The latter (group) includes victims of both traditional and cyberbullying who use the internet for revenge (Specht, 2010).

Operationalisation of cyberbullying

The EU Kids Online questionnaire describes bullying as follows:

> Sometimes children or teenagers say or do hurtful things to someone and this can often be quite a few times on different days over a period of time, for example. This can include: teasing someone in a way this person does not

like; hitting, kicking or pushing someone around; leaving someone out of things.

Both the questionnaire description and the interviewer explained to the child that these activities could refer to events that occurred face to face (in person), by mobile phone (for example, texts, calls or video clips) or on the internet (for example, via email, social networking sites, etc). Following Slonje and Smith's (2008) definition of cyberbullying, throughout the analysis section of this chapter we employ the term *cyberbullying* to refer to the incidence of bullying via mobile phone and on the internet, and *online bullying* to refer to bullying on the internet.

Cyberbullying experiences among 9- to 16-year-olds in Europe

Incidence of cyberbullying across Europe

Among children in Europe, 19 per cent of 9- to 16-year-olds claimed to have experienced some form of bullying in the previous 12 months (Livingstone et al, 2011, p 62), 7 per cent of which was cyberbullying. Table 11.1 shows that 6 per cent of all the surveyed children had been victims of cyberbullying (but had not cyberbullied others), 2 per cent had cyberbullied others (but had not been victims of cyberbullying), and 1 per cent had been both victims and perpetrators of cyberbullying (*cyberbully/victim*). The incidence of cyberbully/victimisation increases with age, peaking at the ages of 13-16.

Table 11.1 shows that, although low, there are gender differences, but only for the group of cybervictims: 5 per cent of boys had been victims of cyberbullying compared to 7 per cent of girls. With regard to gender, it is unclear whether this difference is related to a difference in the incidence of cyberbullying or to differences in perceptions between boys and girls of what is 'hurtful' or 'nasty': 'As a consequence of their interpersonal engagement, girls demonstrate heightened concerns about the status of relationships and about peer evaluations' (Rose and Rudolph, 2006, p 108). Girls' greater anxiety concerns about social relationships could help explain why girls more often state that they have been cybervictims than boys.

Regarding psychological variables, children with a higher level of psychological difficulties and children who feel ostracised more often report being victims of cyberbullying (see Table 11.1).

As regards country differences, the findings show that incidence of cyberbullying is highest in Estonia, Romania and Sweden, with

Table 11.1: Comparison between cyberbullies and cybervictims (%)

	Not a cyberbully/ not a cybervictim	Cyberbully (not a victim)	Cybervictim (not a bully)	Cyberbully and cybervictim
Cases	19,941	503	1295	349
Row percentages	90	2	6	1
*Age**				
9-10	96	1	3	0
11-12	92	1	5	1
13-14	90	2	6	2
15-16	84	5	8	3
*Gender**				
Male	91	2	5	2
Female	89	2	7	2
*Psychological difficulties**				
Low	95	1	3	1
High	86	3	9	2
*Self-efficacy**				
Low	92	1	5	2
High	89	3	7	1
*Sensation-seeking**				
Low	94	1	5	1
High	83	5	8	4
*Ostracism**				
Low	91	2	5	2
High	85	3	10	2
Offline bullying victim**	65	3	24	8
Offline bullying perpetrator**	69	13	8	10

Base: All children aged between 9 and 16.

Note: Variables with 'low and high' categories are dichotomised by median-split
Chi-square test: * $p<0.01$; ** $p<0.01$ and Cramers V>0.3.

percentages of both cyberbullies and cybervictims above the European average (see Figure 11.1, top right quadrant). The lowest rates are in Portugal, Italy and Turkey. These differences seem to be related to the prevalence of offline bullying; the incidence of cyberbullying is highest in those countries where traditional bullying is more frequent (Livingstone et al, 2011, p 63).

Forms and impact of cyberbullying

Of all children who use the internet, 6 per cent had been bullied online in the past 12 months, mostly on social networking sites (3 per cent of

Figure 11.1: Cyberbullies and cybervictims in Europe, by country (have/have been bullied via the internet or mobile phone in the last 12 months)

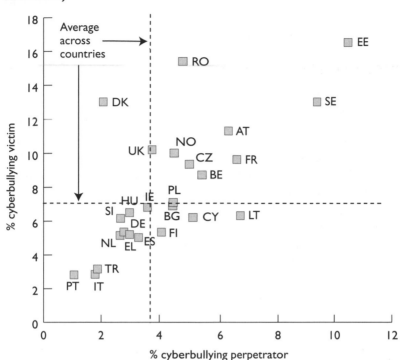

Base: All children who use the internet.

all children who use the internet) and instant messaging (3 per cent). Cyberbullying via email (1 per cent), gaming websites (1 per cent) and chatrooms (1 per cent) was less common. As far as the form of online aggression is concerned, 4 per cent reported having received nasty or hurtful messages from others and 2 per cent realised that such messages about them were being circulated to other children. Exclusion from other activities or threats of exclusion were reported less often (1 per cent) (Livingstone et al, 2011, p 63).

Although online bullying concerns a relatively small number of children, most victims were upset by it, ranging from 'very upset' (31 per cent), 'a bit upset' (24 per cent) to 'fairly upset' (30 per cent); only 15 per cent said it had not upset them. Girls and younger children (11–12 years old) tended to feel more upset and/or upset for a longer time. Once again, girls' greater concerns about social relationships could explain why the impact of online bullying was felt more strongly by them than by boys.

In relation to the perpetrators of online bullying, more children had been involved in face-to-face bullying (10 per cent) than online bullying (3 per cent) or cyberbullying (via mobile phone) (2 per cent).

Factors affecting children's involvement in cyberbullying

We conducted two logistic regression analyses to examine how sociodemographic variables (gender and age), psychological variables (psychological difficulties, self-efficacy and sensation-seeking) and cyberbullying experiences (either as a perpetrator, first regression, or as a victim, second regression) predict the risk of cyberbullying (either as victim, first regression, or as perpetrator, second regression) (see Tables 11.2 and 11.3). The analyses indicate that being a cyberbully is the strongest predictor for being a victim of cyberbullying (Exp(B)=8.45, $p<0.001$), followed by psychological difficulties (Exp(B)=7.58, $p<0.001$). Further, being a cybervictim (Exp(B)=8.64, $p<0.001$) is the strongest predictor for being a cyberbully, followed by psychological difficulties (Exp(B)=3.58, $p<0.001$). Thus, children who experience more psychological difficulties are more likely to be victims or perpetrators of cyberbullying.

Table 11.2: Logistic regression to predict cyberbullying *victims* in Europe

Variables	B	SE	Wald	Sig	Exp(B)
Age (9-16)	0.10	0.01	58.64	0.000	1.109
Sex (1 = male, 2 = female)	0.45	0.06	56.02	0.000	1.573
SDQ (range 1-3)	2.03	0.11	367.17	0.000	7.581
Self-efficacy (range 1-3)	0.33	0.07	23.49	0.000	1.385
Sensation-seeking (range 0-4)	0.15	0.03	29.98	0.000	1.158
Cyberbully	2.13	0.08	659.31	0.000	8.451

Note: Nagelkerkes R^2=0.181.

Table 11.3: Logistic regression to predict cyberbullying *perpetrators* in Europe

Variables	B	SE	Wald	Sig	Exp(B)
Age (9-16)	0.22	0.02	136.67	0.000	1.251
Sex (1 = male, 2 = female)	0.06	0.08	0.52	0.471	1.060
SDQ (range 1-3)	1.28	0.14	78.43	0.000	3.580
Self-efficacy (range 1-3)	0.20	0.09	4.96	0.026	1.223
Sensation-seeking (range 0-4)	0.41	0.32	157.60	0.000	1.500
Cybervictim	2.16	0.08	666.65	0.000	8.637

Note: Nagelkerkes R^2=0.245.

How do children cope with online bullying?

Among children's individual coping strategies, the most common response was to try to solve the problem on their own (31 per cent of those bullied (online)), followed by hoping that the problem would go away (24 per cent) (Livingstone et al, 2011, p 70).[1] Around 12 per cent of those bullied (online) felt slightly guilty about such incidents. The percentage of children that used neither of these coping strategies was 16. Four out of five children (77 per cent) adopted the strategy of 'seeking personal social support' and talked to someone about the incident. Friends seemed to be the most common source of support (52 per cent), followed by parents (42 per cent), siblings (14 per cent) and other adults (9 per cent). Technical coping strategies, such as blocking the perpetrator, seemed to be the most common and relatively most effective strategy employed by children (confirming previous studies; see, for example, Smith et al, 2008). Further, 46 per cent blocked the senders of nasty or hurtful messages, although only 35 per cent stated that they had found the strategy successful (Livingstone et al, 2011, p 71). Some deleted all messages from the bully (41 per cent), which helped in more than half of the cases (23 per cent). Less popular coping responses included not using the internet for a time (20 per cent) or changing the filter/contact settings (18 per cent). Only a few children (9 per cent) reported the problem to an internet adviser or service provider, and only 5 per cent of these perceived this strategy as successful.

Conclusion

Compared to forms of (offline) bullying where the roles of victim, perpetrator and bystander are fairly clear, the boundaries between these roles in cyberbullying are less evident. Our data show that many perpetrators and victims of cyberbullying are not just acting in one or the other role; they sometimes engage in both functions. Also, the boundaries between traditional forms of bullying and cyberbullying are less clear-cut since some children report experience of both online and offline bullying, and as aggressors and/or victims. These findings can be interpreted in several ways. They would seem to support the so-called 'revenge of the nerds' hypothesis (Aftab, 2005). However, there are other plausible interpretations; for instance, it might be that, in order to counteract feelings of vulnerability and powerlessness resulting from being a victim of traditional bullying, children become cyberbullies to achieve 'empowerment' and 'de-victimisation'. This motivation may be stronger than mere revenge. Another interpretation might be that victims of cyberbullying might have more opportunities to react to online bullying due to the social character of the platforms employed, whereas in offline bullying episodes superior physical strength is usually critical.

Another interesting finding is that incidents of offline bullying (as perpetrator and/or victim) are strong predictors of cyberbullying, even stronger than sociodemographic and psychological variables. That a group of children is being confronted with both online and offline bullying raises several questions; for instance, are offline bullies bullying the same victims both offline and online? Or do they choose different bullying mechanisms for different victims? Are online bully/victims motivated to bully others as revenge only, or are there more intricate causes for their aggressive behaviour? Are victims of offline bullying bold enough to take revenge by cyberbullying their offline bullies? Are they afraid of the offline repercussions should they become cyberbullies? What is clear from these questions is that further research is needed to investigate the complex relationships between offline and cyberbullying and between the different roles taken by victims and perpetrators in each environment.

Note
[1] Coping strategies refer only to those children bullied on the internet, not via mobile phone.

References

Aftab, P. (2005) *Common sense to cybersense. Stop cyberbullying* (www. stopcyberbullying.org/parents/howdoyouhandleacyberbully.html).

Festl, R. and Quandt, T. (2011) 'Social relations and cyberbullying. The influence of individual and structural attributes on victimization and perpetration via the internet', Paper presented at the International Communication Association Conference, Boston, 26-30 May.

Gradinger, P., Strohmeier, D. and Spiel, C. (2009) 'Traditional bullying and cyberbullying. Identification of risk groups for adjustment problems', *Zeitschrift für Psychologie* [*Journal of Psychology*], vol 217, no 4, pp 205-13.

Hinduja, S. and Patchin, J.W. (2008) 'Cyberbullying: an exploratory analysis of factors related to offending and victimization', *Deviant Behavior*, vol 29, pp 129-56.

Kowalski, R.M., Limber, S.P. and Agatston, P.W. (2008) *Cyberbullying. Bullying in the digital age*, Oxford: Blackwell Publishing.

Li, Q. (2007) 'New bottle but old wine: a research of cyberbullying in schools', *Computers in Human Behavior*, vol 23, no 4, pp 1777-91.

Livingstone, S., Haddon, L., Görzig, A. and Ólafsson, K. (2011) *Risks and safety on the internet. The perspective of European children. Full Findings*, London: London School of Economics and Political Science.

Mora Merchán, J.A. and Ortega Ruiz, R. (2007) 'The new forms of school bullying and violence' in R. Ortega-Ruiz, J.A. Mora Merchán and T. Jäger (eds) *Acting against school bullying and violence: The role of media, local authorities and the internet* [e-book] (pp 7–34) (www. bullying-in-school.info/uploads/media/e-book_-_Acting_against_ school_bullying_and_violence.pdf).

Olweus, D. (1999) 'Sweden', in P.K. Smith, Y. Morita, J. Junger-Tas, D. Olweus, R. Catalano and P. Slee (eds) *The nature of school bullying: A cross-national perspective*, London: Routledge, pp 7-27.

Patchin, J.W. and Hinduja, S. (2006) 'Bullies move beyond the schoolyard. A preliminary look at cyberbullying', *Youth Violence and Juvenile Justice*, vol 4, no 2, pp 148-69.

Rose, A.J. and Rudolph, K.D. (2006) 'A review of sex differences in peer relationship processes: potential trade-offs for the emotional and behavioral development of girls and boys', *Psychological Bulletin*, vol 132, no 1, pp 98-131.

Schrock, A. and Boyd, D. (2008) 'Online threats to youth: Solicitation, harassment, and problematic content' in *Internet safety technical task force, enhancing child safety and online technologies: Final report of the internet safety task force to the multi-state working group on social networking of state attorneys* (pp 63-142). Durham, NC: Carolina Academic Press (http://cyber.law.harvard.edu/sites/cyber.law.harvard.edu/files/ ISTTF_Final_Report.pdf).

Slonje, R. and Smith, P. (2008) 'Cyberbullying: another main type of bullying?', *Scandinavian Journal of Psychology*, vol 49, pp 147-54.

Smith, P.K. (2011a) 'Cyberbullying and cyberaggression', in S.R. Jimerson, A.B. Nickerson, M.J. Mayer and M.J. Furlong (eds) *The handbook of school violence and school safety: International research and practice* (2nd edn), New York: Routledge, pp 93-103.

Smith, P.K. (2011b) 'Bullying in schools: thirty years of research', in I. Coyne and C.P. Monks (eds) *Bullying in different context*, Cambridge: Cambridge University Press, pp 36-59.

Smith, P.K., Mahdavi, J., Carvalho, M. and Tippett, N. (2006) 'An investigation into cyberbullying, its forms, awareness and impact, and the relationship between age and gender in cyberbullying', *Research Brief No RBX03-06*, London: Department for Education and Skills.

Smith, P.K., Madavi, J., Carvalho, M., Fisher, S., Russell, S. and Tippett, N. (2008) 'Cyberbullying: its nature and impact in secondary school pupils', *The Journal of Child Psychology and Psychiatry*, vol 49, no 4, pp 376-85.

Specht, T. (2010) 'Vernetzt, verletzt? Cyberbullying unter Jugendlichen in Deutschland' ['Connected, harmed? Cyberbullying within adolescents in Germany'], Unpublished masters thesis (www.imb-uni-augsburg.de/files/Masterarbeit_TamaraSpecht.pdf).

Steffgen, G., Pfetsch, J., König, A. and Melzer, A. (2010) 'Effects of traditional bullying and empathy on cyberbullying', in R. Zukauskiene (ed) *Proceedings of the XIV European Conference on Developmental Psychology ECDP, Vilnius, Lithuania, August 18-22, 2009*, Pianoro: Medimond, pp 485-90.

Tokunaga, R.S. (2010) 'Following you home from school: a critical review and synthesis of research on cyberbullying victimization', *Computers in Human Behavior*, vol 26, no 3, pp 277-87.

Vandebosch, H., van Cleemput, K., Walrave, M. and Mortelmans, D. (2006) *Cyberpesten bij jongeren in Vlaanderen* [*Cyberbullying among Flemish youths*], Brussel: Vlaams instituut voor Wetenschappelijk en Technologisch Aspectenonderzoek.

Whitney, I. and Smith, P.K. (1993) 'A survey of the nature and extent of bullying in junior/middle and secondary schools', *Educational Research*, vol 35, pp 3-25.

Wolak, J., Mitchell, K. and Finkelhor, D. (2006) *Online victimization of youth: Five years later*, Alexandria, VA: National Center for Missing and Exploited Children, #07-06-025 (www.unh.edu/ccrc/pdf/CV138.pdf).

Ybarra, M. and Mitchell, K. (2004a) 'Online aggressor/targets, aggressors, and targets: a comparison of associated youth characteristics', *Journal of Child Psychology and Psychiatry*, vol 45, pp 1308-16.

Ybarra, M. and Mitchell, K. (2004b) 'Youth engaging in online harassment: associations with caregiver–child relationships, internet use, and personal characteristics', *Journal of Adolescence*, vol 27, pp 319-36.

TWELVE

'Sexting': the exchange of sexual messages online among European youth

Sonia Livingstone and Anke Görzig

Sexting': a new cultural phenomenon?

> School boards are grappling with a vexing problem – how to curb proliferation of sexually explicit texts and photos sent between teens. (*Toronto Sun*, 24 March 2011)[1]

> A dangerous "sexting" trend seems to be on the rise among minors after six teenagers were probed by police over explicit images sent over the web or mobile phones, police said. (*The Sydney Morning Herald*, 22 March 2011)[2]

The invention of a new term – for example, the portmanteau integration of sex and texting into the concept 'sexting' – may or may not identify a new phenomenon. Despite the public attention attracted by media announcements, such as those that open this chapter, it is unclear whether sexting is new and problematic or merely the latest moral panic related to youth and technology (Critcher, 2008). Although sexting is not unlike earlier telephonic, written or face-to-face exchanges (Chalfen, 2009), these quick-fire exchanges that occur largely 'under the radar' have been greatly enabled, perhaps transformed, by the advent of convenient, affordable, accessible and mobile access to the internet (boyd, 2008). Also, the privacy and anonymity of much online communication would seem to proliferate the possibilities for youthful sexual communication (Subrahmanyam and Šmahel, 2011).

Focus group discussions with teenagers suggest that sexting is primarily a form of electronically mediated flirtation (Lenhart, 2009). However, there have been revelations in some news stories of sexual activity among young people, made visible through the exchange of explicit, even possibly illegal images (if the images are of minors; Arcabascio, 2010; Sacco et al, 2010). Some argue that sexting is problematic only if the messages reach unintended recipients or are manipulated to produce hurtful effects, which is opening a new chapter in the history of sexual harassment (Barak, 2005; Ybarra et al, 2006). Concerns include, on the one hand, sexting as part of the much-claimed sexualisation of childhood (Greenfield, 2004) or the 'hyper, (hetero)sexual commodification and objectification of girl's bodies' (Ringrose, 2010, p 179) and, on the other, sexting as an activity that forms part of the abusive, usually adult-instigated, process of grooming (Davidson and Gottschalk, 2010). The boundary between what is fun and what is coercive may be difficult to distinguish, given the routine, often humorous exchange of sexual innuendo, rude jokes and swearing endemic in teenage conversation (National Campaign to Support Teen and Unplanned Pregnancy, 2008; Ringrose, 2010). Thus, at the other end of the scale of severity, sexting may be part of the developmentally necessary exploration and experimentation that enables the emergence of sexual identity (Stern, 2002; Buckingham and Bragg, 2004) and the identification of valuable sexual information and advice (Brown et al, 2005).

Sexting can, therefore, refer to communication that is voluntary or involuntary, serious or humorous, public or private, trivial or significant, pleasurable or hurtful. Wolak and Finkelhor (2011) distinguish between aggravated (including criminal or abusive elements in the creation of sexual images) and experimental (youth-produced) sexting, further dividing the latter by motivation (romantic, sexual attention-seeking, other). Although the questions in the EU Kids Online survey do not capture all these nuances in meaning, we recognise the ambiguous nature of sexting. Recalling the core distinction in our theoretical framework between risk and harm (see Chapter 1), rather than assuming that all instances of sexting are problematic or should be prevented, we explore first, which children receive online sexual messages, and second, why some experience them as upsetting. Although our child-centred approach suggests that it is in cases where the children themselves report being upset that policy intervention is most obviously justified, the nature of that intervention – empowering children to cope, advising parents on how to mediate, ensuring websites contain appropriate support and guidance, or any other policy approach – demands careful, evidence-based discussion (see Chapter 26 later in this volume).

Sexting among European youth

'If people take a picture of you and they edit it and make you look bad and they put it on the internet.' (girl, 9, Ireland)

'A person asked me to show my breasts on the webcam.' (girl, 11, Belgium)

'In online games where you can get some bonus points. When a child meets someone unknown in such game and that person offers him or her buying those points if the child sends him some naked photos.' (boy, 12, Czech Republic)

'In social networking sites it bothers me if there are foreigners who start bothering you and writing to you. They often ask for your MSN in order to see your webcam.' (girl, 16, Estonia)

These quotes are taken from children's responses to the open-ended survey question, 'What things on the internet would bother people about your age?'. Exploring the possible pleasures of sexual messaging was not one of the objectives of the EU Kids Online survey. The survey question asked 11- to 16-year-olds, in private, about the nature and incidence of sexual messaging. Given uncertainties of interpretation and translation, the term 'sexting' was not used in the questionnaire. Instead, we said: "People do all kinds of things on the internet. Sometimes, they may send sexual messages or images. By this we mean talk about having sex or images of people naked or having sex". Respondents were reminded that such messages "could be words, pictures or videos" and that they could be sent peer-to-peer directly or posted online (for example, on a social networking site or message board) where they could be seen by others. Lastly, we asked about sending/receiving messages (passive, potentially 'victim' activities) and posting/seeing messages (active, potentially 'perpetrator' activities).

Among the 18,709 internet-using children aged 11-16 in Europe who were selected randomly to participate in the EU Kids Online survey, 15 per cent said that they had seen or received sexual messages on the internet in the 12 months previous to the survey, and 3 per cent had sent or posted such messages. This tallies with figures reported by a nationally representative sample of US mobile-owning 12- to 17-year-olds, 15 per cent of whom had received sexually suggestive nude or nearly nude images of someone they knew, via text messaging on their mobile phones, while 4 per cent had sent such messages (Lenhart, 2009). Less rigorous survey samples produce higher estimates: one in three UK teenagers, according to Cross, Richardson and Douglas (2009; see also Phippen, 2009), 48 per cent of 13- to 19-year-olds, according to the US National Campaign to Support Teen and Unplanned Pregnancy (2008). While there is little variation by gender or socioeconomic status, across Europe twice as many older as younger children have received sexual messages (see Table 12.1; see also Livingstone et al, 2011).

Despite the difficulties of determining exactly what children have seen, it seems that 5 per cent of 11- to 16-year-olds (or 34 per cent of those who received a sexual message, most of whom are teenagers) say they had seen other people perform sexual acts on the internet, while 2 per cent (or 13 per cent of those who received a sexual message) had been asked to talk about sexual acts with someone on the internet or to show a photo or video of their genitals to someone via the internet.

Table 12.1 also shows that parents underestimate the amount of sexual messaging. Only 6 per cent of parents, compared with 15 per cent of children, said the child had seen or received a sexual message in the previous year. To put it differently, among the 15 per cent of children who had encountered sexual messages, 21 per cent of parents were aware of this, half (52 per cent) said their child had not encountered this and 27 per cent said they 'didn't know' if it had happened. This misunderstanding between parents and children may impede parents' abilities to support their children should this experience be problematic or distressing.

In terms of evidence of harm, the EU Kids Online project relies on children's self-reports of being upset by sexual messaging. Although 15 per cent of children have seen or received a sexual message online, only 4 per cent of internet-using children aged 11-16 (or a quarter of those who received such messages) responded positively when asked, has this 'bothered you in any way? For example, made you feel uncomfortable, upset, or feel that you shouldn't have seen it?'. Nearly half of these (or one in ten of all those who received sexual messages) were 'fairly' or 'very upset' (Livingstone et al, 2011). Among those who had received sexual messages, girls were much more likely to be bothered or upset (33 per cent) than boys (17 per cent), as were younger compared to older children (41 per cent of 11- to 12-year-olds compared with 25 per cent of 13- to 14-year-olds and 20 per cent of 15- to 16-year-olds).

Only 3 per cent of 11- to 16-year-olds said that they had posted or sent a sexual message in the previous 12 months. This may be underreported for reasons of social desirability, since, for some young people, sending and receiving may be linked and considered part of a peer interaction. Among those 3 per cent, most (46 per cent) had sent a sexual message, 33 per cent talked about sexual acts with someone, 15 per cent had posted a sexual message, 9 per cent had asked someone to send a photo or video showing their genitals and fewer had themselves sent such messages or images.

Explaining sexting

Why are older teenagers more likely to receive, but less likely to be upset by, sexual messages? Recognising that 'age' on its own does not explains this finding, we formulate two hypotheses, based on the theoretical model presented in Chapter 1 (Livingstone and Görzig, submitted). Figure 12.1 shows that the *usage hypothesis* (horizontal dotted arrow) suggests that the broader children's use practices, the more likely they are to encounter online risk. This hypothesised relation may be due to greater access, freedom and privacy in using the internet, or to the disinhibiting nature of much online communication (Suler, 2004), enabling certain kinds of 'risky opportunities' (Livingstone, 2008).

The *risk migration hypothesis* (vertical dashed arrow) recognises that children encounter a range of risks in their everyday lives, either because they are disadvantaged (or 'at risk') or because adolescents tend to take risks to test themselves against the world and develop resilience (Coleman and Hagell, 2007). The idea of risk migration is that since the virtual/real boundary is ever less significant to the so-called 'digital generation', risk experiences occur not only offline, but also online. Moreover, those who are older, or psychologically prone to take risks (diagonal dashed arrow) and opportunities (horizontal dotted arrow), would be expected to encounter more online risks.

In statistical terms, we hypothesise that either or both of usage practices and risky offline activities mediate the relationship between age and online risks. As explained in Livingstone and Görzig

Figure 12.1: Model to explain risk and harm, applied to sexting

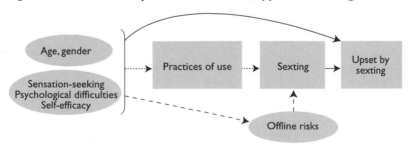

Table 12.1: Child has seen or received sexual messages online, by age, message type and country

	Internet users who have seen/been sent sexual message (country figures show % difference from all)			Among those who have seen/been sent sexual messages, internet users who have encountered the following (country figures show % difference from all):						
	All	11-13	14-16	Been sent	Seen posted	Seen other people perform sexual acts	Been asked to talk about sexual acts	Asked for a photo or video showing private parts	Was bothered by being sent	Parent knows this happened
Austria	+2	+1	+2	-5	11	+7	-9	-7	-9	-2
Belgium	+3	+1	+4	+8	10	-8	-6	-9	-10	+2
Bulgaria	-1	-	-1	-3	+7	-9	-4	-5	-7	+4
Cyprus	-4	-6	-1	-3	-15	+4	-6	-8	-6	+5
Czech Republic	+6	+2	11	+7	+2	+8	+4	-	-7	+19
Germany	+1	-2	+3	-14	-11	+2	-	-2	+2	-8
Denmark	+1	-2	+5	19	-10	+9	+8	+8	-3	-6
Estonia	+4	+3	+5	-	10	-4	+27	+13	+9	-2
Greece	-4	-6	-4	+4	14	-5	+6	-11	-6	+4
Spain	-6	-5	-7	-	-4	-2	-2	-6	-	+3
Finland	+3	-1	+6	-3	14	+2	+8	+9	-15	-
France	+4	+7	+3	-	-5	+3	-4	-4	-5	-3
Hungary	-7	-4	-9	-	-6	+9	-	-3	+4	-15
Ireland	-4	-5	-3	+19	-5	-2	+13	+8	-7	-6
Italy	-11	-8	-14	-5	-5	+25	-9	-	-	-5

(continued)

Table 12.1: Child has seen or received sexual messages online, by age, message type and country (continued)

	Internet users who have seen/been sent sexual message (country figures show % difference from all)			Among those who have seen/been sent sexual messages, internet users who have encountered the following (country figures show % difference from all):						
	All	11-13	14-16	Been sent	Seen posted	Seen other people perform sexual acts	Been asked to talk about sexual acts	Asked for a photo or video showing private parts	Was bothered by being sent	Parent knows this happened
Lithuania	+4	−1	+7	−	14	−5	+2	−	−7	−3
Netherlands	−	−2	+2	−4	−2	−12	+4	−4	−8	−
Norway	+5	−	11	−5	−15	11	17	17	−6	−6
Poland	+2	+3	+1	−21	10	−11	−10	−5	+3	+5
Portugal	−	−2	+1	+4	−9	+2	+3	−3	−3	−18
Romania	+7	+4	12	−	+5	−19	−12	−9	13	−8
Sweden	+3	−	+7	+20	+6	+14	+8	14	−4	−3
Slovenia	+2	+1	+4	−12	17	−7	−8	−5	−13	+5
Turkey	−1	−	−1	+14	+8	+8	+15	+9	15	11
UK	−3	−3	−3	+17	−2	−5	−	+4	−4	+9
All	15	9	20	46	40	34	13	12	25	29

Base: Children aged 11-16 who use the internet.

(submitted), these hypotheses are broadly confirmed. Practices of use (for example, range of online activities and risky online activities) and risky offline activities, together, mediate between, on the one hand, demographic (age) and psychological factors (sensation-seeking, self-efficacy, psychological difficulties)[3] and, on the other hand, the range of types of sexual messages received (see Appendix). Older children, those with higher sensation-seeking and self-efficacy, and those with more psychological problems, are likely to receive a wider range of sexual-type messages. Importantly, this is mediated by practices of use and risky offline activities: children who engage in more online activities, especially more risky online activities, and more risky offline activities (this in turn is influenced by psychological and demographic factors) are particularly likely to encounter more sexual messaging.

The explanations for risk and harm may not be the same. Since only a minority of those who encounter sexual messaging are upset by it, we also examine the *vulnerability hypothesis*, namely, that among those who encounter risk online, the more vulnerable the child (for psychological or demographic reasons), the more likely harm will result (the curved arrow in Figure 12.1). Harm is measured by multiplying how upset the child was by how long the child was upset (resulting in a scale from 0-12 ; see also *Harm Index* in Appendix). As expected, younger children and girls are more upset by receipt of sexual messages. Further, children with more psychological difficulties are more likely to find sexual messages upsetting. Last, although higher scores on sensation-seeking are associated with receiving more types of sexual messaging, this is also associated with less harm: in other words, children who are more upset are lower on sensation-seeking, possibly because over time sensation-seeking provides opportunities to develop resilience.

Country differences

What is common across Europe, and to what extent do children's experiences differ by country? Figure 12.2 shows country averages for the percentage of children who have encountered sexting versus those who were bothered or upset by sexual messages. Countries in which risk and harm are above average (top right quadrant) merit particular attention. It is possible that in Romania, Estonia and Poland, national and familial protection for children is less developed, despite recent adoption of domestic internet access. Harm is also relatively high in Turkey, Hungary and Italy, although the incidence of sexting is lower: are children less resilient in these countries or are the messages they receive more sexually explicit or hostile? In countries where risk is

Figure 12.2: Children who encountered sexting (%), and the percentage of those who were bothered or upset, by country

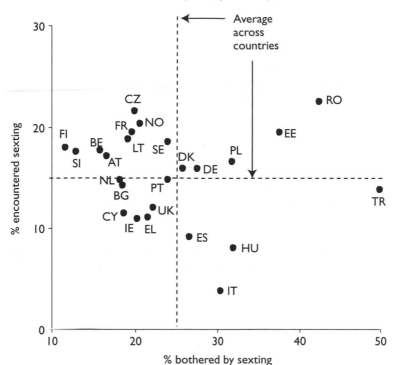

Note: See page 13 for explanation of country codes.

higher, but harm is lower (top left quadrant, for example, the Czech Republic, Finland, France and Lithuania), are children more resilient, or are the messages less extreme or upsetting?

Given the importance of age in relation to online risk and harm, we conducted multilevel regression analysis to check whether, among those who had received sexual messages, younger children reported more harm than teenagers, in all countries.[4] Intriguingly, the relationship is different across countries ($LR(2)=8.52, p=0.03$) – while older teenagers reported similar levels of harm from sexting across Europe, country differences for younger children were marked. In Finland, and to a lesser degree in Cyprus and Greece, children who encountered sexting were equally upset (or not) whatever their ages. In the UK, Estonia and the Czech Republic, younger children were more upset than older teenagers. We then explored whether younger children in more religious cultures were particularly shocked or upset by sexual messages. Using the European Social Survey's (2008) measure of religiosity, we found that this helped explain the varying age differences for harm from sexting among countries (that is, there was a significant interaction effect between age and religion in predicting harm; $B=0.003$; $p<0.05$).

Contrary to our expectations, however, it seems that the stronger the culture of religion in a country, the smaller (not larger) the age differences for harm. Figure 12.3 splits countries into three groups for top third, middle or bottom third for religiosity.[5] For example, in the Czech Republic, which scores particularly low for religiosity, the difference in harm between younger and older children is among the greatest. Countries with a strong religious culture, such as Cyprus, show much smaller differences in harm by age. This could be because there are more sexually explicit messages circulating in less religious countries, and they upset the younger children who encounter them. Or it may be that in more religious countries, children feel more protected by their parents and less vulnerable to sexual messages. More research is needed to understand these cross-national differences.

Figure 12.3: Relationship between child's age, and harm from sexting, by countries grouped according to population religiosity

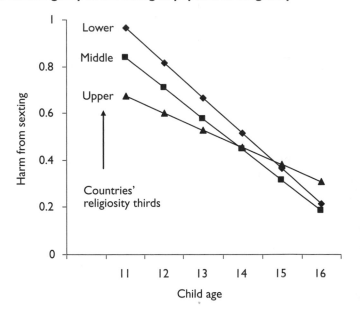

From evidence to policy

The EU Kids Online survey findings suggest that, in the case of most children, we should not be overly concerned about the rise in online sexual messaging among young people. For a minority, however, these experiences are upsetting, and may even signal a threat to the child's safety; for both reasons, sexting merits policy attention. In an effort to avoid top-down interventionist approaches, the preference of policy makers is to equip children to manage online risks themselves insofar as they are able, and insofar as it is reasonable and practical to expect this of them. Politically, this makes for an interesting, possibly constructive, alliance between children's rights advocates who seek to empower children, an industry seeking to avoid top-down regulation and governments concerned about over-regulating a fast-moving and global infrastructure such as the internet.

Children faced with upsetting sexual messages online use a range of coping strategies including individual, social and technical solutions if available (see Table 12.2). Among respondents who had both received sexual messages and been bothered or upset by them, it seems that girls

Table 12.2: Children's coping responses when upset by sexual messages online, by gender and age (%)

	All	Girls	Boys	11-13	14-16
Individual coping (did you do any of these?)					
Try to fix the problem	27	29	23	27	26
Hope the problem would go away by itself	22	**13**	**36**	20	23
Try to get the other person to leave me alone	12	**16**	**6**	11	13
Feel a bit guilty about what went wrong	6	7	3	**12**	**2**
Try to get back at the other person	2	2	3	1	3
None of these things	32	34	30	30	33
Social support (who did you talk to...?)					
Talked to anybody at all	60	**66**	**48**	63	58
A friend[a]	38	**50**	**69**	**46**	**73**
My mother or father[a]	30	50	49	**69**	**38**
My brother or sister[a]	9	15	13	14	15
Another adult I trust[a]	5	10	9	**16**	**6**
Some one whose job it is to help children[a]	3	7	3	6	3
A teacher[a]	2	**9**	**2**	**8**	**1**
Someone else[a]	1	2	2	2	2
Technical responses (did you do any of these?)					
I blocked the person who had sent it to me	40	**33**	**45**	39	41
I deleted any messages from the person who sent it to me	38	33	41	**31**	**42**
I changed my filter/contact settings	24	24	23	**13**	**30**
I stopped using the internet for a while	18	13	21	12	21
I reported the problem	18	15	21	15	20
None of these	7	**10**	**5**	7	7

Base: Children aged 11-16 who have been bothered or upset by seeing or receiving a sexual message on the internet. [a]*Base*: Children aged 11-16 who have been bothered or upset by seeing or receiving a sexual message on the internet and have talked to anybody at all.

Note: Numbers in **bold** show statistically significant gender or age differences (*p*<0.05).

adopt more proactive or social coping strategies while boys either try technical responses or are fatalistic. Future awareness-raising efforts should take account of the finding that four in ten children told no one when sexting had upset them, and some younger children feel guilt at having somehow caused the problem in the first place. In the main, children who try technical solutions find them effective at helping to resolve the problem, although reporting the problem officially was not seen as very efficient – one in five had done this, but only around half of those thought that it helped (see Livingstone et al, 2011).

To conclude, we find that public anxiety over sexting is overstated in that its incidence is relatively low and, among its recipients, most do not find it harmful or upsetting. More types of sexual messages are received online by older than by younger children, partly because they use the internet more and partly because they encounter or indulge in risky behaviour offline. Generally, the consequences are unproblematic – possibly pleasurable, possibly building resilience. However, for some younger children, for girls, and for children with psychological difficulties, receiving sexual messages can be upsetting. These few who experience the harm, we suggest, rather than the larger minority who encounter the risk, should be the target of future policy initiatives, whether preventative, supportive or controlling; notably, this group is already in need of social and psychological support.

Notes

[1] See www.torontosun.com/news/canada/2011/03/24/17734866.html

[2] See www.smh.com.au/technology/technology-news/six-teenagers-investigated-over-sexting-and-webcam-porn-20110322-1c4v9.html

[3] This measure is based on selected items from the four 'difficulties' subscales of the Strengths and Difficulties Questionnaire (SDQ), which assesses emotional problems, conduct problems, hyperactivity/inattention and peer relationship problems (Goodman, 1997). See the Appendix at the end of this book.

[4] One rationale reflects the fact that we cannot discount the possibility that country differences are artefactual, due to differences in the translation of 'upset' or 'bothered' into different languages. However, this explanation might be discounted if an external factor is found to predict cross-country differences in the relation between harm and some other variable.

[5] Religiosity is measured in terms of the percentage of the population who say that they belong to a particular religion or denomination in each country. Countries were split as follows: lower – Czech Republic, Estonia, Sweden, Netherlands, Belgium, UK, France; middle – Slovenia, Norway, Finland,

---

Denmark, Germany, Hungary, Spain, Bulgaria; upper – Ireland, Portugal, Greece, Poland, Romania, Turkey, Cyprus. Austria, Italy and Lithuania are excluded from the analysis since there is no measure of religiosity for these countries.

References

Arcabascio, C. (2010) 'Sexting and teenagers: OMG R U GOING 2 JAIL???', *Richmond Journal of Law & Technology*, vol 16, no 3, pp 1-43.

Barak, A. (2005) 'Sexual harassment on the internet', *Social Science Computer Review*, vol 23, no 1, pp 77-92.

boyd, d. (2008) 'Why youth ♥ social network sites: the role of networked publics in teenage social life', in D. Buckingham (ed) *Youth, identity, and digital media, vol 6*, Cambridge, MA: The MIT Press, pp 119-42.

Brown, J.D., Halpern, C.T. and L'Engle, K.L. (2005) 'Mass media as a sexual super peer for early maturing girls', *Journal of Adolescent Health*, vol 36, no 5, pp 420-7.

Buckingham, D. and Bragg, S. (2004) *Young people, sex and the media*, Basingstoke: Palgrave Macmillan.

Chalfen, R. (2009) '"It's only a picture": sexting, "smutty" snapshots and felony charges', *Visual Studies*, vol 24, no 3, pp 258-68.

Coleman, J. and Hagell, A. (eds) (2007) *Adolescence, risk and resilience*, Chichester: Wiley.

Critcher, C. (2008) 'Making waves: historic aspects of public debates about children and mass media', in K. Drotner and S. Livingstone (eds) *International handbook of children, media and culture*, London: Sage Publications, pp 91-104.

Cross, E.J., Richardson, B. and Douglas, T. (2009) *Virtual violence: Protecting children from cyberbullying*, London: Beatbullying.

Davidson, J. and Gottschalk, P. (2010) *Internet child abuse: Current research and policy*, London: Routledge.

ESS (European Social Survey) (2008) *ESS Round 4* (http://ess.nsd.uib.no/ess/round4/).

Goodman, R. (1997) 'The Strengths and Difficulties Questionnaire: a research note', *Journal of Child Psychology and Psychiatry*, vol 38, pp 581-86.

Greenfield, P.M. (2004) 'Inadvertent exposure to pornography on the internet', *Journal of Applied Developmental Psychology*, vol 25, no 6, pp 741-50.

Lenhart, A. (2009) *Teens and sexting: How and why minor teens are sending sexually suggestive nude or nearly nude images via text messaging*, Washington DC: Pew Internet and American Life Project.

Livingstone, S. (2008) 'Taking risky opportunities in youthful content creation: teenagers' use of social networking sites for intimacy, privacy and self-expression', *New Media & Society*, vol 10, no 3, pp 393-411.

Livingstone, S. and Görzig, A. (submitted) 'When adolescents receive sexual messages on the internet', Manuscript.

Livingstone, S., Haddon, L., Görzig, A. and Ólafsson, K. (2011) *Risks and safety on the internet: The perspective of European children. Full findings*, London: London School of Economics and Political Science.

National Campaign to Support Teen and Unplanned Pregnancy (2008) *Sex and tech: Results from a survey of teens and young adults*, Washington, DC: National Campaign to Support Teen and Unplanned Pregnancy.

Phippen, A. (2009) *Sharing personal images and videos among young people*, Exeter: South West Grid for Learning.

Ringrose, J. (2010) 'Sluts, whores, fat slags and Playboy bunnies: teen girls' negotiations of "sexy" on social networking sites and at school', in C. Jackson, C. Paechter and E. Renold (eds) *Girls and education 3-16*, Maidenhead: Open University Press, pp 170-82.

Sacco, D.T., Argudin, R., Maguire, J. and Tallon, K. (2010) *Sexting: Youth practices and legal implications*, Cambridge, MA: Berkman Center for Internet and Society.

Subrahmanyam, K. and Šmahel, D. (2011) *Digital youth: The role of media in development*, New York: Springer.

Stern, S. (2002) 'Sexual selves on the world wide web: adolescent girls' home pages as sites for sexual self-expression', in J. Brown, J. Steele and K. Walsh-Childers (eds) *Sexual teens, sexual media*, Mahwah, NJ: Lawrence Erlbaum Associates, pp 265-85.

Suler, J. (2004) 'The online disinhibition effect', *CyberPsychology and Behavior*, vol 7, pp 321-6.

Wolak, J. and Finkelhor, D. (2011) 'Sexting: a typology', *Research Bulletin* (March), Durham, NH: Crimes Against Children Research Center, University of New Hampshire.

Ybarra, M.L., Mitchell, K. and Wolak, J. (2006) 'Examining characteristics and associated distress related to internet harassment', *Pediatrics*, vol 118, no 4, pp 1169-77.

THIRTEEN

Pornography

Antonis Rovolis and Liza Tsaliki

Harm, childhood and appropriate media content: an ongoing debate

We live in an era of contested conceptualisations of childhood. On the one hand, the commercial imperative of contemporary capitalism has expanded into marketing for and to children. On the other hand, the predominant view of childhood as a natural, universal and biologically inherent period of human development, imagined as an age of innocence where the child is vulnerable to the threat of deviant sexuality, means that we experience a nervous dialectic in which children are held to be 'naturally' innocent yet, at the same time, implicated in dangerous sexuality. This means that rather than seeing them as humans going through a complex and contradictory maturation process, we posit children as inherently pure, yet easily corrupted by exposure to explicit image material (Kleinhans, 2004, p 72).

However, the assumed harmful influence of pornography on children goes back to a long and still ongoing tradition of media effects, and has been exacerbated with the advent and unprecedented proliferation of online pornography. Children need to be protected from harmful content, which includes pornographic content. We live, the argument goes, in a culture saturated and depraved by uncontrolled sexuality, in which childhood innocence is debauched by media and consumer culture within which the availability of sexual information to children is rarely treated as positive. Alongside a growing acceptance that young viewers interpret pornography in complex ways and claims that media 'effects' are simplistic and overly deterministic – especially when pornography is also seen as having desirable effects, as in the case of challenging restrictive sexual norms and offering positive expressions of non-heterosexual sexualities – there is a need to be cautious about the harmful effects associated with pornography[1] (Flood, 2007). The ubiquity of children's encounters with internet pornography has been discussed by various researchers and institutions, in different national contexts (Freeman-Longo, 2000; Kaiser Family Foundation, 2001; Thornburgh and Lin, 2002; NetRatings Australia, 2005; McKee et al, 2008; Ey and Cupit, 2011; among others).

There is a grey area on the public agenda that covers child sexuality and child pornography, which are, however, separate issues. The confusion is further confounded because public discussion of pornography often conflates three areas that are quite distinct: child abuse images (the depiction of children in sexually explicit contexts), 'grooming' (adults trying to lure children into sexual activity online) and online pornography (adult pornography that children and teens may access on purpose or by accident) (McKee et al, 2008). The interest in this chapter is online pornography since, despite considerable academic interest in the possibility that accidental exposure to sexually explicit material may harm children, there has been very little direct research in this area for ethical reasons (Heins, 2001; Helsper, 2005). Helsper (2005) argues that there is no conclusive empirical evidence of a causal relationship between exposure to over-18[2] material and the impairment of mental, physical or moral development in minors.

Nevertheless, the extent to which pornographic websites are experienced as problematic for young people and their families is unclear, since the link between risks, incidents and actual harm is genuinely tenuous: not all risk-taking results in worrying incidents, not all worrying incidents result in actual or lasting harm (Livingstone, 2009). Millwood Hargrave and Livingstone (2006) show that many questions about harm are difficult to address because research provides evidence based on the balance of probabilities rather than on irrefutable proof. In fact, what is at stake is the likelihood of risk rather than of inevitable harm.

Media representations across Europe affect perceptions of the prevalence of risk by envisaging the online world as hazardous to children, and by focusing public attention disproportionately on risks – as evidenced by a content analysis of news coverage in 14 of the 21 countries participating in EU Kids Online *I* (Haddon and Stald, 2009). Thus, the media contribute to the proliferation of public anxieties that can easily escalate into moral panic (Critcher, 2008; Tsaliki, 2011). That said, it is worth noting that concerns about pornography are relative in the sense that pornography is a bigger issue in some countries than others[3] and, therefore, media representations vary. Also, what was regarded as obscene in one era may be considered as culturally valuable in another, and vice versa (McKee et al, 2008, p 4)[4] and, in this sense, what exactly constitutes pornography remains relatively vague.

Looking into the online activities and behaviour of representative samples of a thousand children per country aged 9-16, across 25 European countries, the EU Kids Online II network found that less than a quarter (23 per cent) had encountered sexual images, online or offline. The greater frequency of older children and teenagers (compared to younger children who encounter more online risks) means that it is this group that has most such experiences; 14 per cent had encountered sexual images online, mostly as a result of accidental pop-ups rather than deliberately, 12 per cent encountered them on television, video or film, and 7 per cent did so in magazines. Also, it is older teenage boys (13-16 years) who are more likely to have seen online sexual content (24 per cent). Of all those exposed to sexual content online, about one third (32 per cent) were bothered by it, which translates into only 4 per cent of the total population of children. Among those few who reported being upset, 16 per cent were 'very upset' by what they saw, 28 per cent were 'fairly upset' and 41 per cent were 'a bit' upset. In all cases, the majority coped well and got over the experience immediately. National variation in the incidence of exposure to sexual content online is considerable, as may be expected, ranging from 34 per cent of children in Norway, followed by Finland and Estonia (29 per cent), Denmark and the Czech Republic (28 per cent), Sweden (26 per cent), Latvia and Slovenia (25 per cent), and Italy (7 per cent). Only a small minority of children in Europe who have encountered sexual content online were bothered by the experience, with percentages of self-reported harm below 10 per cent in all the countries surveyed, with the exception of Estonia (14 per cent) (Livingstone et al, 2011).

The EU Kids Online network contextualises the relationship between risk and harm, whereby risk does not necessarily result in harm, although harm cannot occur without the incidence of risk. This chapter mainly focuses on research on children's experience of risk.[5] In our case, this refers to the risk of exposure to online sexual images. We explore the factors that may determine this exposure and ask which children are more likely to be harmed by such an experience.

Following the theoretical approach taken in Chapter 12 of this volume, we formulate hypotheses regarding the factors that influence the incidence of experiences of online sexual images, arguing that these factors are mediated by practices of use and risky offline activities. Thus the first hypothesis is a *usage hypothesis*, which suggests that the proliferation of private internet usage by children is positively correlated with the likelihood of exposure to online sexual images. The second hypothesis is a *risk migration hypothesis*, that since the boundaries between the online and offline are increasingly blurred, children's risky experiences may occur online as well as offline, so that those children who encounter more risks offline will be likely to encounter more risks online. In order to identify what makes some children more vulnerable to harm than others, the third hypothesis assesses the factors that affect the probability of harm (again, see Chapter 12). This *vulnerability hypothesis* argues that among those children who have seen sexual images online, those reporting resulting harm are more likely to be vulnerable due to psychological and demographic factors. We present the method used, followed by a presentation and discussion of our findings.

Method

In order to test our hypotheses related to risk, we employed the dependent variable 'seeing sexual images',[6] calculated as exposure to sexual images online or not, among all children aged 9-16 who use the internet (values 1/0 respectively). For the vulnerability hypothesis (for those children who encountered sexual images online and self-reported feeling bothered[7] by the experience), we focused on the two dependent variables, 'intensity of harm' and 'duration of harm'.[8]

Following the finding that older teenage boys are more likely to encounter online sexual images, we included the independent variables age (9-16) and gender,[9] in addition to parental level of education, as demographic predictors, and also restrictive mediation.[10] In the case of parents' level of education, we expect that children from a higher educational level home background will be more likely to encounter online sexual images because they will be better equipped and connected (digitally) by comparison with children from lower educational level households. We also expect that children with fewer parental controls will be more likely to encounter online sexual images. We included sensation-seeking ('I do dangerous things for fun', 'I do exciting things, even if they are dangerous') and self-efficacy ('I am confident I can deal with unexpected problems')[11] as psychological predictors. The rationale is that we expect that, while children who are high sensation-seekers may be more likely to encounter online sexual images, the likelihood of them feeling *upset* by such encounters will be lower among children higher in self-efficacy.

We used logistic regression analysis to determine the direct effects of the independent variables 'private practices of use' and 'engagement in any risky offline activities', on children's online exposure to sexual images.

Private practices of use include:

- 'Private devices of use': this was calculated from the responses to the question 'Which of these devices do you use for the internet these days?', offering eight response options (own PC–desktop; own laptop that can be taken to own room; PC shared with others in the family; laptop shared with others that cannot be taken to own room; mobile; games console; TV; other portable device). We assume that children using devices that allow private access to the internet will be more likely to encounter sexual content online because they will be free of adult monitoring. This variable was turned into a binary variable by estimating the options 'own desktop', 'own laptop', 'mobile' and 'other portable device' as means that allow *private* use of the internet, and the options 'PC shared with others in the family', 'laptop shared with others', 'games console' and 'TV' as means that allow *non-private* use of the internet (where 1 is private use and 0 is non-private use).

- 'Private places of use' was calculated from the responses to the question 'Where do you use the internet these days?'. It offers eight response options as follows: 'own bedroom/other private room' and 'when out and about, that is, via a mobile, Blackberry, iPod etc' as allowing for *private* use of the internet; other places, such as 'living room/other public room at home', 'school/college', 'internet café', 'public library', 'other homes', as allowing for *non-private* use of the internet (where 1 is private use and 0 is non-private use); as in the case of private devices of use, we assume that children accessing the internet in private places of use will be more likely to experience online sexual images.

- 'Engagement in any risky online activities',[12] which was turned into a binary variable (1 when any these activities occurred, 0 for no activities); we assume that children practising risky online activities will be more likely to experience online sexual images.

Risky offline activities[13] was included as another independent variable.[14] We assume that children who engage in risky activities will be more likely to have seen online sexual images.

Results and discussion: encountering online sexual content

Of those children (*n*=22,875, not weighted) aged 9-16, who reported having and not having seen sexual images anywhere (offline or online), only 5,907 (not weighted) of them were routed on to the question regarding *online* sexual content (see Table 13.1).

Table 13.1: Children who have seen sexual images in the past year, anywhere and online

	Have you seen sexual images anywhere in past 12 months?	Have you seen sexual images on websites in past 12 months?
Yes	5,302 (23%)	3,228 (14%)

Base: All children aged 9-16 who use the internet.

A regression analysis for seeing sexual images among 9- to 16-year-olds (Table 13.2) shows that having private devices for internet use is not a statistically significant predictor of exposure to online sexual images, contrary to our prediction.

The regression analysis shows that our remaining expectations are supported. We found that the more children engage in risky online activities, the more online sexual images they see; the same applies for those engaging in risky offline activities. Also, more boys rather than girls experience sexual content online, and children who have more self-efficacy about their ability to cope with unexpected situations online and sensation-seekers encounter more online sexual images, which is not a surprising result. In our view, this is evidence of children's resilience when encountering online sexual images, and it should be taken into account when weighing alarmist claims about children being at risk from sexual content online. Encounters with online sexual images increase with age – which is also not surprising since explorations of sexuality, and hence pornography, are part of growing up, and will inevitably increase as children's internet usage abilities increase. Finally, the regression analysis shows that children accessing the internet in private places of use encounter online sexual images; the children of more highly educated parents are more likely to

Table 13.2: Regression analysis for seeing sexual images

	B	SE	Wald	df	Sig	Exp(B)
Gender (0 = female)	0.30	0.04	50.66	1.00	0.00	1.35
Self-efficacy (1-3)	0.32	0.05	46.28	1.00	0.00	1.38
Sensation-seeking (1-3)	0.45	0.04	130.97	1.00	0.00	1.56
Age child (9-16)	0.14	0.01	139.90	1.00	0.00	1.15
Parents' education (1-7)	0.09	0.01	36.20	1.00	0.00	1.09
Restrictive mediation (1-3)	−0.47	0.05	91.73	1.00	0.00	0.63
Private places of use (0/1)	0.17	0.05	10.75	1.00	0.00	1.18
Private devices of use (0/1)	−0.03	0.06	0.33	1.00	0.56	0.97
Risky online activities (0-5)	0.29	0.01	402.20	1.00	0.00	1.34
Risky offline activities (0-5)	0.32	0.02	217.11	1.00	0.00	1.38
Constant	−5.11	0.24	459.91	1.00	0.00	0.01

Base: All children aged 9-16 who use the internet.

encounter more online sexual images (perhaps also as a result of a more advanced and nuanced understanding of sexually explicit material); and less restrictive parental mediation results in children seeing more online sexual images. It appears, then, that while the usage hypothesis is partially supported, the risk migration hypothesis applies to both the online and offline worlds.

Our findings about harm arising as a consequence of seeing sexual images online show that we need to be careful about making sweeping claims. First, the number of children and teenagers self-reporting that they were 'bothered' by sexual content is low. Table 13.3 shows that only 870 young people reported having been upset, to various degrees, by online sexual images – with only 15 per cent of children who saw online sexual images (or less than 1 per cent of all the children in the survey) feeling 'very upset' by it; 57 per cent of children who saw sexual images online (or 2.5 per cent of all children) were either 'not at all' or 'a bit' upset by the experience.

Table 13.4 shows that the majority of those who saw online sexual images (93 per cent), recovered either immediately or in a few days; only 7 per cent (or 52 out of all children) took longer to recover.

Table 13.5 shows that for intensity of harm, among all the predictors, level of parental education plays no role as regards the discomfort the child might experience. On the other hand, the younger and lower in self-efficacy the child, the more likely that seeing sexual images will be upsetting; girls also are more likely to be more upset by online sexual images than boys. Parental level of education is not statistically significant.

Age and parental level of education are not statistically significant in the case of the duration of effect of harm; girls and children with less self-efficacy feel upset for longer after exposure to online sexual images (see Table 13.6).

Table 13.3: Intensity of harm from seeing sexual images

Thinking about the last time you were bothered, how upset were you?	Freq	%[a]	%[b]
Very upset	156	15	0.62
Fairly upset	283	28	1.00
A bit upset	431	43	2.00
Not at all upset	138	14	0.55
Total	1,008	100.00	

Notes: [a] Of children who have seen online sexual images.
[b] Of all children.

Table 13.4: Duration of harm from seeing sexual images

Thinking about this time, how long did you feel like that for?	Freq	%ᵃ	%ᵇ
I got over it straight away	489	63	2.00
For a few days	236	30	1.00
For a few weeks	38	5	0.15
For a couple of months or more	14	2	0.06
Total	777	100.00	

Notes: ᵃ Of children who have seen online pornography.
ᵇ Of all children.

Table 13.5: Regression analysis for intensity of harm from seeing sexual images

Linear regression predicting being upset by seeing sexual images online (0-3)	B	SE	Beta	t	p
(Constant)	1.29	0.16		8.15	0.00
Gender (0 = female)	−0.18	0.03	−0.11	−6.39	0.00
Age child (9-16)	−0.07	0.01	−0.16	−8.54	0.00
Self-efficacy (1-3)	−0.10	0.03	−0.05	−3.09	0.00
Sensation-seeking (1-3)	0.06	0.02	0.05	2.80	0.01
Parents' education (1-7)	0.00	0.00	0.00	−0.19	0.85
Restrictive mediation (1-3)	0.21	0.03	0.12	6.34	0.00

Notes: $R^2=0.08$; $n=3,385$

Base: All children aged 9-16 who use the internet and have seen sexual images online.

Table 13.6: Regression analysis for duration of harm from seeing sexual images

Linear regression predicting length of being upset by seeing sexual images online (0-4)	B	SE	Beta	t	p
(Constant)	0.50	0.15		3.31	0.00
Gender (0 = female)	−0.17	0.03	−0.12	−6.58	0.00
Age child (9-16)	−0.01	0.01	−0.01	−0.74	0.46
Self-efficacy (1-3)	−0.14	0.03	−0.09	−4.84	0.00
Sensation-seeking (1-3)	0.05	0.02	0.04	2.26	0.02
Parents' education (1-7)	0.00	0.00	0.00	−0.19	0.85
Restrictive mediation (1-3)	0.21	0.03	0.13	6.71	0.00

Notes: $R^2=0.05$; $n=3,162$

Base: All children aged 9-16 who use the internet and have seen sexual images online.

Overall, our research shows that few children are vulnerable in the sense that among children who have seen sexual images online, few report being harmed by the experience. The findings lend some support to the vulnerability hypothesis that age (younger), gender (girls) and self-efficacy (lower) play the strongest roles in predicting which children report among harm. Therefore, although we would argue that claims about the 'devastating' effects of online sexual images to young people are overstated, it is also noteworthy that those children who are more vulnerable offline also appear to be more vulnerable online.

Conclusion

Our focus in this chapter was to address the social anxiety around children and teenagers' encounters with adult pornography, and in particular online sexual images. The EU Kids Online survey shows that from this chapter's sample of children who use the internet (out of the total 25,000 children surveyed), only a minority (about 6,000) encountered these. These findings confirm empirically what cultural studies-oriented approaches have been arguing for some time − that social, policy and academic concerns regarding the impact of pornographic content on young people are seriously overstated.

There are some policy-related implications from our findings. First, there is nothing new in young people trying to access adult sexual material − they have always tried to do this. The difference is that instead of trying to access it from print material belonging to parents, relatives or friends, or material found in parks and on the high street, for example, children are finding it on the internet. The comparative lack of censorship and control of the circulation of this material on the internet, and the ease with which pornography has come out from 'under the bed' and 'onto your screens', is causing concern. The perceived powerlessness to monitor children's behaviour, accompanied by mounting social pressure to contain child sexuality, are contributing to a media alarmist and sensationalist culture. This is fed largely by conservative approaches to legal action and social policy (Kleinhans, 2004; Paasonen, 2007).[15]

Recent research on young consumers of pornography (Buckingham and Bragg, 2004; McKee et al, 2008) shows that young people are capable of expressing strong personal opinions without feeling intimidated, powerless or maimed for life by the experience of pornography. Furthermore, it seems that children and teenagers are well aware that not everything they see in the media is true or should be accepted: they often challenge media representations. Ethnographic research shows that experiences with online pornography are rarely traumatic for children and teenagers; they are more likely to be part of a rite of passage or educational, in relation to their own bodies and giving their partners pleasure (McKee et al, 2008, p 164; Buckingham et al, 2010).

What do these findings tell us? Perhaps in a culture engulfed by sexually explicit representations we should opt for filtering software for primary school-aged children (who have limited online research capacities). This would not be suitable for older children with the capability to bypass any protection. It would be unlikely to curtail the type of sexual information older children find on the internet. Perhaps age-appropriate uses of the internet should be advocated. More significant, however, would be discussion of what is considered appropriate in relation to pornography, with parents and educators, which would need to be part of a larger sex education programme. As McKee et al (2008) argue, as with other media, pornography does not exist in a social vacuum; hence, children educated and brought up in a cultural climate where assault and harassment are wrong and where men and women are social equals, will acquire values and attitudes to pornography, and refuse to accept denigrating pornographic representations of men and women as a given. Ultimately, this implies building resilience and a critical stance among young people.

Notes

[1] Within this particular context, what constitutes harm from pornography is neither clear nor consensually accepted; overall, such claims of harm, made by adults in relation to children, may involve several things, from encountering any sexuality at all or particular representations of it, to the long-term effect on children's perceptions of the social world. None of these accounts can be easily measured by this survey; the same applies for children's readings of such encounters, for which an ethnographic approach is needed, something to be dealt with in EU Kids Online III.

[2] What is classified as over-18 material changes over time and across national contexts.

[3] See, for example, Paasonen et al, 2007, p 16, on Finnish debates on porn.

[4] Look, for example, at how connotations around young children's images have changed since the 1950s and 1960s. An image that once seemed tender is now terrifying because it reads as explicitly erotic. At the same time, however, the sensitisation process to child porn also forces us to eroticise children (Kleinhans, 2004, p 79).

[5] Here we see children's experience of online pornographic material as a socially constructed risk; how the children themselves view it, and whether they actually consider it a risk is something to be followed up using ethnographic methods.

[6] See key variables in the Appendix at the end of this book for variable description.

[7] A qualitative follow-up analysis could broach the question of online porn experiences in a different frame, whereby children are not asked if such encounters bothered them, but what they found interesting or extraordinary.

[8] See key variables in the Appendix at the end of this book for variable description.

[9] A binary variable, 1 for boys/0 for girls.

[10] The average level of restriction applied by parents, ranging from 1 ('can do this anytime') to 3 ('can never do this'), was taken across six activities (listed under restrictive mediation in the Appendix at the end of this book).

[11] See key variables in the Appendix at the end of this book for variable description.

[12] See key variables in the Appendix at the end of this book for variable description.

[13] See key variables in the Appendix at the end of this book for variable description.

[14] Also a binary variable – 1 of any of the above options have occurred, 0 if not.

[15] The American Psychological Association report, for example, has been widely cited as an authoritative source on the sexualisation of children; see Buckingham et al (2010) for a critique.

References

Buckingham, D. and Bragg, S. (2004) *Young people, sex and the media: The facts of life?*, Basingstoke: Palgrave Macmillan.

Buckingham, D., Willett, R., Bragg, S. and Russell, R. (2010) *External research on sexualised goods aimed at children*, Equal Opportunities Committee Report (www.scottish.parliament.uk/s3/committees/equal/reports-10/eor10-02.htm).

Critcher, C. (2008) 'Making waves: historic aspects of public debates about children and mass media', in K. Drotner and S. Livingstone (eds) *International handbook of children, media and culture*, London: Sage Publications, pp 91–104.

Ey, L.A. and Cupit, C.G. (2011) 'Exploring young children's understanding of risks associated with internet usage and their concepts of management strategies', *Journal of Early Childhood Research*, vol 9, no 1, pp 53-65.

Flood, M. (2007) 'Exposure to pornography among youth in Australia', *Journal of Sociology*, vol 43, no 1, pp 45-60.

Freeman-Longo, R.E. (2000) 'Children, teens and sex on the internet', *Sexual Addiction & Compulsivity*, vol 7, pp 75-90.

Haddon, L. and Stald, G. (2009) 'A comparative analysis of European press coverage of children and the internet', *Journal of Children and Media*, Special Issue, vol 3, no 4, pp 379-93.

Heins, M. (2001) *Not in front of the children: 'Indecency', censorship and the innocence of youth*, New York: Hill & Wang.

Helsper, E. (2005) *R18 material: Its potential impact on people under 18. An overview of the available literature*, London: Ofcom.

Kaiser Family Foundation (2001) *Generation Rx.com: How young people use the internet for health information*, Menlo Park, CA: Henry J. Kaiser Family Foundation.

Kleinhans, C. (2004) 'Virtual child porn: the law and the semiotics of the image', in P. Church Gibson (ed) *More dirty looks: Gender, pornography and power* (2nd edn), London: BFI, pp 71-84.

Livingstone, S. (2009) *Children and the internet*, Cambridge: Polity Press.

Livingstone, S., Haddon, L., Görzig, A. and Ólafsson, K. (2011) *Risks and safety on the internet: The perspective of European children*, London: London School of Economics and Political Science.

McKee, A., Albury, K. and Lumby, C. (2008) *The porn report*, Melbourne: Melbourne University Press.

Millwood Hargrave, A. and Livingstone, S. (2006) *Harm and offence in media content: A review of the evidence*, Bristol: Intellect.

NetRatings Australia (2005) *Kidsonline@home: Internet use in Australian homes*, Sydney: Australian Broadcasting Authority and NetAlert Limited.

Paasonen, S., Nikunen, K. and Saarenmaa, L. (2007) 'Pornification and the education of desire', in S. Paasonen, K. Nikunen and L. Saarenmaa (eds) *Pornification: Sex and sexuality in media culture*, Oxford: Berg, pp 1-22.

Thornburgh, D. and Lin, H.S. (eds) (2002) *Youth, pornography, and the internet*, Washington, DC: National Academy Press.

Tsaliki, L. (2011) 'Playing with porn: Greek children's explorations in pornography', *Sex and Education*, Special Issue, vol 11, no 3, pp 293-392.

FOURTEEN

Meeting new contacts online

Monica Barbovschi, Valentina Marinescu,
Anca Velicu and Eva Laszlo

Introduction

This chapter investigates children's practices related to meeting face-to-face (offline), contacts previously met on the internet. 'Stranger danger' has been part of the collective imaginaries of citizens, the media, concerned parents and caregivers, teachers and youth workers, non-governmental organisations and regulators. It has frequently been exaggerated by the media based on a relatively few cautionary tales that have sparked disproportionate concerns and reactions. Without minimising the risks of these practices, this chapter, through an in-depth, contextual, exploratory approach, tries to put into perspective the phenomenon of meeting face-to-face with contacts made online. The generic categories of online 'stranger' and, especially, 'meeting strangers', can encompass a variety of situations, from a child who wants to exchange a video game with a 'new online friend' who may be an immediate physical neighbour, to a random person offering a Blackberry for sale in a local advertisement, to the cute 10th-grader from another high school, located through Facebook, to the extremely rare cases of online predators attempting to groom children for sexual purposes.

The EU Kids Online survey posed descriptive questions about children's communication with people newly met online (3 out of 10 of all children), and children's face-to-face meeting with those people originally met online. Among these face-to-face (that is, offline) meetings (9 per cent of all children), 57 per cent met someone with a connection to a friend or a family member (5 per cent of all children), while 48 per cent (4 per cent of all children) met someone with no connections to themselves beyond mutual use of computers – the typical case of the new online contact. Of those 9 per cent who met an online contact offline, almost 12 per cent declared that they had been 'bothered' by the encounter (which translates into fewer than 1 per cent of all the children interviewed).

The main objective of this chapter is to investigate, in depth, children's behaviour related to contacting new people online, to follow those contacts that led to offline meetings – especially meetings with 'complete strangers' – and to examine those cases where the experience had been harmful. Investigation of children's coping strategies and parental mediation is the subject of Chapters 16 and 18 in this volume.

Previous research

Previous studies investigating the characteristics of adolescents who talk with strangers on the internet and their motives for doing so have produced conflicting results. A Dutch survey (Peter et al, 2006) found that early adolescents (aged 12-14) are more prone to talking to strangers online. Frequency of online communication is a negative predictor of communicating with strangers (with the exception of long chat sessions). Introversion was found not to be associated with talking to strangers online, where entertainment and social compensation were the main motivations. A study of Singaporean young people (aged 12-17) indicates that age, frequency of internet use, frequency of chatting and gaming behaviour, parental rules, type of personal information given out, number of inappropriate messages received, whether inappropriate websites are accessed and type of internet safety advice received are predictors of face-to-face meetings with someone previously encountered online (Kienfie Liau et al, 2005). Also, a study of UK children (Livingstone and Helsper, 2007) shows that children who feel more confident communicating online than offline, and value the anonymity of the internet, are more likely to meet someone offline.

Several theories have been advanced about the practice of contacting strangers online and then meeting them offline. Specific hypotheses have been formulated about children's risky online behaviours based on these and some more general theories about children's internet use are also relevant.

General theoretical models

Among the general theories, a 'rich get richer' model of online communication (Bonebrake, 2002; Kraut et al, 2002; McKenna et al, 2002) considers the practice of contacting strangers online to be a consequence of a more general pattern of very intense communication. Indicators, such as the number of online contacts, frequency of internet use and extraversion, can be related to communicating with a more diverse range of people, a number of whom may be strangers.

Conversely, the *social compensation hypothesis* (Tsao, 1996; Livingstone and Helsper, 2007, p 9; Peter and Valkenburg, 2007) is that socially isolated adolescents try to compensate for an unsatisfactory offline social life through online communications, which will inevitably involve communication and contact with strangers. Measures of emotional and peer problems are suitable indicators to explore this relationship. *The rehearsal hypothesis* (Peter and Valkenburg, 2011) is a corollary to the compensation hypothesis and states that children with high levels of social anxiety might use the online environment to 'rehearse' online later face-to-face encounters with others.

Another plausible framework is the *usage paradigm*, which connects internet use with online opportunities and risks (Livingstone and Haddon, 2009, p 17; de Haan, 2009, p 188). A 'more opportunities, more risks' approach (Livingstone and Helsper, 2010; Livingstone et al, 2011, p 7) implies that the more children use the internet, the more they learn to reap its benefits and deal in a healthy and non-harmful way with potential risks.

A general explanatory model might be the *risk migration hypothesis*. Since children encounter different degrees of risk, those who encounter more risks in their daily (offline) lives tend also to encounter more risks in their online lives (Livingstone and Görzig, 2011, submitted). However, risk does not always result in harm; and risk-taking can be beneficial in terms of building resilience (Masten et al, 1990).

Explanations related to harm include a general *vulnerability hypothesis* (see Livingstone and Görzig's chapter in this volume), in which psychological difficulties and demographic factors are important predictors of harm from exposure to the risk of meeting offline someone originally met only online. In addition, lack of self-efficacy, conceptualised as a measure of personal agency and degree of locus of control (Schwarzer et al, 1999), has been found to be associated with more and wider internet usage (Eastin and LaRose, 2000) and more online risks (Livingstone and Helsper, 2010).

Finally, the adolescent's *desire for autonomy and independence* from parental authority (Elder, 1963) might play an important role in children's online and offline activities, notably in establishing and expanding their social circles.

Specific theoretical models

Other theories come from the area of interpersonal relationships and sexuality research. For example, in the context of internet dating, the *recreation hypothesis* relates a sexually permissive attitude and sensation-seeking to looking for casual dates online (Peter and Valkenburg, 2007). Sensation-seeking in adolescents and young adults is viewed as connected to risky behaviour (Newcomb and McGee, 1991).

Method

Drawing on the literature on the topic, we explore the following hypotheses applying exploratory rather than explanatory methods:

H1: Social compensation hypothesis
H2: Rehearsal hypothesis
H3: Risk migration hypothesis
H4: Vulnerability hypothesis
H5: Recreation hypothesis
H6: Usage hypothesis: including the 'the more opportunities, the more risks' hypothesis
H7: Rich get richer hypothesis
H8: Autonomy and independence

Our dependent variables relate to children making new contacts online (including people with connections to a friend or family member), meeting these online contacts in person (including people with connections to a friend or family member), face-to-face meetings with someone with connections to the child's life apart from the internet, and harm as a result of an offline meeting (intensity of harm). Detailed descriptive measures across countries can be found in previous EU Kids Online reports (Livingstone et al, 2011; Lobe et al, 2011; see also the Appendix to this volume).

Dependent variables

• Risk of meeting new people online not met face to face (all children) – dummy variable, 0 = no risk, 1 = risk.
• Risk of meeting new online contacts offline (all children who made a contact online with people not met face-to-face) – dummy variable, 0 = no risk, 1 = risk.

- Risk of meeting 'complete strangers': 'In the previous 12 months, which of these types of people have you met face-to-face that you first met on the internet?' 'Someone who had no connection with my life before I met them on the internet' (all children who have met offline an online contact) – dummy variable, 0 = no, 1 = yes.
- Intensity of harm – 'Thinking about the last time you were bothered by [experiencing the risk], how upset did you feel about it (if at all)?' – four-point variable.

Results

Risk of contacting online people never met face to face

The risk migration, usage and rich get richer theories were considered simultaneously on the assumption that children who use the internet more are prone to sensation-seeking, engage in more risky activities both online and offline and tend also to contact more new people online. The logistic regression model includes demographic factors, psychological and internet use variables, risky online and offline activities and parental restriction. Table 14.1 presents the impact of each factor on the likelihood of children making new contacts online, *ceteris paribus*.

In terms of demographics, age plays a significant role, with every additional year of age resulting in a 10 per cent increase in the odds that a child will contact new people online. Also, boys are less likely than girls to make new contacts online (odds decrease by 15 per cent). Children engaging more in risky online and offline activities have 56 and 17 per cent higher odds, respectively, of contacting new people online for each additional risky activity.

The logistic regression model includes psychological variables: self-efficacy and sensation-seeking are positively related to making new contacts online. However, psychological difficulties (composed of subscales of emotional, conduct and peer problems as well as hyperactivity) have no influence on whether children make new contacts online. The number of online activities, the number of hours spent online daily and the number of places where the internet is used, however, play a significant role, providing support for the usage paradigm. For every additional place where the internet is used (for example, an internet café, friend's home, public library, other public place, etc) there is a 5 per cent increase in the odds that the child will contact new people online. Any additional online activity (for example, using instant messaging, visiting a chatroom) results in an

Table 14.1: Regression models for variables risk of meeting new people online, risk of meeting new people offline and going to meetings with complete strangers

Variables	Logistic regression for the risk of contacting online people never met face to face[a]			Logistic regression for the risk of meeting online people offline[b]			Logistic regression for likelihood of meeting offline complete strangers (from children that met an online contact offline)[c]		
	Mean	Range	Exp(B)	Mean	Range	Exp(B)	Mean	Range	Exp(B)
Age of child	12.5	9-16	1.10**	13.6	9-16	1.11**	14.17	9-16	1.09*
Gender (female = 0)	–	–	0.85**	–	–	0.80**	–	–	0.96
Self-efficacy	2.19	1-3	1.49**	2.31	1-3	1.20*	2.35	1-3	1.07
Sensation-seeking	1.35	1-3	1.27**	1.52	1-3	1.15*	1.66	1-3	1.14
Psychological difficulties	1.4	1-3	1.07	1.42	1-3	1.76**	1.46	1-3	0.9
Number of places where the internet is used	3.18	0-8	1.05**	3.72	0-8	0.98	3.89	0-8	0.96
Hours online/day	1.6	0.1-4.5	1.20**	2.1	0.1-4.5	1.09**	2.32	0.1-4.5	1.06
Online activities	7.26	0-17	1.11**	9.55	0-17	1.04**	10.37	0-17	1.04*
Risky online activities	1.29	0-5	1.56**	2.24	0-5	1.31**	2.8	0-5	1.21**
Risky offline activities	0.41	0-5	1.17**	0.72	0-5	1.31**	1.13	0-5	1.14*
Number of parental restrictions	2.74	0-6	0.93**	1.71	0-6	0.90**	1.27	0-6	0.97
Constant	–	–	0.06**	–	–	0.09**	–	–	0.08**

Notes:
[a] Base: All children aged 9-16 who use the internet.
[b] Base: All children aged 9-16 who have met new contacts online.
[c] Base: All children aged 9-16 who have met new contacts offline.
*$p < 0.05$; **$p < 0.001$.

11 per cent increase in the odds of establishing new contacts online. Finally, children subject to more parental restrictions are less likely to contact new people online.

The overall pattern of children communicating on the internet with people they have not met in person seems to fit the usage paradigm, where more diverse, broad use implies more communication and contact with more people, including some 'strangers'.

The compensation and rehearsal hypotheses cannot be confirmed, since psychological problems do not play a role in the model; on the other hand, those with higher scores for self-efficacy and sensation-seeking tend to communicate more with 'strangers' online, lending support to the rich get richer and recreation theories.

Going to meetings with people first met online

Not all online encounters translate into offline meetings, and those that do lead to meetings do not all have harmful effects: 9 per cent of all children said they had had a face-to-face meeting with someone they met online. However, this percentage includes meetings with friends of someone the child knew face to face (5 per cent), as well as meetings with complete strangers (4 per cent). We can assume that in the case of meeting up with someone met online, the spectrum of motivations would be different, and especially between younger and older children.

The factors considered for contacting new people online were included in the regression model for offline meetings with people originally met online (see Table 14.1). The factors point in the same direction as for meeting new people online, the only additional significant factor being psychological difficulties, with the odds of meeting online contacts offline increasing by 76 per cent for every additional point on the scale. It seems that although psychological difficulties are not associated with making new contacts online, they are relevant for distinguishing those children who kept new contacts to the online world from those who met up offline, suggesting that the compensation and the risk migration hypotheses are plausible.

As in the previous model, older children are more likely to meet face-to-face with new online contacts. Moreover, measures of use seem to play a role in the model: for every additional hour spent online the odds of the child having an offline meeting with someone met online increase by 9 per cent, and every additional online activity results in a 4 per cent increase in the odds of meetings offline, although the number of places where the internet is used has no influence in the model.

Again, risky online and offline activities are both significant. Also, sensation-seeking seems to have a moderate influence on meeting online contacts offline, indicating the plausibility of the recreation hypothesis. However, children higher in self-efficacy are 20 per cent more likely to meet people offline, which, coupled with longer time spent online and more activities undertaken, suggest a rich get richer paradigm, with extensive users of the internet who are higher in self-efficacy and more outgoing in terms of exploring their online and offline social worlds.

The most relevant finding is the impact of psychological difficulties, which, according to the logic of the vulnerability hypothesis, suggests that those children who are already vulnerable offline will become vulnerable online.

Going to meetings with complete strangers

Since there is much public concern about the danger of meeting strangers, the characteristics of children who agree to such meetings are important. We again included demographic aspects, use, psychological variables, risky online and offline activities and parental restrictions in the logistic regression model (see Table 14.1). Among those who meet new online contacts offline, older children, those who engage in online and offline risky activities and those whose internet use is very broad are more likely to go to offline meetings with 'complete strangers'. The results substantiate the usage hypothesis (more risks, more opportunities) and the risk migration theory. All other factors being equal, the psychological variables have no impact in the model. However, they are relevant in the few cases of children negatively affected by these encounters.

Harm resulting from meeting new online contacts offline

A small number of children reported going to an offline meeting and being bothered by the experience. Factors that influence meetings offline might differ from those that are relevant for harm, therefore, as in other chapters (see Chapter 12 in this volume), correlations were computed to see if the same demographic and psychological factors relevant for harm resulting from exposure to other risks (for example, sexting) are also relevant for harm as the result of meeting new online contacts offline (see Table 14.2). Intensity of harm is operationalised by how upset the child felt after meeting a new online contact offline, ranging from 'not at all upset' (0) to 'very upset' (3).

Table 14.2: Correlations among factors predicting intensity of harm resulting from meeting new people offline

| Variables | Range or number (scale) of items | M | Correlations | | | | |
			Age	Gender	Self-efficacy	Psycho-logical difficulties	Sensation-seeking
Age	9-16	12.48	1.00				
Gender	Female = 0	–	–0.01	1.00			
Self-efficacy	4 (1-3)	2.19	0.23**	0.05**	1.00		
Psychological difficulties	16 (1-3)	1.40	–0.03**	–0.01	–0.14**	1.00	
Sensation-seeking	2 (1-3)	1.35	0.17**	0.18**	0.18**	0.25**	1.00
Intensity of harm (offline meetings)	0-3	0.10	–0.13**	–0.01	–0.11**	0.19**	0.02

Note: **Correlations significant at the 0.01 level (2-tailed).

Base: All children aged 9-16 who have met a new online contact offline.

Intensity of harm is negatively correlated to age and self-efficacy, positively correlated to psychological difficulties, and not significant correlated to gender and sensation-seeking. These findings confirm the vulnerability hypothesis of younger children, and those with more psychological difficulties and lower in self-efficacy being more likely to experience harm as a result of meeting new people offline following an original online contact.

Country distributions of types of people children met offline

We discussed the fact that face-to-face meetings with people contacted first online cover a diverse range of contacts and reasons for meeting offline; they include meeting friends of family members to borrow a tent for the summer holiday, to meeting 'complete strangers' to buy a smartphone on the cheap or, what adults dread, for sexual purposes. Figure 14.1 shows that among all children who use the internet, encounters with friends of friends, or a friend of a family member, is strongly correlated to encounters with 'complete' strangers, suggesting that children expand their social circles using all means available. Lithuania, Austria, Sweden and the Czech Republic (but not only these countries) score high for meeting 'complete strangers', which calls for more research at the national level on the specific characteristics of children reporting these types of encounters, their motives and their attitudes.

Figure 14.1: Percentages of meeting offline 'complete strangers' versus people who have a connection with the child's life outside the internet

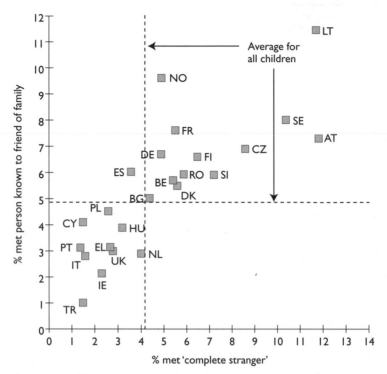

Survey question: I have met someone who is a friend or family member of someone else I know in person face to face; I have met someone who had no connection with my life before I met them on the internet (%).
Base: All children aged 9-16 who use the internet.

Conclusion

The EU Kids Online findings show that 'stranger danger', although high on the internet safety agenda, affects only a few children in Europe. The actual risk and harm resulting from contacting people online and then meeting them offline need to be put into perspective. A range of theories has been proposed to make sense of this practice: the EU Kids Online data suggest that the 'rich get richer' hypothesis, the usage paradigm and the 'more opportunities, more risk' view of children's internet use seem to account for children's practices of contacting new people online, challenging the stereotypical concern about socially ill-adjusted children engaging in online communication with new people. Children are using the internet and new media more and more to expand their social circles and to enrich their life experiences. Children with higher self-efficacy, and with longer and more extensive internet use, contact new people online. Few children engage in this practice for the thrill of doing something dangerous for fun.

The findings suggest that, as a communication practice deeply embedded into children's life, contacting new people online provides few grounds for (exaggerated) concern. However, meeting online contacts in the offline world could be a worry: in addition to sensation-seeking behaviour, self-efficacy and risky online and offline activities, psychological difficulties are relevant in this context, suggesting that the children who are most vulnerable generally might seek emotional and social compensation in risky offline encounters with people originally met online. Contacting new people, online and offline, is generally confined to older children. Children who meet up with complete strangers engage in risky online and offline activities. The few children who experience harm from meeting new people offline tend to be younger children or those lower in self-efficacy or those who experience psychological difficulties, pointing to a generalised pattern of vulnerability. Nevertheless, it should be stressed that these children are a small proportion of the entire European sample.

Without exaggerating the relevance of children's practice of meeting strangers online, policy interventions should be oriented towards the few cases where intensity of harm resulting from offline meetings with people first met online is highest, namely, younger children and the most vulnerable children offline and online. Similar to the risk and harm resulting from sexting, policy initiatives should be aimed at the small number of young people who agree to meet with complete strangers and experience harm, with integrated strategies to control or mediate online behaviour and to address children's social and psychological difficulties in their daily lives.

References

Bonebrake, K. (2002) 'College students' internet use, relationship formation, and personality correlates', *CyberPsychology & Behavior*, vol 5, pp 551-7.

de Haan, J. (2009) 'Maximising opportunities and minimising risks for children online', in S. Livingstone and L. Haddon (eds) *Kids online: Opportunities and risks for children*, Bristol: The Policy Press, pp 188-99.

Eastin, M.S. and LaRose, R. (2000) 'Internet self-efficacy and the psychology of the digital divide', *Journal of Computer-Mediated Communication*, vol 6, no 1 (online).

Elder, G.H. Jr (1963) 'Parental power-legitimation and its effect on the adolescent', *Sociometry*, vol 25, pp 241-62.

Kienfie Liau, A., Khoo, A. and Hwaang, P. (2005) 'Factors influencing adolescents engagement in risky internet behaviour', *CyberPsychology & Behaviour*, vol 8, no 6, pp 513-20.

Kraut, R., Kiesler, S., Boneva, B., Cummings, J., Helgeson, V. and Crawford, A. (2002) 'Internet paradox revisited', *Journal of Social Issues*, vol 58, pp 49-74.

Livingstone, S. and Görzig, A. (under review) 'When adolescents receive sexual messages on the internet: explaining experiences of risk and harm'. Manuscript.

Livingstone, S. and Haddon, L. (2009) *EU Kids Online: Final report*, London: London School of Economics and Political Science, EU Kids Online (EC Safer Internet Plus Programme Deliverable D6.5).

Livingstone, S. and Helsper, E.J. (2007) 'Taking risks when communicating on the internet: the role of offline social-psychological factors in young people's vulnerability to online risks', *Information, Communication & Society*, vol 10, no 5, pp 619-43.

Livingstone, S. and Helsper, E.J. (2010) 'Balancing opportunities and risks in teenagers' use of the Internet: the role of online skills and family context', *New Media & Society*, vol 12, no 2, pp 309-29.

Livingstone, S., Haddon, L., Görzig, A. and Ólafsson, K. (2011) *Risks and safety on the internet: The perspective of European children. Full findings*, London: London School of Economics and Political Science.

Lobe, B., Livingstone, S., Ólafsson, K. and Vodeb, H. (2011) *Cross-national comparison of risks and safety on the internet: Initial analysis from the EU Kids Online survey of European children*, London: London School of Economics and Political Science.

McKenna, K.Y.A., Green, A.S. and Gleason, M.E.J. (2002) 'Relationship formation on the internet: what's the big attraction?', *Journal of Social Issues*, vol 58, pp 9-31.

Masten, A., Best, K. and Garmezy, N. (1990) 'Resilience and development: contributions from the study of children who overcome adversity', *Development and Psychopathology*, vol 2, pp 425-44.

Newcomb, M.D. and McGee, L. (1991) 'Influence of sensation seeking on general deviance and specific problem behaviours from adolescence to young adulthood', *Journal of Personality & Social Psychology*, vol 61, no 4, pp 614-28.

Peter, J. and Valkenburg, P.M. (2007) 'Who looks for casual dates on the internet? A test of the compensation and the recreation hypotheses', *New Media & Society*, vol 9, no 3, pp 455-74.

Peter, J. and Valkenburg, P.M. (2011) 'Online communication among adolescents: an integrated model of its attraction, opportunities, and risks', *Journal of Adolescent Health*, vol 48, pp 121-7.

Peter, J., Valkenburg, P.M. and Schouten, A.P. (2005) 'Developing a model of adolescent friendship formation on the internet', *CyberPsychology and Behavior*, vol 8, pp 423-30.

Peter, J., Valkenburg, P.M. and Schouten, A.P. (2006) 'Characteristics and motives of adolescents talking with strangers on the Internet', *CyberPsychology & Behaviour*, vol 9, pp 526-30.

Schwarzer, R., Mueller, J. and Greenglass, E. (1999) 'Assessment of perceived general self-efficacy on the internet: data collection in cyberspace', *Anxiety, Stress, and Coping*, vol 12, pp 145-61.

Tsao, J. (1996) 'Compensatory media use: an exploration of two paradigms', *Communication Studies*, vol 47, pp 89-199.

Valkenburg, P.M. and Schouten, A.P. (2006) 'Characteristics and motives of adolescents talking with strangers on the internet', *CyberPsychology & Behaviour*, vol 9, pp 526-30.

FIFTEEN

Excessive internet use among European children

David Šmahel and Lukáš Blinka

Introduction

The internet has become an integral part of adolescents' lives. Children and young people are engaging in a broad range of activities online, chatting with friends, playing online games, watching videos, listening to music, doing schoolwork, browsing for information, etc (Subrahmanyam and Smahel, 2010). The rapid increase in fast and cheap internet connections since the end of the 1990s has helped to increase the amount of time individuals spend online. Adolescents growing up in the contemporary digital era are among the most prominent internet users and more frequent users than among the older age categories (Lupac and Sladek, 2008). Their online and offline lives are strongly interconnected (Subrahmanyam and Smahel, 2011).

The increased time spent online is prompting questions about whether all individuals are in control of their increasing internet usage. Excessive time spent online has been deemed to influence several aspects of youths' lives: declining school results or even dropping out of school; increased family tension; abandoned hobbies; psychological problems such as depression, anxiety and low self-esteem; and physical health problems due to sleep deprivation and lack of physical activity (Young, 1996; Shapira et al, 2000).

The term 'internet addiction' emerged when the above-mentioned negative outcomes began to be associated with repetitive, compulsive and uncontrollable use of the technology. Different researchers use different terms to describe the same or similar phenomena: pathological internet use (Young, 1996, 1998), problematic internet use (Shapira et al, 2000), internet addiction disorder or addictive behaviour on/to the internet (Widyanto and Griffiths, 2006). In this chapter we use the term 'excessive internet use' to describe this phenomenon.

Although there is agreement about how to describe the symptoms of this phenomenon, researchers are not agreed about the extent to which it can be considered an addiction and, thus, a pathology. Widianto and Griffiths (2006, 2007) maintain that it is unclear when speaking about excessive internet use how often the technology is blamed for causing the problem versus how much the technology is mediating problems with origins elsewhere. Also, excessive internet use is not acknowledged as an official disorder and is not included in diagnostic manuals, for example, in the American Psychiatric Association Diagnostic and Statistical Manual IV (DSM IV), and will also not be included in the revision DSM V (Block, 2008).

Excessive internet use has been reported among all age groups, but is especially prevalent among adolescents and emerging adults (Tsai and Lin, 2003; Smahel et al, 2009a). Increased concerns about the negative impact of internet use focus especially on adolescence, since this is a formative period, and misuse of the internet in adolescence might be more harmful than later in life (Kaltiala-Heino et al, 2004). The reported prevalence of pathological excessive use varies, due mainly to a lack of agreement on the 'cut-off point' distinguishing 'addicts' from 'non-addicts'. Within the population of European youth the number of excessive internet users is said to be within the range of 10 per cent. Johansson and Götestam (2004) surveyed 3,237 Norwegians aged 12-18 using Young's (1996) Diagnostic Questionnaire and evaluated 2 per cent of their sample as having an 'internet addiction', and an additional 8.7 per cent to be exhibiting at-risk internet use. Within a sample of Czech youth, 8 per cent of young adolescents aged 12-15 and 4.5 per cent of 16- to 19-year-olds were considered to be demonstrating all the symptoms of 'addictive behaviour' (Smahel et al, 2009b).

Components of excessive internet use

The components of 'internet addiction', proposed by Mark Griffiths (2000; Widyanto and Griffiths, 2007), based on Brown's (1993) concept of behavioural addiction, are often used to determine pathological extensive internet use. An internet user can be considered addicted if he or she fulfils or scores highly for all the following factors: *salience*, when the activity becomes the most important thing in an individual's life; *mood change*, or euphoria, where subjective experiences are significantly affected by the activity; *tolerance*, the process of requiring continually higher doses of the activity to achieve the original sensations; *withdrawal symptoms*, negative feelings and sensations which occur when unable to perform the activity or after termination of the required activity;

conflict, usually with the individual's closest social surroundings (family), typically accompanied with a significant decrease in school results or dropping out; and *relapse and reinstatement*, the tendency to return to the damaging activity even after periods of relative control. Different scales and factors to measure excessive internet use or 'internet addiction' have been proposed (see Shapira et al, 2000; Ko et al, 2005); however, their basic premise is similar.

Research questions and hypotheses

Although several studies of European samples show no gender differences in tendencies to become addicted (Johansson and Gotestam, 2004; Milani et al, 2009), there is a gender gap in some online applications. A typically male–dominated application, online gaming (MMORPGs), is often claimed to be the type of application with the greatest addictive potential (Ko et al, 2007). Since online gamers are a predominantly male group of excessive internet users, they may be the cause of identified gender gaps. Most studies in this area originate in East Asia and show that adolescents display addictive behaviour on the internet more often than older age categories; however, the differences within this group are unknown. Thus, our first research question focuses on the role of demographic characteristics.

RQ1: Can excessive internet use be predicted by gender and age?

Our hypotheses are:

H1: Boys will score higher use than girls for excessive internet use.

H2: Older children will score higher than younger children for excessive internet use.

According to Young (2010), internet addiction is often connected to phenomena such as poor self–esteem and feelings of isolation. These connections have been identified in excessive online gamers (Bessière et al, 2007) and Cao and Su's (2007) study of Chinese 12- to 18–year–olds reveals that participants who display symptoms of addictive internet behaviour score higher on the subscales of neuroticism, psychosis, lying, emotional symptoms and conduct problems.

Thus, psychological impairment, whether caused by or the cause of pathological overuse of the internet, plays a significant role. According to Ko and colleagues (2006), internet addiction among adolescents is associated with high novelty seeking. Mehroof and Griffiths (2010) show that sensation-seeking is one of the factors strongly associated with addiction to online games. Lower self-efficacy may also play a role. Davis (2001) states that lower self-efficacy is a cognitive distortion in self, and an individual may use the internet to regain a positive evaluation of their own abilities that is lacking in the offline environment. This leads to our second research question:

RQ2: Can excessive internet use be predicted by psychological variables?

We hypothesise that:

H3: Children who score higher for excessive internet use will have lower self-efficacy.

H4: Children who score higher for excessive internet use will have more psychological difficulties.

H5: Children who score higher for excessive internet use will be greater sensation-seekers.

The personality trait of sensation-seeking is reported to be connected to offline behavioural problems. Ko et al (2006) find that internet addicts more frequently report substance and alcohol use. Internet addiction is also considered a member of the impulse control disorder family. To some extent, the association between internet addiction, sensation-seeking and offline behavioural problems such as aggression and alcohol misuse/abuse lies in the individual's problematic self-control mechanisms. Since there is a correlation between offline and online problematic behaviour (for more details see Chapter 23, and also Chapter 12, this volume), a close relationship between addictive internet use and other types of potentially risky online activities, such as pornography consumption or cyberbullying, can be expected (Juvonen and Gross, 2008; Vandebosch and Cleemput, 2009). The third research question thus is:

RQ3: Can excessive internet use be predicted by risky activities offline and online?

H6: Children who score higher for excessive internet use will display more risky offline activities (behaviour).

H7: Children scoring higher for excessive internet use will display more active risky online activities, where active behaviour means that the individual not only encounters risky material online, but also generates some kind of dangerous behaviour, that is, online perpetration. We expect that active participation could be connected to higher excessive internet use.

(H7a: Meeting strangers from the internet, H7b: Cyberbullying aggression, H7c: Sending sexual messages.)

While the phenomenon of excessive internet use has been studied intensively, most work analyses the relationships of only a few variables. This chapter looks more closely at the connections between online risky activities and excessive internet use, and also at the context of psychological traits. We also study a very large sample that shows the extent of excessive internet use across 25 countries.

Methodology

The study uses data from the international research EU Kids Online II project (details on the project methodology are provided in Chapter 2). This chapter focuses on a subsample of children aged 11-16 (n=18,709) (younger children completed a shorter questionnaire that does not include questions about excessive internet use).

Measures

The following variables are described in the Appendix at the end of the book: psychological difficulties, self-efficacy, risky offline activities and sensation-seeking.

- *Frequency of internet use:* this item measures time spent online. Possible answers include: 'less than once a month', 'once or twice a month', 'once or twice a week' or 'every day or almost every day'. In our data, a higher value of the scale indicated more time spent online.
- *Meeting new online contacts offline:* this variable is a combination of the following three variables: having met strangers online (yes/no), having met strangers offline (yes/no) and number of strangers met offline (see the Appendix). '1' indicates no meetings with strangers online, '2' indicates only meeting strangers online, '3' indicates meeting 1-2 strangers from the internet, offline, and '4' indicates having met 3 or more strangers offline.

- *Bullying others online:* this variable is a combination of the following four variables: prevalence of cyberbullying perpetration, measured through a yes/no question about experiencing it; methods of cyberbullying, including mobile phone bullying; prevalence of perpetrating online bullying, measured through a yes/no question about being the perpetrator of bullying; and frequency of online bullying perpetration (see the Appendix). Bullying through mobile phones and the internet are described as 'bullying others online'. The values are '1' – no online aggressive behaviour; '2' – less frequent ('less often') aggressive behaviour; '3' – aggressive behaviour 'once or twice a month', '4' – aggressive behaviour 'once or twice a week', and value '5' – aggressive behaviour 'every day or almost every day'.

- *Sending sexual messages:* this combines two variables for prevalence and frequency of sending sexual messages (see the Appendix), scored as follows: '1' – never, '2' – 'not often', '3' – 'once or twice a month', '4' – 'once or twice a week', and '5' – 'every day or almost every day'.

- *Excessive internet use:* participants were asked to respond to five questions referring to the six factors of addictive behaviour adjusted by Griffiths (2000): mood change and withdrawal symptoms: 'I have felt bothered when I cannot be on the internet'; salience: 'I have gone without eating or sleeping because of the internet'; tolerance: 'I have felt bothered when I cannot be on the internet'; potential conflicts or a decline in social bonds: 'I have spent less time than I should with family, friends or doing schoolwork because of time spent on the internet'; and relapse and reinstatement: 'I have tried unsuccessfully to spend less time on the internet'. These questions were scored on a four-point Likert scale from 'never' to 'very often'. An excessive internet use index was created as the mean value of these five items. The Cronbach's alpha is 0.767.

Results

Table 15.1 shows the occurrence of 'very often' and 'fairly often' responses as percentages for each of the five items in the excessive internet usage index, across all countries. Table 15.1, column 2 reports the values of the index; higher values are more excessive internet usage in that country. The highest value of the index was for Estonia, followed by Bulgaria, Portugal and the UK. The lowest values were for Italy, Hungary and Belgium.

For the distribution of items on the scale, the highest percentage was for children who responded that they 'very often' or 'fairly often' had found themselves surfing when they were not really interested

Table 15.1: Percentages of excessive internet use among European countries

Country	Excessive internet usage index (Mean)	I have gone without eating or sleeping because of the internet Very/ fairly often (%)	I have felt bothered when I cannot be on the internet Very/ fairly often (%)	I have caught myself surfing when I am not really inter- ested Very/ fairly often (%)	I have spent less time than I should with either family, friends or doing school- work because of time I spent on the internet Very/ fairly often (%)	I have tried unsuccess- fully to spend less time on the internet Very/fairly often (%)
Austria	0.14	4	7	13	9	8
Belgium	0.11	2	9	15	8	8
Bulgaria	0.22	8	30	14	12	17
Cyprus	0.20	10	16	23	13	19
Czech Republic	0.18	3	12	17	12	13
Germany	0.14	6	7	10	11	8
Denmark	0.16	2	5	21	15	14
Estonia	0.23	2	16	30	14	21
Greece	0.16	5	12	20	8	15
Spain	0.18	4	15	31	8	12
Finland	0.16	2	7	14	11	9
France	0.12	2	10	16	10	11
Hungary	0.10	2	8	8	7	9
Ireland	0.21	9	16	19	20	20
Italy	0.09	2	v4	7	10	11
Lithuania	0.15	6	9	10	12	10
Netherlands	0.14	3	7	14	6	12
Norway	0.20	4	13	27	15	14
Poland	0.13	3	7	12	8	9
Portugal	0.22	11	24	23	23	22
Romania	0.17	5	9	13	14	18
Sweden	0.16	2	6	24	19	14
Slovenia	0.13	2	12	13	6	11
Turkey	0.15	6	10	12	11	12
UK	0.21	5	19	20	27	18
Total	0.16	4	11	15	13	12

(15.3 per cent across all European countries); the lowest percentage was for children who responded that they had 'very often' or 'fairly often' gone without eating or sleeping because they were using the internet (4.4 per cent across all European countries).

A hierarchical, three-step, linear regression (see Table 15.2) was used to determine associations and to test the proposed hypotheses relating to excessive internet usage and children's demographic variables, relevant psychological concepts and online/offline risks. In step 1, we include the demographic variables (see model 1), the psychological variables are added in step 2 (see model 2), and variables for online and offline risks are added in step 3 (see model 3). The demographic variables included are age and gender; pre-analysis shows that other demographic variables, such as size of locality, population density and the level of education of household head are not associated with excessive internet use.

In the first step of the regression, both age and gender are associated with excessive internet use (confirming H1 and H2). Boys scored very slightly higher than girls. Since gender differences are only significant in model 1 and not other models, it seems that the gender differences are explained by the psychological variables. The psychological concepts self-efficacy, psychological difficulties and sensation-seeking are added to the regression in model 2.

Table 15.2: Linear regression: factors associated with excessive internet usage

	Model 1		Model 2		Model 3	
	B	β	**B**	β	**B**	β
(Constant)	−0.082**		−0.369**		−0.457**	
Age	0.018**	0.175	0.015**	0.147	0.007**	0.066
Gender	−0.011**	−0.032	−0.004	−0.012	−0.005	−0.013
Self-efficacy			0.010*	0.025	−0.001	−0.003
Psychological difficulties			0.201**	0.274	0.179**	0.245
Sensation-seeking			0.029**	0.165	0.017**	0.095
Risky offline activities					0.084**	0.100
Meeting new online contacts offline					0.028**	0.124
Bullying others online					0.024**	0.055
Sending sexual messages					0.024**	0.040
Frequency of internet use					0.044**	0.137
R^2		0.032		0.155		0.214**
F		199.273**		445.619**		331.554**
ΔR^2		0.032		0.123		0.059

Notes: * $p<0.05$, ** $p<0.01$.

Psychological difficulties and sensation-seeking are positively associated to excessive internet use; the association for self-efficacy is not significant in model 3 (H3 is rejected). We find confirmation that youth with more psychological difficulties and greater need for sensation-seeking are at greater risk of excessive usage (confirming H4 and H5). Among the psychological variables, the highest associations are between psychological difficulties and excessive use. In model 3, online and offline risks and frequency of internet use are added to the regression. Risky offline activities, meeting new online contacts offline, bullying others online, sending sexual messages and frequent internet use are positively associated to the excessive usage index. The highest association is for risky offline activities. Hypotheses H6 and H7 (a–c) are confirmed.

Discussion

This chapter has analysed the associations between excessive internet usage and demographic, psychological and risky behavioural variables. Boys scored slightly higher than girls for excessive internet usage, but the difference is not significant when psychological variables are taken into account. This finding is in line with other research on Europe (Johansson and Gotestam, 2004; Milani et al, 2009) that does not find gender differences. However, it contrasts with the stereotype of boys having problems controlling time spent online, or as constituting a 'nerd culture' (Kendall, 2002). We found that a stronger predictor of excessive use is age: older children tended to score higher than younger children. This may be related to the reduced monitoring of older children by their parents (Eastin et al, 2006), with the result that their time and activities online are less controlled. Although younger adolescents have fewer self-controlling mechanisms and may therefore be more vulnerable to excessive internet use, it is presumed that parental monitoring and rearing styles are important here. The greater knowledge of and experience with digital technology of older adolescents may also contribute to their higher excessive internet use scores, since, overall, older children use the internet more and are therefore more 'dependent' on both its negative (overuse of online games) and positive (information gains, communication with peers) aspects (see Chapter 2 for more details).

The strongest predictor of excessive internet usage among the psychological variables seems to be psychological problems, but sensation-seeking and risky offline activities are also associated with excessive usage, and this has been confirmed in other studies (Ko et al,

2006; Cao and Su, 2007). This is perhaps an indication that psychological predictors of excessive use are similar for Asian and for European children. The Taiwan study shows relations between excessive internet use and substance use (Ko et al, 2006) and also, aggressive behaviour (Ko et al, 2009). This supports the hypotheses that adolescents' online and offline problems are interconnected (Subrahmanyam and Smahel, 2011). The analysis in this chapter shows weak connections between risky offline activities and excessive usage. Further research is needed to investigate the relations between offline risky activities and excessive internet use, since the available data on risky offline activities is not sufficiently detailed to allow firm conclusions. Studies of the relationships between excessive internet use and other online risks are scarce. A study of a representative sample of Czech youths aged 12–18 reveals moderate correlations between cyberbullying experiences and two components of addictive behaviour: conflict and salience (Smahel et al, 2009c). These results might indicate that not only are offline risks and excessive internet usage interconnected, but also that other online risks can be related to excessive use. This is confirmed by the findings in this chapter of associations with active online risky activities, including making new contacts online, being the perpetrator of cyberbullying and sending sexual messages. Among the online risk variables, the strongest relation is between excessive internet usage and meeting strangers encountered on the internet in the real world; this is among the more risky behaviours since it could have physical consequences. This finding is in line with research showing that the stronger the preference among youths for online communication, and the greater the number of friends met online, the more symptoms of excessive use that will be demonstrated. Conversely, the more online addictive behaviour that young people demonstrate, the greater will be the number of their online friends (Smahel et al, 2012).

The analysis in this chapter has some limitations. First, since it involved 25 countries and 20 different languages, there are some methodological limitations (as discussed in Chapter 2 and 3). Second, the five-item scale used to assess excessive internet use allows only one item per factor of excessive use; this enabled us to operationalise the scale as an index, but measuring more items would allow deeper analysis of the serious cases of excessive internet use.

Conclusion

This chapter set out to discover associations between excessive internet use and demographic, psychological and risky behaviour variables.

Excessive internet use was described using the five factors of addictive behaviour (Griffiths, 2000). Excessive internet use among European children is shown to be associated with psychological, online and offline risky activities and, to some degree, demographic variables. The best predictors of excessive use seem to be psychological difficulties. However, there are associations between risky offline and active online risky activities. These risky online activities include more numerous meetings with new contacts ('strangers') online, and being an active perpetrator of cyberbullying or sexting.

Acknowledgment

The authors acknowledge the support of the Czech Science Foundation (GAP407/11/0585 and GAP407/12/1831), and the Faculty of Social Studies, Masaryk University. The preparation of this chapter was also supported by grant No 8527, financed by the Estonian Science Foundation.

References

Bessière, K., Seay, A.F. and Kiesler, S. (2007) 'The ideal elf: identity exploration in world of warcraft', *CyberPsychology & Behavior*, vol 10, no 4, pp 530-5.

Block, J.J. (2008) 'Issues for DSM-V: internet addiction', *American Journal of Psychiatry*, vol 165, pp 306-7.

Brown, R.I.F. (1993) 'Some contributions of the study of gambling to the study of other addictions', in W.R. Eadington and J.A. Cornelius (eds) *Gambling behavior and problem gambling*, Reno, NV: Institute for the Study of Gambling and Commercial Gaming, University of Nevada, pp 241-72.

Cao, F. and Su, L. (2007) 'Internet addiction among Chinese adolescents: prevalence and psychological features', *Child: Care, Health and Development*, vol 33, no 3, pp 275-81.

Davis, R.A. (2001) 'A cognitive–behavioral model of pathological internet use', *Computers in Human Behavior*, vol 17, no 2, pp 187-95.

Eastin, M.S., Greenberg, B.S. and Hofschire, L. (2006) 'Parenting the internet', *Journal of Communication*, vol 56, no 3, pp 486-504.

Griffiths, M. (2000) 'Does internet and computer "addiction" exist? Some case study evidence', *CyberPsychology & Behavior*, vol 3, no 2, pp 211-18.

Johansson, A. and Gotestam, K.G. (2004) 'Internet addiction: characteristics of a questionnaire and prevalence in Norwegian youth (12-18 years)', *Scandinavian Journal of Psychology*, vol 45, no 3, pp 223-9.

Juvonen, J. and Gross, E. (2008) 'Extending the school grounds? Bullying experiences in cyberspace', *Journal of School Health*, vol 78, no 9, pp 496–505.

Kaltiala-Heino, R., Lintonen, T. and Rimpela, A. (2004) 'Internet addiction? Potentially problematic use of the internet in a population of 12-18 years-old adolescents', *Addiction Research and Theory*, vol 12, no 1, pp 89-96.

Kendall, L. (2002) *Hanging out in the virtual pub masculinities and relationships online*, Berkeley, CA: University of California Press.

Ko, C.-H., Yen, J.-Y., Chen, C.-C., Chen, S.-H. and Yen, C.-F. (2005) 'Proposed diagnostic criteria of internet addiction for adolescents', *Journal of Nervous and Mental Disease*, vol 193, no 11, pp 728-33.

Ko, C.-H., Yen, J., Liu, S., Huang, C. and Yen, C. (2009) 'The associations between aggressive behaviors and internet addiction and online activities in adolescents', *Journal of Adolescent Health*, vol 44, no 6, pp 598-605.

Ko, C..H., Yen J.-Y., Yen C.-F., Lin, H.-C., Yang, M.-J. (2007) 'Factors predictive for incidence and remission of Internet addiction in young adolescents: a prospective study', *CyberPsychology & Behavior*, vol 12, no 4, pp 545-51.

Ko, C.-H., Yen, J.-Y., Chen, C.-C., Chen, S.-H., Wu, K. and Yen, C.-F. (2006) 'Tridimensional personality of adolescents with internet addiction and substance use experience', *The Canadian Journal of Psychiatry/La Revue canadienne de psychiatrie*, vol 51, no 14, pp 887-94.

Lupac, P. and Sladek, J. (2008) 'The deepening of the digital divide in the Czech Republic', *Cyber-psychology: Journal of Psychosocial Research on Cyberspace*, vol 2, no 1, article 2.

Mehroof, M. and Griffiths, M.D. (2010) 'Online gaming addiction: the role of sensation seeking, self-control, neuroticism, aggression, state anxiety and trait anxiety', *Cyberpsychology, Behavior, and Social Networking*, vol 13, no 3, pp 313-16.

Milani, L., Osualdella, D. and Di Blasio, P. (2009) 'Quality of interpersonal relationships and problematic internet use in adolescence', *CyberPsychology & Behavior*, vol 12, no 6, pp 681-84.

Shapira, N.A., Goldsmith, T.D., Keck, P.E., Khosla, U.M. and McElroy, S.L. (2000) 'Psychiatric features of individuals with problematic internet use', *Journal of Affective Disorders*, vol 57, nos 1-3, pp 267-72.

Smahel, D., Blinka, L. and Sevcikova, A. (2009c) 'Cyberbullying among Czech internet users: prevalence across age groups', Paper presented at 'E-Youth: Balancing between Opportunities and Risks', Antwerp, 27-28 May.

Smahel, D., Brown, B.B. and Blinka, L. (2012) 'Associations between online friendship and internet addiction among adolescents and emerging adults', *Developmental Psychology*, vol 48, no 2, pp 381-88.

Smahel, D., Vodrackova, P., Blinka, L. and Godoy-Etcheverry, S. (2009b) 'Comparing addictive behavior on the internet in the Czech Republic, Chile and Sweden', in G. Cardoso, A. Cheong and J. Cole (eds) *World Wide Internet: Changing societies, economies and cultures*, Macau: University of Macau, pp 544-79.

Smahel, D., Sevcikova, A., Blinka, L. and Vesela, M. (2009a) 'Abhängigkeit und Internet-Applikationen: Spiele, Kommunikation und Sex-Webseiten' ['Addiction and internet applications: games, communication and sex websites'], in B.U. Stetina and I. Kryspin-Exner (eds) *Gesundheit(spsychologie) und neue Medien* [*Health psychology and new media*], Berlin: Springer, p 235-60.

Subrahmanyam, K. and Smahel, D. (2011) *Digital youth: The role of media in development*, New York: Springer.

Tsai, C.-C. and Lin, S.S.J. (2003) 'Internet addiction of adolescents in Taiwan: an interview study', *CyberPsychology & Behavior*, vol 6, no 6, pp 649-52.

Vandebosch, H. and Cleemput, K.V. (2009) 'Cyberbulling among youngsters: profiles of bullies and victims', *New Media & Society*, vol 11, no 8, pp 1349-71.

Widyanto, L. and Griffiths, M. (2006) 'Internet addiction: a critical review', *International Journal of Mental Health & Addiction*, vol 4, no 1, pp 31-51.

Widyanto, L. and Griffiths, M. (2007) 'Internet addiction: does it really exist? (revisited)', in J. Gackenbach (ed) *Psychology and the internet: Intrapersonal, interpersonal, and transpersonal implications*, San Diego, CA: Academic Press, pp 141-63.

Young, K.S. (1996) 'Internet addiction: the emergence of a new clinical disorder', *CyberPsychology & Behavior*, vol 1, no 3, pp 237-44.

Young, K.S. (1998) *Caught in the net*, New York: John Wiley & Sons.

Young, K. (2010) 'Clinical assessment of internet-addicted clients', in K.S. Young and C.H. de Abreu (eds) *Internet addiction: A handbook and guide to evaluation and treatment*, Hoboken: John Wiley & Sons, pp 19-34.

SIXTEEN

Coping and resilience: children's responses to online risks

Sofie Vandoninck, Leen d'Haenens and Katia Segers

Theoretical background

There is an impressive body of behavioural science research, beginning in the 1950s, which focuses primarily on '[w]hat makes a difference in the lives of children threatened by adversity or burdened by risk' (Masten and Powell, 2003, p 4). Exposure to risks is part of everyday life and potentially contributes to increased ability to cope with threats; however, children's resilience to risks varies, and some cope with adversity better than others (Smith and Carlson, 1997). Resilience, defined as 'positive patterns of adaptation in the context of risk or adversity', is considered one of the most complex and provocative aspects of human development (Masten and Gewirtz, 2006, p 24). Masten and Gewirtz (2006, p 24) define the concept of 'coping' as 'efforts to adapt to stress or other disturbances created by a stressor or adversity'. Interestingly, risk and protective factors can work together to enhance overall resilience (Coleman and Hagell, 2007, p 15). Very few studies focus specifically on resilience to risks in the online world, and also little work has been done on investigating whether the risks encountered offline also extend to the online world.

Contextualising online risks: from risk to harm

As children grow older and as their level of digital literacy increases, they are more exposed to all types of online risks (Livingstone et al, 2011). Psychological characteristics are related to the effect of online risks: children with more self-efficacy and more psychological difficulties, who are sensation-seeking, experience more exposure (see Table 16.1).

Exposure to risk, however, is not necessarily related to more harm. Despite their higher levels of exposure, older children, children from more affluent homes and children with high self-efficacy are frequently

Table 16.1: Exposure to and being bothered by online risks, and intensity of being upset (among those feeling bothered) (%)

		Sexual images			Sexual messages			Online bullying		Meeting online contact		
		Exposure	Bothered	Fairly/very upset	Exposure	Bothered	Fairly/very upset	Bothered (victim)	Fairly/very upset	Exposure	Bothered	Fairly/very upset
Gender	Boy	15[c]	28[c]	43	16[c]	19[c]	40[a]	4[c]	47[c]	8[a]	14[b]	35[a]
	Girl	11	42	45	13	36	49	6	61	7	9	53
Age	9-10	5[c]	59[c]	50[b]	–	–	–	3[c]	48	2[c]	33[c]	64[a]
	11-12	8	46	54	7[c]	46[c]	55[a]	5	54	3	21	52
	13-14	15	35	44	13	28	44	6	58	8	10	43
	15-16	23	25	36	22	22	41	8	57	15	9	30
Socio-economic status	Low	11[c]	42[c]	55[c]	14[c]	36[c]	42[b]	5[c]	62[c]	5[c]	15[b]	49[b]
	Medium	12	32	39	13	25	54	5	57	8	13	33
	High	17	32	40	17	22	38	6	46	8	8	64
Self-efficacy	Low	7[c]	52[c]	34	11[c]	31[b]	55	3[c]	63	3[c]	33[c]	63[b]
	Medium	11	35	44	13	29	46	5	55	6	11	48
	High	18	31	46	17	24	43	7	54	10	10	29
Psychological difficulties	Few	8[c]	24[c]	24[c]	10[c]	21[c]	49	2[c]	46[c]	5[c]	2[c]	17
	Moderate	13	27	40	14	21	41	5	50	7	11	35
	A lot	16	45	50	19	35	47	9	60	9	17	48
Sensation-seeking	No	8[c]	40[c]	46	9[c]	34[c]	49	4[c]	60[b]	4[c]	12	43
	Low	16	32	42	17	24	48	6	55	10	9	55
	High	26	29	43	27	22	39	9	49	16	13	38

(continued)

Table 16.1: Exposure to and being bothered by online risks, and intensity of being upset (among those feeling bothered) (contd.)

		Sexual images			Sexual messages			Online bullying		Meeting online contact		
		Exposure	Bothered	Fairly/very upset	Exposure	Bothered	Fairly/very upset	Bothered (victim)	Fairly/very upset	Exposure	Bothered	Fairly/very upset
Online activities	Low	4ᶜ	53ᶜ	63ᶜ	4ᶜ	37ᶜ	38	1ᶜ	54	1ᶜ	19	25ᶜ
	Medium	14	34	44	13	30	46	7	56	8	12	55
	High	32	29	33	32	22	46	11	53	20	10	20
Total		13	34	44	15	27	45	5	55	7	12	42

Notes: χ^2-test; ᵃ$p<0.05$; ᵇ$p<0.01$; ᶜ$p<0.001$.

Online bullying: no difference between exposure and being bothered, since being a victim is assumed to be bothering anyway.

Bothered: percentage of children feeling bothered among those being exposed to the online risk.

Intensity of harm: 'Not at all/a bit upset' vs 'fairly/very upset'.

less bothered by sexual risks (seeing sexual images or receiving sexual messages) or offline meetings with online contacts. High sensation-seeking and a wide range of online activities also seem to increase children's resilience towards online sexual risks. Experiencing psychological difficulties may threaten the development of children's resilience to online risks: emotionally troubled children are subject to higher exposure to online risks and are more likely to feel bothered by the experience. Although boys more often see or receive sexual images and messages, girls are more sensitive about sexual risks.

Psychological characteristics have a particularly strong impact on a child's level of perceived harm, irrespective of the type of risk. Self-confident children are more likely to recover from the experience immediately, while children with psychological difficulties may experience more intense, longer-lasting harm (that is, they are more upset and for longer).

There are some personal characteristics that are related to resilience: sensation-seekers are more resilient to online bullying and undertaking a wider range of online activities seems to have a mainly positive impact on resilience to disturbing sexual images. Younger children are more intensely upset by sexual risks (both images and messages). Girls tend to find it more difficult to cope with contact risks (online bullying, sexting and meeting online contacts). Children from lower socioeconomic status families are more upset by online bullying. Overall, children with psychological difficulties manifest in the offline world are likely to be more vulnerable online, and children who are generally more resilient are likely to develop resilience offline to online situations.

Online bullying is the online risk that most upsets young people: more than half of the children who had been victims of cyberbullying said they were very or fairly upset by it. In relation to sexual risks, more children were upset after seeing sexual images than after receiving sexual messages. Meeting online contacts offline is less likely to produce negative feelings: among those children who felt bothered by the experience, the majority were only slightly upset. These findings illustrate why it is important to differentiate between exposure to risk and actual harm. While quite a few young people come across sexual images and/or receive sexual messages, these incidents cause less harm than being exposed to acts of online bullying. Adults tend to overestimate the risks related to meeting online contacts, since in most cases these meetings are pleasant experiences involving age group peers. Moreover, what adults might consider risky young people may perceive as opportunities.

Coping strategies: who adopts what strategy when encountering different risks

In this section we discuss for each type of response which children are most likely to adopt it, and under what circumstances (see Table 16.2).

Fatalistic response

Children can respond in passive, rather fatalistic ways, hoping simply that the problem will go away, or they can stop using the internet for a while. The former group may be upset for a short time, and any harm is not substantial or long term, or they may feel indifferent, accepting that sometimes they will encounter unpleasant things. One in four of those bothered by an experience hope the problem will go away, and this reaction is related less to specific sociodemographic or psychological characteristics. Deciding to stop using the internet can be interpreted as ignoring the problem without eliminating the actual cause, and involves missing online opportunities or the chance to build resilience. This strategy is more common among younger children, lower socioeconomic status children, children with little self-efficacy or with psychological difficulties, young people who engage in only a few online activities and those who are more intensely upset.

Younger children are more likely to adopt a fatalistic reaction to unwelcome *sexual images*. Boys and children from higher socioeconomic status families more often hope simply that the problem will go away. Girls, lower socioeconomic status children, those with psychological issues and the less active internet users more often decide to go offline for a while, a more radical decision that indicates that they feel more upset. Indeed, those feeling upset to a more intense degree stop using the internet more often. Boys receiving unwelcome *sexual messages* online are more likely to do nothing and wait until the problem goes away; girls are more likely to react by going offline for a time. Children with low self-confidence, and older children, are more likely to stop using the internet. Children upset by sexting are more likely to turn off their computers for a while. Among victims of *online bullying*, psychologically troubled children and those more upset and upset for longer by the experience are more likely to respond fatalistically. Girls more often simply hope that the problem will disappear without intervention.

These findings indicate that more vulnerable groups are more likely to use a strategy that may further reduce their capacities for resilience and online opportunities. However, about seven in ten children who

Table 16.2: Use of coping strategies among those feeling bothered (%)

| | Fatalistic/passive coping strategies | | | | | | Communicative strategy | | | | | | Proactive strategies | | | | | |
| | Hope the problem would go away | | | Stop using the internet for a while | | | Talk to somebody | | | Try to fix the problem | | | Delete the message | | | Block the person who sent the message | | |
	Sexim	Bullying	Sexting	Sexim	Bullying	Sexting	Sexim	Bullying	Sexting	Sexim	Bullying	Sexting	Sexim	Bullying	Sexting	Sexim	Bullying	Sexting
Boys	30[b]	18[c]	36[c]	22[b]	19	13[a]	50[a]	67[c]	48[c]	25[a]	30[c]	23	25	39	33	24	43	33[b]
Girls	22	28	14	29	20	21	56	85	66	19	41	29	26	43	41	22	48	45
Age																		
9-10	–	–	–	50[c]	41[c]	–	61[b]	78[a]	–	–	–	–	20[b]	37	–	20[b]	34[a]	–
11-12	33[a]	23	21[a]	21	24	13[b]	62	76	72[c]	23	27[c]	35[a]	21	43	31[a]	26	43	45[b]
13-14	26	21	28	21	16	14	53	82	48	22	43	21	32	42	34	17	50	30
15-16	21	26	18	21	14	24	45	74	62	21	36	27	25	40	44	28	47	46
Socioeconomic status																		
Low	17[c]	25	26	37[c]	25[b]	22	60[b]	74[b]	61[b]	26	47[c]	36[b]	39[c]	52[c]	41	31[c]	52	43
Medium	28	25	18	24	21	14	46	82	52	23	34	21	24	38	33	22	44	36
High	32	21	22	17	16	19	57	73	70	19	33	25	18	36	41	17	44	46
Self-efficacy																		
Low	35	20[c]	22	26	47[c]	33[c]	46	71	48	18[a]	42[c]	10[a]	32	52[b]	28	32	37	37
Medium	23	31	25	25	17	21	53	77	59	19	29	26	25	44	40	21	46	38
High	26	16	18	26	18	11	56	78	63	26	44	32	25	36	36	23	47	44

(continued)

| | Fatalistic/passive coping strategies | | | | | | Communicative strategy | | | | | | Proactive strategies | | | | | |
| | Hope the problem would go away | | | Stop using the internet for a while | | | Talk to somebody | | | Try to fix the problem | | | Delete the message | | | Block the person who sent the message | | |
	Sexim	Bullying	Sexting	Sexim	Bullying	Sexting	Sexim	Bullying	Sexting	Sexim	Bullying	Sexting	Sexim	Bullying	Sexting	Sexim	Bullying	Sexting
Personal difficulties																		
Few	26[b]	15[c]	21	15[c]	12[a]	14[b]	56	80[a]	59	11[c]	35	35[b]	23[a]	41	40	12[b]	50	44
Moderate	33	17	23	21	18	11	55	81	58	19	34	18	20	38	37	22	48	38
A lot	22	30	22	30	22	23	52	74	61	26	38	29	29	43	37	26	44	41
Sensation-seeking																		
No	31[b]	23[c]	26	25	19	10[c]	57[a]	83[c]	65[b]	18[c]	37	26	27	43	37	20	49[a]	39
Low	18	39	16	22	21	27	48	87	66	16	36	23	23	40	47	25	38	44
High	22	20	20	28	19	25	50	66	49	29	36	31	25	40	35	25	45	42
Online activities																		
Low	23	26	36	44[c]	40[c]	28	56	78[b]	52	13[a]	34	12[b]	23[c]	38	10[c]	12[c]	33[a]	10[c]
Medium	25	24	21	25	19	18	55	80	61	21	37	23	20	43	37	22	46	43
High	27	23	22	16	16	14	50	71	58	26	36	35	36	39	44	29	48	42
f/v upset	31[a]	30[c]	21	37[c]	26[c]	22[b]	63[c]	88[c]	69[c]	30[c]	46[c]	31[a]	29[a]	46[c]	40	27[b]	49[b]	39
n/b upset	23	18	23	16	13	12	47	65	54	15	26	23	23	34	37	19	40	43
Got over	23[b]	18[c]	23	19[a]	10[c]	11[c]	48[b]	67[c]	55[c]	14[c]	24[c]	27	32[b]	37[b]	39	26	46	46[a]
Longer	32	27	23	25	22	22	60	85	72	35	44	30	21	46	38	21	50	35
Total	26	24	22	25	20	18	53	77	60	22	36	27	26	41	38	23	46	40

Notes: χ^2-test; [a]p<0.05; [b]p<0.01; [c]p<0.001.

f/v upset: very/fairly upset; n/b upset: not/a bit upset; got over: got over it straight away; longer: feeling upset for at least a couple of days. Sexim: sexual images, Bullying: online bullying. The number of children bothered by meeting online contacts was too low to conduct valid X^2-analysis on coping strategies.

went offline for a while following an upsetting experience indicated this strategy was 'helpful', although in this case it is important to understand that 'helpful' refers to lack of further exposure to online risks during that time.

Communicative response

Children can adopt a communicative approach, seeking social support and talking to someone. For all online risks, children prefer to talk to their peers (63-68 per cent) or to parents (48-54 per cent). Only a few children turned for advice to teachers (4-10 per cent) or professional childcare workers (2-4 per cent).

Regardless of the type of online risk, girls, children not interested in sensation-seeking and those experiencing more intense feelings of being upset tend to be more communicative. About half of children talk to someone about an upsetting sexual image and one in six discuss the receipt of an unwelcome sexual message. Younger children are more likely to talk to someone when they feel bothered by sexual risks. Children from lower socioeconomic backgrounds tend to talk to someone when they are bothered by sexual images, while children from more affluent families will talk to someone about sexting-related problems. Among victims of online bullying, 77 per cent report talking to somebody about this. Interestingly, children who engage in fewer digital activities are more likely to talk to someone about being bullied online.

These findings might be an indication that awareness-raising campaigns that emphasise communicative coping strategies are having an impact. Communicative strategies are broadly adopted by members of sociodemographic groups identified as vulnerable (girls, younger children, lower socioeconomic status children). However, children with psychological difficulties or low self-efficacy – identified as most vulnerable – are no more likely to talk about their negative experiences than children with no psychological issues.

Proactive response

Children who are proactive are regarded as displaying the best adaptation (most resilience) to adversity, because their actions are intended to reduce or eliminate harm in the future. Although this reaction is not limited to the more resilient groups, the willingness to tackle problems independently is stronger among children with high self-efficacy. This suggests that self-confidence is a key component of greater resilience. Internet-specific coping strategies, that is, deleting messages or blocking senders, require minimal digital skills. Hence, as expected, the number of a child's online activities is positively related to these coping strategies. Our findings also confirm that if the feeling of being upset is strong and persistent, this motivates the child 'to fix' the problem.

Children are more likely to respond proactively to being bothered (upset) by sexual images if they use the internet for a wide range of activities. Trying to fix the problem is a more likely response among more resilient groups, such as boys, self-confident children and sensation-seekers, as well as those experiencing more intense harm. Online proactive coping strategies are also common among lower socioeconomic status children. Thus, a proactive response to upsetting sexual images is not limited to the more resilient groups. Also, the child's level of online activities is again related positively to a proactive response to unwelcome sexual messages. Self-confident children are more likely to try to fix problems, but more vulnerable groups, such as younger children and children from lower-class families, also favour this approach. There is no straightforward relationship with other personal characteristics. Children are most proactive when the victims of bullying online, and the number of online activities is positively related to the strategy of blocking the senders of upsetting messages.

There is a self-reported success rate of around 80 per cent for deleting messages and blocking senders, which are perceived as very effective strategies to cope with sexting. For victims of online bullying, blocking the sender is more effective (78 per cent) than simply deleting the message (58 per cent). In the case of experiences of unpleasant sexual images, it is more helpful to delete the content (82 per cent) than to block the source or sender (71 per cent). Overall, the strategy adopted depends on the risk at stake.

Coping strategies: predictive factors

To provide a more complete picture of the relative predictive value of sociodemographics, psychological difficulties (emotional, conduct and peer problems) and the range of online activities for children's coping strategies, we conducted linear regression analyses for three of the four online risks (seeing sexual images, online bullying and receiving sexual messages)[1] (see Table 16.3). In Table 16.3, empty cells refer to non-significant beta values. Emotional, conduct and peer problems were added separately to the regression model. The relative impact of these different types of psychological problems varies across different

Table 16.3: Relative predictive values of factors for coping strategies with online risks (standardised betas)

	Sexual images						Online bullying						Sexual messages (sexting)					
	Hope the problem would go away	Stop using the internet	Talk to somebody	Try to fix the problem	Delete message(s)	Block the sender of message(s)	Hope the problem would go away	Stop using the internet	Talk to somebody	Try to fix the problem	Delete message(s)	Block the sender of message(s)	Hope the problem would go away	Stop using the internet	Talk to somebody	Try to fix the problem	Delete message(s)	Block the sender of message(s)
Gender	-0.106[b]	0.147[c]	0.088[b]	-0.068[a]					0.142[c]	0.086[b]		0.070[b]	-0.277[c]	0.092[a]	0.156[c]	0.131[b]	0.148[c]	0.115[b]
Age	-0.106[b]	-0.103[b]	-0.128[c]			0.071[a]		-0.176[c]				-0.070[a]		0.132[b]		-0.139[c]		
Socioeconomic status					0.148[c]					0.084[b]	0.196[c]				-0.294[c]			
Education (parents)	0.121[c]										0.169[b]					-0.153[c]		
Self-efficacy			0.074[a]	0.088[a]				-0.111[c]		0.132[c]	-0.074[a]		-0.127[b]	-0.229[c]	-0.245[c]	0.182[c]		
Emotional problems				0.079[a]		0.091[a]	0.219[c]							-0.231[c]	0.119[c]	-0.128[b]	-0.235[c]	
Conduct problems										-0.110[c]				0.146[b]	0.241[c]	0.192[c]		
Peer problems		0.153[c]		0.124[b]	0.108[b]			0.138[b]	-0.080[b]	0.128[c]				0.259[c]			0.153[c]	
Sensation-seeking	-0.123[b]	0.082[a]		0.093[b]	-0.120[c]				-0.143[c]						-0.182[c]			
Online skills		-0.183[c]		0.119[b]		-0.090[a]					0.099[b]	0.212[c]	-0.110[b]			0.217[c]	0.133[b]	0.117[b]
Online activities	0.137[c]				0.190[c]	0.253[c]											0.106[a]	
Intensity of harm	-0.124[b]	-0.200[c]	-0.133[c]	-0.179[c]	-0.086[b]	-0.120[b]	-0.103[b]	-0.138[c]	-0.241[c]	-0.180[c]	-0.130[c]	-0.082[b]		-0.124[b]	-0.115[b]	-0.098[a]		
Adjusted R^2	0.060	0.146	0.044	0.088	0.072	0.061	0.064	0.097	0.127	0.083	0.044	0.044	0.096	0.172	0.111	0.140	0.091	0.024

Notes: [a]$p<0.05$; [b]$p<0.01$; [c]$p<0.001$.
The number of children bothered by meeting online contacts was too low to conduct valid regression analyses on coping strategies.
Gender: boy = 1, girl = 2/SES (socio-economic status): high = 1, low = 6/Education parents: low = 1, high = 7.
Being upset: fairly/very upset = 1, a bit/not at all upset = 2.

coping strategies and different online risks. For example, in the case of online bullying, it is peer problems that show the main influence on children's coping reactions; in the case of sexting, children's strategies are explained by a broader range of psychological difficulties. These nuances are better captured by looking at emotional, conduct and peer problems separately rather than psychological problems combined.

Sexual images

Children who feel very upset when confronted by sexual images are more likely to respond in some way – passively, communicatively or proactively. Girls, younger children, children who have problems with peers, sensation-seekers and children with few online activities more often take the route of going offline for a time following an upsetting experience with sexual images. Adoption of a proactive problem-solving strategy increases children's resilience and is more common among self-confident children and children who are very active online. Also, sensation-seekers and those who experience peer problems are more likely to look for some solution to their problem. The use of specific online coping strategies, such as deleting or blocking messages, increases with the range of children's online activities. Girls, younger children and very self-confident young people prefer a communicative approach.

Online bullying

More intense feelings of being upset have a strong impact on the whole range of children's responses to online bullying. Children with higher self-efficacy are more willing to try to fix the problem and not to stop using the internet. The children most vulnerable to online bullying are children with peer problems, low self-efficacy and younger children: all are more likely just to stay offline for a period. Experiencing peer problems, being a boy and coming from a more affluent home is linked to responding proactively to problems. The children that seem to experience serious harm are apparently more motivated to look for a (long-term) solution to bullying. Self-confident children are also proactive at dealing with bullying. Deleting messages and blocking senders of upsetting messages happens more often among children who are highly skilled online. Those who prefer a communicative response following an experience of bullying online tend to be girls, low sensation-seekers and children with no peer problems.

Sexual messages (sexting)

Negative experiences with sexual messages produces the response in boys of hoping that the problem will go away, whereas girls stop using the computer and talk to someone or be proactive. Girls, and children with low self-efficacy, more conduct problems and more peer problems, are more likely to decide to go offline for a while after a sexting incident. It is noticeable that older children and children with no emotional problems often adopt a fatalistic approach to sexting. Presumably, the more resilient children go offline for short periods, while those groups less able to cope may stop using the internet for much longer. Although girls, children with conduct problems and children with no emotional problems are more likely to abandon the internet for a time, they are also more motivated to look for solutions. Also, children engaged in a broad range of online activities, higher socioeconomic status children and younger age groups tend to respond proactively. The group most vulnerable to harm from sexting are children with low self-confidence: this group more often stops using the internet and less often searches for solutions. Internet-specific coping strategies (deleting messages and blocking senders) are practised more often by girls, children with no emotional problems, children with peer problems and, as might be expected, children who are more skilled and active online (who engage in more activities). These findings indicate that the likelihood of using online coping strategies increases with the intensity of distress from the experience, a certain state of mind and mastery of the necessary skills.

Conclusion

Exposure to risk does not necessarily result in harm, and not every risk is equally upsetting. Some online risks, such as seeing sexual images, provoke mainly minor negative responses. Other risks, such as meeting online contacts offline, are perceived mainly as opportunities and are rarely upsetting for those involved. In order to understand the negative effects of online risks, it is crucial to take account of the child's understandings and characteristics. Children reporting more psychological difficulties, particularly those with low self-efficacy and emotional problems, are more likely to be upset by the risks they encounter. For each type of risk, individual characteristics (gender, age, online activities) play a definite role in the intensity of the harm that children feel following exposure to that risk. Our results are indicative of a type of 'Matthew effect' (in which the rich get richer and the poor get poorer), in that those children who experience more difficulties coping with offline risks seem to find it more difficult to cope with online risks.

In tackling the problem of online risks in relation to young people, it is essential that educators and policy makers know what young people actually perceive as most risky and upsetting. From the four risks discussed in this chapter, online bullying has the strongest negative impact. However, it is the online risk that engenders the most proactive and communicative coping responses. Young people who encounter disturbing sexual images are less inclined to look actively for a solution to the problem. Online problem-solving coping strategies, such as deleting unwelcome messages or blocking contacts, are much more common if children are upset by the risks. This suggests that children are able to build online resilience through the use of different strategies when confronted with something that upsets them. However, it should be borne in mind that some children are significantly less likely than others to be able to respond adequately. Across all risks, the 'more vulnerable' children will often stop using the internet for a time, which then slows their progress up the ladder of digital opportunities (see Chapter 6).

Our findings show that more than half of children (including less resilient groups such as girls and primary school children) talk to someone about online problems, which implies that awareness-raising efforts already in place are playing a positive role. However, we need other initiatives to encourage children with psychological difficulties and/or low self-efficacy to talk about the online risks they encounter and the harms they suffer. As more and more children perceive talking to someone to be an acceptable coping strategy, those providing the support could become key agents in the transition from using communicative to applying proactive strategies.

Notes
[1] The number of children bothered by offline meetings with online contacts is too small for a valid regression analysis.

References

Coleman, J. and Hagell, A. (eds) (2007) *Adolescence, risk and resilience: Against the odds*, Chichester: John Wiley & Sons Ltd.

Livingstone, S., Haddon, L., Görzig, A. and Olafsson, K. (2011) *Risks and safety on the internet: The perspective of European children. Full findings*, London: London School of Economics and Political Science.

Masten, A.S. and Gewirtz, A.H. (2006) 'Vulnerability and resilience in early child development', in K. McCartney and D. Philips (eds) *Blackwell handbook of early childhood development*, Oxford and Carlton: Blackwell Publishing, pp 22-43.

Masten, A.S. and Powell, J.L. (2003) 'A resilience framework for research, policy and practice', in S. Luthar (ed) *Resilience and vulnerability: Adaptation in the context of childhood adversities*, New York: Cambridge University Press, pp 1-25.

Smith, C. and Carlson, B.E. (1997) 'Stress, coping and resilience in children and youth', *Social Service Review*, vol 71, no 2, pp 231-56.

SEVENTEEN

Agents of mediation and sources of safety awareness: a comparative overview

Dominique Pasquier, José Alberto Simões and Elodie Kredens

Defining mediation

The question of mediation raises many issues since it entails a normative view about children's socialisation. How do media enter children's lives and who has responsibility for regulating their potential risks or benefits? Parents, teachers, policy makers and the media – all seem to have an opinion. However, the role of parents is prominent since most media use occurs within the home. Structural changes in family life (James et al, 1998; Beck and Beck-Gernsheim, 2002) may explain certain transformations within family dynamics (from less to more 'democratic' styles of parenting) and account for changes in parental styles of mediating online activities (Eastin et al, 2006). Parents' strategies toward media consumption reflect these dynamics and the family tensions and power relations that underlie the rules set and the way they are negotiated in different situations.

New media appear to undermine the effectiveness of some parental strategies through the individualisation and segmentation of media consumption within the home. There has been an emergence of 'media-rich homes' and a 'bedroom culture' among children and young people (Livingstone, 2002) and a tendency towards 'living together separately' (Flichy, 2002). The apparent contradiction that needs to be resolved is related to media uses within the family becoming increasingly segmented and individualised, but family socialisation in relation to media is still regarded as being crucial.

Although most authors agree that mediation involves some sort of effort to manage children's relations with media, they are not in complete agreement about what kinds of practices should be considered and how they should be classified (Livingstone and Helsper, 2008). Most theoretical discussions focus on parents, which harks back to their role in relation to traditional media (such as television; see, for example, Austin, 1990, 1993; Valkenburg et al, 1999; Nathanson, 2001a, 2001b). Mediation strategies regarding new media are still being explored (and adapted from previous research) although evidence on their effectiveness is scarce (Eastin et al, 2006; Livingstone and Helsper, 2008; Livingstone, 2009).[1]

In discussing whether parental mediation of internet use can be analysed in the same terms as television, Livingstone and Helsper (2008) note that the conditions are obviously different. It is difficult to share an activity on the internet (in contrast to co-viewing television), and many parents are not very familiar with the internet (in contrast to traditional mass media). Monitoring is more difficult: a glance at the screen is not enough to determine what the child is doing on the internet. Also, the internet and television have a different social image and social history. The internet is a medium linked to writing and reading and, as Meyrowitz underlines, the world of print is more adult-controlled than television (Meyrowitz 1985). The internet is associated with education: it is used at school (and at workplaces), only rarely the case for television, which might make teachers influential. Upper-class families, traditionally reluctant to accept television, were among the first to access the internet at home, and to allow their children to access it in their bedrooms. This compares to a once rather low tolerance of private television sets (Jouët and Pasquier, 1999). However, the internet brings new risks and, among them, with the recent social networking phenomenon, uncontrolled diffusion of personal data and photographs. In brief, the mediation landscape is framed by ambivalent feelings on the part of adults: the internet is not a medium you can simply try to ban because children need it for schoolwork. However, it is more risky than television viewing.

In line with these debates, EU Kids Online distinguishes among five types of mediation:[2]

- *Active mediation of the child's internet use:* mediation practices that include talking to children about particular media activities or sharing these activities with them. Although the latter has been described as 'active co-use' (Austin, 1990; Livingstone, 2009), it is included in active mediation, since sharing an activity usually involves talking about it.
- *Active mediation of the child's internet safety:* mediation activities that specifically include parents' initiatives (before, during or after internet use) to guide their children and introduce the idea of online safety,

by helping them in the case of difficulty, or by telling them what to do should an upsetting or disturbing situation occur.

- *Restrictive mediation:* mediation that includes regulating internet use, for example, through clear instruction about what children can or cannot do (for example, limiting access and specific types of uses).
- *Monitoring:* mediation strategies that include checking the computer to see what children have been doing, checking the child's social networking profile or looking at emails or instant messaging accounts. Since these mediation strategies are rather furtive, it has been suggested that these forms of mediation might lead to children employing tactics to evade parental control (Livingstone, 2006; Livingstone and Bober, 2006). The issues of trust and privacy are central here; it is important that parents do not lose their opportunity to influence their children's online practices.
- *Technical mediation of child's internet use:* mediation that includes specific filtering software that restricts certain types of uses or monitors the child's actual use. Technical means of controlling children's internet use face the same privacy and trust issues as other mediation activities (for example, simple monitoring), and might motivate the child to employ avoidance tactics.

Some of these strategies may be adopted by other agents in other contexts and situations:

- *Teachers' mediation:* since several of the restrictive practices or shared online activities described may be adopted by school teachers, and most schools use technical solutions, the questionnaire included questions to children about their teachers.
- *Peer mediation of children's internet safety:* assuming that children talk with peers about their online activities, some questions focused on peer mediation especially of safety practices.
- *Other sources of safety awareness:* which include traditional media, websites, internet safety experts, internet service providers, etc.

However, these contexts are inherently different and may have an influence on the effectiveness of the practices adopted. Mediation from parents takes place predominantly within the (private) home and may involve many alternative strategies. Mediation at school or by teachers is defined primarily at the institutional level, occurs in a public, formal context, and is carried out by agents with institutional roles. Mediation by peers involves young people with shared, common understandings and experience of media use.

First, we examined the main agents of mediation, the parents, through the following research question:

RQ1: Are there significant variations in parental mediation?

We tested three hypotheses:

H1: Parental mediation depends on parents' sociocultural profile.
H2: Parental mediation depends on parents' own internet use.
H3: The pattern of parental mediation varies by country.

We examined the balance between parental and others' mediation through the research question:

RQ2: Does the role of mediation agents depend on the situations encountered by the child?

We tested two hypotheses:

H4: The role played by potential mediation agents varies depending on the type of problem or risk encountered by the child.

H5: The balance between adult and peer mediation will vary depending on the type of coping strategy used by the child.

Variations in parental mediation

The internet appears to be highly mediated by parents; almost nine out of ten European children whose parents use the internet receive advice from them about internet use and safety and have to abide by restrictive rules. Monitoring is less frequent, experienced by only one in two children. Only a third of parents use technical mediation to block and filter some types of websites. Parents who are internet users are more proactive about mediation than parents who are not (see Table 17.1), but the gap is not as large as might be expected. The fact that non–internet–using parents practise mediating activities to some extent is an indication of the considerable attention in the domestic sphere given to mediation.

Higher levels of mediation by parent users occurs for all types of mediation, but the gap is largest in relation to advice about safety, while it is least in relation to restrictive mediation. We need to distinguish between forms of mediation that require technical skills relating to

Table 17.1: Differences in parental mediation between parents who are internet users and who are non-users

	% of mediated children where parents use internet	% of mediated children where parents do NOT use internet	Phi-coefficient
At least one form of active mediation of use	91	72	0.24
At least one form of active mediation of safety	92	65	0.34
At least one form of restrictive mediation	86	82	0.05
At least one monitoring activity	53	37	0.11
At least one for of technical mediation	30	18	0.10

Base: All children who use the internet.

Notes: All data are statistically significant ($p<0.001$). The data in this and subsequent tables are based on the response of the child.

the internet (for example, helping the child to do something difficult or suggesting ways to behave and act on the internet), and forms of mediation that rely on general rules that can be formulated without experience of the internet (for example, forbidding the child to give out personal information or download material).

Parental mediation is also related to children's demographics, especially age. Table 17.2 shows that it decreases as children grow older. This is particularly evident in the case of restrictive strategies: 95 per cent of 9- to 10-year-olds versus 71 per cent of 15- to 16-year-olds. Parents also restrict girls' use (87 per cent) slightly more than boys' use (83 per cent). Parents' level of education only has a significant effect on certain types of active mediation: parents with higher levels of education are more active at mediation related to advice about internet safety and use than parents with lower levels of education. This is directly related to better-educated parents being more likely to be internet users and more technically competent. The fact that more highly educated parents put less emphasis on monitoring and restrictive rules shows the difference in these families' attitudes towards television compared to the internet. A decade ago, the Young People New Media study showed there were wide differences in rules about television use according to socioeconomic status (Livingstone and Bovill, 1999).

Finally, differences by country as regards the balance between active mediation and restrictive rules show that a large majority of European parents prioritise the former, especially in northern Europe, for example, Norway, where mediation to maintain internet safety is high (see Table 17.3). In contrast, some countries, especially in southern Europe, have

Table 17.2: Types of parental mediation, by sociodemographics (%)

Socio-demographics	At least one form of mediation activity of the child's internet use	At least one form of active mediation of safety	At least one form of restrictive mediation	At least one monitoring activity[a]	Use of parental controls or filtering software[a]
9-10 years	92	89	95	58	[b]
11-12	88	88	92	57	37
13-14	86	86	84	51	29
15-16	81	79	72	37	21
Cramer's V	*0.11*	*0.11*	*0.26*	*0.17*	*0.14*
Boys	86	85	83	50	28
Girls	87	86	87	51	28
Cramer's V	*0.02*	*0.02*	*0.05*	*0.01 (ns)*	*0.01 (ns)*
Primary or less	79	69	83	39	18
Lower secondary	83	82	86	44	22
Upper and post-secondary	88	88	85	47	20
Tertiary	91	93	87	47	19
Cramer's V	*0.12*	*0.20*	*0.05*	*0.05*	*0.06*
Total	**87**	**86**	**85**	**50**	**28**

Base: All children who use the internet.
Notes: [a]All children who use the internet at home. [b]It does not include this age group.
All data are statistically significant (p<0.001), except otherwise noticed.

high levels of parental restrictive mediation: this is the case in Portugal, France, Italy, Greece, Turkey and Cyprus, but also in Ireland and Germany. Of course, these variations might be due to many different reasons: parental style of education, whether the child has bedroom access to the internet or not, how long ago the internet was introduced in the country (and the type of connection), how much parents know about and use the internet, national campaigns about internet risks, etc.

Different agents of mediation for different types of mediation

In most cases, parents are the main agents of mediation related to safety, but the role of teachers is also very important (see Table 17.4), and more important than that of other professionals such as librarians.[3] The data show that teachers are more important than parents for older teenagers (60 per cent of 15- to 16-year-olds say their teacher suggested ways of using the internet safely compared to 55 per cent for parents; among 9- to 10-year-olds the figures are 50 and 68 per cent). The figures for children from lower socioeconomic status homes are 63 and

Table 17.3: Type of parental mediation, by country

Country	At least one form of active mediation of the child's internet use	At least one form of active mediation of safety	At least one form of restrictive mediation	At least one monitoring activity[a]	Use of parental controls or filtering software[a]
Austria	80	83	81	39	20
Belgium	85	87	84	45	25
Bulgaria	91	84	84	42	9
Cyprus	94	91	91	36	23
Czech Republic	93	93	72	44	17
Denmark	87	90	79	29	10
Estonia	87	89	61	54	12
Finland	89	94	84	39	15
France	89	90	91	50	38
Germany	88	90	92	47	26
Greece	84	82	87	51	15
Hungary	89	78	78	52	15
Ireland	92	92	93	57	41
Italy	87	86	87	54	21
Lithuania	87	75	54	26	9
Netherlands	97	94	87	50	37
Norway	94	97	89	54	15
Poland	94	88	65	61	17
Portugal	90	82	93	38	22
Romania	89	80	84	36	5
Sweden	88	92	84	53	12
Slovenia	86	79	77	27	11
Spain	89	89	88	48	20
Turkey	73	70	85	55	38
UK	89	90	87	55	46
Cramer's V	*0.19*	*0.21*	*0.21*	*0.14*	*0.27*
Total	**87**	**86**	**85**	**50**	**28**

Base: All children who use the internet. [a]All children who use the internet at home.
Note: All data are statistically significant (*p*<0.001).

58 per cent, compared to 56 per cent for teachers and 69 per cent for parents in the case of children from high socioeconomic status homes. This finding suggests public policy should focus on more information campaigns and teacher training in internet use, especially in countries where teachers do not currently have much input. The data show major differences by country: for example, teachers in the UK are extremely active in giving safety advice (83 per cent of children), while teachers in France and Romania are much less so (only 40 per cent of children refer to the teacher).

Table 17.4: Different sources of advice on safety (%)

Different sources of advice on safety	Gave advice or suggested ways to use the internet safely
Parents	63
Teachers	58
Other relatives (adults or young)	47
Peers	44
Television, radio newspapers or magazines	20
Websites	12
Someone whose job is to give advice over the internet	9
Internet service provider	6
Youth or church or social worker	6
Librarian	6

Base: All children who use the internet.

Other relatives, adults or other young people are slightly more important (47 per cent) for safety advice than peers (44 per cent). Compared to those involved in children's everyday lives, the role of the mass media is low (20 per cent), and resources available on the web are exploited even less. Overall, safety advice comes from the adults who are most prominent in children's everyday lives.

The influence of mediation agents also varies by the *type of problem concerned* (see Table 17.5). If children are bothered by something on the internet, the tendency is not to consult a teacher. Although the data do not provide in-depth details on this aspect, they show that teachers primarily exercise restrictive mediation. An average of 62 per cent of children say that their teachers set rules for use of the internet, but there are major differences between northern Europe, where teachers are very strict (for example, over 80 per cent of teachers in Norway, the UK and Finland set rules) and southern countries, where teachers

Table 17.5: Help from parents versus teachers versus peers (%)

% who say that parents/teachers/peers....	Parent	Teacher	Peer
Explained why some websites are good or bad	68	58	41
Helped you when something is difficult to do or to find on the internet	66	58	64
Suggested ways to use the internet safely	63	58	44
Suggested ways to behave towards other people	56	48	37
Talked to you about what to do if something on the internet bothered you	52	40	na
Helped you in the past when something has bothered you on the internet	36	24	28

Base: All children who use the internet.

are more permissive (less than 40 per cent of teachers in Spain, Greece and Italy set rules).

There are also variations in the coping strategies used by children.[4] One of the strategies is to talk to someone about a risk that has been encountered. Table 17.6 shows that, on the whole, children talk to others less about risks linked to sex (sexual images or sexual messages) than risks linked to unpleasant communications or unpleasant meetings: 77 per cent of those children who are bullied talk to someone versus 53 per cent of children exposed to sexual images.

Table 17.6 shows the major role of peers for providing support: children turn first to their friends, whatever the type of risk, and friends are more important than siblings in these cases. Intragenerational social support in the family is low compared to the roles played by peer groups or parents. Around a quarter of children talk to their parents about seeing sexual images and receiving sexual messages, 40 per cent tell parents about bullying and 28 per cent consult parents about feeling bothered following an offline encounter with an online contact. There are no other adults than parents who play such an important role in mediation related to internet safety.

Table 17.6: Who the child talked to when encountering different risks (%)

Who the child talked to when....	Seeing sexual images	Being bullied	Seeing or receiving sexual messages	Being bothered when meeting offline an online contact
% talked to someone	53	77	60	62
To a friend	34	52	38	35
Mother/father	26	42	30	28
Brother/sister	9	14	9	11
Another adult I trust	5	9	5	10
A teacher	3	7	3	6
Someone whose job is to help children	1	2	2	2
Someone else	–	–	1	4

Base: All children who use the internet.

Conclusion

The most surprising finding is the important role of parents for giving advice, setting rules and providing social support to a child who has been upset by something related to the internet. It is surprising since most studies highlight the autonomous nature of children's culture on the internet. danah boyd (2010), in a study of social networking among adolescents, highlights the desire to keep this world secret from adults, and especially parents, and the findings in Cedric Fluckiger's (2006) work on pre-adolescents blogging are similar – that it is only within the peer culture that such use makes sense. Moreover, some studies on youth culture stress the decline of parental cultural guidance and the rising role of peer group authority (Pasquier, 2008). In the EU Kids Online study the pattern seems to be different: parents are more present, more accepted as qualified authorities and more often consulted about problems. The importance of teachers is also surprising even though it is less important in southern Europe, and there are limits to it. Teachers are seen as trusted advisers in terms of avoiding risks, but not as reliable people from whom to seek support if upset about something related to the internet. This was the situation in 2010; the wider diffusion of mobile access to the internet might reduce the influence of adults at home or at school, and increase the role of peers.

Notes

[1] See Chapter 18 on the effectiveness of parental mediation.

[2] For exact questions asked, see the Appendix to this volume.

[3] For more data about teachers' roles, see Chapter 19.

[4] For more data about coping strategies, see Chapter 16.

References

Austin, E.W. (1990) 'Effects of family communication on children's interpretation of television', in J. Bryant and J.A. Bryant (eds) *Television and the American family*, Hillsdale, NJ: Lawrence Erlbaum, pp 377-95.

Austin, E.W. (1993) 'Exploring the effects of active parental mediation of television content', *Journal of Broadcasting & Electronic Media*, vol 37, pp 147-58.

Beck, U. and Beck-Gernsheim, E. (2002) *Individualization*, London: Sage Publications.

boyd, d. (2010) 'Social network sites as networked publics: affordances, dynamics and implications', in Z. Papacharissi (ed) *Networked self: Identity, community, and culture on social network sites*, New York: Routledge, pp 39-58.

Eastin, M., Greenberg, B.S. and Hofschire, L. (2006) 'Parenting the internet', *Journal of Communication*, vol 56, pp 486-504.

Flichy, P. (2002) 'New media history', in L. Lievrouw and S. Livingstone (eds) *Handbook of new media: Social shaping and consequences of ICTs*, London: Sage Publications, pp 136-50.

Fluckiger, C. (2006) 'La sociabilité juvenile instrumentée. L'appropriation des blogs dans un groupe de collegiens' ['Appropriation of blogs by high school students'], *Réseaux*, vol 4, pp 109-38.

James, A., Jenks, C. and Prout, A. (1998) *Theorizing childhood*, Cambridge: Polity Press.

Jouët, J. and Pasquier, D. (1999) 'Les jeunes et la culture de l'écran. Enquête nationale auprès des 6-17 ans' ['Young people and screen culture. French survey on 6-17 years old'], *Réseaux*, vol 92/93, pp 25-103.

Livingstone, S. (2002) *Young people and new media: Children and the changing media environment*, London: Sage Publications.

Livingstone, S. (2006) 'Children's privacy online: experimenting with boundaries within and beyond the family', in R. Kraut, M. Brynin and S. Kiesler (eds) *Computers, phones, and the internet: Domesticating information technology*, New York: Oxford University Press, pp 145-67.

Livingstone, S. (2009) *Children and the internet. Great expectations, challenging realities*, Cambridge: Polity Press.

Livingstone, S. and Bober, M. (2006) 'Regulating the internet at home: contrasting the perspectives of children and parents', in D. Buckingham and R. Willett (eds) *Digital generations*, Mahwah, NJ: Lawrence Erlbaum Associates, pp 93-113.

Livingstone, S. and Bovill, M. (1999) *Young people, new media*, Research Report, London: London School of Economics and Political Science.

Livingstone, S. and Helsper, E.J. (2008) 'Parental mediation of children's internet use', *Journal of Broadcasting & Electronic Media*, vol 52, no 4, pp 581-99.

Meyrowitz, J. (1985) *No sense of place. The impact of electronic media on social behavior*, Oxford: Oxford University Press.

Nathanson, A.I. (2001a) 'Parent and child perspectives on the presence and meaning of parental television mediation', *Journal of Broadcasting & Electronic Media*, vol 45, no 2, pp 201-20.

Nathanson, A.I. (2001b) 'Parents versus peers: exploring the significance of peer mediation of antisocial television', *Communication Research*, vol 28, no 3, pp 251-74.

Pasquier, D. (2008) 'From parental control to peer pressure: cultural transmission and conformism', in S. Livingstone and K. Drotner (eds) *International handbook of children, media and culture*, London: Sage Publications, pp 448-60.

Valkenburg, P.M., Krcmar, M., Peeters, A.L. and Marseille, N.M. (1999) 'Developing a scale to assess three different styles of television mediation:"instructive mediation","restrictive mediation", and "social coviewing"', *Journal of Broadcasting & Electronic Media*, vol 43, no 1, pp 52-66.

EIGHTEEN

The effectiveness of parental mediation

Maialen Garmendia, Carmelo Garitaonandia, Gemma Martínez and Miguel Ángel Casado

Introduction

A child's relationship with the internet is shaped by multiple factors. Chapter 17 showed that individual characteristics (demographic, psychological), national context (socioeconomic stratification, legal framework, technological infrastructure, education system, cultural values) and social mediation influence the way that children use the internet and, thus, the risks and opportunities they encounter. The actions of parents, siblings and peers and teachers are part of that social mediation (see Livingstone et al, 2011).

Since parents are responsible for their children's education, they play a vital role in limiting the risks and harm to which children may be exposed. In the specific case of the internet, it should be remembered that although children's use of handheld devices is growing, the household is still the main locus of internet access (see Chapter 4 in this volume). Research has examined the role of parents in children's media use, distinguishing different types of parental mediation strategies (see classifications in Valkenburg et al, 1999; Livingstone and Helsper, 2008; Kirwil et al, 2009). This chapter explores which strategies are the most effective for minimising online risks and harm and maximising online opportunities for children, using the classifications in Chapter 17 – summarised as: (i) co-use – parent is present/sharing the activity with the child; (ii) active mediation – parent discusses content (for example, interprets, criticises) to guide the child; (iii) restrictive mediation –parent sets rules to restrict the child's use (for example, time or activity); (iv) monitoring – parent checks available records of child's internet use; and (v) technical restrictions – use of software to filter, restrict or monitor the child's use.

In practice, it is difficult to distinguish co-use and active mediation, since sharing an activity generally involves talking about it. Therefore, in this chapter, instead of distinguishing between 'active mediation' of internet use generally, and active mediation of internet safety in particular, we combine these classifications. This combined classification probably represents the main sources of support available to children. For policy makers, it enables them to differentiate by demographic factors and by country when providing support for children.

Overall, all these mediation types are fairly widespread among children. Nearly 90 per cent of European children state that their parents carry out some kind of active mediation of their use of the internet, 85 per cent say parents set some kind of restriction on internet use, and even the least extensive type of mediation, monitoring, affects 50 per cent of children (see Chapter 17). Different types of mediation imply different behaviours regarding a child's relationship with the internet. It is important, therefore, to determine which behaviours are more beneficial and which mediation strategies contribute to reducing risks without reducing the opportunities available to children on the internet.

Theoretical framework

How families are facing the process of adopting the internet in the household (see Silverstone et al, 1992; Silverstone and Haddon, 1996), and the effectiveness of parental mediation activity (to prevent children from potential risks and harm from using the internet) have become concerns for policy, the public sphere and families. Public and individual anxiety, worry or fear (see Livingstone and Bober, 2006; Lwin et al, 2008) are often heightened by the recognition that children are especially vulnerable actors in the process of media consumption, which can have a negative impact on their behaviour, attitudes, well-being and safety (see Buckingham, 2000; Bushman and Anderson, 2001; Selwyn, 2003; Livingstone, 2007).

Parents' responsibility for their children's education includes supervising use of the internet in the most effective way. Parents' efforts to balance the educational and social advantages of the internet with its negative effects are characterised by Livingstone and Helsper (2008, p 581) as a 'constant battle'. In early research into parental mediation styles, Bybee et al (1982, p 697) found that 'industry officials and some regulators have tended to place increasing emphasis or parental responsibility in guiding their children's viewing and researchers have begun to explore the benefits of such guidance'. This is paralleled by academic arguments that this tendency of attributing to parents responsibility for supervising children's media consumption might be excessive (Ribak and Turow, 2003; Selwyn, 2003; Hasebrink et al, 2009). Parents need and are calling for guidance from policy makers, public bodies and stakeholders in order to distinguish and apply the most effective parental mediation strategies to their children's internet use (see European Commission, 2008).

There is a stream of evidence showing that the notions of 'digital natives' and 'digital immigrants', proposed by Prensky (2001), do not entirely hold. Since the early 2000s, for instance, parents' internet use and access have increased, resulting in levels of internet literacy being higher among parents than children (Duimel and de Haan, 2009; Hasebrink et al, 2009). However, it has been shown that parents usually underestimate the risks that children quite clearly state they are facing (Livingstone and Bober, 2006; Livingstone et al, 2011). There is an inconsistency or disagreement between parents and children about different forms of parental mediation; parents usually try to present themselves as sociably acceptable 'good' fathers or mothers (Lin and Atkin, 1989; Oswell, 1999; van der Bulck and van den Bergh, 2000). This striving for social acceptability might help to clarify the effectiveness of parental mediation strategies. For this reason, we focus especially on children's perceptions and experiences of parental mediation strategies.

Despite the vast body of research on parental regulation of children's and young people's media consumption (see van der Voort et al, 1992; Nathanson, 1999, 2001; Eastin et al, 2006), the concept of effectiveness (maximise opportunities, minimise potential risks and avoid harm to children) is applied by scholars rather cautiously. Research by Kirwil et al (2009, pp 211-13) on parental mediation and the effectiveness of parents' mediation strategies shows that the type of strategies parents use is influenced especially by parents' personal characteristics (gender, education level), and also by children's personal characteristics (gender, age). It seems that mothers engage in all types of parental mediation to a greater extent than fathers, and that parents with higher levels of education use social mediation and monitoring software less, but tend to adopt the strategy of being nearby when their children are using the internet. Among children, boys are subject to more parental mediation than girls, and older children are monitored less than younger ones (for factors influencing types of parental mediation strategies, see Chapter 17).

Kirwil et al (2009, p 219) also address the effectiveness issue. They conclude that generally restrictive strategies seem to be the most effective for protecting children from risks, but maintain that 'multiple strategy parental mediation might be more effective than single strategy mediation'. It is worth noting that some research claims that active mediation through direct communication rather than restrictions (Weaber and Barbour, 1992; Austin, 1993; Nathanson, 1999; Hasebrink et al, 2009) is far less effective. Kirwil et al (2009) assess effectiveness simply by taking account the risks that children have to cope with. In our view, the effectiveness of parental mediation strategies should be assessed by also taking account of two other variables: the harm that can be avoided by parental strategies, and the increasing number of opportunities that children may encounter online. In this chapter, the effectiveness of parental strategies is evaluated in relation to their influence on reducing or avoiding risk and harm, and helping children to develop skills and abilities through use of the internet.

It should be noted that the findings in this chapter do not take account of such factors as family dynamics, structure, rules or roles. Research on family systems shows that these factors influence the type of mediation strategies that parents adopt towards their children (see Goodman, 1983; Varenne, 1996; Yeung et al, 2001). Also, although not analysed in this chapter, we should stress that parent's attitudes (positive or negative) towards the content that children consume seem to predict the type of parental mediation strategy, which, at the same time, is related to parents' concerns or worries (see Valkenburg et al, 1999, which develops an important set of classifications of parental mediation strategies and identifies concern as the main predictor of type of parental mediation strategies exploited).

Hypotheses

In order to evaluate the influence of the different types of mediation, we analyse the relationship between different mediation strategies and children's exposure to different risks, harm suffered and children's online opportunities. Before presenting the results of our analysis we discuss three issues that may affect them. First, mediation is only one among other factors that influence exposure to risks and opportunities. We would expect, therefore, neither a large decrease in risk nor an increase in opportunities. Second, nearly all children report some kind of mediation by parents. This makes it impossible to isolate strategies and achieve a valid sample in order to evaluate each strategy used, in an independent way. Third, we cannot ignore the influence on the results of children's attitudes to mediation strategies. For instance, 7 per cent of children state that they completely ignore what their parents say about the internet, 29 per cent ignore it to some extent and 30 per cent state that parental mediation is no help to them.

Taking account of previous research on parental mediation, the analysis in this chapter tests the following hypotheses:

H1: Parental mediation strategies contribute to reducing children's exposure to risks.

H2: Parental mediation strategies contribute to reducing children's exposure to harm.

H3: Parental mediation strategies contribute to increasing children's online opportunities.

The EU Kids Online survey asked children and their parents about the mediation strategies practised by parents (see the Appendix at the end of this volume). To find support for our hypotheses, we considered the children's responses in relation to all mediation types except technical mediation. In this case, since the parents installed the software, they knew more about it. Technical mediation may influence children's exposure to risks without their being aware of it, such as in the case of content filters for sexual images or inappropriate content.

For exposure to risks, harm or opportunities, we considered the children's responses. For risks, we included: access to sexual images, reception of sexual messages, reception of bullying messages, acting as the perpetrator of sexual or bullying messages, online contacts with people not met face to face and meeting people face to face only previously met on the internet. We considered children to have suffered harm if they said that they felt upset after exposure to any of these risks.

Analysis of opportunities is important because some strategies might reduce some risks effectively, but might have other consequences such as limiting the benefits available from the internet. It is difficult to measure this concept in terms of children's online activities, but there are two relevant indicators: number of different activities (out of a total of 17, see Chapter 5) conducted online in the previous week, and number of digital skills (from a total of 8, see Chapter 6) reported by the child.

Analysis

Risks

In order to check for a significant relationship between parental mediation strategies and children's exposure to risks we employed a

2×2 Chi-Square analysis for each risk (experienced: yes/no) and the respective mediation strategy (as reported by child: yes/no). In the EU Kids Online survey we considered the six main types of risk analysed (seeing sexual images, receiving sexual messages, being bullied online, acting as a perpetrator of sexual and bullying messages, contacting other people on the internet and meeting face to face with people only contacted on the internet). We explored children's roles as perpetrators of potentially damaging messages, and focused on those children who said they had sent sexual and/or bullying messages.

Table 18.1 shows that most mediation strategies have a negative relationship with the different risks considered. In most cases, children reporting any of these mediation strategies show a lower incidence of risk. However, restrictive and monitoring are the only strategies that show a significant relationship to risks. In the case of restrictive mediation, the relationship is significant for all cases except being bullied online; in the case of monitoring, there is only a significant relationship for the risks of new online contacts.

For the other mediation strategies, the percentages in Table 18.1 show there are only very small differences in the level of risk exposure among children who report mediation strategies and those who do not.

Regarding the role of children as perpetrators, all mediation types show a negative relationship for the child acting as a perpetrator (sending bullying messages or sexual messages); only restrictive mediation shows a significant relationship.

Harm

For harm, we analysed the relationship between parental mediation strategies and children's experiences of harm. We examined only those children who said they had been upset after exposure to some kind of risk in order to try to determine whether the existence of a mediation strategy reduced the experience of harm in children after exposure to risk.

Table 18.2 shows that, in most cases, the relationship between harm and mediation is positive, that is, children who suffer harm are subject to higher levels of mediation. The EU Kids Online survey also included a question about changes in parental mediation after a child's risk experience, which shows that parents tend to change their strategies if their children experience risks. However, this relationship is significant only for children who suffer harm after seeing sexual content or receiving sexual messages. In the first case, children report higher levels of restrictive mediation, monitoring and active mediation

Table 18.1: Parental mediation as reported by the child and risk exposure

% risk	Active mediation of internet use			Restrictive mediation			Active mediation of internet safety			Monitoring			Technical mediation		
	No	Yes	Phi	No	Yes	Phi	No	Yes	Phi	No	Yes	Phi	No	Yes	Phi
Sexual images seen	15	14	−0.01	25	12	−0.13c	15	14	−0.01b	16	13	−0.05c	17	18	0.02
Sexual messages received*	17	14	−0.02b	24	13	−0.12c	16	14	−0.02	17	12	−0.07c	15	15	0.00
Been bullied online	6	6	0.00	9	5	−0.06c	4	6	0.03c	6	6	0.00	8	7	−0.02b
New online contact	35	29	−0.04c	44	27	−0.14c	34	29	−0.03c	36	27	−0.10	34	37	0.03b
Met new online contact face to face	11	8	−0.03c	17	7	−0.14c	10	8	−0.02b	12	7	−0.07c	12	11	−0.01
Act as a perpetrator (sent sexual or bullying messages)	5	4	−0.02b	9	3	−0.10c	5	4	−0.02a	5	4	−0.04c	7	5	−0.02b

Notes: a $p<0.05$; b $p<0.01$; c $p<0.001$.

Phi coefficients with an effect size which can be considered small or above (Cohen, 1992) in italics. The Phi coefficient (φ or r_φ) is a measure of association for two binary variables. This measure is similar to the Pearson correlation coefficient (r) in its interpretation.

Base: All children who use the internet (* only children aged from 11-16).

Table 18.2: Parental mediation as reported by the child and harm experiences (only children who have reported risk exposure)

% harm	Active mediation internet use			Restrictive mediation			Active mediation of internet safety			Monitoring			Technical mediation		
	No	Yes	Phi	No	Yes	Phi	No	Yes	Phi	No	Yes	Phi	No	Yes	Phi
Sexual images seen	24	36	0.08c	25	38	0.12c	23	36	0.10c	28	41	0.13c	28	31	0.03
Sexual messages received*	19	28	0.08c	20	30	0.10c	15	29	0.11c	22	30	0.09c	26	25	-0.01
Been bullied online	84	85	0.02	83	86	0.04	82	86	0.03	82	87	0.07a	81	85	0.06
Met new online contact face to face	7	13	0.06a	12	11	-0.01	13	11	-0.02	10	15	0.08b	14	10	-0.07a

Notes: [a] p<0.05; [b] p<0.01; [c] p<0.001.

Phi coefficients with an effect size which can be considered small or above (Cohen, 1992) in italics. The Phi coefficient (φ or r_φ) is a measure of association for two binary variables. This measure is similar to the Pearson correlation coefficient (r) in its interpretation.

Base: All children who use the internet and reported the specific risk (* only children aged from 11-16) for internet safety; in the second case, the relationship was significant only for restrictive mediation and active mediation in internet safety.

Opportunities

For opportunities, we tested the relationship between type of mediation applied by parents (for each parental mediation strategy, see Chapter 17) and level of activities and digital skills developed by children. For each mediation type we analysed the variance, which considers whether parents apply (at least) one mediation strategy or no strategy, and child's age (9–12 versus 13–16) to test for a significant difference in the average number of activities and skills developed among mediated and non-mediated children and whether this difference varies with age.

As far as the number of activities is concerned (see Figure 18.1), in all cases the difference between means was significant ($p<0.001$), except for monitoring among 13- to 16-year-old children, where the number of activities engaged in by monitored and non-monitored children

Figure 18.1: Parental mediation and children's online activities

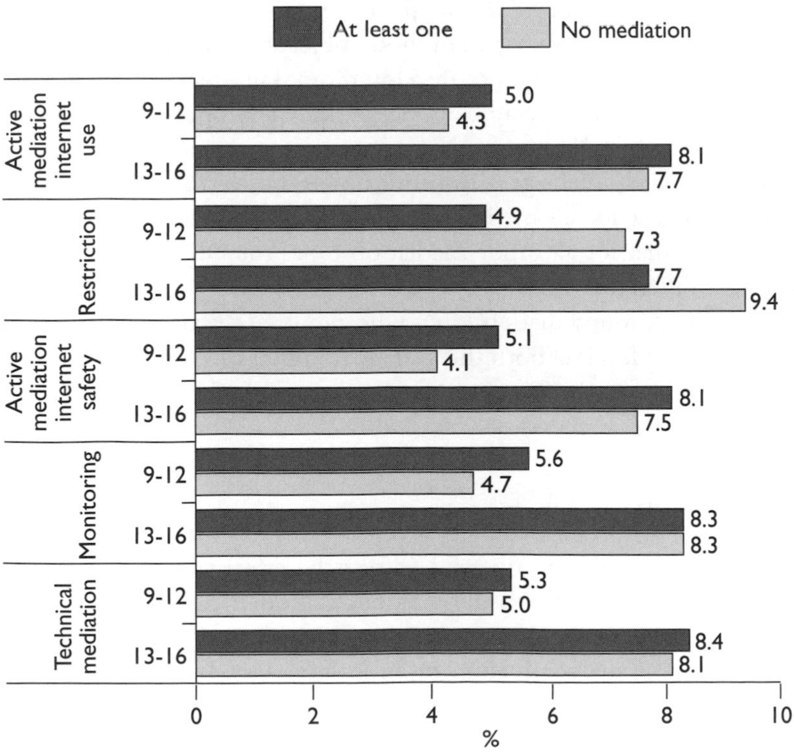

Base: All children who use the internet.

was very similar. Although differences in means were not very high, in most cases mediation seemed to coincide with more activities as the average number of activities was higher among mediated children. There is an exception to this tendency: children subject to restrictive mediation engaged in a much smaller number of activities than non-mediated children. Also, while for other mediation types differences between means were small, in the case of restrictive strategies, there were clear differences among mediated and non-mediated children. The interaction term of age and mediation is significant for all mediation types. We conducted separate one-way analyses of variance tests for each mediation type and each age group. Most mediation types stimulate children to develop more activities online, but restrictive mediation has the opposite effect, and for all children. Thus, restrictions reduce opportunities for children on the internet while other mediation strategies seem to stimulate activities, with higher numbers of activities among children subject to mediation and especially younger children. In this case, the relationship may suggest that parents' monitoring of their child's use of the internet gives the child more freedom when online or encourages them to spend more time online.

For skills (see Figure 18.2), the pattern was very similar to mediated children – with the exception of those subject to restrictive mediation. Mediated children seemed to develop more skills than other children. The difference in the average number of skills developed was significant ($p<0.001$) for all mediation types and age groups. Again the interaction in terms of age (noted age groups are 11-12 and 13-16) and mediation was significant for all mediation types except restrictive mediation, suggesting that for all other mediation types the effect of mediation on skills differed by age.

Overall, we found that children who reported restrictive mediation showed lower levels of both the average numbers of activities and skills, whereas other mediation types tended to increase both activities and competencies.

Conclusion

It is difficult, as already noted, to assess the effectiveness of different types of mediation due to the incidence of other influencing factors in children's relationships with the internet and because of the complexity of analysing them in an isolated way. It is also not clear which strategies are used to prevent risk and harm and which strategies are a response to them. Nonetheless, the findings point towards some valuable conclusions.

Figure 18.2: Parental mediation and children's online skills

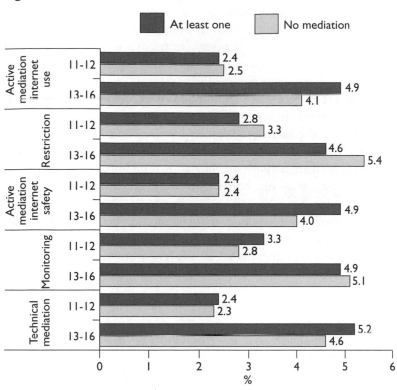

Base: All children aged 11-16 who use the internet.

First, regarding children's exposure to different risks, only some of the mediation strategies – mainly restriction and monitoring – show a significant relationship with risks, but in most of the cases children who report at least one type of mediation show a lower incidence of risk experiences. Differences in exposure to risk are not generally large, except for monitoring and, especially, restrictive mediation, where mediated children show a much lower risk incidence. These results confirm the findings in Livingstone and Helsper (2008) and Kirwil et al (2009) that show that restrictive mediation reduces children's exposure to risks.

However, among those who have encountered risks, children are more likely to report harm if their use has been mediated by their parents. Although it is difficult to explain this result, changes in parental mediation as a consequence of some exposure to risk may explain this finding. In other words, it seems more likely that the experience of harm results in increased parental mediation than the other way around.

Regarding opportunities, the most significant finding is the negative effect of restrictive mediation on the average number of children's online activities and digital skills. As Livingstone and Helsper's (2008, p 596) findings also show, although restrictive mediation has some benefits, 'the costs in terms of reducing teenagers' freedom to interact with peers online must be weighed against the advantages in developing safety guidance directed at parents and teenagers'.

Based on these findings, and in line with previous research on television and the internet (Weaber and Barbour, 1992; Nathanson, 1999; Hasebrink et al, 2009), it is difficult to identify an ideal model of parental mediation; however, they allow one important conclusion. Although restrictions on internet use may reduce risk, parents need to carefully weigh this benefit against the degree to which mediation, especially restrictive mediation, reduces the number of opportunities available to their children from using the internet. It would seem advisable that restrictive mediation especially should be confined to very particular cases.

References

Austin, E.W. (1993) 'Exploring the effects of active parental mediation of television content', *Journal of Broadcasting & Electronic Media*, vol 37, no 2, pp 147-58.

Buckingham, D. (2000) *After the death of childhood: Growing up in the age of electronic media*, Cambridge: Polity Press.

Bushman, D.J. and Anderson C.A. (2001) 'Media violence and the American public: scientific facts versus media misinformation', *American Psychologist*, vol 56, no 6/7, pp 477-89.

Bybee, C., Robinson, D. and Turow, J. (1982) 'Determinants of parental guidance of children's television viewing for a special subgroup: mass media scholars', *Journal of Broadcasting*, vol 26, pp 697-710.

Cohen, J. (1992) 'A power primer', *Psychological Bulletin*, vol 112, no 1, pp 155-9.

Duimel, M. and de Haan, J. (2009) *ICT en Cultuur: Het gebruik door tieners* [*ICT and culture: How teenagers use the opportunities*], The Hague: Netherlands Institute for Social Research.

Eastin, M.S., Greenberg, B.S. and Hofschire, L. (2006) 'Parenting the internet', *Journal of Communication*, vol 56, pp 486-504.

European Commission (2008) *Towards a safer use of the internet for children in the EU: A parents' perspective*, Luxembourg: European Commission.

Goodman, I.R. (1983) 'Television's role in family interaction: a family systems perspective', *Journal of Family Issues*, vol 4, no 2, pp 405-24.

Hasebrink, U., Livingstone, S., Haddon, L. and Ólafsson, K. (2009) *Comparing children's online opportunities and risks across Europe: Cross-national comparisons for EU Kids Online*, London: London School of Economics and Political Science.

Kirwil, L., Garmendia, M., Garitaonandia, C. and Martinez Fernandez, G. (2009) 'Parental mediation', in S. Livingstone and L. Haddon (eds) *Kids online: Opportunities and risks for children*, Bristol: The Policy Press, pp 99-115.

Lin, C.A. and Atkin, D.J. (1989) 'Parental mediation and rulemaking for adolescent use of television and VCRs', *Journal of Broadcasting & Electronic Media*, vol 33, no 1, pp 53-67.

Livingstone, S. (2007) 'Strategies of parental regulation in the media-rich home', *Computers in Human Behavior*, vol 23, no 3, pp 920-41.

Livingstone, S. and Bober, M. (2006) 'Regulating the internet at home: contrasting the perspectives of children and parents', in D. Buckingham and R. Willett (eds) *Digital generations*, Mahwah, NJ: Lawrence Erlbaum Associates, pp 93-113.

Livingstone, S. and Helsper, E.J. (2008) 'Parental mediation of children's internet use', *Journal of Broadcasting & Electronic Media*, vol 52, no 4, pp 581-99.

Livingstone, S., Haddon, L., Görzig, A. and Ólafsson, K. (2011) *Risks and safety on the internet: The perspective of European children. Full findings*, London: London School of Economics and Political Science.

Lwin, M.O., Stanaland, A.J.S. and Miyazaki, A.D. (2008) 'Protecting children's privacy online: how parental mediation strategies affect website safeguard effectiveness', *Journal of Retailing*, vol 84, pp 205-17.

Nathanson, A.I. (1999) 'Identifying and explaining the relationship between parental mediation and children's aggression', *Communication Research*, vol 26, pp 124-43.

Nathanson, A.I. (2001) 'Parent and child perspectives on the presence and meaning of parental television mediation', *Journal of Broadcasting & Electronic Media*, vol 45, pp 210-20.

Oswell, D. (1999) 'The dark side of cyberspace: internet content regulation and child protection', *Convergence: The Journal of Research into New Media Technologies*, vol 5, no 4, pp 42-62.

Prensky, M. (2001) 'Digital natives, digital immigrants', *On the Horizon*, vol 9, no 5, pp 1-2.

Ribak, R. and Turow, J. (2003) 'Internet power and social context: a globalization approach to web privacy concerns', *Journal of Broadcasting & Electronic Media*, vol 47, no 3, pp 328-49.

Selwyn, N. (2003) 'Doing IT for the kids: re-examining children, computers and the information society', *Media, Culture & Society*, vol 25, no 3, pp 351-78.

Silverstone, R. and Haddon, L. (1996) 'Design and the domestication of ICTs: technical change and everyday life', in R. Silverstone and R. Mansell (eds) *The politics of information and communication technologies: Communication by design*, Oxford: Oxford University Press, pp 44-74.

Silverstone, R., Hirsch, E. and Morley, D. (1992) 'Information and communication technologies and the moral economy of the household', in R. Silverstone and E. Hirsch (eds) *Consuming technologies: Media and information in domestic spaces*, London: Routledge, pp 15-31.

Valkenburg, P.M., Krcmar, M., Peeters, A.L. and Marseille, N.M. (1999) 'Developing a scale to assess three styles of television mediation: "instructive mediation", "restrictive mediation", and "social coviewing"', *Journal of Broadcasting & Electronic Media*, vol 43, no 1, pp 52-66.

van der Bulck, J. and van den Bergh, B. (2000) 'Parental guidance of children's media use and conflict in the family', in B. van den Bergh and J. van der Bulck (eds) *Children and media: Interdisciplinary approaches*, Leuven-Apeldoorn: Garant, pp 131-50.

van der Voort, T., Nikken, P. and van Lil, J.E. (1992) 'Determinants of parental guidance of children's television viewing: a Dutch replication study', *Journal of Broadcasting & Electronic Media*, vol 36, pp 61-74.

Varenne, H. (1996) 'Love and liberty: the contemporary American family', in A. Burguiere, C. Klapisch-Zuber et al (eds) *A history of the family volume II: The impact of modernity*, Cambridge, MA: Harvard University Press, pp 416-41.

Weaber, B. and Barbour, N. (1992) 'Mediation of children's televiewing', *Families in Society*, vol 73, pp 236-42.

Yeung, W.J., Sandberg, J.F., Davis-Kean, P.E. and Hofferth, S.L. (2001) 'Children's time with fathers in intact families', *Journal of Marriage and Family*, vol 63, pp 136-54.

NINETEEN

Effectiveness of teachers' and peers' mediation in supporting opportunities and reducing risks online

Veronika Kalmus, Cecilia von Feilitzen and Andra Siibak

Introduction

A distinctive feature of the EU Kids Online survey is that it asked children about mediation of internet use practised by parents, teachers and peers (Livingstone et al, 2011). This chapter starts from the assumption that these three agents, by virtue of their different social relationships with children, play distinct roles in influencing children's online experiences, both positively and negatively. The chapter evaluates the effectiveness of mediation by teachers and peers in supporting online opportunities and in reducing risks and harm.

Teachers' mediation

Parents often expect teachers to act as coach or facilitator in relation to their children's internet use, in other words to act 'in loco parentis' (Wishart, 2004, p 200). There is a quite long tradition of research examining the role of parental mediation of their children's (new) media use. Work on teachers' mediation, however, is more recent (cf Hasebrink et al, 2009; Inan et al, 2010; Zhao et al, 2011), and most studies (see, for example, Wishart, 2004; Berrier, 2007) do not differentiate between different types of mediation, or ask how teachers' mediation is related to online risks and harm experienced by children.

Research indicates that teachers are concerned mainly with internet safety. Rather than engaging in active mediation, teachers tend to apply rules that restrict children's internet use, but which also hinder the development of good internet safety practices and reduce the chances for children to explore online opportunities (Wishart, 2004).

Although the support given by teachers has been shown to have a weak influence on children's intrinsic motivation to go online, some of the motivation for children to explore the internet is related to use of this technology for school assignments (Zhao et al, 2011). In relation to more advanced usage than is required for schoolwork, however, teachers' mediation is the weakest predictor of children's online content creation (Kalmus et al, 2009b).

Peer mediation

The role played by peers may also be important for shaping the online practices of young people (cf Hasebrink et al, 2009; see also Chapter 1 in this volume), although relatively little is known about their influence. Livingstone and Bober (2005) found that compared to parents and teachers, peers may be less important for help related to using the internet, but may have a significant impact on young people's intrinsic motivations for going online (Zhao et al, 2011). Peers are also the main sources of information about new opportunities on the internet (Kalmus, 2007). For instance, they are the biggest influence on establishing a social networking site profile and contributing to a blog (Kalmus et al, 2009b). In some cases, however, this positive influence may become confused with more ordinary peer pressure, often referred to as the most frequent reason for taking up creative (for example, blogging, social networking) and interactive (for example, instant messaging) uses of new media (boyd, 2008; Siibak, 2009). To our knowledge, there are no studies that focus on the possible relations between peer mediation and risky and harmful experiences online.

Research questions and measures

First, we explore the extent to which support from teachers and peers is related to children's uptake of online opportunities and their levels of digital literacy and safety skills. Second, we investigate whether and how teachers' mediation and peer mediation are related to the main online risks and harm experienced by children. We address this through several focused research questions. These questions enquired about the strength of the relationship between teachers' mediation compared to peer mediation, and children's digital skills and range of online opportunities and whether particular mediating activities worked in the same direction. We analyse sociodemographic variations in the effectiveness of teachers' and peers' mediation: do a child's age and gender affect the relation between support from teachers and friends, and his or her digital skills and online opportunities? We also examine how strongly teachers' mediation versus peer mediation is related to children's experiences of online risks and harm and investigate whether particular mediating activities work in the same direction.

Finally, we explore whether there are substantial differences among European countries with regard to correlations between teachers' and peers' mediation on the one hand, and children's digital skills and online opportunities, and experiences of risks and harm on the internet on the other.

Teachers' mediation was measured by the responses to eight questions that asked about *restrictive mediation, active mediation of the child's internet use* and *active mediation of the child's internet safety* (see the Appendix at the end of this volume for more details). Positive responses to the eight questions were summed into an *index of teachers' mediation.* Average intercorrelation among the eight items (the Cronbach's alpha) was 0.86.

Peer mediation was measured by the responses to five questions on *active mediation of internet safety* (see the Appendix at the end of this volume). Positive responses were summed into an index of peer mediation; the Cronbach's alpha was 0.80.

To measure the scope of *online opportunities* we used the cumulative index of 17 online activities undertaken by children in the month previous to the survey (see Chapter 6 in this volume). The level of children's *digital literacy and safety skills* was measured by the cumulative index of eight specific skills (only 11- to 16-year-olds were included in these questions) (see Chapter 7).

For *risks* online, we used a general measure indicating whether the child experienced any of seven risks listed in the EU Kids Online survey: that is, seeing a sexual image on the internet; being bullied on the internet; seeing or receiving sexual messages on the internet ('sexting'); contacting someone on the internet not met with face to face; meeting an exclusively online contact offline; seeing potentially harmful user-generated content; and suffering misuse of personal data (41 per cent of children had encountered at least one of these risks – see Livingstone et al, 2011).

As the measure of *harm* we used the general question: 'In the past 12 months, have you seen or experienced something on the internet that has bothered you in some way?' (12 per cent answered 'yes' to this question – see Livingstone et al, 2011).

Teachers and peers supporting children's digital skills and online opportunities

Table 19.1 shows that the indexes of teachers' and peers' mediation are positively correlated to the number of children's digital literacy and safety skills, and the number of online activities engaged in, in the previous month. The correlations are statistically significant also if we control for age. Thus, support from teachers and friends is related to increased digital skills and range of online activities that children engage in. The effect size of the correlations is small, however, which suggests there are other aspects that influence children's digital skills and opportunities.

The very small difference between teachers' and peers' effectiveness, particularly with regard to supporting digital literacy and safety skills, is surprising; it might be expected that teachers' mediation of children's internet use would be directed towards safeguarding and coaching, while friends might be more likely to influence their peers to explore the 'digital jungle' further and exploit more online opportunities.

To analyse whether particular mediating activities practised by teachers and peers work in the same direction, we compared the mean values of the indexes of children's digital skills and online activities, between two groups: children who reported a specific mediating activity, and children who did not. Almost every one of the mediating activities undertaken by teachers and peers was positively related to children's digital skills and online activities: the mean values of the indexes were significantly higher ($p<0.001$) among the group of children who reported a specific mediating activity, compared to those who did not. In the case of one item of peer mediation ('Have your friends ever explained why some websites are good or bad?'), the difference of the mean values of the index of digital skills was not significant. Only one mediating activity practised by teachers ('Have your teachers ever helped you in the past when something has bothered you on the internet?') showed opposite directions: children who

Table 19.1: Correlations between the indexes of children's digital skills and online activities, and mediation by teachers and peers

	Teachers' mediation		Peer mediation	
	Pearson's *r*	Partial correlations (controlling for age)	Pearson's *r*	Partial correlations (controlling for age)
Skills	0.12	0.10	0.10	0.07
Activities	0.10	0.07	0.15	0.12

Note: All correlations are significant at $p<0.001$.
Base: All children who use the internet.

reported this mediating activity showed a lower mean value for skills (*M*=4.09, *SD*=2.76) than children who did not (*M*=4.21, *SD*=2.64; *p*<0.01). It is likely that less skilled children consult their teachers for help if something online bothers them.

To analyse sociodemographic influences we compared the correlations of the indexes of children's digital skills and online activities, and mediation by teachers and peers, among age groups (see Figure 19.1) and among boys and girls (see Figure 19.2). To test the significance of the interaction effect between child's age and teachers' and peers' mediation, and child's gender and teachers' and peers' mediation, we employed linear regression analysis where the dependent variables were digital skills and online activities, and teachers' mediation, peer mediation, age, gender and interactions between them were the predictors.

The role of teachers in advancing children's skills does not change much with children's increasing age; the part they play in widening horizons and increasing children's online opportunities diminishes as children get older (see Figure 19.1). The importance of peer mediation for increasing skills and opportunities decreases as children get older. Table 19.2 demonstrates that there are significant interaction effects between peer mediation and age, and between teachers' mediation and age.

Figure 19.1: Correlations between the indexes of children's digital skills and online activities, and mediation by teachers and peers (in age groups)

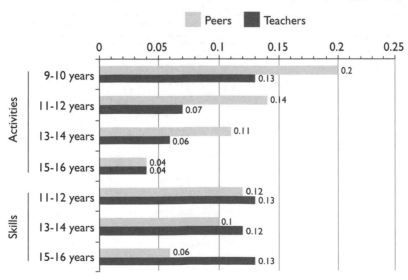

Base: All children who use the internet.
Note: Pearson's correlations; all significant at *p*<0.001.

Figure 19.2: Correlations between the indexes of children's digital skills and online activities, and mediation by teachers and peers (among boys and girls)

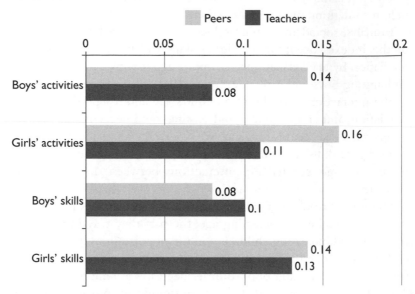

Base: All children who use the internet.
Note: Pearson's correlations; all significant at *p*<0.001.

Table 19.2: Teachers' mediation, peer mediation, a child's age and gender, and interaction effects in predicting children's digital skills and online activities

Predictors	Dependent variable: skills	Dependent variable: activities
Teachers		
Teachers' mediation	0.248***	0.043***
Age	0.425***	0.489***
Gender[1]	0.085***	0.060***
Teachers' mediation × age	–0.123*	–0.115***
Teachers' mediation × gender	–0.037**	–0.011
R^2	0.179	0.232
Peer		
Peer mediation	0.381***	0.317***
Age	0.440***	0.493***
Gender[1]	0.081***	0.049***
Peer mediation × age	–0.277***	–0.191***
Peer mediation × gender	–0.036**	0.010
R^2	0.177	0.246

Notes: [1] 0 = female, 1 = male.
Beta coefficients; * *p*<0.05, ** *p*<0.01, *** *p*<0.001.
Base: All children who use the internet.

Support from teachers and friends is slightly more important for girls than for boys in relation to increasing digital skills (Figure 19.2). This is expected, since girls tend to be less self-confident about their digital skills (see, for example, Henwood et al, 2000) and are more likely to seek and be more receptive to social support. Table 19.2 shows that the interaction effects between teachers' mediation and gender, and between peer mediation and gender, are significant for predicting skills. Boys are more likely to report higher levels of digital skills and a greater number of online activities compared to girls.

Teachers' and peers' mediation related to online risks and harm

The general measure for whether the child has experienced any of seven online *risks* is strongly positively correlated to the child's age (r_{pb}=0.37), total time per week on the internet (r_{pb}=0.32), number of online activities (r_{pb}=0.45) and number of digital skills (r_{pb}=0.34; all significant at $p<0.001$). These four variables are correlated positively, but much more weakly with harm (age – r_{pb}=0.06; time on the internet – r_{pb}=0.11; online activities – r_{pb}=0.15; and digital skills – r_{pb}=0.12; all significant at $p<0.001$). In the following correlations for teachers' and peers' mediation, and online risks and harm, we control for these four variables.

Table 19.3 presents the indexes of teachers' mediation and peer mediation, which are very weakly, but positively related to online risks and harm, that is, both risks and harm are slightly more likely with higher levels of teacher or peer support. When we include the control variables, three of the positive correlations are even more weakly significant. The findings are similar for different combinations of the control variables, although the coefficients vary slightly in size.

Table 19.3: Correlations between children's experiences of online risks and harm, and mediation by teachers and peers

	Teachers' mediation		Peer mediation	
	Point biserial correlations r_{pb}	Partial correlations*	Point biserial correlations r_{pb}	Partial correlations*
Risks	0.05	ns	0.09	0.03
Harm	0.06	0.05	0.07	0.05

Notes: * Controlled for a child's age, total time spent on the internet per week, the number of online activities and the number of digital skills.
All correlations are significant at $p<0.001$.
Base: All children who use the internet.

Table 19.4 (*phi* coefficients) shows that the correlations between particular mediating activities and the measure of children's experience of any risks are mostly not significant, but that the correlations with children's experience of harm are mostly positive, although weak. One of the stronger positive correlations is for harm, and the statement: 'Friends have helped you in the past when something has bothered you on the internet' (*phi*=0.13). The correlation is stronger among 13- to 14-year-olds (*phi*=0.16) and 15- to 16-year-olds (*phi*=0.15; all significant at *p*<0.001). Children who had experienced harm on the internet more often responded positively (46 per cent) to this statement than children who had not (24 per cent). This finding suggests that when children have experienced harm, they often turn to their friends to discuss it. This is supported by the analysis of the main sources of social support (see Chapter 17), which shows that following a negative online experience, children are more likely to discuss it with their friends. (Analogical findings and conclusions about parental mediation changing after a child has experienced online harm are presented in Chapter 18.) It would therefore seem that important mediation by peers (as well as parents and teachers) occurs *retroactively*, with children being active agents in this process and initiating the mediation when needed.

Table 19.4: Correlations (*phi* coefficients) between the indicators of mediation by teachers and peers, and children's experiences of online risks and harm

	Teachers' mediation		Peer mediation	
	Risks	**Harm**	**Risks**	**Harm**
Helped you when you found something difficult to do or find on the internet	ns	0.03	0.05	0.03
Explained why some websites are good or bad	−0.02*	0.04	ns	0.03
Suggested ways to use the internet safely	ns	0.04	ns	ns
Suggested ways to behave towards other people online	ns	0.02*	ns	0.03
Helped you in the past when something has bothered you on the internet	ns	0.05	0.07	0.13
Made rules about what you can do on the internet at school	0.02*	0.03	na	na
Talked to you about what you do on the internet	ns	0.04	na	na
In general, talked to you about what you would do if something on the internet ever bothered you	ns	0.04	na	na

Notes: * Correlation is significant at *p*<0.05; all other correlations are significant at *p*<0.001.
Base: All children who use the internet.

Comparing countries

Significant positive correlations between mediation by teachers and peers, and children's digital skills and online opportunities are universal across the countries with only a few exceptions. The effectiveness of teachers' mediation for advancing children's digital and safety skills is relatively high in Denmark and Portugal (r=0.24, p<0.001), but not discernible in France, Lithuania, Slovenia and Turkey. The strongest positive correlations between teachers' mediation and children's range of online activities are in Denmark (r=0.25), Austria (r=0.24) and Norway (r=0.23; all significant at p<0.001), while there is no significant correlation in Turkey. The irregularity of these cases makes their explanation difficult. While the lack of effectiveness of teachers' mediation in some countries may in part be because in these countries a relatively small percentage of teachers describe themselves as computer and internet-competent in classroom situations (41 per cent in France and 51 per cent in Lithuania compared to the average of 60 per cent in 21 European countries), this does not apply to Slovenia where the same indicator (76 per cent) is the second highest in Europe (there are no data for Turkey; Empirica:LearnInd, 2006).

Correlations between peer mediation and digital skills are highest for Germany (r=0.26), Norway and Romania (r=0.23; all significant at p<0.001), but support from friends does not contribute significantly to children's digital skills in the Czech Republic, France and Slovenia. The influence of peers for increasing online opportunities is universal across all European countries: significant positive correlations ranging from r=0.06 (p<0.05) for Turkey to r=0.29 (p<0.001) for Germany, Hungary and Norway.

It is also difficult to discern any specific country patterns for the relation between teachers' or peers' mediation, and online risks or harm. There are few significant correlations between *teachers' mediation* and *risks*. Four countries show significant weak negative correlations: Cyprus (r_{pb}=–0.13, p<0.01), Denmark (r_{pb}=–0.11, p<0.05), Greece (r_{pb}=–0.08, p<0.05) and Spain (r_{pb}=–0.14, p<0.001). And five countries show significant, but weak positive correlations between *teachers' mediation* and *harm*: the Czech Republic (r_{pb}=0.12, p<0.01), Germany (r_{pb}=0.08, p<0.05), the Netherlands (r_{pb}=0.10, p<0.01), Romania (r_{pb}=0.11, p<0.01) and Slovenia (r_{pb}=0.10, p<0.05).

Significant weak negative correlations between *peer mediation* and *risks* occur for four countries: Bulgaria (r_{pb}=–0.07, p<0.05), Finland (r_{pb}=–0.10, p<0.05), Lithuania (r_{pb}=–0.12, p<0.01) and Spain (r_{pb}=–0.08, p<0.05), and the correlations for Belgium (r_{pb}=0.08, p<0.05) and

Germany (r_{pb}=0.09, p<0.05) are significant and weakly positive. The correlations are significant and weakly positive for *peer mediation* and *harm*: in Austria (r_{pb}=0.11, p<0.01), Denmark (r_{pb}=0.17, p<0.001), Estonia (r_{pb}=0.10, p<0.01), Greece (r_{pb}=0.11, p<0.01), Italy (r_{pb}=0.11, p<0.01), the Netherlands (r_{pb}=0.08, p<0.05), Norway (r_{pb}=0.15, p<0.001), Portugal (r_{pb}=0.09, p<0.05), Sweden (r_{pb}=0.11, p<0.01), Slovenia (r_{pb}=0.10, p<0.01) and the UK (r_{pb}=0.13, p<0.001).

Conclusion

Support from teachers and from friends has a positive effect on increasing children's digital skills and the range of their online activities. However, this importance decreases for older children, and especially with regard to increasing opportunities. We can conclude that social support from teachers and friends for learning about new online activities is stronger when children begin their climb up the 'ladder of online opportunities' (cf Livingstone and Helsper, 2007). More advanced uses of the internet, particularly in relation to creative online activities, likely depend more on children's individual agency and priorities (cf Kalmus et al, 2009a), and are not easily fostered by social learning and support.

Given that parents, teachers and peers play distinct roles in influencing children's online experiences, the very small difference between the effectiveness of teachers' and peers' mediation is surprising. The universal pattern of a significant and positive correlation between peer mediation and online activities, however, might indicate the stronger role of peers in encouraging children's advance on the 'ladder of online opportunities'. While many parents expect their children will acquire primary digital literacy and safety skills at school (cf Chapter 1 in this volume), very few teachers in several European countries are equipped to provide them.

We also found that teachers' and peers' mediation are weakly, although significantly positively correlated with harm experienced on the internet. Perhaps, contrary to common expectations, teachers' and peers' mediation does not reduce children's negative online experiences. However, without this mediation, it is possible that, over time, more children would experience risks and harm. It would seem that, often, mediation by peers (and parents and teachers) is triggered after a child had a negative online experience. This hypothesis, and considering children as active agents initiating mediation when required, should be investigated in future research.

An implication for policy is that these types of social mediation, particularly the role played by teachers, have a great, and unrealised, potential for reducing online risks and harm by improving children's online competences.

Acknowledgements

Cecilia von Feilitzen wishes to thank The International Clearinghouse on Children, Youth and Media at Nordicom, University of Gothenburg, Sweden, for supporting her work with this chapter. Veronika Kalmus and Andra Siibak acknowledge support from the Estonian Science Foundation (grant No 8527) and the Estonian Ministry of Education and Research (target financed project No 0180017s07).

References

Berrier, T. (2007) 'Sixth-, seventh-, and eighth-grade students' experiences with the internet and their internet safety knowledge', Unpublished doctoral dissertation (http://wenku.baidu.com/view/13add01455270722192ef7a9.html?from=related).

boyd, d. (2008) 'Why youth ♥ social network sites: the role of networked publics in teenage social life', in D. Buckingham (ed) *Youth, identity, and digital media*, London: The MIT Press, pp 119-42.

Empirica:LearnInd (2006) *Benchmarking access and use of ICT in European schools 2006: Final report from Head Teacher and Classroom Teacher Surveys in 27 European Countries*, Bonn: Empirica (http://ec.europa.eu/information_society/eeurope/i2010/docs/studies/final_report_3.pdf).

Hasebrink, U., Livingstone, S., Haddon, L. and Ólafsson, K. (2009) *Comparing children's online opportunities and risks across Europe: Cross-national comparisons for EU Kids Online*, London: London School of Economics and Political Science (http://eprints.lse.ac.uk/24368/1/D3.2_ReportCross_national_comparisons-2nd-edition.pdf).

Henwood, F., Plumeridge, S. and Stepulevage, L. (2000) 'A tale of two cultures? Gender and inequality in computer education', in S. Wyatt, F. Henwood, N. Miller and P. Senker (eds) *Technology and in/equality: Questioning the information society*, London, New York: Routledge, pp 111-28.

Inan, F.A., Lowther, D.L., Ross, S.M. and Strahl, D. (2010) 'Pattern of classroom activities during students' use of computers: relations between instructional strategies and computer applications', *Teaching and Teacher Education*, vol 26, no 3, pp 540-6.

Kalmus, V. (2007) 'Estonian adolescents' expertise in the internet in comparative perspective', *Cyberpsychology: Journal of Psychosocial Research on Cyberspace*, vol 1, no 1 (www.cyberpsychology.eu/view.php?cisloclanku=2007070702).

Kalmus, V., Runnel, P. and Siibak, A. (2009a) 'Opportunities and benefits online', in S. Livingstone and L. Haddon (eds) *Kids online: Opportunities and risks for children*, Bristol: The Policy Press, pp 71-82.

Kalmus, V., Pruulmann-Vengerfeldt, P., Runnel, P. and Siibak, A. (2009b) 'Online content creation practices of Estonian schoolchildren in a comparative perspective', *Journal of Children and Media*, vol 3, no 4, pp 331-48.

Livingstone, S. and Bober, M. (2005) *UK children go online. Final report of key project findings* (www.citizensonline.org.uk/site/media/documents/1521_UKCGO-final-report.pdf).

Livingstone, S. and Helsper, E.J. (2007) 'Gradations in digital inclusion: children, young people and the digital divide', *New Media & Society*, vol 9, no 4, pp 671-96.

Livingstone, S., Haddon, L., Görzig, A. and Ólafsson, K. (2011) *Risks and safety on the internet: The perspective of European children. Full findings*, London: London School of Economics and Political Science.

Siibak, A. (2009) *Self-presentation of the 'digital generation' in Estonia*, Tartu: Tartu University Press.

Wishart, J. (2004) 'Internet safety in emerging educational contexts', *Computers & Education*, vol 43, no 1/2, pp 193-204 (http://bitbee44.myweb.uga.edu/portfolio/article.pdf).

Zhao, L., Lu, Y., Wang, B. and Huang, W. (2011) 'What makes them happy and curious online? An empirical study on high school students' internet use from a self-determination theory perspective', *Computers & Education*, vol 56, no 2, pp 346-56.

TWENTY

Understanding digital inequality: the interplay between parental socialisation and children's development

*Ingrid Paus-Hasebrink, Cristina Ponte,
Andrea Dürager and Joke Bauwens*

Introduction

Across Europe, economic restructuring and immigration from disadvantaged countries show that relations related to inequality are dynamic and persistent. Given the diversity of European countries, in social, cultural and economic terms, the gaps between rich and poor take various forms and occur to differing degrees. However, in all countries social inequalities are a major concern in social politics. Political economists point to the dynamics of inclusion and exclusion that continue to affect the communicative rights and competencies of considerable numbers of citizens (Murdock and Golding, 2004). Hence, the increasing emergence of a society that is mediated, experienced and encountered more and more through the internet is raising continuous questions about whether and how vulnerable families are getting the best out of the social, informational, educational and cultural opportunities of online technologies (Livingstone, 2009).

The younger children are, the more parental education is required for them to use the internet safely and exploit its potentials. Since lower parental educational status often leads to less confidente parental mediation, we need to provide the resources for children to draw on to build competencies for using the internet and coping with online risks. As children get older, they achieve more unrestricted access to and use of the internet, and parents tend to refrain from intervening in their personal time and space (see, for example, Wang et al, 2005; Livingstone and Helsper, 2008; Bauwens et al, 2009). However, the degree of liberty children enjoy and how they deal with it is often the product of a particular family culture. Drawing on sociological and psychological theoretical perspectives, this chapter investigates two research questions:

How does parents' formal education influence children's internet use?

How does children's development (by age) interact with their family background in terms of an autonomous and competent use of the internet?

The interrelation between these two processes, that is, parental socialisation and development by age, helps us understand the interplay between children's activities in dealing with the internet and how their parents mediate this.

Building on existing empirical work, first, we discuss the persistent importance of social inequality in information and communications technology (ICT) use in industrialised countries; second, we propose a theoretical framework that includes children and parents' individual agency and how they are interlinked with respect to their societal status. The focus here is on parents' formal education as a key indicator of socioeconomic status. Finally, based on a multilevel analysis of the EU Kids Online data set, we test our theoretical ideas and hypotheses and ask how parental socialisation shapes young people's online competences, and how children's development by age interacts with structural processes and the dynamics of socialisation.

Social inequality, children's vulnerability and internet use

National levels of modernisation affect which digital tools are available in the home, but patterns of children and adolescents' internet use seem to differ not so much across countries as across social positions (see Rothbaum et al, 2008; Vekiri, 2010). Adolescents with higher socioeconomic status and two-parent households are more likely to have internet access in the home than single-parent and lower-status families. Also, it is more likely that the former group will use it more often for specific informational purposes, whereas (especially) young people from lower-status family backgrounds use the internet more for utilitarian information, communication and gaming (Peter and Valkenburg, 2006; Notten et al, 2009). However, among vulnerable youth, the results are not clear-cut. For example, minority ethnic groups use ICT for both entertainment and more functional reasons (see Mertens and d'Haenens, 2010).

In Europe, where most countries show high levels of internet penetration in households that include children and young people, the traditional binary division (access/no access) is inevitably being replaced by a 'more nuanced description that considers differing levels of access and how they limit and enable actual use of the online environment' (Clark et al, 2005, p 410), envisaged in the notion proposed by these authors of an 'access rainbow'. Therefore, an evaluation of the quality of children's internet use should pay attention to 'the array of opportunities in people's everyday lives' and a contextualisation of 'the online with the offline' (Livingstone and Helsper, 2007, p 692). Examples of this broader approach stress the social divide (see, for example, Livingstone and Helsper, 2007; Lebens et al, 2009). However, digital inequality and vulnerability are not only a straightforward matter of manifest, objectifiable parameters (for example, infrastructure, access, diploma); they are also related to the cultural-cognitive, latent processes of sense-making, which are often complex and contradictory.

For example, socially disadvantaged parents tend to join in the main discourses about the educational potential of the internet, but frequently lack knowledge about computers and, because ICT is not part of their everyday lives, lack support from their social circles. They tend to couch what they think the importance of ICT might be for their children, in generic terms, influenced by various sources within the culture; they would like to support their children's use of ICT, but find it difficult due to their lack of cultural resources and digital experience (Paus-Hasebrink and Bichler, 2008). Some parents clearly categorise themselves as not an ICT-type person, and apply to the internet the prevailing 'public scripts' (Hoover et al, 2004; Clark et al, 2005) or concerns about children and media (that is, the invasion of media in children's life and the necessity to control content). In general, less well educated parents express 'more reservations and ambivalences [towards] ... the rhetoric on ICT proficiency for their children's prospects for success' (Clark et al, 2005, p 423). Likewise, they are more concerned about ICT as entertainment than as informational media. Within families, the different approaches of family members to screen media might also reflect the knowledge gap between those with and those without digital expertise; familial tension and shame can result from parents being less experienced and knowledgeable about digital media than their children (Clark, 2009).

Empirical knowledge about social inequality and ICT use reveals that differences among families often coincide with societal status and position. However, there is insufficient research on how children and young people themselves respond to their parents' strategies and orientations towards digital media, how their 'access rainbows' are affected by material resources and cultural dispositions, and the interactions with age.

Understanding the linkage between social disadvantage and developmental tasks

It has been argued, from different perspectives, drawing on Gramsci, Bourdieu and Giddens' ideas, that structures become resources for subjective sense-making, individual agency and knowledgeable action (see, among others, Willis, 1977, p 171). Hence, macro determinants, such as class location, region and educational background, are not only reproduced in everyday life, but are also negotiated and worked through in subjective feelings of confidence, trust, self-esteem and self-worth. It is precisely in the linkage between sociostructural and psychological aspects that children's capabilities to cope with their developmental tasks need to be understood (see Havighurst, 1972 [1953]). Bridging between sociological and psychological theories avoids a social-reductionist perspective on commonalities and especially on differences among children and parents from socially disadvantaged milieux. Although the socioeconomic conditions of everyday life are the main context for the consideration of internet usage and parental mediation, psychological aspects of individual sense-making are as important to identify the configurations of parents and children's internet usage and the challenges that emerge – risks as well as harm.

The obvious first core starting point is Bourdieu's work, which provides a theoretical framework for the interaction between structure and action. Bourdieu (1977) explains how in the social field, in which social action takes place, certain aims are established, particular patterns of action are socially 'accepted' (Weiß, 2000, p 47) and certain patterns of orientation and perspectives can be built (see Paus-Hasebrink and Bichler, 2008). Patterns of action and orientation are culturally routed and refer to people's societal status. When they are transformed into everyday opportunities and competences, they not only influence individual actions and processes of social and personal identity development, but also interact with people's own subjective sense-making of societal conditions.

What does this mean for parents' mediation of their children's internet use, and children's own capacities to deal with the internet? Studies that look at the connection between socioeconomic factors and parental mediation of adolescents' internet use show that supportive socialisation conditions are found mainly in families with higher levels of formal education (Grundmann, 2000, p 97). The chances of developing more resilience to cope with the challenges of everyday life and its related media and internet offers are unequally distributed (Paus-Hasebrink and Bichler, 2008). It is important to point out that it is not the socioeconomic and sociocultural conditions per se, but rather the (inter)acting capabilities of parents that play a role in shaping the development and experiences of children (Paus-Hasebrink and Bichler, 2008). Paus-Hasebrink and Bichler's longitudinal study on media socialisation of socially disadvantaged children in Austria shows that lower educated parents use inconsequent mediation strategies, such as aggressive banning of media use on one occasion, and then allowing it on another. The authors highlight that there are no systematic and transparent rules on media education that children can learn.

The second core set of work draws on developmental psychology and the concept of developmental tasks (Havighurst, 1972 [1953]). Within this theoretical framework the focus is on how children develop and learn to deal with specific challenges encountered in everyday life and the day-to-day environment. In order to cope with the developmental tasks related to different age stages, and their accompanying daily life experiences, young people seek to acquire expertise. Thus, the growing up process is built on dealing un/successfully with developmental tasks, for example, building stable social relationships with peers and dealing with the self. Developmental tasks — closely linked to the child's age, gender and social background — shape perceptions and action when dealing with the environment. Studies show that children use the internet to acquire a view of the world, to build contacts with peers and friends, and to deal with the self (see Paus-Hasebrink, 2010; Subrahmanyam and Šmahel, 2011).

Hypotheses and data analysis

From the research overview and theoretical framework we can derive a set of hypotheses, which start from the idea that there are tangible social differences in parental mediation. All the hypotheses aim to test the interaction between parental socialisation (structuring children's experiences) and development by age (leaving room for children's agency). Although other parental variables, such as gender, age and internet use, are considered, we operationalise social differences in terms of education, since this is an important indicator of social stratification.

First, the education systems differ across Europe, as does the number of years of compulsory/expected education (Eurostat, 2008), thus, the distribution of parental education in Europe varies significantly. According to the data on the highest educational level achieved within a household,[1] in around 46 per cent of European households education falls into the upper or post-secondary level category. In almost a quarter of households the education level is lower secondary or tertiary. In 14 per cent of households the highest level of education is primary. In terms of the expected duration of education (Eurostat, 2008), we can build five clusters of countries that differ significantly (see Figure 20.1). For example, people in Belgium, Finland and Sweden continue in education for the longest time (almost 20 years on average), whereas in Turkey (13.6 years) – which constitutes a single cluster – and in Bulgaria and Cyprus (15.5 years in average) they continue in education for the shortest time. At both country and cluster level the EU Kids Online data are very similar to Eurostat data. Some countries, for example, Bulgaria and France, Portugal and Germany, differ from the Eurostat clusters (the first pair are categorised as higher educated, the second pair lower educated).[2]

> H1: Higher educated parents are more confident about using the internet[3] than lower educated parents.

The correlation between parental education and internet confidence is highly significant ($r=0.17$;[4] $p=0.00$); the higher the educational level of the household, the higher the level of confidence reported by the respondent. To test this hypothesis further, we considered other parental indicators that might influence parents' internet confidence, that is, age, gender and frequency of use.[5] Regression analysis shows[6] that frequency of use has the highest influence on confidence ($\beta=0.29$; $p=0.00$). Education level has a smaller impact ($\beta=0.08$; $p=0.00$), but higher than age ($\beta=-0.07$; $p=0.00$) and gender ($\beta=0.07$; $p=0.00$). Hence, the model as a whole was highly significant ($R^2=0.11$; $p=0.00$) and shows that parents who use the internet more frequently, who live in households with a higher level of education, who are younger and who are male, are more confident about using the internet ($R^2=0.11$). If we control for the effects of single countries in the regression, we find a significant impact of country on internet confidence; the R-squared rises to almost 20 per cent if we include country as a control variable and the beta weight of the education variable rises to 0.12.

Figure 20.1: Distribution of the highest educational level within the household, by country and Eurostat cluster (2008)

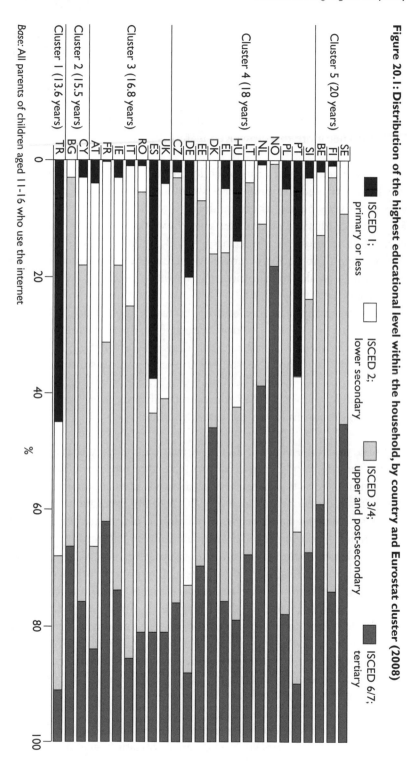

Base: All parents of children aged 11-16 who use the internet

H2: Because higher educated parents can give their children more help than less educated parents (because they are more confident), the children of better educated parents will be more competent at dealing with the internet than the children of lower educated parents.

H2.1: More highly educated parents mediate their children's use of the internet more than lower educated parents.

To evaluate active mediation of children's internet use,[7] we find that the higher the educational level within the household, the more parents actively mediate their children's internet use (r=0.18; p=0.00). For active mediation of internet safety,[8] we find a highly significant correlation in the same direction (r=0.13; p=0.00). There are weak, but still significant, positive correlations between the education and mediation subscales for monitoring[9] (r=0.04; p=0.01) and technical mediation[10] (r=0.09; p=0.00).

It is interesting that in the case of restrictive mediation[11] (r=–0.07; p=0.00) our hypothesis is not supported, since in this case the correlation is in the other direction. Thus, the lower the educational level within a household, the higher the score on this subscale.

H2.2: Children from higher educated families are more competent[12] than children from lower educated households.

The scale of children's (aged 11+) internet competency, that is, digital literacy and safety skills, measured through eight items (see Chapter 7 in this volume), shows that parental education is significantly correlated to the child's internet competence (r=0.17; p=0.00). It might be assumed, therefore, that especially active mediation leads to greater internet competency. However, the data provide a nuanced picture, in which active mediation of the child's internet safety (r=0.10; p=0.00) seems to have the biggest association with increasing internet competence. Active mediation of the child's internet use (r=0.03; p=0.00) and technical mediation (r=0.06; p=0.00) show a weak significance for increased competence. The other two subscales of mediation show that restrictive mediation (r=–0.39; p=0.00) lead to lower level internet competency, whereas monitoring has no significant effect (r=–0.01; p=0.39), but this does not mean that they cannot contribute to decreasing the possibility of encountering online risks.

H2.3: Children's internet competency is influenced by child's age and by parental factors such as parents' education, age and gender, frequency of internet use, confidence in using the internet, as well as all the mediation subscales.

Finally, if we consider all the relevant indicators (parental education, age and gender, frequency of internet use, confidence in using the internet as well as all the mediation subscales and child's age) in one model for children's digital literacy and safety skills, we find it is highly significant (0.00), with an R-squared of 0.26. After parental confidence in using the internet, parental education is the only non-significant variable in the model ($p=0.13$). The most influential variable is child's age ($\beta=0.30$; $p=0.00$); in a single model child's age explains 18 per cent of the variance: the older the child, the more their internet competence. The second most influential variable is the mediation subscale for restrictive mediation ($\beta=-0.29$; $p=0.00$); using aspects of restrictive mediation tends to reduce internet competence. Child's age and restrictive mediation together explain 24 per cent of the variance. All other factors have only a small impact on internet competence (see Table 20.1). It would seem that parents' education is a moderating variable since it is significantly correlated with several variables. Also, children's internet competence seems to be influenced more by child-related factors, such as child's age, than by parental socialisation. If we control for country in the regression, the R-squared increases to 29 per cent.

Table 20.1: Regression for predicting internet competency (digital literacy and safety skills)

Variables	Unstandardised regression-coefficients (b)	Standardised regression-coefficients (β)	Significance (p)
(Constant)	−2.46		0.00
Child's age	0.46	0.30	0.00
Restrictive mediation	−0.23	−0.29	0.00
Technical mediation	0.19	0.08	0.00
Active mediation of internet safety	0.09	0.06	0.00
Parent's age	0.02	0.06	0.00
Monitoring	0.07	0.04	0.00
Frequency of parental internet use	0.18	0.03	0.00
Active mediation of internet use	−0.05	−0.03	0.00
Parent sex	−0.12	−0.02	0.00
Parental confidence in using the internet	0.05	0.02	0.08
Education (highest in household)	0.06	−0.01	0.13

Questions: Which of these things do you know how to do on the internet? Please say yes or no to each of the following... (Scale shows the sum of all eight skills answered with yes.)
Base: All children aged 11-16 who use the internet.

H3: The likelihood of children feeling more competent than their parents[13] decreases with children's age and parental level of education.

Comparing children's self-assessment of their internet knowledge with that of their parents, we find a highly significant, and quite high correlation between the statement 'I know more about the internet than my parents' and the child's age (r=0.42; p=0.00). The older the child, the higher the level of agreement with this statement. Moreover, the lower the educational level within a household, the greater the children's belief that they know more about the internet than their parents (r=–0.13; p=0.00).

Also, the older the age of the parents, the more competent the child considers him or herself to be in comparison (r=0.19; p=0.00). Older parents also feel less confident than younger parents about using the internet (r=–0.05; p=0.00). And there is a correlation between the way children assess their internet competency compared to their parents' abilities, and parents' frequency of internet use and confidence in using the internet. The higher the frequency of parents' use of the internet (r=0.14; p=0.00) and the more confident they feel (r=–0.14; p=0.00), the less children claim to know more than their parents.[14]

H4: The competency gap[15] between the children of highly and less well educated parents is higher for younger than for older children.

There are highly significant differences in the way children's internet competence depends on parents' education and age development. Table 20.2 shows internet competence increases significantly with age, but the family's educational background continues to play a determining role as children get older. Thus, contrary to our hypothesis, the digital gap among children increases with age. Children from lower educational level backgrounds claim to know more about the internet than their parents, but compared to children of their own age who come from more privileged educational milieux, they have fewer skills.

Conclusion

As expected by our theoretical framework, we found evidence of the influence of children's age and parental education on children's internet competency. Our results stress the dynamic interplay between children's age and parental education. Also, the findings from this chapter suggest that, in order to understand the intricate interplay between child-related and social factors and their relevance for improving children's

Table 20.2: Internet competence (digital literacy and safety skills) in dependency of the child's age and the highest education of the parents within a household

Children's age	Parents' education				
	Primary or less	Lower secondary	Upper or post-secondary	Tertiary	All
11-12	2.04 (+/–0.15)	2.71 (+/–0.12)	2.91 (+/–0.10)	3.25 (+/–0.12)	2.81 (+/–0.06)
13-14	3.63 (+/–0.16)	4.10 (+/–0.12)	4.42 (+/–0.09)	4.90 (+/–0.12)	4.33 (+/–0.06)
15-16	4.03 (+/–0.18)	5.05 (+/–0.13)	5.38 (+/–0.09)	5.99 (+/–0.11)	5.24 (+/–0.06)
All	3.29 (+/–0.10)	3.95 (+/–0.08)	4.29 (+/–0.07)	4.73 (+/–0.06)	4.16 (+/–0.04)

Questions: Which of these things do you know how to do on the internet? Please say yes or no to each of the following 0... (Scale shows the sum of all eight skills answered with yes.)

Note: 95% confidence intervals in brackets.

Base: All children aged 11-16 who use the internet.

internet competencies, more complex levels of both quantitative and qualitative analysis are needed.

Confirming previous studies, the data show that better-educated parents try to support and mediate their children through more active mediation, whereas lower-educated families tend to set regulations and use technical means (see Rothbaum et al, 2008; Vekiri, 2010). The reason for this might be that they feel less sure about actively mediating their children because they are less knowledgeable and confident about using the internet, which also means that they use it less often. However, there is likely to be a social desirability bias, as especially higher educated parents tend to answer survey questions in line with socially, politically and culturally correct views on parenthood. Other studies on the media socialisation of socially disadvantaged children show that parents have less time and competencies to actively support their children through face-to-face discussion. Hence they fall back on restrictive regulations, which, most of the time, are relatively inconsequential (Paus-Hasebrink and Bichler, 2008; Bauwens et al, 2009).

Our results show that children from lower socioeconomic backgrounds tend to claim to know more about the internet than their parents, and generally acquire internet skills independently or from other people than their parents; see also Sonck et al (2012), Chapter 7 in this volume. However, Sonck et al point out that children with more highly educated parents show higher levels of self-reported skills and diversity of use, but lower levels of self-confidence. Although children are often described as 'digital natives', who 'naturally' acquire the skills to engage successfully with the newest media technologies, the facts show that the structural inequalities in the information society that prevent socially vulnerable citizens from participating fully in economic, political and cultural life also affect children. These inequalities are highly relevant to the notion of the access rainbow, and parents and children's ability to engage with their online surroundings or not.

Notes

[1] Although we have information on the educational level of the interviewee, the other parent or carer and the household head if not the interviewee, we focus on the variable measuring the highest level of education within the household.

[2] As the distribution of education varies widely among countries, the country variable might correlate to the education variable. Therefore, focusing only on parental education might divert attention from the influence of country. In the regression analysis we try to control for country effects and show their impact, through the increase in the R-squared, which means that adding single countries in the regression explains more of the variance of the derived variable.

[3] QP218: How confident are you in using the internet? (Four-step scale: not at all confident to very confident.)

[4] All correlations are based on a Spearman calculation.

[5] QP217 recoded: How often do you use the internet? (Almost every day – once or twice a week – once or twice a month – less often.)

[6] Beta-weights are reported.

[7] Sum of QP220a–e answered with yes. (Scale from 0–5.)

[8] Sum of QP222a–e answered with yes. (Scale from 0–5.)

[9] Sum of QP223a–d answered with yes. (Scale from 0–4.)

[10] Sum of QP2241–d answered with yes. (Scale from 0–4.)

[11] Sum of QP221a–f answered with 'can do this anytime' or with 'can only do this with permission'. (Scale from 0–12.)

[12] Internet competency is measured through a combination of children's digital literacy and safety skills. (QC320a–d and QC321a–d: Which of these things do you know how to do on the internet? Please answer yes or no to each of the following... *[Scale shows the sum of all eight skills answered with yes (DCskillsNM)]*.)

[13] DCwebableA: I know more about the internet than my parents (9-16). (Scale: not true – a bit true – very true.)

[14] QP218: How confident are you in using the internet? (Four-step scale: not at all confident to very confident.) QP217: How often do you use the internet? (Four-step scale: almost every day to less often.)

[15] Measured through digital literacy and safety skills (see note 12 above).

References

Bauwens, J., Pauwels, C., Lobet-Maris, C., Poullet, Y. and Walrave, M. (2009) *Cyberteens, cyberrisks, cybertools. Tieners en ICT, risico's en opportuniteiten.* [*Cyberteens, cyberrisks, cybertools. Teenagers and ICT, risks and opportunities*], Gent: Federaal Wetenschapsbeleid/Academia Press.

Bourdieu, P. (1977) *Outline of a theory of practice on the basis of ethnological Kabyle society*, Cambridge: Cambridge University Press.

Clark, L.S. (2009) 'Digital media and the generation gap: qualitative research on US teens and their parents', *Information, Communication & Society*, vol 12, no 3, pp 388-407.

Clark, L.S., Demont-Heinrich, C. and Weber, S. (2005) 'Parents, ICT, and children's prospects for success: interviews along the digital "access rainbow"', *Critical Studies in Media Communication*, vol 22, no 5, pp 409-26.

Eurostat (2008) *Expectancy of education. Tables* (http://epp.eurostat.ec.europa.eu/tgm/table.do?tab=table&init=1&language=de&pcode=tps00052&plugin=1).

Grundmann, M. (2000) 'Kindheit, Identitätsentwicklung und Generativität' ['Childhood, identity development and generativity'], in A. Lange and W. Lauterbach (eds) *Kinder in Familie und Gesellschaft zu Beginn des 21sten Jahrhunderts* [*Children in family and society at the beginning of the 21st century*], Stuttgart: Lucius & Lucius, pp 87-104.

Havighurst, R.J. (1972 [1953]) *Developmental tasks and education* (3rd edn), New York: McKay.

Hoover, S., Clark, L.S. and Alters, D. (2004) *Media, home and family*, New York: Routledge.

Lebens, M., Graff, M. and Mayer, P. (2009) 'Access, attitudes and the digital divide: children's attitudes towards computers in a technology-rich environment', *Educational Media International*, vol 46, no 3, pp 255-66.

Livingstone, S. (2009) *Children and the internet*, London: Polity Press.

Livingstone, S. and Helsper, E.J. (2007) 'Gradations in digital inclusion: children, young people and the digital divide', *New Media and Society*, vol 9, no 4, pp 671-96.

Livingstone, S. and Helsper, E.J. (2008) 'Parental mediation of children's internet use', *Journal of Broadcasting & Electronic Media*, vol 52, no 4, pp 581-99.

Mertens, S. and d'Haenens, L. (2010) 'The digital divide among young people in Brussels: social and cultural influences on ownership and use of digital technologies', *The European Journal of Communication*, vol 35, no 2, pp 187-207.

Murdock, G. and Golding, P. (2004) 'Dismantling "the digital divide": rethinking the dynamics of participation and exclusion', in A. Calabrese and C. Sparks (eds) *Towards a political economy of culture: Capitalism and culture in the twenty-first century*, Lanham, MD: Rowman & Littlefield, pp 244-60.

Notten, N., Peter, J., Kraaykamp, G. and Valkenburg, P.M. (2009) 'Research note: digital divide across borders – a cross-national study of adolescents' use of digital technologies', *European Sociological Review*, vol 25, no 5, pp 551-60.

Paus-Hasebrink, I. (2010) 'Das Social Web im Kontext der Entwicklungsaufgaben junger Menschen' ['On the role of the social web in the framework of young people's developmental tasks'], *Medien Journal*, vol 34, no 4, pp 20-34.

Paus-Hasebrink, I. and Bichler, M. (2008) *Mediensozialisationsforschung. Theoretische Fundierung und Fallbeispiel sozial benachteiligte Kinder* [*Research on media socialisation. Theoretical basis and case study socially disadvantaged children*], Innsbruck: Studienverlag.

Peter, J. and Valkenburg, P.M. (2006) 'Adolescents' internet use: testing the "disappearing digital divide" versus the "emerging digital differentiation" approach', *Poetics*, vol 34, pp 293-305.

Rothbaum, F., Martland, N. and Beswick Jannsen, J. (2008) 'Parents' reliance on the web to find information about children and socio-economic differences in use, skills and satisfaction', *Journal of Applied Developmental Psychology*, vol 29, no 2, pp 118-28.

Subrahmanyam, K. and Šmahel, D. (2011) *Digital youth. The role of media in development*, New York: Springer.

Vekiri, I. (2010) 'Socioeconomic differences in elementary students' ICT beliefs and out-of-school experiences', *Computers & Education*, vol 54, no 4, pp 941-50.

Wang, R., Bianchi S.M. and Raley, S.B. (2005) 'Teenagers' internet use and family rules: a research note', *Journal of Marriage and Family*, vol 67, no 5, pp 1249-58.

Weiß, R. (2000) 'Praktischer Sinn, soziale Identität und Fern-Sehen. Ein Konzept für die Analyse der Einbettung kulturellen Handelns in die Alltagswelt' ['Practical meaning, social identity and television], *Medien und Kommunikationswissenschaft*, vol 48, no 1, pp 42-62.

Willis, P. (1977) *Learning to labor: How working class kids get working class jobs*, Tiptree: Anchor Press Ltd.

TWENTY-ONE

Similarities and differences across Europe

Bojana Lobe and Kjartan Ólafsson

Introduction

Funding bodies and policy makers have increasingly called for comparative research. The result is that many researchers have initiated or participated in projects aimed at achieving some kind of multinational comparison (Livingstone, 2003). The EU Kids Online project is an example of such a study. In a review of about 400 studies of children and the internet, Hasebrink et al (2009) concluded that although it was possible to conduct a systematic and structured analysis of the existing research, it was both demanding in terms of research efforts and the claims made should be 'treated as indicative rather than conclusive' (see Hasebrink et al, 2009, p 95). At the same time, the analysis indicated that there are important cross-country differences in terms of children's risks and opportunities on the internet. However, building on this uneven evidence base (Staksrud et al, 2009) it was difficult to extract the information required to conduct cross-national comparisons of other than the most commonly studied issues. Therefore, the second EU Kids Online project was designed to produce a rigorous, cross-nationally comparative quantitative evidence base of children's internet use across Europe. This chapter investigates similarities and differences across countries in children's usage of the internet and their encounters of risk. Countries are clustered, and national contexts are explored, to show how contextual factors at country level shape children's patterns of online use, opportunities and risks.

Logic of cross-country comparison

There are several reasons for conducting comparative research. One is to investigate the universality and uniqueness of findings based on nation-specific data. This requires comparison with data on other countries.

Broadening the research perspective and providing fresh insights into the issues applying to a particular national context are part of the value of such research, and show how this approach can reveal significant knowledge gaps and point to new (or previously hidden) variables and factors that affect the phenomenon under scrutiny (Hantrais and Mangen, 1996, p 2; Livingstone, 2003, p 478). However, cross-national research must cope with many methodological as well as practical challenges. Methodological problems include selection of the research unit (mostly the nation-state), sampling and comparability of data issues and more practical issues (which also may have serious methodological implications) such as differences in professional academic culture, and standards of writing and communication (cf Livingstone, 2003).

Mervin Kohn (1989) proposed a popular typology of cross-national comparison. It distinguishes between four approaches according to their principal focus: (i) nation as the object of study (juxtaposition of data/reports from particular nations); (ii) nation as the context of study (testing universal hypotheses across a sample of contrasting nations); (iii) nation as the unit of analysis (relations among the dimensions along which nations vary systematically); and (iv) nation as part of a larger international/global system.

The analysis in this chapter applies the first and third of these principles. Countries are the objects of analysis in a cluster analysis determining what is distinctive (or not) about a country, and are the units of analysis in a multilevel analysis. The objective is to explain patterns of similarities and, particularly, differences among countries, by examining the national-level contextual factors that explain how and why nations vary systematically.

Country versus individual-level data

Understanding country-level differences is important for at least two reasons. First, some of the variance that appears at the individual level might be a function of country-level factors. An investigation of individual-level factors only could promote an 'individualist fallacy' (Subramanian et al, 2009) created by macro-level inferences based on micro-level relations. For example, we might find that at the individual level, family income is positively related to encountering online risks, and then notice that GDP per capita is higher in the UK than in Spain. The assumption might follow that children in Spain are less likely to encounter risks online than their UK counterparts, which is not necessarily the case. Also, focusing only on individual-level variables might suggest that contextual effects either do not matter or are simply summaries of individual-level factors. Thus, it is important to link individual-level analyses to the relevant cross–country context.

Second, it is important for the cross–country perspective to take account of individual-level information in trying to explain country-level differences. Variance observed at country level can be a function of individual-level factors; if we focus on national-level findings only, this could prompt an ecological fallacy (Steenbergen and Jones, 2002), in which inferences are made about micro-level (individual-level) relations based on relations between macro-level averages. '

It is also important to recognise that it is meaningful to analyse children's internet use at the national level. Our reason for analysing the country level is not because we do not have information on individuals but because, in our view, specific country-level factors matter for individual-level outcomes. Important structures that can be related theoretically to important outcome variables at the individual level (education system, internet regulation) are organised by country. We hypothesise that the ways in which countries organise such systems as education and internet regulation influences how children experience risks and opportunities online. The focus on country-level factors is therefore not just to remove 'noise' (for example, possible correlation between socioeconomic status and country), but also to understand how country-level and individual-level factors behave.

Country-level differences in online use and risks

The EU Kids Online project concluded that northern European countries tend to be 'high use, high risk', southern European 'low use, variable risk' and countries in eastern European countries 'new use, new risk' (Hasebrink et al, 2009). The analysis in this chapter, based on directly comparable measures applied across all countries, proposes a comparable classification based on the EU Kids Online survey data, generated through analysis of countries clustered[1] according to levels and types of usage and risk. Our proposed classification is presented in Table 21.1.

Broadly speaking the results are in line with what Hasebrink et al (2009) concluded in their review of the existing evidence base, that high levels of use in a particular country seem to go hand in hand with a higher probability of children in a particular country encountering risks. However, using data from the 2010 EU Kids Online survey it is possible to take a step further and also look at the types of risks. Based on a cluster analysis, the countries participating in the survey have been grouped into four categories (for a further discussion of the analysis,

Table 21.1: Country classification based on children's online use and risk (based on the *EU Kids Online* survey findings)

Risk	Level of usage	
	Lower	**Higher**
Lower	Spain, Ireland, Portugal, Turkey (Group 1, lower use, some risk) Austria, Belgium, Germany, France, Greece, Hungary, Italy (Group 2, lower use, lower risk)	
Higher		Cyprus, Finland, the Netherlands, Poland, Slovenia, the UK (Group 3, higher use, some risk) Bulgaria, Czech Republic, Denmark, Estonia, Lithuania, Norway, Romania, Sweden (Group 4, higher use, higher risk)

see Lobe et al, 2011). The categories should be regarded as ideal types rather than fixed and non-overlapping groups.

- Group 1: low use but some risks. In these countries the level of usage is below average and also the overall likelihood of encountering risks. However, for some particular risks, the likelihood of encountering them is higher than would be expected given the overall level of usage.
- Group 2: low use and low risks. In these countries the level of usage is below average, and the overall likelihood of encountering risks is also relatively low.
- Group 3: high use and some risks. In these countries the level of usage is high, and also the overall likelihood of encountering risks. However the likelihood of encountering risks is somewhat lower than would be expected, given the level of usage, or it does not apply to all risks.
- Group 4: high use and high risks. These countries follow the general pattern where higher levels of usage go hand in hand with a higher likelihood of encountering risks.

Perhaps the most interesting group of countries are those where relatively high levels of use are not associated with a similarly high likelihood of encountering risks. Compared with previous findings, children in Greece, Italy and Cyprus seem to have increased their usage without a commensurate increase in risk, while in the UK and Poland, risks have been reduced alongside maintenance of already high use of the internet. This may reflect national differences in awareness-raising campaigns, or the strategies used by parents to mediate their children's internet use (see Livingstone et al, 2011).

Explaining country differences

Various national contexts may shape children's patterns of online use, opportunities and risks (Hasebrink et al, 2009; Livingstone et al, 2011). We therefore examined national socioeconomic stratification, regulatory framework, technology infrastructure, education system and cultural values. For this part of the comparative process, countries were the units of analysis.

Secondary-level data in the form of contextual factors that constitute the national context were collected from various sources. In the first stage of the comparative process, we tested several contextual factors for each area. Based on assumptions about the effects of specific contextual factors (see Hasebrink et al, 2009), we retained one or two factors per area, although we had concerns about the quality and availability of external indicators available for each factor in each country. The following contextual factors were tested in the analysis (we did not include contextual factors for cultural values due to lack of data for a number of countries):

- *GDP per capita* as a contextual factor for *socioeconomic stratification*. GDP in US dollars refers to the total market value of all final goods and services produced in a country in a given year, which is equal to total consumer investment and government spending plus the value of exports, minus the value of imports.

- *Press Freedom Index* and the responses to a question in the 2005 Eurobarometer survey of parents in Europe ('Are filtering/blocking tools barring access to certain websites when your child uses the internet?') serve as contextual factors for the *regulatory framework*. The Press Freedom Index reflects the freedom of expression afforded to journalists and news organisations, and the efforts made by state authorities to ensure respect for this freedom. In this scale a lower score is greater press freedom. The 2005 Eurobarometer (2006) question refers to the percentage of parents (whose children accessed the internet from their own computers or the family's computer at home) who said they used filtering software.

- *Broadband penetration* and *number of years since 50 per cent of households had access to the internet* as contextual factors for the *technological infrastructure*. The first refers to the percentage of households in each country with a broadband connection. The second refers to the number of years (from 2004 to 2010) since 50 per cent of households in the country had access to the internet (minimum 0 years, maximum 7 years).

- *Expected years of schooling* and *percentage of schools that offer and use computers in classrooms* as contextual factors for *educational system*. The first contextual factor is based on the years of compulsory schooling in a country. The second refers to the percentage of schools that provide and use one or more computers in classroom teaching (among all schools that use computers for educational purposes).

Table 21.2 presents the effects of each contextual factor on risk and usage. A multilevel analysis was conducted using the mixed linear models available in SPSS. Individual-level dependent variables were checked using the multilevel unstructured modelling method, with the national-level independent variable defined as a fixed effect. We did not define random effects because there was only one independent variable.

None of the contextual factors at country level had a statistically significant effect on children's internet use at the individual level. However, there were some interesting patterns that are discussed below. In contrast to usage, risk seems to be significantly affected by contextual factors, at least to some degree.

Table 21.2: Contextual factors effects on usage and risk

National context area	Contextual factors	Usage	Risk
Socioeconomic stratification	GDP	No significant effect	Small positive and statistically significant effect (6.2% variance of risk explained on a country level)
Regulatory framework	Press Freedom Index	No significant effect	Small negative and statistically significant effect (4.4% variance of risk explained on country level)
Technological infrastructure	Broadband penetration	No significant effect	Small positive and statistically significant effect (6.2% variance of risk explained on a country level)
Technological infrastructure	Number of years since 50% of households had internet access	No significant effect	Small positive and statistically significant effect (6.2% variance of risk explained on a country level)
Education system	Expected years of schooling	No significant effect	No significant effect
Cultural values	Lack of availability	Not tested	Not tested

Socioeconomic stratification

In the previous EU Kids Online work (see Hasebrink et al, 2009), it was hypothesised that national wealth would be related to internet use, and that higher socioeconomic status households would be more likely to provide their children with access to the internet, which, in turn, would lead to more and more frequent use of the internet among more advantaged children.

Our analysis shows that GDP has no statistically significant influence on children's internet use. However, we can see that the wealthier Nordic countries, the UK and the Netherlands, along with countries with low levels of GDP and recent broadband introduction, such as Bulgaria, Romania, Lithuania, Estonia and the Czech Republic, have very high usage.

For risk, the analysis suggests a positive and statistically significant effect of GDP per capita on the degree of risk from using the internet. Children in the wealthier Nordic countries are significantly more likely to encounter a higher degree of online risk. For Italy, Spain, Ireland and the UK, however, higher GDP is not associated with a higher level of online risk, and children in Lithuania, Estonia and the Czech Republic encounter more risk despite a low GDP.

Regulatory framework

The previous EU Kids Online project research found no straightforward relation between development of a regulatory framework and children's experience online. Our multilevel analysis shows that parental use of filtering and blocking, measured at country level, has no statistically significant effect on either usage or risks. This finding may be disconcerting for policy makers. However, there are indications that, in certain countries such as the UK, Ireland and Portugal, high levels (over 43 per cent) of use of filtering/blocking tools are associated with low levels of online risk.

Press freedom has no statistically significant effect on internet usage, despite expectations that a freer media might mean more widespread usage of the internet. However, our analysis suggests that countries with the lowest Press Freedom Index and, therefore, greater press freedom, such as Norway, Denmark and Sweden, are more likely to have high internet use. Turkey, the country with least freedom of the press, has one of the lowest internet usage levels among children in Europe.

Our analysis also suggests that in countries with greater freedom of the press, such as the Nordic and Baltic countries, there is a statistically significantly greater likelihood that children will encounter more risks. It is possible that more freedom of expression means less censorship of the internet, which might result in more online risk for children. However, Slovenia has low levels of press freedom, but relatively high online risks from using the internet.

Technological infrastructure

The first EU Kids Online project hypothesised that cross-national variations in the amount of children's use and online risks depended mostly on cross-national variations in the technology infrastructure as a crucial dimension influencing children's online experience.

Our analysis shows that neither broadband penetration nor the number of years since 50 per cent of households had access to the internet has a statistically significant effect on usage. Nevertheless, there are some interesting patterns. In the Nordic countries and the UK, where 50 per cent of households have had access to the internet for six years or more, daily internet use is among the highest and daily use is similarly relatively high in countries with more recent internet access, such as the Baltic and eastern European countries.

Broadband penetration has a positive and statistically significant effect on online risks. Children from countries with higher broadband penetration are significantly more likely to encounter more online risks. In the Nordic countries and Estonia there is high broadband penetration and children encounter more online risks. There are many initiatives to promote children's rights and freedoms in the Nordic countries, which may explain the higher risks in these countries.

At the same time, children in eastern European countries, such as Bulgaria and Romania, encounter more online risk despite lower national broadband penetration, while in Ireland, Spain, the UK and Germany, which have high broadband penetration, the risks are lower, which is perhaps due to active efforts to reduce risk and to raise safety awareness.

Thus, broadband access contributes to more online risk in both 'new risk' countries, such as the countries of eastern Europe, and 'high risk' countries, such as the Nordic countries. Also, in most countries where 50 per cent of households have had access to the internet for more than 3.7 years, it is statistically significantly more likely that children will experience more online risks. These countries are Slovenia, the Nordic countries and Estonia; Ireland and the UK have longer years of usage and a lower degree of risk. Likewise, for countries where 50 per cent of households have had internet access for less than approximately three-and-a-half years, it is statistically more likely that children will experience fewer online risks. The two countries where more recent access is accompanied by more risks are the Czech Republic and Lithuania. This might suggest that in the group of countries where low risk is associated with very recent mass internet use, the risks will rise to the levels in longer internet-using countries.

Educational system

The previous EU Kids Online project (Hasebrink et al, 2009) showed that cross-country differences in children's online use can be explained, in part, by difference in general education. It was hypothesised that higher levels of general education (more years) in a country would lead to higher use of the internet among children. It was also assumed that higher education would increase children's digital literacy and safety skills.

The present analysis shows that neither expected years of schooling nor percentage of schools that offer and use computers in classrooms has a statistically significant effect on online usage or online risks. However, when we include education system contextual factors in our analyses we find that education has a positive and significant effect on children's digital skills (considered as ability to delete records of which sites visited; changing privacy settings on social networking sites; blocking unwanted messages; and searching for information on safe use of the internet). In countries with 15 years of schooling or more, children are more likely to have above-average digital skills.

Similarly, among children from countries where a higher percentage of schools provide computers and use computers in the classroom (45 per cent or more of schools), it is statistically significantly more likely that they will have better digital skills. These countries are the Nordic countries, wealthy north west European countries (the UK, the Netherlands, France, Belgium and Denmark), and Portugal and Slovenia. However, there are some countries where levels of computer use in the classroom are low but the children have good digital skills (the Baltic countries, Poland and Spain). Hungary and Italy have the lowest number of computers in classrooms and the lowest level of digital skills among children.

Conclusion

The EU Kids Online survey of 2010 showed considerable differences in children's risks and opportunities across countries. Compared with differences across demographics such as age, gender and socioeconomic status, the magnitude of the differences observed across countries is comparable to those observed by age. It has been hypothesised (see Hasebrink et al, 2009) that these differences can be attributed to country-level factors. In this chapter we tested four contextual factors: socioeconomic stratification, regulatory framework, technological infrastructure and education system using available country-level data. The fifth contextual factor (cultural values) could not be tested. The overall pattern that appears is that these factors have a small but significant correlation with risks but not with the level of use.

We also looked at how the individual countries group together in terms of risks and level of internet use. The overall conclusions in the full findings report (see Livingstone et al, 2011) are applicable to the findings from this analysis: the more children in a country who use the internet daily, the more children in that country will encounter one or more risks. This also holds at the individual level: children who use the internet on a daily basis are more likely than those who do not to experience one or more risk factors.[2] In addition, private and/ or mobile access may be an important factor explaining variations in risk encounters across countries.

The country-level analysis reveals that factors associated with socioeconomic stratification, regulatory framework, technological infrastructure and education system all have significant effects on children's experience of online risk, across countries. Specifically, children in wealthier countries (measured by GDP) encounter more online risk but, arguably, these countries are also well placed to provide more accessible and user-friendly safety resources for children and parents. Also, countries with more press freedom, such as the Nordic and Baltic countries, are more likely to have children who encounter online risk. This may be because of lower internet regulation, and strategies that ensure safety without introducing censorship are thus needed. Degree of broadband penetration, and length of time in which most people have had internet access, are associated with greater online risks, but not greater online activities among children. This suggests that, while children are motivated to use the internet everywhere in Europe, higher quality access is bringing more risks than are adequately dealt with by policy makers (whether industry, state or education). In countries with 15+ years of schooling on average, children are more likely to have better digital skills, as are children from countries where more schools use computers in the classroom. Education clearly has a positive role to play in supporting digital skills, literacies and citizenship, and should be supported across all countries.

It is clear that there are a large number of factors that play a role in accounting for differences across countries, and the task of constructing clear patterns or strong associations among variables is difficult. The effect-size of the country-level factors is generally not very big, and it has to be considered that the indicators available are either quite general or even only indirectly linked to the factors of interest. In particular, identifying comparable cultural values indicators on a country level and including them into analysis might uncover further significant patterns explaining varieties not only in risk but also in use. Further, identifying alternative country-level indicators for regulatory framework (such as targeted country measures that are used to regulate internet use) and educational system (more closely linked to what children learn in schools on how to use internet) might offer clearer patterns of use. The findings in this chapter only indicate the current balance of similarities and differences across countries. Therefore, further analysis is required to uncover more subtle trends affecting children's experiences in particular countries or regions within Europe.

Notes

[1] K-means clustering procedure on country means with usage and risk variables. The objective is to find centres of natural clusters in the data set to identify countries with similar characteristics in terms of use, activities and risks on the internet. Note that the cluster analysis is based on the patterning of variables rather than on absolute values.

[2] Correlation at country level, $r=0.74$ and at individual level, $r=0.30$; both statistically significant, $p<0.001$.

References

Eurobarometer (2006) *Safer internet*, Eurobarometer 64.4, Special No 250, Luxembourg: Directorate General, Information Society and Media, European Commission.

Hantrais, L. and Mangen, S. (1996) 'Method and management of cross-national social research', in L. Hantrais and S. Mangen (eds) *Cross-national research methods in the social sciences*, London: Pinter, pp 1-12.

Hasebrink, U., Livingstone, S., Haddon, L. and Ólafsson, K. (eds) (2009) *Comparing children's online opportunities and risks across Europe: Cross-national comparisons for EU Kids Online* (2nd edn), London: London School of Economics and Political Science.

Kohn, M.L. (1989) *Cross-national research in sociology*, Newbury Park, CA: Sage Publications.

Livingstone, S. (2003) 'On the challenges of cross–national comparative media research', *European Journal of Communication*, vol 18, no 4, pp 477-500.

Livingstone, S., Haddon, L., Görzig, A. and Ólafsson, K. (2011) *Risks and safety on the internet: The perspective of European children. Full findings*, London: London School of Economics and Political Science.

Lobe, B., Livingstone, S., Ólafsson, K. and Vodeb, H. (2011) *Cross-national comparison of risks and safety on the internet: Initial analysis from the EU Kids Online survey of European children*, London: London School of Economics and Political Science.

Staksrud, E., Livingstone, S., Haddon, L. and Ólafsson, K (2009) *What do we know about children's use of online technologies? A report on data availability and research gaps in Europe*, London: London School of Economics and Political Science (http://eprints.lse.ac.uk/24367/).

Steenbergen, M.R. and Jones, B.S. (2002) 'Modelling multilevel data structures', *American Journal of Political Science*, vol 46, no 1, pp 218-37.

Subramanian, S.V., Jones, K., Kaddour, A. and Krieger, N. (2009) 'Revisiting Robinson: the perils of individualistic and ecological fallacy', *International Journal of Epidemiology*, vol 38, pp 342-60.

TWENTY-TWO

Mobile access: different users, different risks, different consequences?

Gitte Stald and Kjartan Ólafsson

Introduction

Online communication and information is increasingly accessible to young people, from several other platforms than traditional personal computers. While mobile phones may be primary sources of online access to some and supplementing access to others, all mobile platforms offer the benefits of being personal, portable and always on and to hand. The increased online access from mobile phones raises two questions: does more access to the internet from mobile phones expose children to more risk and harm, and are there different risks and harm if children use mobile access rather than traditional personal computers? This chapter explores and analyses potential correlations between online access through mobile platforms, and patterns of exposure to risks.

The original purpose of the chapter was to look into patterns of and relations among risk, actual harm and coping strategies, related to using the internet accessed via a mobile device. Based on the questions asked and the size of the relevant groups we cannot, however, find evidence in the dataset that show that specific mobile uses result in higher levels of harm than 'traditional' internet use, and the same is the case for findings regarding coping strategies. Deeper explorations of these topics would have been possible if we could compare groups of users who access the internet only from mobile devices and those that use multiple platforms. However, the data set do not enable such comparison because very few respondents fall into these groups.

New opportunities, new challenges

This chapter builds on theories about how media landscapes are changing and how young people are adapting digital media. When we look at how new opportunities are being integrated at various rates and in various – different and similar – ways across Europe, it is clear that we must see 'media as part of the changing context, the environment or the ecology of everyday life' (Livingstone, 2002, p 71). Although, in principle, the introduction of new technological opportunities provides the same opportunities in terms of access to information and communication and social factors, our data show that despite their similarities, new technologies should be analysed in the context of the social landscape they become part of (Silverstone and Hirsch, 1992; Livingstone, 2002, 2009; Haddon, 2004). Every country has a different media culture and history, and every child fits media into his or her everyday life in different ways. It is important that, even when studying aspects of children's media culture, we need to place them 'in the context of a given social structure' (Castells et al, 2007, p 127).

We also need to look critically at the phenomena and technologies behind the consequences that we study in order to understand the interplay between different media platforms and formats, and the specific affordances and restraints of each additional new medium. For example, the obvious characteristics of mobile phones and 'smartphones' are that they are handheld, personal devices that optimise mobility. However, an essential consequence of these characteristics is that we are connected constantly (Castells et al, 2007; Ling, 2008), and we need to consider how this changes the way we interact, and the risks that our children encounter in everyday life with digital media.

Access to the internet from mobile phones

The *EU Kids Online* survey asked children about the devices they use to access the internet (see Table 22.3; Livingstone et al, 2011) including 'mobile phone' and 'other handheld or portable device'. The latter category was defined further as iPod Touch, iPhone or Blackberry. The term 'smartphone' was deliberately not used in the question, but distinguishing between 'mobile phone' and 'other handheld or portable device' was important since the accessibility and usability differ between a push-button mobile phone and an advanced smartphone.[1] We did not ask about iPads or other reading devices.

Around a third of 9- to 16-year-olds who use the internet say that they use a mobile phone *or* a handheld device to go online. Almost all of these children also access the internet using other means (mostly through a computer at home). Twelve per cent of all children go online using some kind of smartphone, and 22 per cent go online using a mobile phone (but not other kinds of handheld devices). However, we do not know how often or how much these alternative means are used. Use of both mobile phones and other handheld devices increases by age, but gender differences are small. Using *only* mobile devices to access the internet is not common: 9 children reported another handheld device as their only device and 85 reported a mobile phone as their only means of access. So mobile access seems to be additional to other possibilities.

Some children use their mobiles to access the internet 'just because they want to'. They have access at home (often in multiple locations), but also use their mobile phones. Some children use mobiles because their other means of access are limited. However, there are substantial country differences in both the percentage of children using a mobile phone or some other mobile device to go online, and the overall use of any mobile device. For handheld devices other than a mobile phone the top three countries are Norway, the UK and Sweden. At the same time, substantially more children in Norway (66 per cent) and Sweden (68 per cent) have internet access in bedrooms than in the UK (52 per cent), so lack of bedroom access does not alone explain the pattern of internet access using a mobile device. The explanation may be related to cheap access, a youth culture 'on the move', or simply a deeper interest in being online when 'out and about'. Interestingly in Denmark, which scores high for access at home, time spent online, etc, only 17 per cent of children access the internet using a smartphone, compared to 31 per cent in Norway. This might be explained by the fact that almost all 15-year-old Danes and an increasing number of younger children in Denmark have their own laptops equipped with WiFi. Thus, they may have less motivation to go online using a mobile device. However, this picture seems to be changing rapidly (Bertel and Stald, 2011).

Only 8 per cent of children in Spain use any kind of mobile device to go online compared with 78 per cent of children in Greece. However, the high combined use of any kind of mobile device for Greece is mainly due to a very large group of Greek children using mobile phones to go online. In Spain, 42 per cent of children have access to the internet in own bedrooms compared to 52 per cent in Greece. So the difference, in this case, is not due to lack of internet access. Other factors such as cost and internet and mobile phone cultures play an essential role in individual countries. Other studies indicate that the motivation to go online from a mobile phone is affected by various country-level factors, such as availability of services, cost of using the services, ease of use and use imitating peers (Klastrup and Stald, 2009; Bertel and Stald, 2011). If going online is expensive in a country, children may prefer to use their own or a shared computer. As we do not know how frequently

and for how long Greek and Spanish children use different devices to
go online, or if the mobile device is the main point of access, there may
be quite simple explanations for the difference. It may be that Greek
children go online using their mobile phone once in a while to join
in a particular mobile game popular in Greece, or that some service
or activity has become 'smart' among young Greeks. This is perhaps
confirmed to an extent by the finding that the top three countries for
children going online using mobile phones are in the same area: Greece,
Slovenia and Cyprus. However, our data do not allow us to confirm
or refute this or other hypotheses based on surprising or unexpected
dissimilarities and similarities among surveyed countries.

Country differences underline the importance of distinguishing
between different kinds of mobile access. Figure 22.1 shows the
percentages of children in each country using mobile phones and/or
using other handheld devices.

Countries fall roughly into four groups: first, countries where both
use of mobile phones and other handheld device to access the internet is

**Figure 22.1: Use of handheld devices versus use of mobile phones to go
online**

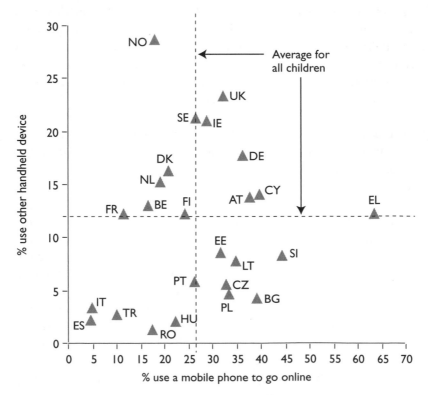

below average, which include Spain, Italy and Turkey. Second, countries where use of mobile phones is above average, but use of other handheld devices is below average, which includes Slovenia, Bulgaria and to an extent, Greece. Third, countries where mobile access is characterised by use of other handheld devices than mobile phones, which includes Norway, Sweden and Denmark. Fourth, countries where use of other handheld devices as well as mobile phones is above average, which includes the UK and Germany.

Since smartphones are most often used by children who already have access to the internet from more personal platforms, the explanation is as indicated above most likely to be related to extent of use as it is simpler and of higher quality to go online from a smartphone than from an ordinary mobile.

It would seem that one of the determinants of mobile use as supplementary as well as primary personal access to the internet is the type of access to the internet available to the child. Table 22.1 shows the percentage of children who go online using each device by type of mobile device. It shows that 41 per cent of children who go online using a mobile phone also use a personal computer to go online. Of those children who access the internet using another handheld portable device, 42 per cent also use their own computers. For the group that uses no type of mobile device, 31 per cent use their own computers. It is interesting that, for all devices, the group that uses neither a mobile phone nor a handheld device is less likely to use any other type of device.

In relation to access it is important to look at how many activities children undertake when they also go online from mobile devices. The breadth of online activities undertaken by the children is based

Table 22.1: Devices used to go online by type of mobile device

% who also use...	Type of mobile device used to go online		
	Mobile phone	Other handheld device	Neither of these
Own PC	41	42	31
Own laptop	35	47	18
Shared PC	60	63	56
Shared laptop	26	31	20
Mobile phone	100	74	0
Games console	56	64	11
Television set	71	67	13
Other handheld portable device	28	100	0

Question: Which of these devices do you use for the internet these days?
Base: All children aged 9-16 who use the internet.

on asking children about the 17 activities, from which we derived a variable range of online activities (see Appendix) ranging from 0 to 17: the average number of activities across Europe is about 7.1 activities. On average those who use a mobile phone to go online engage in about 1.2 more activities than those who do not use a mobile device to go online. For those who use other handheld devices the difference, on average, is almost 2.6 activities. When we control for time spent online, we find (not surprisingly) that gender, age, frequency, home access and country reduce the differences between mobile users and others in terms of the number of online activities. Compared to those who do not use a mobile device to go online, children who use a mobile phone to go online engage in around 0.5 more activities and those who use other handheld devices in 1.3 more activities. Again, the data indicate that smartphones make a difference.

The difference in the number of activities between internet access by mobile and non-mobile device users might, in part, be due to age and country differences in mobile internet use. There is an average difference of three activities between 9-year-olds and 16-year-olds. Daily internet users engage in 1.8 more activities than more intermittent users. Children who do not have internet access in their own bedrooms report fewer activities: this applies both to children who have access at home in some other room, as well as children who have no home access. The difference between mobile users and others is fairly substantial for number of online activities, but, as already noted, there is a connection between extensive access, time spent online, frequency of access and mobile phone access.

Mobile access and time spent online

Time spent online is estimated in minutes based on the responses to the question: 'About how long do you spend using the internet on a normal school day/normal non-school day?'. We derived a variable ranging from 5 to 270 minutes per day, and with the average time for European countries of 88 minutes a day.

We performed a linear regression model to assess whether mobile use is related to time spent on the internet. On average, those children who use a mobile phone to go online use the internet for 18 minutes longer than those who do not use a mobile device to go online. For use of other handheld devices the difference, on average, is almost 27 minutes per day. The immediate conclusion is that some young European children have multiple, personal opportunities to go online and some have very few and, often, shared opportunities. The first group is more likely to spend more time online.

When we control for gender, age, frequency of use, home access plus country, the differences between mobile users and others are much smaller: under six minutes for those using a mobile phone to go online, and around eight minutes for those using some other handheld device, compared to those who do not use any mobile device. Gender differences are not huge, but age differences are more marked, with the average time spent online each day increasing by almost 7 minutes with each additional year of age, leading to an average difference of 46 minutes between 9-year-olds and 16-year-olds, with girls spending between 5-6 minutes less online than boys. Not surprisingly, children who are daily internet users spend considerably more time (37 minutes) on the internet than those who are not. Children who do not have access to the internet in their own bedrooms use the internet less, and that goes both for those who have access at home but just not in their own bedroom as those with no home access. The difference between mobile users and others is not substantial for time spent online, especially considering that the vast majority of mobile users also have other means of access.

Mobile access and online risks

One of the questions we would like to be able to answer – or at least provide indicators of – is whether going online from a mobile phone or a smartphone results in exposure to more and different types of risk than 'traditional' online access.

We used a logistic regression model to estimate the difference between children with the two different types of mobile access on the likelihood of experiencing four types of risks. The largest difference is for seeing sexual messages; the smallest difference is the likelihood of being bullied. It may be that the harmful effects of bullying on the mobile are more serious than when experienced through other media or face to face since the mobile phone is the ultimate personal communication device, which leaves no room to escape the bullying apart from turning it off. However, this is not supported by the data, and should be investigated in more depth.

For all the risks listed, using other handheld devices compared to using mobile phones is associated with a bigger increase in risk experiences. The likelihood of encountering risk on the internet is also related to a host of other factors. The same applies when we look at time spent online and the range of other activities that children engage

Table 22.2: Logistic regression models predicting four types of risks by type of mobile access, controlling for time spent online, gender, age, daily use, type of access at home and country*

	Sexual images	Being bullied	Meeting strangers	Sexual messages (only 11+)
Intercept	0.05	0.04	0.11	0.02
Uses mobile phone to go online	1.14	ns	1.09	ns
Uses other handheld device to go online	1.31	1.35	1.19	1.42
Girls	0.63	1.55	ns	0.83
Age	1.34	1.10	1.33	1.55
Child uses the internet daily	1.88	1.97	2.58	2.20
No access at home	0.79	ns	ns	ns
At home but not in own bedroom	0.84	0.80	0.81	0.83
Austria	1.68	ns	2.31	1.71
Belgium	2.08	ns	1.22	2.33
Bulgaria	2.16	0.68	1.26	1.66
Cyprus	ns	0.43	0.43	ns
Czech Republic	3.25	ns	2.64	2.43
Germany	0.39	0.59	1.77	1.95
Denmark	2.89	ns	2.24	1.72
Estonia	3.18	1.58	2.97	2.07
Greece	1.34	0.43	0.60	ns
Spain	ns	0.64	ns	ns
Finland	2.82	0.55	2.71	1.90
France	2.85	ns	1.46	2.68
Hungary	1.30	ns	ns	ns
Ireland	ns	0.49	ns	ns
Italy	0.68	0.17	ns	0.35
Lithuania	2.59	0.55	3.44	2.08
The Netherlands	2.29	0.53	1.41	1.78
Norway	3.48	0.65	2.47	2.25
Poland	ns	0.70	ns	1.67
Portugal	1.49	0.36	0.57	1.91
Romania	2.23	1.91	1.49	2.98
Sweden	2.20	ns	3.21	1.83
Slovenia	2.68	0.54	1.53	1.98
Turkey	1.97	0.58	0.74	1.78
−2 Log likelihood	18,564	9947	24,699	13,205
Cox and Snell R^2	0.10	0.03	0.17	0.10
Nagelkerke R^2	0.18	0.07	0.25	0.20
Model χ^2	2671	637	4677	2469
Degrees of freedom	31	31	31	31

Notes: * For the four risks investigated, children were coded '1' for those who had experienced the risk, and 0 for those who had not. Results in the tables are reported as odds ratios, which indicate how a certain change in an independent variable is related to a change in the proportionate likelihood that a child experienced that particular risk. For ease of interpretation all continuous variables in the model are centred on a number close to their means.

in. Table 22.2 presents the results of the logistic regression models which include time spent online, gender, age, daily internet use, type of home access and country in addition to mobile access, to predict the likelihood of children experiencing the four types of risks. Controlling for these factors shows that there is little difference in the likelihood of experiencing risks on the internet, between those children who use a mobile phone to go online and those who do not have mobile access. Children who use other handheld devices, however, have an increased likelihood of experiencing risks over and above what would be expected based on time spent online, gender, age, daily internet use, type of home access and country. As already noted, use of other handheld device is related to more intense use, which, again, is related to increased exposure to risk.

Table 22.2 depicts some country-specific issues. It shows clearly that the mobile access and exposure to risk are country-specific. In the countries where children have extensive online access, more devices, higher frequency of use and more time spent online, the significance of going online from mobile devices – in terms of time spent online and likelihood of encountering risks – is higher than in countries with low access and use. However, the four risk types we asked about are not equally represented in either group.

We would like to be able to say whether increased exposure to risk due to going online from smartphones causes increased experience of harm, and to identify which types of harm. However, our findings do not allow this. In order to interpret the findings in more depth we need to look at the variables shown to make a difference, that is, age, extent of access, frequency of online use, time spent and country-specific issues. For example, we know that the extent of internet access using various types of mobile devices is different in each of the countries surveyed. When we break the data down taking these factors into consideration, the figures are too small to identify significant findings related to mobile use and experience of harm. We can hypothesise that there must be some children, in some contexts, who have more, and other, bad experiences than the average user, from going online from their mobile devices, but we need to identify these cases in some other way, especially in country-level analyses.

Conclusion

There are three main conclusions from the analysis in this chapter. First, it appears that personal access to the internet from more than one platform is generally more important than the actual platform, because increased access means increased extent of use and more extensive use results in more exposure to risk. Mobile phones and smartphones have different affordances and restraints from other types of digital communication devices. Going online on a mobile phone is not necessarily the same as going online on a desktop or laptop computer, since the perception of content, context and connectivity may be different. However, the overall effect of the integration of various types of new online opportunities seems to be an increase in the extent of use. The data do not provide evidence that going online from a mobile device causes *specific* risk, but seems to result in a slightly higher incidence of seeing sexual images. We cannot say whether this is related to the mobile phone being notably different from other access platforms, in terms of general exposure to risk. The possibility of new risks from going online from mobile phones and smartphones would seem, based on our data, to be on the risk of 'more of the same'.

Second, it is evident that the introduction of smartphones into everyday life has some impact. We find slightly increased exposure to risk related to using a smartphone compared to going online from a mobile phone. This is related, again, to slightly increased time spent online and number of activities related to using a smartphone.

Third, more detailed studies on going online from mobile phones, smartphones and other types of new devices are needed, in order to be able to provide evidence-based knowledge about the relation between type of access, risk factors, experience of harm and coping strategies in the context of the variables that we have identified as determinants of opportunities, risks and harm. Based on the data, we can say that the pattern of access, extent of online activity and uses of online opportunities continues to change. There is likely to be increased numbers of children who encounter risk and experience harm as a result of going online, as increasing numbers of European children get personal access to the internet, including from mobile phones. We have identified a connection between smartphone use and more online opportunities and more exposure to risk. As the extent of online activities increases alongside the integration of cheaper and smarter phones, this area will require more detailed study and more focused surveys. In addition we need more qualitative studies to identify potential cases that could provide insights into the increased incidence of specific risks and harm related going to online from various types of mobile phones, or the reverse.

Note

[1] 'Smartphones' are popularly defined in short as mobile phones with computer-like capabilities, and often with touchscreens (Bertel and Stald, 2011). In the case of the present survey the category also included the Blackberry, which has a push-button keyboard and allows easy access to the internet. Smartphone is used in this chapter to refer to 'other handheld device' than a mobile phone.

References

Bertel, T.F. and Stald, G. (2011) 'From SMS to SNS: the use of the internet on the mobile phone among young Danes', Paper presented to NordMedia 2011, Akureyri, Iceland, 11-13 August.

Castells, M., Fernández-Ardèvol, M., Linchuan Qiu, J. and Sey, A. (2007) *Mobile communication and society*, Cambridge, MA: The MIT Press.

Haddon, L. (2004) *Information and communication technologies in everyday life. A concise introduction and research guide*, Oxford and New York: Berg.

Klastrup, L. and Stald, G. (2009) *Executive rapport. Mobity survey. Danske unges brug af sociale netværk i et mobilt perspektiv* [*Executive report. Mobity survey. Young Danes' uses of social network media in a mobile perspective*] (http://stald.files.wordpress.com/2009/12/facebook-survey-klastrup-stald-181209.pdf).

Ling, R. (2008) *New techs, new ties*, Cambridge, MA and London: The MIT Press.

Livingstone, S. (2002) *Young people and new media. Childhood and the changing media environment*, London, Thousand Oaks, CA and New Delhi: Sage Publications.

Livingstone, S. (2009) *Children and the internet*, Cambridge: Polity Press.

Livingstone, S., Haddon, L., Görzig, A. and Ólafsson, K. (2011) *Risks and safety on the internet: The perspective of European children. Full findings*, London: London School of Economics and Political Science.

Silverstone, R. and Hirsch, E. (eds) (1992) *Consuming technologies. Media and information in domestic spaces*, London and New York: Routledge.

TWENTY-THREE

Explaining vulnerability to risk and harm

Alfredas Laurinavičius, Rita Žukauskienė and Laura Ustinavičiūtė

Introduction

Although the internet brings a wide range of opportunities for online communication, not all of it is positive and it may leave children vulnerable to numerous online hazards. Previous research, as other chapters show, points to encounters with material considered risky and potentially harmful being related to a range of sociodemographic and psychological variables. For example, age correlates with more intensive internet use and with more risky behaviour, and age can also moderate the relationship between internet use and psychological well-being (Shapira et al, 2000). Gender differences in relation to risk are supposed to be strong but unpredictable – in the case of bullying, for example, the findings are inconsistent across studies. Some studies find that boys are more likely than girls to engage in cyberbullying (Katzer et al, 2009); Li (2006) finds that more boys than girls report being cyberbullied; but other research finds no significant gender differences for online bullying (Aricak, 2009).

Results from personality research help to clarify the facets of personality that may produce a predisposition for problematic internet use. Several traits are identified as being associated with problematic internet use, including shyness (Chak and Leung, 2004), (lack of) self-efficacy (Eastin and LaRose, 2000; LaRose et al, 2001) and sensation-seeking (Lin and Tsai, 2002). There is also a growing body of scientific evidence on the relationship between certain offline and online risks – research related mostly to cases of online and offline bullying rather than seeing sexual material. For example, Ybarra et al (2007) report that 36 per cent of youth harassed online are also bullied at school; Smith et al (2008), in a sample of UK youth, find that 26 per cent of traditional victims of bullying are also bullied online; and Gradinger and colleagues (2009), in an Austrian sample, report an overlap of 12 per cent between online and offline bullying. A study conducted by Erentaite, Bergman and Zukauskiene (2012) addresses a large sample of high school students in Lithuania (*n*=1,667, 58 per cent girls, aged 15-19, *M*=16.29, *SD*=0.95). They consider three forms of traditional bullying – verbal, physical and relational – and seven forms of cyberbullying victimisation, measured at two time points. Their findings reveal that one third of victims of traditional bullying are victimised in cyberspace. In particular, the experiences of verbal and relational/mixed bullying victimisation at school predicts cyberbullying victimisation one year later. In Juvonen and Gross' (2008) study, 72 per cent of respondents aged 12-17 reported at least one incident of online bullying; of these, 85 per cent also experienced bullying at school. In another study, 432 students in Canadian school grades 7-9 were surveyed about their experiences of bullying; the results indicate that students who are bullied in cyberspace are also likely to be bullied at school (56 per cent) (Beran and Li, 2007). Beran and Li show that bullying online is just an indirect form of bullying in which the aggressor does not harass the victim in a face-to-face interaction, but through a computer screen. It is very likely that bullying at school is related to bullying online (Beran and Li, 2007).

In contrast to other chapters in this book, this chapter compares two problem areas, online bullying and sexual content online, in terms of the factors that predict these risks and the factors that predict harm. This chapter also compares experience of these risks offline and online. The general hypothesis is that children who encounter a particular risk offline will be prone to encounter the same type of risk online.

Method

The EU Kids Online project interviewed a random stratified sample of approximately 1,000 internet-using children aged 9-16 in each of 25 European countries participating in the EU Kids Online II project. For more details regarding our procedure, see Chapter 2 in this volume, and Ipsos/EU Kids Online (2011).

To evaluate online bullying we asked: 'Has someone acted in this kind of hurtful or nasty way to you in the past 12 months?' and 'At any time during the last 12 months, has this happened on the internet?'. In the case of seeing images with sexual content online, we asked: 'In the past year, you will have seen lots of different images…. Sometimes these might be obviously sexual…. Have you seen anything of this kind in the past 12 months?' and 'Have you seen these kinds of things on any websites in the past 12 months?'. The children who responded positively to the questions about each type of risk were asked about the impact of their encounters, through the question: 'Thinking about the last time this happened to you, how upset were you about what happened, if at all?'. Response options were 1 – 'Not at all upset' to 4 – 'Very upset'.

Age, gender, total time spent on the internet per week, being bullied offline and seeing sexual images offline were the predictors examined. Being bullied offline was evaluated based on responses to questions about the experience of being bullied via non-internet means of communication. We asked: 'At any time during the last 12 months, has this happened.... In person or face to face?' and 'By mobile phone calls, texts or image/video texts?'. At least one positive answer indicates an encounter with this type of risk offline. Seeing sexual images offline was evaluated through the responses to questions about seeing sexual images other than online. We used four response options in answer to the question, 'In which, if any, of these places have you seen these kinds of things in the past 12 months?' 'In a magazine or book', 'On television, film or video/DVD', 'By text (SMS), images (MMS), or otherwise on your mobile phone' and 'By Bluetooth'. A 'yes' response to one or more options indicates experience of this type of risk offline.

The psychological measures used to predict risk and harm are:

- *Self-efficacy*, a brief version adapted from Schwarzer and Jerusalem (1995); four items on a scale of 1 – Not true to 3 – Very true (α=0.66).
- *Sensation-seeking*, measured using two items (Stephenson et al, 2003), scored as 1 – Not true to 3 – Very true. (α=0.77).
- *Psychological difficulties*, measured using 16 selected items (α=0.71) from Goodman et al's (1998) Strengths and Difficulties Questionnaire (SDQ) scale: emotional symptoms (five items), conduct problems (five items), peer relationship problems (five items) and hyperactivity (one item). Each statement was scored on a scale from 1 – Not true to 3 – Very true. The average score reflects the level of psychological difficulties. For more detailed information on the variables used in the analysis see the Appendix at the end of this book.

We used a logistic regression to predict risk and multiple regression analysis to predict harm.

Results

At the start of the analysis we calculated correlations between all the variables included in the analysis. Table 23.1 presents descriptive

Table 23.1: Descriptive characteristics of variables used in statistical analysis and their intercorrelations

Name	M (SD) or ratio: positive/valid	1	2	3	4	5	6	7	8	9	10	11
1. Risk 1 (Being bullied online)	1395/23,080	–										
2. Risk 2 (Seeing sexual images online)	3861/22,452	0.209*** (21,093)	–									
3. Being bullied offline	3666/23,303	0.340*** (23,056)	0.188*** (21,237)	–								
4. Seeing sexual images offline	4477/22,856	0.115*** (21,396)	0.536*** (22,446)	0.179*** (21,554)	–							
5. Gender (boys)	12,641/25,142	-0.047*** (23,080)	0.076*** (22,452)	0.003 (23,303)	0.032*** (22,856)	–						
6. Intensity of harm 1 (bullying)	1.47 (1.01)	–	-0.036 (1181)	0.107*** (1315)	0.027 (1206)	-0.177*** (1324)	–					
7. Intensity of harm 2 (sexual images)	0.42 (0.82)	0.211*** (3227)	–	0.165*** (3263)	-0.076*** (3449)	-0.114*** (3452)	0.330*** (510)	–				
8. Age (years)	12.48 (2.28)	0.078*** (23,080)	0.263*** (22,452)	0.016* (23,303)	0.228*** (22,856)	-0.011 (25,142)	-0.006 (1324)	-0.232*** (3452)	–			
9. Internet use (hours/week)	1.56 (1.03)	0.130*** (22,558)	0.230*** (21,934)	0.077*** (22,780)	0.158*** (22,332)	0.050*** (24,548)	-0.032 (1294)	-098*** (3395)	0.377*** (24,548)	–		
10. Sensation-seeking	1.35 (0.52)	0.108*** (22,959)	0.243*** (22,335)	0.138*** (23,180)	0.199*** (22,738)	0.177*** (24,984)	-0.107*** (1318)	0.019 (3445)	0.170*** (24,984)	0.172*** (24,403)	–	
11. Self-efficacy	2.19 (0.47)	0.040*** (23,017)	0.137*** (22,389)	0.014* (23,241)	0.107*** (22,792)	0.045*** (25,049)	-0.078*** (1322)	-0.105*** (3445)	0.226*** (25,049)	0.138*** (24,465)	0.176*** (24,938)	–
12. Psychological difficulties	1.40 (0.26)	0.163*** (23,041)	0.095*** (22,417)	0.231*** (23,264)	0.079*** (22,821)	-0.011 (25,082)	0.128*** (1322)	0.205*** (3449)	-0.028* (25,082)	-0.078*** (24,496)	0.251*** (24,968)	-0.137*** (25,037)

Note: Pearson correlation was used. ***Correlation is significant at the 0.001 level (2-tailed). **Correlation is significant at the 0.01 level (2-tailed). *Correlation is significant at the 0.05 level (2-tailed). Number of cases is given in brackets.

characteristics of the measures used. Because of the large sample size, almost all the variables are significantly correlated in the ways predicted; however, the size of some of these correlations is small. According to Cohen (1992), a correlation of 0.5 is large, 0.3 is moderate and 0.1 is small. The significant correlations between the same kinds of offline and online risk are as predicted: moderate $r=0.34$ for bullying and large $r=0.54$ for sexual images. Age correlates moderately with hours spent online per week ($r=0.38$). The intensities of harm, that is, being upset, reported by the children from both types of risk are moderate ($r=0.33$). Six per cent of respondents (1,395 out of 23,080) reported being bullied online; about 17 per cent (3,861 out of 22,452) saw sexual images online.

The logistic regression investigates the sociodemographic and psychological variables and presence of offline risk as predictors of exposure to each type or risk. The independent variables were entered into the regression computation simultaneously. The logistic regression results for predicting the risk of being bullied online are presented in Table 23.2. These show that all the variables included in the equation significantly predict the risk of being bullied online. Girls report being bullied online more often than boys. Each additional year of age increases the odds of being bullied online by 8 per cent, on average; each additional hour per week spent online increases the odds of being bullied by 37 per cent. Psychological difficulties are positively related to the occurrence of risk. However, being bullied offline is the strongest predictor of online bullying: being bullied offline increases the odds of bullying online by 10 times.

The results of the logistic regression for the risk of seeing sexual images online are shown in Table 23.3. These show that all the variables entered into the equation significantly predict the risk of seeing sexual images online. With the exception of gender, the directions of the relations are the same as for the risk of being bullied online. Boys more often report seeing sexual images online, and being a boy increases the odds of the occurrence of seeing sexual images by 39 per cent. Each year of age increases the odds by 20 per cent; each additional hour per week spent online increases the odds by 34 per cent. The relation between psychological difficulties and seeing sexual images online is positive. The presence of offline experience is the strongest predictor of online experience – almost 15 times more children who watch sexual images offline encounter sexual images online.

We performed two multiple regression analyses to investigate which characteristics of children predict intensity of harm for each of the risks investigated. We used the same predictors as for the prediction of risks. The results of multiple regression analyses are presented in Table 23.4.

Table 23.2: Results of a logistic regression: prediction of being bullied online using psychological, demographical variables and being bullied offline

Predictors	B	SE	Wald	df	Sig	Exp(B)	95% CI for EXP(B) Lower	Upper
Age (years)	0.081	0.015	28.705	1	0.000	1.084	1.052	1.1169
Gender (1 = boy)	-0.542	0.064	71.741	1	0.000	0.582	0.513	0.659
Hours online per week	0.311	0.028	120.765	1	0.000	1.365	1.291	1.442
Sensation-seeking	0.184	0.056	10.902	1	0.001	1.203	0.992	1.078
Self-efficacy	0.361	0.072	24.953	1	0.000	1.435	1.245	1.653
Psychological difficulties	1.354	0.116	136.9561	1	0.000	3.872	3.086	4.857
Being bullied offline (1 = yes)	2.286	0.064	1288.597	1	0.000	9.831	8.678	11.138
Constant	-7.934	0.305	677.394	1	0.000	0.000		

Note: Number of cases used in the analysis n=22,392.

Table 23.3: Results of logistic regression: prediction of the prevalence of seeing sexual images online using psychological, demographic variables and seeing sexual images offline

Predictors	B	SE	Wald	df	Sig	Exp(B)	95% CI for EXP(B) Lower	Upper
Age (years)	0.182	0.011	265.793	1	0.000	1.200	1.174	1.226
Gender (1 = boy)	0.327	0.046	50.092	1	0.000	1.386	1.266	1.518
Hours online per week	0.293	0.021	190.639	1	0.000	1.340	1.285	1.397
Sensation-seeking	0.519	0.042	154.329	1	0.000	1.681	1.548	1.824
Self-efficacy	0.395	0.053	55.302	1	0.000	1.485	1.338	1.648
Psychological difficulties	0.681	0.092	54.996	1	0.000	1.976	1.651	2.366
Seeing sexual images offline (1 = yes)	2.689	0.046	3489.770	1	0.000	14.724	13.467	16.098
Constant	–8.097	0.235	1190.708	1	0.000	0.000		

Note: Number of cases used in the analysis *n*=21,791.

Table 23.4: Results of multiple regression analyses: prediction of the intensity of two types of harm using psychological and demographical variables

DV	Predictors						
	Age	Gender	Time online	Sensation-seeking	Self-efficacy	Psychological difficulties	Risk offline
Standardised coefficients (β) for intensity of harm 1 (bullying)	0.012	–0.145***	–0.018	–0.122***	0.011	0.144***	–0.102***
Standardised coefficients (β) for Harm 2 (sexual images)	–0.179***	–0.087***	–0.043*	–0.004	–0.020	0.175***	–0.052**
R^2 (Harm 1)			0.069				
R^2 (Harm 2)			0.096				

Note: ***Coefficient is significant at the 0.001 level (2-tailed). **Coefficient is significant at the 0.01 level (2-tailed). *Coefficient is significant at the 0.05 level (2-tailed). Number of cases used in the analysis: n=1,281 for bullying and n=3,381 for sexual images. Gender: 1 = boy, 0 = girl. Risk offline: 1 = present, 0 = not present.

The results show that the intensity of harm from encountering online bullying is significantly related to gender, sensation–seeking, psychological difficulties and offline bullying. Girls are more upset by online bullying. Children with lower levels of sensation–seeking and more psychological difficulties are more vulnerable to online bullying. Being bullied offline reduces the intensity of harm from being bullied online.

The level of harm reported from seeing sexual images online is significantly related to age, gender, time spent online, psychological difficulties and watching sexual images offline. The predictors explain 6.9 and 9.6 per cent respectively of the variance of the dependent variables.

Discussion

The results show that the likelihood that children will experience these two types of risk is small: only 6 per cent of children reported being bullied online, a much smaller proportion than the results for North American children (72 per cent) (Juvonen and Gross, 2008). Seeing sexual images online is more frequent, with about 17 per cent of children reporting seeing sexual images online. This is a similar proportion to the findings for the US of 15 and 25 per cent of children deliberately or unintentionally encountering sexual content online (Mitchell et al, 2003; Ybarra and Mitchell, 2005).

Exposure to either risk online is related to numerous sociodemographic and psychological variables. The strongest correlations are between online and offline risks of the same type. There is some scientific evidence that some kinds of online risks, for example, risk of being bullied online, are continuations of other forms of offline risks/activities (Beran and Li, 2007; Juvonen and Gross, 2008). The correlations support these arguments. We found a moderate relationship between two types of subjectively evaluated intensities of harm. This relationship suggests that there is some personality trait related to general vulnerability to different types of risks.

The results of the logistic regressions for both types of risk, although similar, show some differences. Age, hours spent online, sensation-seeking, self-efficacy and psychological difficulties are predictors of both risks. Being older and spending more time online is related to the variety of internet experiences, and this includes more frequent exposure to risks. There are some gender differences in the occurrence of the two online experiences. Under the same sociodemographical and psychological conditions, girls are more often victims of online bullying and boys more often see sexual material online. These results are consistent with previous research (Mitchell et al, 2003; Kowalski and Limber, 2007).

However, the strongest predictor of both risks is experience of the same risks offline. Being bullied offline increases the odds of being bullied online by 10 times. Seeing sexual materials offline increases the odds of seeing sexual content online by 15 times. The results of the logistic regressions show that those children who encounter risks in their daily lives offline are more vulnerable to encountering the same types of risks online.

The results for harm show that lower scores for sensation-seeking and higher scores for psychological difficulties and being a girl predict a greater intensity of subjectively evaluated harm. Having psychological difficulties and lower sensation-seeking renders children more vulnerable to online bullying. Although being bullied offline is a significant predictor of experiencing harm from being bullied online, the direction is negative: that is, the occurrence of offline bullying decreases the intensity of harm experienced from online bullying.

The intensity of harm from seeing sexual images online is significantly predicted by age, gender, time spent online, psychological difficulties and presence of offline risk. The results show that younger children are especially likely to say they are upset after encountering sexual material online. Having psychological difficulties also predicts more intense negative emotions promoted by encountering material with sexual content online. The presence of offline risk predicts the intensity of harm: but, again, having seen sexual images offline actually decreases the harm reported from seeing such images online.

In other words, for both types of harm (being bullied and seeing sexual images) the presence of offline risk is associated with less harm. This can be explained by habituation to certain types of experience, defined as risks. Those children who are bullied offline will likely be less sensitive to being bullied online. Those children who have seen sexual images elsewhere are not so affected by seeing similar images online. The results of both multiple regressions explain only 6 and 10 per cent of subjectively evaluated intensity harm and so should not be overestimated.

Conclusion

This chapter investigated the sociodemographic and psychological factors associated with online risk and harm. The results show that although being bullied online and seeing sexual images online are quite different types of experiences, age, gender, time spent online, sensation-seeking, self-efficacy, psychological difficulties and presence of offline risk are common predictors and are influential in both cases. Gender plays a different role as a predictor for the two different types of risk. Also, our findings show that the intensity of harm from an encounter with both online risks is associated with gender, the presence of psychological difficulties and an experience of the same type of risk offline. Age, time spent online and sensation-seeking play a different role as a predictor of intensity of harm resulting from encountering different risks online. However, the explanatory power of the variables is quite low. In sum, this research shows that there is a strong connection between online and offline risks. As the internet comes into more frequent use, online and offline risks are tending to coincide. There are therefore arguments for treating children's online reality not as separate from, but rather as part of, their usual reality.

References
Aricak, O.T. (2009) 'Psychiatric symptomatology as a predictor of cyberbullying among university students', *Journal of Educational Research*, vol 8, pp 167–84.

Beran, T. and Li, Q. (2007) 'The relationship between cyberbullying and school bullying', *Journal of Student Wellbeing*, vol 1, no 2, pp 15–33.

Chak, K. and Leung, L. (2004) 'Shyness and locus of control as predictors of internet addiction and internet use', *Cyberpsychology & Behavior*, vol 7, pp 559-70.

Cohen, J. (1992) 'A power primer', *Psychological Bulletin*, vol 112, no 1, pp 155-9.

Eastin, M.A. and LaRose, R.L. (2000) 'Internet self-efficacy and the psychology of the digital divide', *Journal of Computer Mediated Communication*, vol 6, no 1 (www.ascusc.org/jcmc/vol6/issue1/eastin.html).

Erentaite, R., Bergman L. R. and Zukauskiene, R. (2012) 'Cross-contextual stability of bullying victimization: a person-oriented analysis of cyber and traditional bullying experiences among adolescents', *Scandinavian Journal of Psychology*, vol 53, no 2, pp 181-90.

Goodman, R., Meltzer, H. and Bailey, V. (1998) 'The Strengths and Difficulties Questionnaire: a pilot study on the validity of the self-report version', *European Child & Adolescent Psychiatry*, vol 7, pp 125-30.

Gradinger, P., Strohmeier, D. and Spiel, C. (2009) 'Traditional bullying and cyberbullying: identification of risk groups for adjustment problems', *Zeitschrift für Psychologie/Journal of Psychology*, vol 217, no 4, pp 205-13.

Ipsos/EU Kids Online (2011) *EU Kids Online II: Technical report*, London: London School of Economics and Political Science (www2.lse.ac.uk/media@lse/research/EUKidsOnline/EUKidsII%202009-11)/Survey/Technical%20report.PDF).

Juvonen, J. and Gross, E. (2008) 'Extending the school grounds? Bullying experiences in cyberspace', *The Journal of School Health*, vol 78, no 9, pp 496-505.

Katzer, C., Fetchenhauer, D. and Belschak, F. (2009) 'Cyberbullying: who are the victims? A comparison of victimization in internet chatrooms and victimization in school', *Journal of Media Psychology*, vol 21, pp 25-36.

Kowalski, R.M. and Limber, S.E. (2007) 'Electronic bullying among middle school students', *Journal of Adolescent Health*, vol 41, pp S22-S30.

LaRose, R., Mastro, D.A. and Eastin, M.S. (2001) 'Understanding internet usage: a social cognitive approach to uses and gratifications', *Social Science Computer Review*, vol 19, no 3, pp 395-413.

Li, Q. (2006) 'Cyberbullying in schools: a research of gender differences', *School Psychology International*, vol 27, no 2, pp 157-70.

Lin, S.S.J. and Tsai, C.C. (2002) 'Sensation seeking and internet dependence of Taiwanese high school adolescents', *Computers in Human Behavior*, vol 18, no 4, pp 411-26.

Mitchell, K.J., Finkelhor, D. and Wolak, J. (2003) 'The exposure of youth to unwanted sexual material on the internet', *Youth & Society*, vol 34, no 3, pp 330-58.

Schwarzer, R. and Jerusalem, M. (1995) 'Generalized self-efficacy scale', in J. Weinman, S. Wright and M. Johnston (eds) *Measures in health psychology: A user's portfolio. Causal and control beliefs*, Windsor: NFER-Nelson, pp 35-7.

Shapira, N.A., Goldsmith, T.D., Keck, P.E., Khosla, U.M. and McElroy, S.L. (2000) 'Psychiatric features of individuals with problematic internet use', *Journal of Affective Disorders*, vol 57, pp 267-72.

Smith, P.K., Mahdavi, J., Carvalho, M., Fisher, S., Russell, S. and Tippett, N. (2008) 'Cyberbullying: its nature and impact in secondary school pupils', *Journal of Child Psychology and Psychiatry*, vol 49, pp 376-85.

Stephenson, M.T., Hoyle, R.H., Palmgreen, P. and Slater, M.D. (2003) 'Brief measures of sensation seeking for screening and large-scale surveys', *Drug and Alcohol Dependence*, vol 72, pp 279-86.

Ybarra, M.L. and Mitchell, K.J. (2005) 'Exposure to internet pornography among children and adolescents: a national survey', *Cyber Psychology & Behavior*, vol 8, no 5, pp 473-86.

Ybarra, M.L., Diener-West, M. and Leaf, P.J. (2007) 'Examining the overlap in internet harassment and school bullying: implications for school intervention', *Journal of Adolescent Health*, vol 41, pp S42-S50.

TWENTY-FOUR

Relating online practices, negative experiences and coping strategies

Bence Ságvári and Anna Galácz

Introduction

The initial findings of the EU Kids Online survey (as presented in the preceding chapters in this book) provide detailed information on the types and nature of risks that children face when using the internet. In this chapter we focus on the presence of multiple risks in children's lives, using a complex approach that also takes account of the complex characteristics of the different coping strategies employed to obviate potential harm. We investigate the following questions:

- What are the typical risk patterns from the child's perspective? What kinds of risks are related?
- What are the typical risk and harm factors?
- How do children react to exposure to risk? How do they respond to harm and how do they develop resilience to risk and harm? What is the nature of their various coping strategies?

To start, we provide a brief overview of the changing concept of risk in general, and the meaning of risk in the online world.

Changing concept and role of risk in children's lives

The early modernist notion of risk was a neutral concept, denoting the probability of something happening combined with potential losses or gains from its occurrence. By the end of the 20th century this meaning had been almost completely overtaken by a negative concept of risk as involving undesirable, threatening and dangerous outcomes (Lupton, 2005, p 8). The current understanding is generally that risk describes the probability of an unwanted event that may or may not occur (Hansson, 2007).

Opinions on childhood and children's relation to risk have changed throughout history (Cunningham, 2006). Gill (2007) argues that enjoyment of childhood is being undermined by increasing risk-aversion and increasing adult intervention to minimise risk at the expense of childhood experiences. Children have numerous restrictions imposed on them that are intended to support them by minimising or even eliminating risk (Gill, 2007), which leads to the argument that children will be unable to understand risk if society (at the macro level of policy making or the micro level of family) prevents them from experiencing it.

Resilience generally refers to positive adaptation developed in response to negative experiences (Masten and Gewirtz, 2006). The challenge model of resilience suggests that low levels of exposure to risk may have beneficial or 'steeling' effects, and provide opportunities to rehearse problem-solving skills and to mobilise resources. In this model, moderate levels of risk are associated with less negative outcomes, in contrast to high levels of a risk experience, which are associated with negative outcomes. Moderate levels of risk provide opportunities to learn how to overcome adversity. In this model the resilience or protective effect depends on the level of exposure to risk (Schoon, 2006, p 75). Thus, if children are exposed to moderate risks, they will learn how to assess and respond to them. However, determining what should be classified as a moderate level of risk is not straightforward.

Vulnerability is the degree to which children are susceptible to negative outcomes and harm. There is a complex set of contingencies that makes some children more vulnerable (more exposed to harm) than others. The various factors resulting in offline vulnerability or protection from harm has been well researched. There are certain personality types, family background characteristics and factors relevant at the societal level that function as both strong determinants of vulnerability and ability to cope with risks.

The spread of use of the internet among children and the consequent emergence of online risks has moved the question of what difference the internet makes to childhood risks to the top of several agendas. Can we simply accommodate the causal relationships between risk and harm, and resilience and vulnerability in children's offline contexts, in their online environments? Or are the various forms of online activities rewriting the 'old' rules related to risk?

Nature of online risks

As children's everyday life becomes more and more embedded in digital technologies, new kinds of risks are emerging and 'old' risks are re-emerging in new forms and, due to the features of technology, in greater intensities. There is growing evidence that the online environment exacerbates the experience of harm (Livingstone, 2010). However, the constantly developing, but still young technology, and the fast changing means of usage of applications and services, make it difficult to formulate incontestable connections between offline and online risk factors, and patterns of vulnerability related to the internet.

In examining the main characteristics determining risk experience and patterns of resilience related to internet use, the work of Schoon (2006) is informative. Schoon (2006, p 14), based on previous evidence, identifies three broad sets of variables related to protective and risk factors that may decrease or increase the impact of adverse offline experiences. These include characteristics of the individual, the family environment and the wider social context. The EU Kids Online research is based on similar theoretical assumptions.

It should be noted that none of these risk factors in isolation exerts an effect: it is their interaction with other influences that matters. So the effects of risk factors are synergistic and transactional since they are a result of joint influences and bi-directional effects related to the child and his or her context. Schoon believes that exposure to risks and different risk patterns are the results of the interplay among numerous factors:

> What distinguishes a high–risk individual from others is not so much exposure to a particular risk factor, but rather a life history characterised by multiple disadvantages. Serious risk emanates from the accumulation of risk effects, and it has been suggested that it is the number of these factors and their combined effect that exert a deleterious impact on developmental outcomes. (Schoon, 2006, p 9)

Without clear and obvious results on the nature of online risk and harm, micro and macro-level actors (that is, parents and the media, and policy makers) tend to endorse the idea that children should be protected as much as possible from all risks. This general highly risk-averse culture of childhood has penetrated the online world, making it difficult to find the right balance between providing (online) opportunities to children while protecting them from the possibility of encountering risks that might lead to potential harm, by closing certain internet 'gates'.

The results of previous research show that, contrary to commonly held assumptions, children – as members of the 'digital' or 'net' generation – are not equally capable and fluent at using the internet: there are clear dividing lines according to the level of their digital skills.

The first results of the EU Kids Online research indicates that more frequent consumption of online content, more intensive and broader use of internet opportunities and higher levels of (self-perceived) internet skills entail potentially higher exposure to all types of online risks (Livingstone and Helsper, 2009; Livingstone et al, 2010).

Contrary to common assumptions, digitally skilled and experienced young people do not tend to avoid risks. However, their capabilities make them more able to cope with these risks (Livingstone and Bober, 2005). These results support the so-called usage hypothesis, which suggest that more intense and complex internet usage leads to greater indulgence in risky practices (Chapter 12, this volume). However, the risk migration hypothesis holds that offline risky activities predict more risky behaviour in the online environment, which is supported by several accounts in the literature (see Chapter 12). We therefore need to focus on the relevance of 'classic' offline factors and differences in involvement in the digital culture. But it is also important to differentiate between incidents of risk and harm, as suggested by the theoretical framework of the EU Kids Online project (see Chapter 1, this volume). The notion that exposure to risk does not necessarily lead to harm draws attention to the factors determining vulnerability and resilience.

In the next part of this chapter we use data from the EU Kids Online research to elaborate the question of online risk and vulnerability. The earlier chapters in this book have provided detailed analyses of exposure to particular types of risk (see Chapters 11, 12, 13 and 14) and models to explain the role of certain characteristics of risky behaviour and harm (Chapter 23). Our goal is to complete these investigations by proposing models to illustrate the complexities involved in risk exposure and vulnerability to harm.

In our analyses we exploited the full database of 25 countries but, in order to avoid data gaps, we limited the focus to children aged 11–16. We start by providing some insights into the nature of multiple risks by identifying the connections between various risks in the cases of children who were exposed to more than one type of risk. We then propose a complex model of risk and protective factors to explore the background to online risk-taking and vulnerability. Finally, we present a segmentation of the coping strategies employed by children who experienced harm after being exposed to certain risks.

Results

Multiple risks

According to the survey, 48 per cent of European children aged 11-16 had experienced one or more of the six online risks identified in the EU Kids Online research in the 12 months previous to the interviews (including online bullying; seeing sexual images online; receiving sexual messages online; meeting new contacts online [contact with someone on the internet not previously met face to face]; exposure to potentially harmful online user-generated content; and personal data misuse online).[1] Twenty-three per cent had experienced one risk, and 25 per cent had experienced two or more risks. In terms of basic demographic variables, the average number of risks experienced is higher among older children, children from high socioeconomic status households and those who use the internet frequently and intensively.

Among those who had experienced risk, the most frequent risks were contact with someone on the internet not met face to face before (34 per cent), exposed to potentially harmful content (21 per cent), saw sexual images online (17 per cent) or received sexual messages online (15 per cent). Among those children who had been exposed to multiple risks, the order of priority was the same: the most common risk was meeting strangers online and the least common was being bullied online (Table 24.1). In the group of children exposed to only one risk, the most frequent was meeting new contacts online (50 per

Table 24.1: Exposure to online risks

Type of risk	% of children who were exposed to the risk in general	% of children who were exposed to only 1 type of online risk	% of children who were exposed to the risk among those who were exposed to multiple online risks (more than 1)
Meeting new contacts online	34	50	76
Exposure to potentially harmful user generated content	21	25	62
Seeing sexual images online	17	10	57
Receiving sexual messages online	15	6	48
Experience of personal data misuse	9	10	27
Being bullied online	7	5	22

cent) and exposure to harmful user-generated content (25 per cent). These results suggest that the most frequent risk for children exposed to only one risk and to multiple risks is the same.

In order to map the more complex risk patterns, we need to investigate pairs of risks and analyse the associations between each two risk types. To define the strength of the association between different risks we calculated the *Phi* values for all possible 2×2 tables (see Table 24.2.)

According to the results, the strongest association is between seeing sexual images and receiving sexual messages. Based on Cohen's (1992) assumptions, the strength of the association is medium. In all other cases, the correlations are significant, but with only small effect sizes. However, a close to strong effect size is observed for the case of seeing sexual images and receiving sexual messages, and a close to medium effect size for receiving sexual messages and meeting new people online. These results are not surprising and indicate that sexual content (seeing and/or receiving it), meeting new people online and exposure to potentially harmful user-generated content, generally show the strongest association. The main findings in both the EU Kids Online report (Livingstone et al, 2010) and the chapters in this

Table 24.2: Exposure to multiple risks: strength of associations and effect-sizes (bivariate Phi coefficients)

	Online bullying	Seeing sexual images	Meeting new people online	Meeting strangers offline	Receiving sexual messages	Exposure to potentially harmful content
Seeing sexual images	0.19*					
Meeting new people online	0.17*	0.29*				
Meeting strangers offline	0.17*	0.23*	–			
Receiving sexual messages	0.19*	0.49***	0.29**	0.23		
Exposure to potentially harmful content	0.17*	0.28*	0.25*	0.19*	0.25*	
Experience of personal data misuse	0.20*	0.16*	0.14*	0.15*	0.13*	0.21*

Notes: * Small effect size, ** medium effect size.

The strength of the association between meeting strangers offline and meeting strangers online is not calculated since they are linked together in the questionnaire. (Meeting online is a prerequisite of meeting offline.)

book on certain risk types show these risks are more common among older children with more intense online activities. It should also be noted that being bullied online shows the weakest links to other types of risks, indicating that children exposed to this kind of risk cannot be characterised by well-defined patterns. In other words, online bullying represents a slightly different type of risk compared to the other risks analysed. In general it shows weaker links to the other types of risk, one reason being that online bullying is the least frequent type of the risks investigated.

A complex model of risk and protective factors to explore the background of online risk-taking and vulnerability of European children

Risk factors

To explore the factors underlying online risks we created a complex index of risk-taking as our dependent variable. We considered six types of online risk in the analysis (see Table 24.3, column 1, for the list of variables). To avoid the problem of simple aggregates (where only occurrences of the different risks are counted), we used principal component analysis to specify the relative importance of the risk types in the index, and adjusted the simple dummy values for each individual risk according to their factor loadings obtained from the principal component analysis (Table 24.3). The aim, here, is to capture the nature of the online risks in a holistic way – merging the different types of risk together hides their individual attributes, but our risk index allows us to measure exposure to online risk in general.

In a next step we developed a regression model to investigate the most important factors determining how much a child encounters risks. Based on our theoretical considerations and the availability of variables, we identified the following broad groups of risk/protective

Table 24.3: Risk index (factor loadings from the principal component analysis)

Risk type	Factor loading
Seeing sexual images online	0.713
Receiving sexual messages online	0.704
Meeting new people online	0.609
Exposure to potentially harmful content	0.601
Online bullying	0.486
Experience of personal data misuse	0.432

factors as independent variables. The final list of variables is the result of multiple attempts to find variables with the highest explanatory power within the theoretical frame:

- *sociodemographic:* gender, age and parent's level of education (expressed as total years in education);
- *complexity of internet usage:* number of online activities (index 0-17), digital literacy and safety skills (index 0-8);
- *psychological/behavioural factors:* sensation-seeking, psychological problems[2] and risky offline activities (that is, drinking too much alcohol, missing school lessons without parents knowing, having sexual intercourse, being in trouble with teachers for bad behaviour, being in trouble with the police).

The variables in the regression model leave 69 per cent of the deviation of the risk index unexplained, which is a fairly good result considering the complexity of the nature of online risks (Table 24.4).

The results show that the most important independent variables explaining exposure to online risks are number of online activities (β=0.22) and risky offline activities (β=0.22).

Sensation-seeking (β=0.13) and the aggregated variable for psychological problems (β=0.13) are also fairly strong and direct predictors for exposure to online risks.

Note, however, that the basic demographic variables (age and gender, β=0.056 and 0.081) have only minor direct effects on exposure to online risks, and the parent's level of education is a significant but very weak predictor of the dependent variable.

Table 24.4: Regression model of risk experience

	Unstandardised coefficients		Standardised coefficients		
	B	SE	Beta	t	Sig
(Constant)	−1.031	0.061		−16.958	0.00
Number of online activities	0.054	0.002	**0.224**	26.835	0.00
Risky offline activities	0.202	0.008	**0.222**	26.829	0.00
Sensation-seeking	0.105	0.007	**0.132**	16.102	0.00
Psychological problems	0.104	0.006	**0.126**	16.983	0.00
Digital literacy and safety skills	0.034	0.003	**0.110**	12.783	0.00
Child's age	0.039	0.004	**0.081**	10.18	0.00
Child's gender	0.09	0.012	**0.056**	7.739	0.00
Parent's level of education	0.019	0.002	**0.056**	7.662	0.00

Note: Adjusted R^2: 0.31.

The results show that risky offline activities and number of online activities and the intensity of internet use are the main determinants of exposure to online risks in general. Some psychological factors (and sensation-seeking in particular) are quite important, while demographic factors have significant, but relatively small, explanatory power.

Harm (protective) factors

In the next regression model explaining harm and vulnerability, the dependent variable is an index expressing the state of being upset to some extent, after encountering the following four risks: online bullying, seeing sexual images, receiving sexual messages and meeting new online contacts offline.[3] Only data on those children who had experienced at least one of the four types of risks are included in the model.

The regression model includes seven independent variables. Again, based on our theoretical assumptions and on the availability of variables, we use the items describing the child's (i) sociodemographic background (age and gender), (ii) user characteristic (number of online activities, mediation [support] from friends and teachers, risky offline activities), and (iii) psychological problems (a variable aggregating information on peer, conduct and emotional problems). The final mix of the variables is the result of several attempts to capture the nature of the harms using a model with possibly high explanatory power.

The results show that the model's explanatory power is very low: the value of the adjusted R-squared is only 0.096. So the experience of harm in general (in its aggregate form exploited in the model) cannot be traced to well definable factors. The strongest links to harm are with psychological problems and, to a lesser extent, gender. In case of gender, girls are a little more likely to experience harm, while age is in a very weak reverse relationship to harm: younger children are more likely to be upset when exposed to online risk. If we decompose psychological problems into emotional, peer and conduct problems, emotional problems show the strongest association to the harm index. The model also suggests that the characteristics of online usage and risky offline activities have almost no effect on the experience of harm (see Table 24.5).

The results of the two models for risk and harm (protective) factors, similar to the results in the chapters focusing on specific risks (for example, Chapter 12), confirm that both the usage and the risk migration hypotheses have relevance for predicting risk encounters and vulnerability to harm. The models show that complexity of internet

Table 24.5: Regression model explaining vulnerability to harm

	Unstandardised coefficients		Standardised coefficients		
	B	SEr	Beta	t	Sig
(Constant)	0.513	0.208		2.465	0.014
Psychological problems	0.343	0.022	0.242	15.602	0.00
Child's gender	0.329	0.044	0.115	7.464	0.00
Teacher mediation	0.033	0.008	0.063	3.941	0.00
Peer mediation	0.05	0.013	0.062	3.838	0.00
Number of online activities	0.023	0.007	0.048	3.062	0.02
Risky offline activities	0.062	0.024	0.042	2.571	0.01
Child's age	–0.06	0.014	–0.068	–4.247	0.00

Note: Adjusted R^2: 0.096.

use and (to a lesser extent) risky offline activities are the most common strong(er) determinants of being exposed to risk. However, while in case of risk factors sensation-seeking proves to be one of the most important factors, in case of harm psychological problems are very important. This model excludes sensation-seeking and risky offline activities because they show little effect on vulnerability to harm. This result, however, provides further support for the usefulness of the vulnerability hypothesis.

Complex coping strategies

We next investigate the aftermath of being harmed. Using the possible reactions to the four types of harm investigated (online bullying, sexual images, sexual messages and meeting new people) we can identify four different strategies which can be grouped into two broad types of actions:
   Passive coping strategies include:

- *Fatalistic:* "Hoped the problem would go away", "Stopped using the internet".
- *Self-accusatory:* "Feel a bit guilty about what went wrong".

Active coping strategies include:

- *Communicative (seeking social support):* "Talked to someone about what happened".
- *Proactive:* "Tried to fix the problem" and "online defence activities", such as "Deleted any messages from the other person", "Changed filter/contact settings", "Blocked other person", "Reported the problem to an internet adviser or ISP [internet service provider]".

For those coping strategies that fell outside these four broad categories, we used the label 'other or not known'.

The results show that for all four types of risk, the main tendencies of the coping strategies are the same: the most common coping strategies are proactive and communicative, with fewer children adopting fatalistic or self-accusatory schemes. In the case of online bullying, 74 per cent of children talked to somebody about what had happened and tried actively to change the situation. In just over a third of cases there was a fatalistic response. When seeing unwanted and upsetting sexual images, about half of the children chose a communicative strategy, and 52 per cent of them also tried to do something on their own. However, 41 per cent also reported "just waiting" or stopping their use of the internet. In those cases, when the child received sexual messages, communicative and proactive behaviour was more common than in the case of just seeing the images. The occurrence of fatalistic responses was 35 per cent. Children who met online contacts offline also talked to someone (53 per cent), or tried to solve the problem by taking active steps (50 per cent), while the proportion of fatalistic responses was 35 per cent. Feeling guilty, in other words, following the self-accusatory strategy, was the least common response for all types of risk (see Table 24.6).

In the report on the findings of the EU Kids Online project these coping strategies are analysed separately (Livingstone et al, 2010). However, only a small minority of children choose a single coping strategy; most adopt more than one solution, which means that they mix the theoretically separate types of action in developing a coping strategy. Accordingly, fatalism or self-accusation schemes are rarely adopted on their own.

In order to have a clear understanding of the structure of different coping strategies, we identify three broad categories: (i) only passive,

Table 24.6: Characteristics of coping strategies related to different types of risks

	Online bullying (%)	Seeing sexual images (%)	Receiving sexual messages (%)	Meeting new contacts online (%)
Passive				
Fatalistic	36	41	35	35
Self-accusatory	12	9	5	10
Active				
Communicative	74	49	58	53
Proactive	76	52	64	50
Other or not known				
Other	7	18	13	24

(ii) only active and (iii) mixed, with fatalistic and self-accusatory responses in the passive category and communicative and proactive responses in the active category. If one or two active and passive responses are present together, we used the third, mixed category.

Our results show that a sole passive type of coping is very rare among children encountering risks and being harmed to some extent. Only 4 per cent of children who were bullied responded passively. In the case of meeting strangers, this is 7 per cent, but it is still a small minority of children who did nothing specific. The absence of active responses is slightly higher among those who saw sexual images or pornographic content online (13 per cent) or received sexual messages (10 per cent) (see Table 24.7).

The results confirm the findings from the EU Kids Online research, which indicate that children's responses are generally positive: most children feel empowered to seek social support or act on their own.

Table 24.7: Summary of coping strategies

	Online bullying (%)	Seeing sexual images (%)	Receiving sexual messages (%)	Meeting online contacts offline (%)
Total (only) passive	4	13	10	7
Total (only) active	56	45	55	42
Total passive + active	40	42	35	51
	100	100	100	100

Conclusion

This chapter provides a complex overview of risk patterns, potential harm and coping strategies. One of our initial questions was whether there are typical risk patterns: are there some risk types that go together, or are these risky usage forms mainly independent acts? Our results show that certain similar risky activities may go together: for example, children who engage in some kind of online practice related to sexuality may turn to related online activities. However, other risk pairs show significant, but weaker correlations. Notably, online bullying has the weakest links to any other types of risks, suggesting that this kind of online experience has special determinants.

We also investigated typical risk and harm factors. Using two regression models we identified patterns and factors leading to potential exposure to risk and harm. The models included different individual, family and wider social factors. In case of risk our results provide support for the usage and the risk migration hypotheses, since the complexity of internet usage and the presence of risky offline activities have the biggest effect on increasing the probability of exposure to risk. For harm (protective) factors, the most important determinant is emotional problems. This result supports the vulnerability hypothesis (see Chapter 12). Both models confirmed that individual factors are the most important. Family and social context characteristics are of secondary importance only. Of course their indirect effect should not be underestimated, since family background could have a great effect on certain psychological factors, such as emotional problems.

The results in this chapter support the notion that the offline and online environments are not separate activity spheres, but are closely related. Those who tend to participate in risky offline activities are more likely to do so online, and those who have emotional problems are generally more vulnerable to online threats. This suggests that the online activities of children considered to be at risk in general should be monitored by professionals with knowledge of relationships within the family (for example, teachers, social workers, etc). It is also important that professionals involved should have sufficient information and possibilities to develop relevant skills to empower them to handle situations that involve online risks and harm.

Finally, this chapter addressed the complex nature of coping strategies. We found that the majority of children who were upset after being exposed to some kind of risk chose an active response to his or her problem. In other words, they tried to solve the problem by taking action or by talking to someone. This contrasts with common assumptions about how children cope with online risks and supports the thesis that some exposure to risk builds resilience and produces positive responses. However, this relation needs more investigation.

Notes

[1] For *exposure to potentially harmful content* and *personal data misuse* we aggregated the results of multiple-item questions and used a dummy variable for exposure or not to such risks in general. The potentially harmful content includes websites that discuss: (i) ways of physically harming or hurting oneself; (ii) ways of committing suicide; (iii) ways to be very thin; (iv) hate messages that attack certain groups or individuals; and (v) experiences of taking drugs. The items for personal data misuse are: (i) "Somebody used my personal information in a way I didn't like", (ii) "I lost money by being cheated in the internet" and (iii) "Somebody used my password to access my information or to pretend to be me".

[2] We created a composite index variable based on information from separate indexes on peer problems; emotional and conduct problems were aggregated using principal component analysis.

[3] Unfortunately for the remaining variables used in the previous model there are no separate questions that measure their harm. To calculate the index, we summed the values of the four variables for the extent of being upset: 0 = not at all upset, 1 = a bit upset, 2 = fairly upset, 3 = very upset. The values of the resulting index range from 0 to 12.

References

Cohen, J. (1992) 'A power primer', *Psychological Bulletin*, vol 112, no 1, pp 155-9.

Cunningham, H. (2006) *The invention of childhood*, London: BBC Books.

Gill, T. (2007) *No fear. Growing up in a risk averse society*, London: Calouste Gulbenkian Foundation.

Hansson, S.O. (2007) 'Risk', *Stanford Encyclopedia of Philosophy* (http://plato.stanford.edu/entries/risk/).

Livingstone. S. (2010) *E-youth: (Future) policy implications: Reflections on online risk, harm and vulnerability*, London: London School of Economics and Political Science Research Online (http://eprints.lse.ac.uk/27849/1/eYouth_(future)_policy_implications_(LSERO_version).pdf).

Livingstone. S. and Bober. M. (2005) *UK children go online: Final report of key project findings*, London: London School of Economics and Political Science Research Online (http://eprints.lse.ac.uk/archive/00000399).

Livingstone, S. and Helsper, E. (2009) 'Balancing opportunities and risks in teenagers' use of the internet: the role of online skills and internet self–efficacy', *New Media & Society*, vol 11, no 8, pp 1-25.

Livingstone, S., Haddon, L., Görzig, A. and Ólafsson, K. (2010) *Risks and safety on the internet: The perspective of European children. Full findings*, London: London School of Economics and Political Science.

Lupton, D. (2005) *Risk*, New York: Routledge.

Masten, A.S. and Gewirtz, A.H. (2006) 'Vulnerability and resilience in early child development', in K. McCartney and D. Phillips (eds) *Blackwell handbook of early childhood development*, Malden/Oxford: Blackwell Publishing, pp 22-44.

Schoon, I. (2006) *Risk and resilience. Adaptations in changing times*, Cambridge: Cambridge University Press.

TWENTY-FIVE

Towards a general model of determinants of risk and safety

Sonia Livingstone, Uwe Hasebrink and Anke Görzig

Introduction

Rapid adoption of the internet and other online technologies is presenting policy makers, governments and industry with a significant task of ensuring that online opportunities are maximised and the risks associated with internet use are minimised and managed. Online opportunities are the focus of considerable public and private sector activity, and diverse ambitious efforts are underway in many countries to promote digital learning technologies in schools, e-governance initiatives, digital participation and digital literacy. The risks associated with the technologies are receiving similar attention through national and international initiatives that address child protection, cybersecurity and privacy, and through discussions explaining the potential for state and/or self-regulation.

Policy initiatives assume particular circumstances, understandings and practices applying to children, their parents and teachers. These assumptions may be more or less accurate and well judged, and at worst, they may be unnecessarily anxious or already out of date. Herein lies the value of direct research on children's contemporary experiences across diverse contexts. But although technological and regulatory change since the early 2000s has been accompanied by research seeking to understand the social shaping and consequences of internet use, early research tended to be more descriptive than theoretical (Wellman, 2004). However, since researchers seek to understand and predict children's online experiences, mere descriptions of survey findings are insufficient.

Consequently, a central feature of the EU Kids Online project has been to develop a theoretical framework within which its findings can be interpreted because, in the absence of theory, three problems occur. First, it is difficult to say what 'findings' mean since they are open to multiple interpretations – for example, is a certain percentage large or small, surprising or banal? Second, findings tend to be mere lists of percentages that cannot be connected to the findings of other studies, either in the domain of children's internet use or in relation to other studies of risk in childhood, the nature of parenting, or the role of the internet in adolescent development. Third, theory is needed to generate predictions and, so, to go beyond the particularity of any one data set in order to anticipate the consequences of different combinations of factors in future situations. In short, theory enables the judicious evaluation of evidence, it extends its relevance into bordering domains and it allows for generalisations beyond the particular.

However, when framing new lines of investigation, such as that of children's online experiences of opportunities and risks, the theory is somewhat thin on the ground, which has tended to impede analysis of survey data in this area. To put it simply, there is no carefully developed, widely accepted, readily operationalised theory of children's internet use. Thus, when we designed our research initially, despite our substantial review of the literature (Hasebrink et al, 2009), we had only a partly completed jigsaw puzzle, with some obvious pieces in place but also some whose contribution to the larger picture was unclear at the start of our project. Having embarked on our empirical work, the very complexity of the resulting data set then invited exploration from many theoretical perspectives – first in the construction of the variables and then especially in the examination of their interrelations. Even though some of our initial ideas had to be discarded or substantially revised, as charted in the foregoing chapters, we can now observe that, significantly, the results have broadly converged to support the working model proposed in Chapter 1.

This working model had been formalised first by building on a set of basic questions often posed by researchers, policy makers and the public (see, for example, Internet Safety Technical Task Force, 2008; Carr and Hilton, 2009; Livingstone, 2011). These were used to structure the interviews with children and then the data analysis, specifically: how do children use the internet?; what do children do online?; what online factors shape their experiences and their risk experiences in particular?; and what are the outcomes for children (in terms of benefits and harms, our focus being on self-reported harms)? These core questions were examined in terms of child and parental perceptions, and contextualised, first, in relation to the circumstances of the individual (that is, regarding internet use as shaped by demographic and psychological variables) and then in widening concentric circles around the individual, following Bronfenbrenner's (1979) ecological theory of child development.[1] Thus we worked both with the child as the unit of analysis, including the immediate social context as shaped by parents, teachers and peers, and with the country as the unit of analysis, focusing on such national factors as socioeconomic stratification, regulatory framework, technological infrastructure, education system and cultural values.

Our working model is grounded in several linked areas of theory (Livingstone, 2009). A general influence was the historically and culturally sensitive contextualisation of childhood (Cunningham, 2006; James and James, 2008), which is underpinned by the social theory of individualisation and the risk society in late modernity (Beck, 1986, 2005; Giddens, 1991). More specifically, we applied these theories to new media developments to construct a critical account of moral panics about media in children's lives (Critcher, 2008), complemented by an agentic account of media appropriation, by children (Buckingham, 2008) and within the home (Berker et al, 2006). Together, they refuse over-celebratory notions of 'digital natives', panicky accounts of the dangerous internet, technologically determinist accounts of radical societal transformations and idealised visions of family life. However, these theories can be less helpful for understanding the processes of social development from childhood through adolescence to young adulthood (Coleman and Hendry, 1999), or for grasping the specific affordances of digital media and a convergence culture (Jenkins, 2006). Nevertheless, while there are some disagreements about emphasis or direction, taken together, these diverse theories contribute to a framework able to encompass the fast-developing body of research on children and online risk (see, for example, Hope, 2007; Mitchell et al, 2007; Stern, 2008; Valkenburg and Peter, 2009; Patchin and Hinduja, 2010).

On a more practical level, the EU Kids Online survey has produced what is essentially a huge matrix, defined by about 25,000 individual respondents on one dimension, and about 1,000 variables on the other. Typically, theory is built from the relations that structure the variable dimension, although an idiographic account – a typology of individuals – can be derived from the respondent dimension. Ideally, these two should converge in a common account of the important patterns in a data set. Note that this is to operationalise the above theory, metaphorically and literally, in terms of the general linear model. For the most part, then, we extracted from the data set a series of conceptually distinct and reliable measures, and sought to understand their intercorrelations, whether simple bivariate associations or more complex paths, through reference to the working model. Some of the chapters in this volume focused in detail on particular parts of the model; others took a wider overview of patterns of relations among the variables. It will also be observed, however, that the limitations of the general linear model (which underpins the multiple regressions and related analyses widely used in this volume) also became apparent in the process, for many social processes are cyclic, with key variables mutually influencing each other bi-directionally. For example, the nature of children's experiences online leads their parents to increase or reduce their supervisory activities, this in turn shaping the conditions under which children go online. Similarly, the more children encounter risks through their internet use the more they develop skills and resilience, and this in turn alters how much they go online as well as the consequences of their encountering risk. Ideally, future research would undertake longitudinal studies that could track children's changing online experiences over time, identifying the path dependencies that progressively enable or constrain the opportunities and risks before them.

A typology of young internet users

To conclude this book and to draw together the many insights and findings in the foregoing chapters, we examine the similarities and differences among individuals in order to propose a typology of young internet users, and then look at the associations among factors shaping online risk and safety. Our motivation here is the recognition that, on the one hand, it is hardly helpful to consider every different way in which each individual child goes online but, on the other, it is problematic that discourses of childhood and of the internet tend to treat 'children' as a homogeneous category and to construct 'the internet' as something unitary and fixed (Livingstone, 2009; Hasebrink et al, 2011).

Our research recognises that the internet is complex in its affordances and diverse in its uses, and that children are not all the same. We sought a middle way – identifying some broad patterns in children's online use to enable the construction of a typology of young online users that allows for individual differences but also permits some general conclusions. The foregoing chapters in this volume reveal that frequency and amount of internet use correlate with variations in the places children use when going online. Together, they provide a strong indication of their likely online opportunities and risks. A more subtle account is achieved by including the range of online activities that children undertake, which, in turn, is indicative of their diverse motivations and skills, captured by 'the ladder of opportunities' presented in Chapter 6. The end result of combining all these variables was the cluster analysis identifying six 'user types' presented in Chapter 10.

While these user types were initially based on online uses and opportunities, what also emerges strongly from the EU Kids Online findings is the positive association between opportunities and risks, which suggests that efforts to increase opportunities will be likely to increase risks, and that efforts to reduce risks will be likely to restrict opportunities. When we examine the six user types in relation to measures of risk and harm, a more complex relation to online risks is revealed (see Table 25.1, developed from Hasebrink et al, 2011, in turn developing the earlier research in Livingstone, 2006).

- *'Low risk novices':* average age 11.1 years; this group does not use the internet for long or for many activities. The focus is mainly schoolwork, watching video clips and reading/watching news, all fairly popular forms of one-to-many communication in which the internet is more of a mass medium than an interactive or creative one. Few in this group have social networking site profiles, and participation in risky online activities is low. The risk indicators are very low, but indicators for harm (among those who encounter risk) are quite high, particularly for sexual content and meeting new people. Not surprisingly, given their low digital skills, while at low risk this group seems vulnerable to harm. Their parents tend to be rather restrictive of their online activities – understandable in the light of their vulnerability yet in itself a factor that may prevent the exploration that builds resilience.

- *'Young networkers':* on average 12.7 years old and more girls than boys; this group is less likely than the first group to use the internet for schoolwork or news, and more likely to use social networking sites. They include some interactive experiences as well as mass communication uses, so it is not surprising that their incidence of risk is higher than in the first group, especially for meeting new online contacts offline. However, this group's greater resilience (possibly due to their slightly higher digital skills) means they report being upset by online risks less than the first group, so they report a lower risk of harm online.

- *'Moderate users':* a similar age to the second group (on average 12.7 years); they spend about the same time online, but engage in a wider range of activities (although not as many as the three succeeding groups) without the clear focus on social networking sites. They are less likely to encounter online risks directly linked to the communicative

Table 25.1: Six user types classified by risk and harm

	Low risk	High risk
Lower harm	**Moderate users**	**Risky explorers**
Age	Younger (12.7 years)	Older (13.5 years)
% girls	48%	More boys (38% girls)
Use (minutes online/day)	Low (71)	High (118)
Online activities (of 17)	Moderate (7.7)	Very high (13.2)
Risky online activities (of 5)	Low (0.7)	Very high (2.1)
Online skills (of 8)	Moderate (3.9)	Fairly high (5.8)
% restrictive parental mediation (reported by child)	Moderate (87%)	Low (69%)
Note:	Exception: high harm for sexual content	Exception: high harm for meeting new contacts
		Experienced networkers
Age		Oldest (14.1 years)
% girls		More girls (67%)
Use (minutes online/day		High (108)
Online activities (of 17)		High (9.6)
Online skills (of 8)		Fairly high (5.4)
Risky online activities (of 5)		High (1.5)
% restrictive parental mediation (reported by child)		Moderate (81%)
Note:		Exception: high harm for bullying
Medium harm	**Young networkers**	**Intensive gamers**
Age	Younger (12.7 years)	Older (13.6 years)
% girls	55%	More boys (37% girls)
Use (minutes online/day)	Low (72)	Very high (180)
Online activities (of 17)	Low (5.2)	High (9.8)
Risky online activities (of 5)	Moderate (1.0)	High (1.6)
Online skills (of 8)	Moderate (3.8)	Fairly high(5.4)
% restrictive parental mediation (reported by child)	Moderate (87%)	Fairly low (76%)
Higher harm	**Low risk novices**	
Age	Youngest (11.1 years)	
% girls	50%	
Use (minutes online/day)	Very low (50)	
Online activities (of 17)	Very low (3)	
Risky online activities (of 5)	Very low (0.3)	
Online skills (of 8)	Very low (1.7)	
% restrictive parental mediation (reported by child)	High (96%)	

functions of online media, that is, meeting new contacts. The general pattern of the results for this group can be characterised by the notion that opportunities and risks go hand in hand. Thus, some use among this group makes for some opportunities, some risk and, at least in relation to sexual content, some harm.

- *'Risky explorers'*: 13.5 years on average and more boys than girls; these children spend almost two hours a day online and engage in the most diverse range of activities in our study, including far more risky online activities and also the more advanced and creative activities on the ladder of opportunities. Not only are they the most likely to read/watch news, to download music or films, to send or receive emails, to play games with others and to use webcams, they are also the most likely to create avatars, use file-sharing sites, spend time in virtual worlds and write blogs. Although this group is slightly younger than the next two groups, with a lower level of use than in the 'intensive gamers' group (see below), they report the most risk encounters. However, looking at the single risks, the likelihood that those who have encountered a risk are bothered by this is comparatively low, particularly compared with the three younger groups. It is possible that these children who have the highest level of sensation-seeking (see Chapter 10) have become desensitised to harm, but equally that experiencing risk provides opportunities to learn (how) to cope, which renders them more resilient. Nonetheless, high use is clearly associated with high risk for these children. Perhaps unsurprisingly, their parents are the least restrictive as regards their child's internet use.

- *'Intensive gamers'*: on average 13.6 years and more often boys than girls; they are online for the longest of all (around three hours per day) and have a fairly wide range of activities. They like playing games – on their own or against the computer – and watching video clips, and engage in relatively little schoolwork, news or creative activities on the internet. Their exposure to risk is quite high, and some use the internet excessively – and relatively less restricted by their parents. Although high users, they are at lower risk than the previous group (but more than the three younger groups), possibly because the *intensive gamers'* lengthy use is less indicative of risk than the *risky explorers'* comparably high diversity of use.

- *'Experienced networkers'*: the oldest (average 14.1 years), with more girls than boys; they use the internet for less than two hours and have a fairly broad range of activities. They are the most frequent users of social networking sites. They also read/watch news, use instant messaging, post photos or music and write blogs. The most significant difference compared with the other groups is their complete lack of interest in gaming. Their online risk encounters are fairly high, as are their online risky activities, as similar to the previous group. The level of perceived harm is also comparatively low; they are least likely to be bothered by meeting new online contacts offline, but they are more often upset when they encounter bullying online – both may be consequences of the importance they place on social networking and interaction with peers.

What does this typology suggest? First, confirming the emphasis on adolescent social development, the analysis shows that age is the main differentiating factor. Gender is less important except for marking a well-known difference in preferences for social networking and gaming, and socioeconomic status matters mainly in relation to access rather than use.

Second, following the usage hypothesis ('the more, the more'), more use, more opportunities and, it seems to follow, more risk. However, those whose low use is focused largely on one-to-many activities encounter fewer risks than those whose low use includes peer-to-peer communication – thus mode of use matters. Similarly, among high users who encounter more risks, it is the most diverse users rather than those who use the internet for the longest period of time who experience the highest levels of risk. Those who use the internet a lot, but mainly for games or YouTube, report fewer risks than the 'risky explorers' group, suggesting that it is context that affords experimental engagement with Web 2.0 applications which lead to most risk.

Third, as has been stressed throughout this book, risk of harm does not necessarily result in actual harm. Theories of risk (Breakwell, 2007) emphasise that risk is a probabilistic judgement and, for the most part, the EU Kids Online evidence suggests that these probabilities are relatively low. Moreover, the harm from a risk may be greater for some children (low use, low risk) than for others (high use, high risk). Thus, it is crucial to understand how children's vulnerabilities or resilience factors mediate the relationship between risk and harm (Schoon, 2006).

Relationships among factors shaping online risk and safety

The patterning among variables (rather than children) points to some cautionary observations before moving to abstract generalisations. Many results from the statistical analyses in the chapters in this volume are statistically significant, but fairly small in terms of effect size (cf Cohen, 1992). Thus, it is not possible to propose a 'strong' theoretical model, because much of the variance observed remains unexplained. Also, as noted earlier, cross-sectional surveys cannot measure temporal relations (for example, which comes first, an upset child or a restrictive parent?); thus, causal claims remain only hypotheses, and cyclic relations cannot be examined.

Last, cross-national analysis proved particularly difficult, first, because the research literature provides few developed hypotheses (for example, what, at a cultural level, accounts for country differences in parenting?), second, because it was difficult to find reliable external indicators for the factors we hypothesised were important (for example, there are few robust indicators of country differences in regulatory frameworks), and third, because the few external indicators we were able to identify (for example, broadband penetration) ultimately explained rather little in relation to internet use. In what follows, the focus is, therefore, on patterns across Europe, bearing in mind that other causal hypotheses might be tested and new cross-cultural explanations might yet be proposed.

More constructively, the evidence obtained from the very substantial survey of European children largely supports the working model presented in Chapter 1, which does not require substantial revisions. The key features of the model are supported as follows.

In terms of overall structure, usage (breadth and extent) is associated with the range of activities such that both account for degrees of digital inclusion or exclusion (especially by age, but also by socioeconomic status and country); in turn, both usage and activities are correlated with digital skills, resulting in either a virtuous or a vicious circle, depending on the circumstances of the individual child. Also, activities are linked with risk factors, such that more use is connected to more online opportunities and more online risks and, conversely, restrictions on use or opportunities are the most effective but destructive (in terms of resilience building) means of reducing risks.

Finally, there is empirical support for one of the project's initial assertions that risks may or may not result in harm, depending on circumstances (many of them explored in the foregoing chapters); equally, although the project did not seek to measure actual benefits, we would hypothesise that, depending on the child's circumstances, undertaking a wide range of activities may or may not result in actual benefits. It might be more accurate to say that, in the demographic, psychological and social (that is, the offline) context of children's lives, there are both risk factors and protective factors – examples from the research include risk factors such as offline risky activities, and protective factors such as self-efficacy. Similarly, in the online context, both risk factors and protective factors occur – examples from the research include risk factors such as the receipt of unwanted sexual messages, and protective factors such as the use of filters or availability of safety tools.

In terms of Bronfenbrenner's (1979) ecological approach (individual, social and national), a focus on the individual user provides the best explanations – here, we identified the clearest relationships. These include the positive correlations between use, activities, skills and risks (cf the ladder of opportunities). Also, it is important to distinguish between risk and harm, summarised in the overall finding that children who are older, higher in self-efficacy and sensation-seeking, who engage in more online activities (that is, are higher up the ladder of opportunities) and who have more psychological problems, encounter more risks of all kinds online; in contrast, younger children, lower in self-efficacy and sensation-seeking, who undertake fewer online activities, have fewer skills and who have more psychological problems find online risks more harmful. In other words, the explanations for risk and for harm differ and should not be confused.

Overall, clear findings at the individual level are revealed – the primary significance of age as a variable structuring almost all aspects of children's experience of the internet; the importance of the psychological variables of self-efficacy, sensation-seeking and, most of all, psychological difficulties; and last, the importance of the measure of risky offline activities. This was proposed on the basis of consistent arguments in the research literature that a particular medium – such as 'the internet' – is unlikely to introduce entirely new problems into children's lives; rather, it is likely to change the communicative conditions of children's engagement with others and, thus, enable a degree of migration of risk from offline to online (as discussed in Chapter 12). The evidence from the project strongly supports this initial supposition, inviting further analysis of the continuities in children's lives across diverse contexts; future research, therefore, should ask many more questions about aspects of children's lives that seem unrelated to the internet, on the assumption that they will become relevant for understanding the significance of the internet. Also, we would propose that it is in these other aspects of children's lives that measures may be found to improve our observations (that is, effect sizes) and their explanation in relation to internet use.

We explored the level of social mediation primarily in terms of parenting, and future research could further develop the roles of the school, peers and other life contexts in shaping the nature and consequences of online use, activities, risk and harm in children's lives. A particular strength of the EU Kids Online survey was that each interview with children and parents posed matched questions, permitting some insightful analyses. For example, although at the aggregated country level it appeared that levels of risk estimated by children and their parents were similar, examining awareness of risk among individual parents matched with the children who had encountered it, parental awareness was low. We found that the greater the parents' familiarity with the internet, the greater their ability to mediate their child's internet use, and the more active and skilled their children in using the internet – and vice versa. Most important, the responses to the matched questions reveal that the children of more restrictive parents encounter fewer risks, but also make more limited use of the internet which could undermine their resilience to harm; this pinpoints the dilemma for policy makers and awareness-raisers – should they advise the imposition by parents of rules on their children's internet use, or not? Possibly the decision should depend on the child's degree of vulnerability, as this has been shown to make a difference – less in relation to online risk, but especially to the experience of online harm.

Cross-national explanations were the most difficult (see Lobe et al, 2011). Hypotheses that initially seemed plausible revealed evidence that seemed far more diverse. Given a complex situation, a complex conclusion must be drawn.

First, although in practice countries are subtly graded in terms of amounts and types of use and risk, we grouped them into four categories. Overall, we found that high internet use was rarely associated with low risk, and high risk was rarely associated with low use; rather, the more use, the more risk. Specifically, in 'lower use, lower risk' countries (Austria, Belgium, France, Germany, Greece, Italy and Hungary), children show the lowest internet usage and they are below average for all risks except meeting online contacts; however, it can be expected that as levels of use in these countries rise, so too will levels of risk.

Second, 'lower use, some risk' countries (Ireland, Portugal, Spain and Turkey) show low levels of internet usage, although there is some excessive use of the internet, and some problems with user-generated content. The 'higher use, some risk' countries (Cyprus, Finland, the Netherlands, Poland, Slovenia and the UK) show high levels of internet usage, but high levels of only some risks, possibly because of effective awareness-raising campaigns, regulatory strategies or some strategies of parental mediation of children's internet use. Last, 'higher use, higher risk' countries (Bulgaria, the Czech Republic, Denmark, Estonia, Lithuania, Norway, Romania and Sweden) include both wealthy Nordic countries and eastern European countries (better called, 'new use, new risk').

There is also some evidence that socioeconomic stratification, regulatory framework, technological infrastructure and the education system all shape children's online risks. Children in wealthier countries (measured by GDP) encounter more online risk, but, arguably, these countries are also well placed to provide more accessible and user-friendly safety resources for children and parents. Also, in countries where the press has more freedom, such as the Nordic and Baltic countries, children are more likely to encounter online risk. If researchers and policy makers wish to manage risk without introducing more stringent internet regulation, alternative strategies must be found to ensure safety without introducing censorship (as discussed in the next chapter).

At country level, somewhat unexpectedly, we found no systematic relation between level of parental filtering and children's risk experiences, although at the individual level there is a weak relationship – children whose parents use technical filtering are less likely to encounter sexual content, suggesting a useful role for technical solutions. Rather less unexpected is that the degree of broadband penetration, and length of time that most people have had internet access, are associated with higher levels of online risks, but not a wider range of activities among children. This suggests that, while children are motivated to use the internet everywhere in Europe, higher quality access brings more risks than are being adequately dealt with by policy makers. Last, in countries with a comparatively higher level of formal education, where full-time education continues for most of adolescents' lives (that is, for an average of 15 or more years), children are more likely to have better digital skills, as are children from countries where more schools use computers in the classroom; thus education clearly plays a positive role in supporting digital skills, digital literacies and citizenship, and should be supported across all countries.

Time does not stand still

The differences revealed by this pan-European project endorse differences across and within countries and contribute to the wider international effort to understand and influence the changing conditions of childhood. The same questions continue to be asked by researchers, policy makers and the public relating to the value of digital and online media, the digital literacies required to benefit from their use, whether inequalities in access or participation matter, when and how these technologies should be introduced into children's lives, whether the opportunities they afford outweigh the risks, and which risks result in real harm. The EU Kids Online project has sought to balance the commonalities and differences in children's lives as they embrace the internet in almost every dimension of their activities. Arguably, Europe has sufficient common history and political–economic realities as to result in more striking similarities than contrasts in European children's lives, pointing to the value of more international comparisons. Continuing changes in the technological and social landscapes make for a continually shifting research agenda, with new questions emerging. Key dimensions of these changes include:

- *technological environment:* the array of increasingly personalised, networked, convergent and mobile media products and services;
- *social environment:* the changing contexts of media use, as digital and online media are more deeply embedded in diverse spheres of life, blurring the boundaries between home and school, public and private, work and leisure;
- *regulatory regime:* as new forms of national and transnational governance and new kinds of self- and co-regulatory organisation emerge, with varying degrees of accountability and effectiveness;
- *practices of childhood:* as children's agency promotes more digitally literate, creative, participatory and peer-to-peer activities, albeit with considerable variations.

This chapter sought to summarise both what we now know, as a result of the EU Kids Online research, and the new questions that are emerging. The final chapter in this volume reviews the implications of these aspects for the linked agendas of policy makers and researchers.

Note
[1] Bronfenbrenner postulated four types of nested systems: (i) microsystem (for example, family or classroom); (ii) mesosystem (two microsystems in interaction); (iii) exosystem (external environments that indirectly influence development, for example, parental workplace); and (iv) macrosystem (larger sociocultural context). According to Bronfenbrenner, the roles and norms in each system shape development.

References

Beck, U. (1986/2005) *Risk society: Towards a new modernity*, London: Sage Publications.

Berker, T., Hartmann, M., Punie, Y. and Ward, K.J. (eds) (2006) *The domestication of media and technology*, Maidenhead: Open University Press.

Breakwell, G. (2007) *The psychology of risk*, Cambridge: Cambridge University Press.

Bronfenbrenner, U. (1979) *The ecology of human development*, Cambridge, MA: Harvard University Press.

Buckingham, D. (ed) (2008) *Youth, identity, and digital media*, Cambridge, MA: The MIT Press.

Carr, J. and Hilton, Z. (2009) 'Child protection and self-regulation in the internet industry: the UK experience', *Children & Society*, vol 23, no 4, pp 303-8.

Cohen, J. (1992) 'A power primer', *Psychological Bulletin*, 112(1), pp 155-9.

Coleman, J. and Hendry, L. (1999) *The nature of adolescence* (3rd edn), London: Routledge.

Critcher, C. (2008) 'Making waves: historic aspects of public debates about children and mass media', in K. Drotner and S. Livingstone (eds) *International handbook of children, media and culture*, London: Sage Publications, pp 91-104.

Cunningham, H. (2006) *The invention of childhood*, London: BBC Books.

Giddens, A. (1991) *Modernity and self-identity: Self and society in the late modern age*, Cambridge: Polity Press.

Hasebrink, U., Livingstone, S., Haddon, L. and Olafsson, K. (2009) *Comparing children's online opportunities and risks across Europe: Cross-national comparisons for EU Kids Online* (2nd edn), London: EU Kids Online, London School of Economics and Political Science.

Hasebrink, U., Görzig, A.S., Haddon, L.G., Kalmus, V. and Livingstone, S. (2011) *Patterns of risk and safety online: In-depth analyses from the EU Kids Online survey of 9- to 16-year-olds and their parents in 25 European countries*, August, London: EU Kids Online, London School of Economics and Political Science.

Hope, A. (2007) 'Risk taking, boundary performance and intentional school internet "misuse"', *Discourse*, vol 28, no 1, pp 87-99.

Internet Safety Technical Task Force (2008) *Enhancing child safety and online technologies: Final report of the ISTTF to the multi-state working group on social networking of State Attorney Generals of the United States*, Cambridge, MA: Berkman Center for Internet and Society, Harvard University.

James, A. and James, A.L. (eds) (2008) *European childhoods: Cultures, politics and childhoods in Europe*, Basingstoke: Palgrave Macmillan.

Jenkins, H. (2006) *Convergence culture: Where old and new media collide*, New York: New York University Press.

Livingstone, S. (2006) 'Drawing conclusions from new media research: reflections and puzzles regarding children's experience of the internet', *The Information Society*, vol 22, no 4, pp 219-30.

Livingstone, S. (2009) *Children and the internet: Great expectations, challenging realities*, Cambridge: Polity Press.

Livingstone, S. (2011) 'Regulating the internet in the interests of children: emerging European and international approaches', in R. Mansell and M. Raboy (eds) *The handbook on global media and communication policy*, Oxford: Blackwell, pp 505-24.

Lobe, B., Livingstone, S., Ólafsson, K. and Vodeb, H. (2011) *Cross-national comparison of risks and safety on the internet: Initial analysis from the EU Kids Online survey of European children*, London: EU Kids Online, London School of Economics and Political Science.

Mitchell, K.J., Wolak, J. and Finkelhor, D. (2007) 'Trends in youth reports of sexual solicitations, harassment and unwanted exposure to pornography on the internet', *Journal of Adolescent Health*, vol 40, no 2, pp 116-26.

Patchin, J.W. and Hinduja, S. (2010) 'Trends in online social networking: adolescent use of MySpace over time', *New Media & Society*, vol 12, no 2, pp 197-216.

Schoon, I. (2006) *Risk and resilience: Adaptations in changing times*, New York: Cambridge University Press.

Stern, S. (2008) 'Producing sites, exploring identities: youth online authorship', in D. Buckingham (ed) *Youth, identity, and digital media* (vol 6), Cambridge, MA: The MIT Press, pp 95-117.

Valkenburg, P.M. and Peter, J. (2009) 'Social consequences of the internet for adolescents: a decade of research', *Current Directions in Psychological Science*, vol 18, no 1, pp 1-5.

Wellman, B. (2004) 'The three ages of internet studies: ten, five and zero years ago', *New Media & Society*, vol 6, no 1, pp 123-9.

TWENTY-SIX

Policy implications and recommendations: now what?

Brian O'Neill and Elisabeth Staksrud

Introduction

In recent years, the policy agenda concerned with children's use of the internet has assumed an increasingly prominent role, due to sustained efforts on the part of civil society and of various government agencies to raise awareness about the topic. Policy considerations encompass both online opportunities (focused on access to education, communication, information and participation) and the risks of harm posed to children by internet use. In relation to risks and safety, the main focus of this book, the agenda remains a highly contested one. This is partly because evidence about children's experience of internet technologies has to date been patchy, in some countries more than others. It is also because the benefits of particular policy actions, whether focused on state intervention, industry self-regulation, educational initiatives or parent (and child) safety awareness, are as yet unproven. Last, it is contested because children's safety gives rise to considerable public anxiety, even moral panic, over childhood freedom and innocence, all compounded by an uncertainty and fear of the power of new and complex technologies.

Research findings, as detailed throughout this volume, provide new kinds of evidence that are significant for policy makers and raise new questions about how to respond to the fact that the internet is now thoroughly embedded in children's lives. Policy attention in this area has, since the early 2000s, shifted from a focus on content-related risks, for example, exposure to pornographic and violent content, to contact and conduct-related risks, such as grooming and cyberbullying. Arguably, this shift reflects the increase in children's participation in the online environment. Children no longer simply consume content; they are creators of content and encouraging children to be safe and responsible users of online technologies needs to take account of their diverse roles as consumer, participant and creator.

Against the background of sustained policy initiatives, as supported by the EC Safer Internet Programme among others, this chapter examines the following policy-related questions:

- What implications for internet safety arise in the context of a rapidly changing technological environment and shifting patterns of access and use?
- How can stakeholders manage persistent risks to children's welfare that appear to be amplified in the online world, and deal with completely new risks that are now emerging?
- What are the most effective and appropriate ways to mediate and support children's internet use to maximise the benefits and reduce harm?
- How, given the wide diversity of contexts across Europe, can policy goals of equality and inclusiveness be promoted?

Central to the research presented in this volume is its framing within a particular policy context. Informed by a detailed review of existing findings in European research evidence, EU Kids Online offers the first fully comparable, European evidence base of children and parents' experiences of the internet. A central objective at the outset was knowledge enhancement to inform policy making. The need for a rigorous evidence base – with detailed national and European data – to support awareness-raising and safety initiatives and to guide future policy development was identified at an early stage by the European Commission (2004), and following identification of research gaps in its first phase (2006-09), the project developed a detailed survey instrument to investigate the most important issues of risk and safety. In both this and during subsequent phases of implementing the survey and dissemination of its findings, close stakeholder consultation was an integral element of the project. Working with representative civil society groups, government agencies and the network of Safer Internet Centres, individual national teams organised stakeholder meetings in which the most significant research findings were highlighted and policy priorities, particularly within the national context, were identified. Formal presentation of research findings to the European Commission included detailed discussion of policy implications and recommendations (O'Neill and McLaughlin, 2010; O'Neill et al, 2011), in addition to presentation at the Safer Internet Forum, Europe's premier online safety forum, convened by the Safer Internet Programme and bringing together industry, law enforcement authorities, child welfare organisations and policy makers. Finally, the project's International Advisory Panel (IAP), comprising experts and policy makers from around the world, provided an important international benchmark for assessing policy relevance and locating findings and points of policy interest within a global context.

In this chapter, we review the background to the project's policy objectives and highlight the principal recommendations that emerged from the findings of EU Kids Online. The focus in this chapter is primarily on Europe and policy actions framed at a European level and/ or implemented within member states of the European Union (EU). While the European Commission's Safer Internet Programme is the primary point of reference, the Council of Europe, the International Telecommunication Union, various United Nations organisations (UNICEF, UNESCO) and the Internet Governance Forum among other international agencies have also contributed to an increasingly dynamic policy debate on internet safety. Against a background of intense debate regarding the effectiveness of self-regulatory regimes as mechanisms for online child protection, the chapter examines gaps in policy formulations for internet safety, asking whether current policy is effective and how policy makers can address future challenges in an area that continues to evolve and become more complex.

Policy context

A digital agenda for Europe (European Commission, 2010a), the overarching policy framework for the Information Society in Europe, is a central reference point for policy priorities in relation to trust, safety and security in the information environment. Framed as a roadmap for policy to the year 2020, it includes measures to promote the building of digital confidence and digital literacy skills, based on the premise that safer internet use engenders greater public confidence and digital inclusion. Digital competence, including an understanding of how to be safe online, is also a policy priority and one of eight key competences in the European Framework for lifelong learning (European Parliament and the Council of the European Union, 2006) and in Commission policy on the importance of media literacy for all, especially media literacy in the digital environment (European Commission, 2007).

The theme of online child protection has, in fact, been a topic of policy concern ever since the World Wide Web emerged as mass phenomenon in the mid-1990s. With growing commercialisation of the internet and rapid uptake by the general public of user-friendly web services, fears have grown about the spread of harmful and illegal content, about risks from online predators and growing concern about the internet as a potentially dangerous or 'lawless' place, especially for children. Responding to such concerns and amid calls for tighter control, policy makers have sought to balance two competing demands. On the one hand, governments everywhere have sought to encourage, with the least amount of direct interference, the development of the Information Society and the consequent benefits for society as a whole. At the same time, policy makers have been at pains to develop strategies that minimise the apparent downsides of unregulated access and the increased risk to children and families from potentially harmful internet content. This delicate balancing act has resulted in a number of legislative and regulatory dilemmas. Early efforts to extend traditional content regulation to the online world, such as the US Communications Decency Act 1996, have proved largely unsuccessful, foundering on the need to protect the fundamental freedom of expression that characterises the internet (Nesson and Marglin, 1996). In many cases, governments argue that sufficient protection is provided on the basis that what is illegal offline is also illegal online (Akdeniz et al, 2000), yet tensions continue to be felt over the readiness of governments to adopt policies that support and harness the economic potential of information technologies in contrast with the apparent lack of urgency in protecting citizens from exploitation and risk of predation via the internet. More recently, there is a growing recognition that the persistence of pessimism and a lack of trust on the part of the general public actually threaten the development of the internet's full potential (Reding, 2009).

The *Green Paper on the protection of minors and human dignity* (European Commission, 1996a) and communication on *Illegal and harmful content on the internet* (European Commission, 1996b) highlight the EU's early commitment to a protective regime, although successive measures implemented under its various programmes highlight some of the inherent difficulties in multilateral, multi-stakeholder action. The tension exhibited is also illustrated in the two key principles underpinning the European approach to information and communications technology (ICT) in general, and online safety in particular. On the one hand, public policy at the European level is underpinned by the so-called precautionary principle, in that there is a requirement on regulatory agencies to protect the public from exposure to harm, emphasising a 'better safe than sorry' approach to technological innovations (European Commission, 2000; Schomberg, 2006). At the same time, the principles set out in the 1994 Bangemann report on the emerging information society, strongly support self-regulation on the part of industry, coordinated ultimately at European level in order to support the development of a single European market. This broad regulatory framework has coincided with a shift from the traditional 'command and control' model of content regulation to a more diverse and individualised market for online services in which industry, responding to new challenges in a fast-changing technological environment, self-regulates through agreed principles and codes of conduct (Marsden, 2011).

In practice, self-regulation frequently entails varying degrees of partnership between private sector and relevant regulatory agencies. Safety provision has been developed on the basis of regulatory agencies and other stakeholder groups working with industry to agree common principles and codes of practice to which all participating partners subscribe (Tambini et al, 2008). Given the pace of change in the communications environment, industry is viewed as best placed to respond to the latest technologies and use trends, and to their safety implications. As such, industry-led codes are relied on to deal with risk, safety and child protection issues that accompany new technological developments. The *European Framework for safer mobile use by young teenagers and children* (GSMA, 2007), for example, is one such self-regulatory agreement signed by most mobile operators in Europe, and monitored for implementation and compliance (GSMA, 2010). Similarly, the *Safer social networking principles for the EU* (European Commission, 2009) incorporates guidelines signed by most of Europe's major social network providers, although successive evaluations point to deficiencies in default privacy settings, reporting procedures (Staksrud and Lobe, 2010) and age-verification mechanisms (Livingstone et al, 2011a).

In practical terms, EU policy initiatives to ensure internet safety have been coordinated since 1999 within the Information Society Directorate's Safer Internet Programme. Initial efforts were focused on formulating and developing an action plan to create a safer environment for children online, through self-regulatory initiatives such as filtering and content classification, and support hotlines for reporting illegal content (European Commission, 1999). The action plan intended to make 'a link between users, market and technology developments, and EU policy' (European Commission, 2001, p 1; see also Sommer, 2001). This plan developed into a full-scale programme providing support to European organisations through INHOPE, the network of hotlines, and Insafe, the European network of national awareness centres. Awareness centres work with a broad range of partners, including schools, libraries, youth groups and industry, to promote internet safety, and are intended to be the primary, national-level platforms for internet safety awareness. The European Commission also supports knowledge enhancement projects (of which EU Kids Online is one) (European Commission, 2010b, 2011), aimed at informing practical safety work and providing implications for policy. The current Safer Internet Programme (2009-13) has broadened to encompass new Web 2.0 internet services, such as social networking, and to deal with illegal content and harmful conduct, such as grooming and bullying. The objectives of the Safer Internet Programme continue to be to increase public awareness and support for reporting mechanisms, to establish and support information contact points and to continue to foster self-regulatory initiatives (European Commission, 2010b).

Varied European landscape for internet safety

While there may be general consensus on internet safety as a policy goal with several legal instruments giving effect to this across Europe – the *Green Paper on the protection of minors and human dignity* (European Commission, 1996) or the Council of Europe's recommendation on empowering young people online (Council of Europe, 2006), for instance, in practical terms, there is wide variation in its implementation. The 25 European countries included in the EU Kids Online survey differ widely in geography, culture and politics, and vary in physical and population size. They also differ in terms of internet usage and online risk factors (Livingstone and Haddon, 2009). Most, but not all, are members of the EU; all except Turkey are members of Insafe.

Countries in the survey also vary in the degree of governmental importance attached to internet safety as a policy issue, the extent to which there are dedicated statutory or other regulatory bodies with responsibility for internet safety, and in wider societal engagement in safety awareness through non-governmental organisations and other groups concerned with child protection and children's welfare. Legislative provision, likewise, varies substantially across Europe, adding to the complexity of dealing at the pan-European level with such issues as data protection, privacy, copyright and the protection of minors. Stakeholders in Romania and Turkey, for instance, report no substantial national policy on internet safety, while in northern Europe and the UK, internet safety has been the subject of sustained policy interest for many years (Jorge et al, 2010).

In the EU Kids Online survey, several country-level contextual factors were found to have influenced children's encounters with online risk. Factors such as socioeconomic stratification, regulatory framework, technological infrastructure and educational system were found to have a significant effect on shaping children's online risk encounters across countries (Lobe et al, 2011), emphasising the importance of targeted and nationally specific policy recommendations. Responsibility for education, as for media regulation, is an area of responsibility of member states rather than for Europe. Unsurprisingly, there is much variation across the continent in provision for digital skills education. According to EACEA,[1] internet safety education features in school curricula in 24 countries/regions (Eurydice, 2009). However, its implementation diverges considerably. In 11 of 30 countries, internet safety was not part of the school curriculum, and in some countries, schools had local autonomy over whether to include it at all. Internet literacy was viewed as a very recent development in most systems; in 80 per cent of the countries surveyed, internet safety was not introduced until 2007. Teachers responsible for delivering internet safety education, it was found, did not always have specific training, and there was substantial variation in both content and the curriculum framework within which it was implemented.

Implications for risks and safety

To date, safer internet policies have been based on multi-stakeholder strategies that encourage industry to make services and products safer for young people and that support parents and guardians to more effectively mediate and guide their children's internet use. A combination of content labelling, parental software controls and awareness-raising efforts, initially aimed at parents and now increasingly targeted at young people themselves, have been to the fore in an ongoing effort of all partners, public and private. The contribution of a substantial body of new data on young people's use of internet technologies and experience of online risks allows such efforts to be more closely targeted to new and emerging usage trends as well as to those most in need or underserved by existing approaches.

Data from EU Kids Online, rigorously collected and cross-nationally comparable, provides for the first time in a European context a robust evidence base to guide such policy action. In the first instance, it provides a wealth of evidence about children's *access and use* of internet technologies: which children in Europe are fully online, the changing contexts of access within households, schools and public places, the devices and platforms used, and the digital skills practised by children. Second, the research provides evidence on the kinds of *activities* young people engage in and the opportunities they avail of, exploring the balance between content-based activities, contact and communication-oriented activities and conduct or peer participation activities (Hasebrink et al, 2011). Third, accurate data is provided on the extent of exposure to online risks, and identifies those who are most harmed or bothered by such exposure. Fourth, the research gives an indication of to whom children turn for support and which forms of mediation, whether by parents, teachers or peers, prove to be the most effective. Findings, in each case, entail implications for current policy and call attention to new areas requiring intervention.

In relation to *access and use*, with 93 per cent of 9- to 16-year-old users going online at least once a week and 60 per cent almost every day, EU Kids Online provides a strong illustration of just how thoroughly the internet is embedded in children's lives (Livingstone et al, 2011b). However, education, age and gender are significant factors in shaping the quality of children's use of the internet (see Chapter 4, this volume). Evidence of where children use the internet (Chapter 5, this volume), which opportunities they pursue (Chapter 6, this volume) and the skills they practice (Chapter 7, this volume) are critically important for developing more targeted policy interventions. Traditionally, teenagers have been the main subjects of awareness-raising and education. As such, there is now a gap in internet safety support for younger children and their parents. Across Europe, a third of 9- to 10-year-olds use the internet daily. The average age of first internet use in some countries is seven, but many start using the internet before they reach school age. The youngest children lack skills and confidence in areas of internet use that are especially related to risk and safety. Younger children are active on social networking sites and are more likely than older children to have their profiles set to 'public' (over a quarter of 9- to 12-year-olds) (Livingstone et al, 2011b). Younger children are also likely to have fewer skills, less confidence in managing their safety and privacy online and lack the knowledge to realise the importance of doing so (see Chapter 10, this volume; Livingstone et al, 2011b).

Findings in relation to the *activities* children engage in provides a detailed map of the kinds of opportunities young people enjoy as well as the context in which risks occur. The research depicts a 'ladder of opportunities' (Livingstone and Helsper, 2007), a general trend across all children which characterises a gradation of internet opportunities from basic activities such as browsing and watching video clips to more sophisticated uses which call on more advanced skills and draw on the participative and creative potential of the internet. Just half of 9- to 10-year-olds and a third of 11- to 12-year-olds, for instance, use the internet in this passive way. From a policy point of view, it is important to encourage children to do more online, to broaden the range of activities engaged in, particularly in those countries and for those groups which do not progress very far up the ladder of opportunities. Encouraging young people to expand their horizons online improves their digital skill set and their safety skills. More provision of positive online content, especially for younger children, is another dimension of this, drawing on the finding that only a third of younger users find that there are lots of good things for them to do online.

The distinction made by EU Kids Online between *risk* and *harm* is of particular importance for policy makers. The research model recognises that since not all children encounter risks, and that risks do not always lead to harm, it is vital to identify the protective factors that reduce the probability of harm as well as the risk factors that increase it. Children who are older, higher in self-efficacy and sensation-seeking and who do more activities online encounter more risks of all kinds online. However, younger children who are younger, lower in self-efficacy and sensation-seeking, who do fewer online activities, have fewer skills and who have more psychological problems find online risks more harmful and upsetting. Targeting policy initiatives at those smaller groups of more vulnerable children is therefore recommended as being more effective than universal restriction of online opportunities. More attention to support children's capacity to cope themselves, building greater resilience as digital citizens, is likewise an important policy implication. The research also suggests that policy makers need to pay greater attention to the relationship between risks in the offline and online worlds. Lampert and Donoso (Chapter 11, this volume) and Görzig (2011) show that online bullies and online victims of bullies are often the same children who are most vulnerable to these threats offline. Victims of bullying are also sometimes the perpetrators of bullying and providing more support for these children, offline and online, might decrease the occurrence of online bullying.

With regard to mediation and coping strategies, EU Kids Online found that parents are often ignorant of the risks experienced by children in their digital lives. This is not to suggest that more restrictive parental mediation is required, which would limit children's online opportunities and may not be effective in reducing harm (Chapter 18, this volume). Rather parents should be made aware of both the risks and ways of dealing with them; greater awareness should empower them not just to set rules, but to give advice and provide social support (Chapter 17, this volume). The take-up of parental software controls remains low, despite extensive investment and promotion. The use of software filtering may even become less relevant in the face of children's growing skills and increasing access to different ways of going online. More generally, parents seem unaware of the internet sources that have received the most investment: most receive information about internet safety from family and friends and a minority get safety information from websites or traditional media sources (Livingstone et al, 2011b). We also found that social support from teachers and peers has considerable potential for reducing harm and increasing children's online competences (Chapter 19, this volume). Yet the youngest children in the survey reported the least mediation from teachers, pointing to a need for primary schools to increase their critical and safety guidance for pupils.

Policy recommendations

Internet safety policy has to date relied on a cooperative alliance of industry, regulatory and civil society stakeholder groups promoting a strategy of self-regulated practice backed up by awareness-raising aimed at parents and children encouraging them to take greater responsibility for their own safety. Do initiatives such as hotlines and helplines, content labelling schemes and awareness messaging counteract the risks that young people may experience and lead to safer online opportunities? There is evidence that many of these measures continue to be relevant and effective, perhaps even more so than when they were first introduced (European Commission, 2008). However, as discussed, there is considerable scope for further refining policy on children's internet safety, with closer targeting of initiatives to those areas where persistent challenges remain, such as inadequate skills, insufficient opportunities, high exposure to risk or vulnerability to harm.

Drawing on the findings of the EU Kids Online survey and analysis of the existing pillars of internet safety policy (O'Neill and McLaughlin, 2011), we submit that in addition to established efforts, there should be more focus on the contributions that different players can make within this policy space, with a greater attention to monitoring the effectiveness of initiatives. Below we highlight the principal recommendations arising from EU Kids Online and identify relevance for individual policy actors.

Governments

As the policy actors most likely to lead policy development, governments need to ensure equality of access and opportunity for all children, and that sufficient resources are available to support the expansion of children's opportunities and development of their digital literacy skills. Governments provide leadership and support for educational and stakeholder efforts; they also have a crucial role to play in incentivising industry engagement and making sure that it is inclusive, effective and accountable.

Awareness-raising

Awareness-raising efforts coordinated at European level by Insafe and implemented by a network of Safer Internet Centres and multiple stakeholder groups need to adopt a differentiated and sophisticated awareness approach recognising that not all children are the same. Accordingly, raising children's awareness to online risks needs to be balanced and proportionate, and directed at those most at risk of harm. Better targeting of awareness messages to the concerns of children according to age and levels of skill is likely to prove more effective. 'Hard-to-reach' children and those most susceptible to harm are a priority although empowering all children to cope better with online risks through information and better skills is fundamental.

Industry

Calls for more sustained industry engagement have been a consistent theme of evaluations of the Safer Internet Programme (Technopolis, 2003; European Commission, 2006). In accordance with self-regulatory agreements, industry needs to ensure that best practice prevails in providing protection for young people accessing their services, whether on social networking sites, via mobile phone services or more general browsing and online communications services. 'Safety by design principles' should be more widely implemented in the development of new internet services. Industry can also be more proactive in fostering internet safety awareness and promoting safety education in a prominent and accessible manner.

Parents and children

Improving and reinforcing parents and young people's awareness of risk and safety remains an ongoing priority for internet safety policy. Parents need to be alert to the risks, but initiatives should also avoid an alarmist or sensationalist approach. Parents should be helped to mediate in practical ways, and encouraged to develop more active forms of shared activity and mediation with their children. A reliance on restrictive mediation has the effect of limiting children's opportunities and also hampers the development of resilience. Awareness-raising efforts among children and parents should also include emphasis on coping strategies through safety messages highlighting social supports such as talking to parents, friends and teachers, and support from the use of online tools.

Educators

The role of schools in supporting digital skills development and awareness of internet safety is critical and requires further support. Digital literacy education should become a core element of national education frameworks and should include an inventory of digital safety skills. Better integration of ICT in the curriculum will encourage children to practice a wider diversity of online activities, improve their skills, build digital citizenship and enhance their coping strategies and resilience. Given the ever younger ages at which children go online, the need for educational intervention should be extended to primary and even to nursery schools.

Conclusion

The environment in which children go online is one that does not stand still, and one of the overriding challenges for policy in this area is to keep pace with rapidly evolving technologies, new patterns of use and emerging challenges for safety. Many of the existing awareness-raising strategies and much of the internet safety advice developed at a time when internet services were limited, connectivity could be easily controlled and parents could assume a pivotal role in mediating their children's internet use. Clearly, this no longer pertains, and the multiple modalities and contexts of young people's internet use now require more sophisticated policy responses. With inexorable trends towards ubiquitous internet access via mobile devices, more access in privatised settings and the availability of new and emerging location-based services, there is an urgent need to update this approach to ensure internet safety guidance remains relevant to and responds to children's actual experience.

The constituents of such an approach, including those features identified above, require targeted, research-informed and proportionate responses to a changing communications environment, underpinned by an emphasis on children's empowerment rather than restriction of their usage. Encouraging self-management skills, responsible behaviour and digital citizenship, it is increasingly recognised, are key elements of the response to emerging child safety needs in today's complex information ecology. To be effective, internet safety policy will continue to require the collaboration and support of multiple stakeholders. But to be successful, policy must be firmly based on evidence and informed by the latest research on new and emerging trends in order to respond to users' real needs. The effectiveness of initiatives needs to be monitored and evaluated on a consistent basis in order to identify what works best in enhancing online safety. Last but not least, a child-centred perspective, to which the EU Kids Online project stands as a substantial evidence base, is also one that treats children as a competent, participating group, not only as the target of awareness-raising efforts, but also as active agents who must likewise assume a central role in formulating, promoting and implementing safer internet practices.

Note

[1] The Education, Audiovisual and Culture Executive Agency (EACEA) is responsible for the management of certain parts of the EU's programmes in the fields of education, culture and audiovisual.

References

Akdeniz, Y., Walker, C. and Wall, D. (2000) *The internet, law and society*, Harlow: Longman.

Bangemann, M. (1994) *Europe and the global information society: Recommendations to the European Council*, Brussels: DGXII, CEC.

Council of Europe (2006) *Recommendation Rec(2006)12 of the Committee of Ministers to member states on empowering children in the new information and communications environment*, Strasbourg: Council of Europe.

European Commission (1996a) *Green Paper on the protection of minors and human dignity in audiovisual and information services*, Brussels: European Commission.

European Commission (1996b) *Illegal and harmful content on the internet* (COM(96)487), Brussels-Luxembourg: European Commission.

European Commission (1999) *A multiannual community action plan on promoting safer use of the internet by combatting illegal and harmful content on global networks. Four-year work programme 1999-2002*, Luxembourg: European Commission Safer Internet Programme.

European Commission (2000) *Communication from the Commission on the precautionary principle* (COM 2000/001), Brussels: European Commission.

European Commission (2001) *Term of Reference on Workshop 11-12 June 2001, 'Safe use of new interactive technologies'*, Luxembourg: Safer Internet Programme.

European Commission (2004) *Ex ante evaluation Safer Internet Plus (2005-2008)*, Brussels: European Commission.

European Commission (2006) *Final evaluation of the implementation of the multiannual community action plan on promoting safer use of the internet by combating illegal and harmful content on global networks*, Luxembourg: Safer Internet Programme.

European Commission (2007) *A European approach to media literacy in the digital environment. Communication from the Commission to the European Parliament, the Council, the European Economic and Social Committee and the Committee of the Regions*, Brussels: European Commission.

European Commission (2008) *Safer Internet Plus (2005-2008) final evaluation*, Luxembourg: Safer Internet Programme.

European Commission (2009) *Safer social networking principles for the EU*, Luxembourg: European Commission Safer Internet Programme.

European Commission (2010a) *A digital agenda for Europe*, Brussels: European Commission.

European Commission (2010b) *Safer Internet Plus work programme 2010*, Luxembourg: European Commission Safer Internet Programme.

European Commission (2011) 'A wide variety of project funded by the Safer Internet Programme', Europe's Information Society Thematic Portal (http://ec.europa.eu/information_society/activities/sip/projects/index_en.htm#children_internet).

European Parliament and the Council of the European Union (2006) *Recommendation of the European Parliament and of the Council of 18 December 2006 on key competences for lifelong learning*, Brussels: Official Journal of the European Union.

Eurydice (2009) *Education on online safety in schools in Europe*, Brussels: Education, Audiovisual and Culture Executive Agency.

Görzig, A. (2011) *Who bullies and who is bullied online?* LSE, London: EU Kids Online.

GSMA (2007) *European Framework for safer mobile use by younger teenagers and children*, Brussels: GSMA Europe.

GSMA (2010) *Third implementation review of the European Framework for safer mobile use by younger teenagers and children*, Brussels: GSMA Europe.

Hasebrink, U., Görzig, A., Haddon, L., Kalmus, V. and Livingstone, S. (2011) *Patterns of risk and safety online. In-depth analyses from the EU Kids Online survey of 9-16 year olds and their parents in 25 countries*, London: EU Kids Online, London School of Economics and Political Science.

Jorge, A., Cardoso, D., Ponte, C. and Haddon, L. (2010) *Stakeholders' forum general report*, London: EU Kids Online, London School of Economics and Political Science.

Livingstone, S. and Haddon, L. (2009) *EU Kids Online: Final report. EC Safer Internet Plus Programme Deliverable D6.5*, London: EU Kids Online, London School of Economics and Political Science.

Livingstone, S. and Helsper, E. (2007) 'Gradations in digital inclusion: children, young people and the digital divide', *New Media & Society*, vol 9, no 4, pp 671-96.

Livingstone, S., Ólafsson, K. and Staksrud, E. (2011a) *Social networking, age and privacy*, London: EU Kids Online, London School of Economics and Political Science.

Livingstone, S., Haddon, L., Görzig, A. and Ólafsson, K. (2011b) *Risks and safety on the internet: The perspective of European children. Full findings*, London: EU Kids Online, London School of Economics and Political Science.

Lobe, B., Livingstone, S., Ólafsson, K. and Vodeb, H. (2011) *Cross-national comparison of risks and safety on the internet: Initial analysis from the EU Kids Online survey of European children*, London: EU Kids Online, London School of Economics.

Marsden, C.T. (2011) *Internet co-regulation: European law, regulatory governance and legitimacy in cyberspace*, Cambridge: Cambridge University Press.

Nesson, C. and Marglin, D. (1996) 'The day the internet met the First Amendment: Time and the Communications Decency Act', *Harvard Journal of Law and Technology*, vol 10, no 1, pp 113-20.

O'Neill, B. and McLaughlin, S. (2010) *Recommendations on safety initiatives*, London: EU Kids Online, London School of Economics and Political Science.

O'Neill, B., Livingstone, S. and McLaughlin, S. (2011) *Final recommendations. Policy implications, methodological lessons and further research recommendations*, London: EU Kids Online, London School of Economics and Political Science.

Reding, V. (2009) *The future of the internet and Europe's digital agenda*, Brussels: European Commission.

Schomberg, R.V. (2006) 'The precautionary principle and its normative challenges', in E.C. Fisher, J.S. Jones and R. van Schomberg (eds) *Implementing the precautionary principle: Perspectives and prospects*, Cheltenham: Edward Elgar, pp 19-41.

Sommer, P. (2001) *Safer use of interactive technologies workshop, Luxembourg, 11-12 June 2001, Background paper*, Luxembourg: European Commission, DG Information Society.

Staksrud, E. and Lobe, B. (2010) *Evaluation of the implementation of the safer social networking principles for the EU. Part I: General report*, Luxembourg: European Commission Safer Internet Programme.

Tambini, D., Leonardi, D. and Marsden, C.T. (2008) *Codifying cyberspace: Communications self-regulation in the age of internet convergence*, London: Routledge.

Technopolis (2003) *The evaluation of the Safer Internet Action Plan 1999-2002*, Brussels: European Commission.

Appendix:
Key variables used in
EU Kids Online analyses

Use and activities

Concept	Questions/response options	Summaries/variable names
Number of places where the internet is used	At school or college Living room (or other public room) at home At a friend's home Own bedroom (or other private room) at home At a relative's home In an internet café In a public library or other public place When 'out and about'	The number out of eight response options/ DC30INM
Number of devices used to access the internet	Shared PC Own PC Television set Mobile phone Games console Own laptop Shared laptop Other handheld or portable device (eg iPod Touch, iPhone or Blackberry)	The number out of eight response options/ DCdeviceNM
Estimated minutes online each day	About how long do you spend using the internet on a normal school day/ normal non-school day?	DCtimeuse

Digital literacy

Concept	Questions/response options	Summaries/variable names
Digital skills	Bookmark a website	The number out of eight response options/ DCskillsNM
	Block messages from someone you don't want to hear from	
	Find information on how to use the internet safely	
	Change privacy settings on a social networking profile	
	Compare different websites to decide if information is true	
	Delete the record of which sites you have visited	
	Block unwanted adverts or junk mail/ spam	
	Change filter preferences	
Range of online activities	Used the internet for schoolwork	The number out of 17 response options/ DCactNM
	Played internet games on your own or against the computer	
	Watched video clips	
	Visited a social networking profile	
	Used instant messaging	
	Sent/received email	
	Read/watched the news on the internet	
	Played games with other people on the internet	
	Downloaded music or films	
	Put (or posted) photos, videos or music to share with others	
	Used a webcam	
	Put (or posted) a message on a website	
	Visited a chatroom	
	Used file-sharing sites	
	Created a character, pet or avatar	
	Spent time in a virtual world	
	Written a blog or online diary	
Belief about internet abilities	I know lots of things about using the internet. I (not true) to 3 (very true)	DCwebableB

Risky activities

Concept	Questions/response options	Summaries/variable names
Risky offline activities (adapted from the Health Behaviour in School-aged Children survey; Currie et al, 2008)	Missed school lessons without my parents knowing Been in trouble with my teachers for bad behaviour Been in trouble with the police Had so much alcohol that I got really drunk (only asked of children aged 11+) Had sexual intercourse (only asked of children aged 11+)	The number out of three response options for 9- to 10-year-olds and out of five response options for children aged 11+/ DCROB1NM DCROB2NM
Risky online activities (adapted from the UK Children Go Online survey; Livingstone and Helsper, 2007, 2010)	Looked for new friends on the internet Added people to my friends list or address book that I have never met face to face Pretended to be a different kind of person on the internet from who I really am Sent personal information to someone that I have never met face to face Sent a photo or video of myself to someone that I have never met face to face	The number out of five response options/ DCriskactNM

Online risks

Concept	Questions/response options	Summaries/variable names
Online contacts		
Online contacts	Can I just check, have you ever had contact on the internet with someone you have not met face to face before? yes/no	QC147
Meeting online contacts offline	And have you ever gone on to meet anyone face to face that you first met on the internet in this way? yes/no	QC148
Number of online contacts met offline	And how many new people have you met in this way in the last 12 months, if any? 1 to 2, 3 to 4, More than 10	QC149

(continued)

Concept	Questions/response options	Summaries/variable names
Seeing and receiving sexual messages		
Receiving sexual messages	In the past 12 months, have you seen or received sexual messages of any kind on the internet? yes/no	QC167
Frequency of receiving sexual messages	How often have you seen or received sexual messages of any kind on the internet in the past 12 months? Every day or almost every day Once or twice a week Once or twice a month Less often	QC168
Types of sexual messages received	I have been sent a sexual message on the internet	The number out of five response options/ QC169A-E
	I have seen a sexual message posted where other people could see it on the internet	
	I have seen other people perform sexual acts	
	I have been asked to talk about sexual acts with someone on the internet	
	I have been asked on the internet for a photo or video showing my private parts	
Sexual images		
Seeing sexual images	Have you seen these kinds of things [images that are obviously sexual] on any websites in the past 12 months? yes/no	QC131
Types of sexual images	Which types of website have you seen things like this [any kind of sexual images] on in the last 12 months?	The number out of five response options/ QC133A-E
	Images or video of someone naked	
	Images or video of someone's 'private parts'	
	Images or video of someone having sex	
	Images or video of movies that show sex in a violent way	
	Something else	

(continued)

Concept	Questions/response options	Summaries/variable names
Bullying		
BULLYING (introduction)	Sometimes children or teenagers say or do hurtful or nasty things to someone and this can often be quite a few times on different days over a period of time, for example. This can include: • teasing someone in a way this person does not like • hitting, kicking or pushing someone around • leaving someone out of things When people are hurtful or nasty to someone in this way, it can happen: • face to face (in person) • by mobile phones (texts, calls, video clips) • on the internet (email, instant messaging, social networking, chatrooms)	
Cyberbullying (victim of)...		
Being cyberbullied	Has someone acted in this kind of hurtful or nasty way to you in the past 12 months? At any time during the last 12 months, has this happened.... By mobile phone calls, texts or image/video texts? yes/no [and/or] At any time during the last 12 months, has this happened on the internet? yes/no	QC114B and/or QC115
Online bullying (victim of)...		
Being bullied online	Has someone acted in this kind of hurtful or nasty way to you in the past 12 months? At any time during the last 12 months, has this happened on the internet? yes/no	QC115
Types of being bullied online	And in which ways has this [someone has done nasty or hurtful things to you on the internet] happened to you in the last 12 months? Nasty or hurtful messages were sent to me Nasty or hurtful messages about me were passed around or posted where others could see I was left out or excluded from a group or activity on the internet I was threatened on the internet Other nasty or hurtful things on the internet	The number out of five response options/ QC117A-E

(continued)

Concept	Questions/response options	Summaries/variable names
Negative user-generated content		
Number of items reflecting negative user-generated content	Hate messages that attack certain groups or individuals Ways to be very thin (such as being anorexic or bulimic) Ways of physically harming or hurting themselves Talk about or share their experiences of taking drugs Ways of committing suicide	The number out of five response options/ DC142NM
Data misuse		
Number of items reflecting data misuse	Somebody used my password to access my information or to pretend to be me Somebody used my personal information in a way I didn't like I lost money by being cheated on the internet	The number out of three response options/ DC143NM
All risks		
Has experienced any of seven online risks	Online contacts, meeting online contacts offline, receiving sexual messages, seeing sexual images, being bullied online, has come across one or more negative user-generated content, has experienced personal data misuse of any kind	DCirisk2

Online perpetrators

Concept	Questions/response options	Summaries/variable names
Cyberbullying others	Have you acted in a way that might have felt hurtful or nasty to someone else in the past 12 months? In which of the following ways have you acted like this in the past 12 months…? By mobile phone calls, texts or image/video texts [AND/OR] On the internet (yes/no)	QC127B and/or QC127c
Online bullying others	Have you acted in a way that might have felt hurtful or nasty to someone else in the past 12 months? In which of the following ways have you acted like this in the past 12 months…? On the internet (yes/no)	QC127c
Sending sexual messages	In the past 12 months, have you sent or posted a sexual message (example: words, pictures or video) of any kind on the internet? This could be about you or someone else (yes/no)	QC179

Harm from online risks

(overall, sexual images, sexual messages, meeting online contacts offline, being bullied online)

Concept	Questions/response options	Summaries/variable names
Experience of harm on the internet (overall)	In the past 12 months, have you seen or experienced something on the internet that has bothered you in some way? For example, made you feel uncomfortable, upset, or feel that you shouldn't have seen it (yes/no)	QC110
Experience of harm (sexual images, sexual messages, meeting online contacts offline)	And in the last 12 months has [the risk] bothered you in any way? For example, made you feel uncomfortable, upset [...] (yes/no)	QC134, QC152, QC171
Intensity of harm (sexual images, sexual messages, being bullied online, meeting online contacts offline)	Thinking about the last time you were bothered by [experiencing the risk], how upset did you feel about it (if at all)? 0 (not at all upset) to 3 (very upset)	QC118, QC135, QC160, QC172
Duration of harm (sexual images, sexual messages, being bullied online)	How long did you feel like this [upset] for? 1 (I got over it straight away) to 4 (I thought about it for a couple of months or more)	QC119, QC136, QC173
Duration of harm (meeting online contacts offline)	How long did you feel like this [upset] for? 1 (*I got over it straight away*) to 3 (*I felt like that for a few weeks*)	QC161
Harm index (sexual images, sexual messages, being bullied online)	Intensity x duration 0 (low) – 12 (high)	QC118*QC119, QC135*QC136, QC172*QC173
Harm index (meeting online contacts offline)	Intensity x duration 0 (low) – 9 (high)	QC160*QC161

Mediation

Concept	Questions/response options	Summaries/variable names
Active mediation of internet use	*Does your parent/do either of your parents sometimes...* sit with you while you use the internet? stay nearby when you use the internet? encourage you to explore and learn things on the internet on your own? do shared activities together with you on the internet?	Either number of available response options OR if at least one of them was chosen or not/ e.g. QC327a-e, QP220a-e
	Does your parent/do either of your parents sometimes.../Have any teachers at your school ever done any of these things? talk to you about what you do on the internet?	
Active mediation of internet safety	*Does your parent/do either of your parents sometimes.../Have any teachers at your school ever done any of these things? Have your friends ever done any of these things?* Helped you when something is difficult to do or find on the internet Explained why some websites are good or bad Suggested ways to use the internet safely Suggested ways to behave towards other people online Helped you in the past when something has bothered you on the internet	Either number of available response options OR if at least one of them was chosen or not/ e.g. QC329a-f, QP222a-f
	Does your parent/do either of your parents sometimes.../Have any teachers at your school ever done any of these things? In general, talked to you about what to do if something on the internet bothered you	

(continued)

Concept	Questions/response options	Summaries/variable names
Restrictive mediation	*Parents CURRENTLY allow them to do them only with permission/supervision, or never allow.* Use instant messaging Download music or films on the internet Watch video clips on the internet Have your own social networking profile Give out personal information to others on the internet Upload photos, videos or music to share with others	Either number of available response options OR if at least one of them was chosen or not/ e.g. QC328a-f, QP221a-f
	Have any teachers at your school ever done any of these things? Made rules about what you can do on the internet at school	
Parental monitoring	*Does your parent/either of your parents sometimes check any of the following things afterwards?* Which websites you visited The messages in your email or instant messaging account Your profile on a social networking or online community Which friends or contacts you add to your social networking profile/instant messaging service	Either number of available response options OR if at least one of them was chosen or not/ e.g. QC330a-d, QP223a-d
Parents' technical mediation	*Does your parent/do your parents make use of any of the following...?* Parental controls or other means of blocking or filtering some types of website Parental controls or other means of keeping track of the websites you visit A service or contract that limits the time you spend on the internet Software to prevent spam or junk mail/viruses	Either number of available response options OR if at least one of them was chosen or not/ e.g. QC331a-d, QP224a-d

Psychological measures

SELF-EFFICACY (variable: DCSEMN)

Adapted from Schwarzer and Jerusalem (1995) (four items, $\alpha=0.65$)

*Item property analyses, selection and re-phrasing for the adapted **self-efficacy** scale*

Item	Original item phrasing	ITC original items	ITC selected items	Adapted item phrasing for *EU Kids Online II*
1	I can always manage to solve difficult problems if I try hard enough.	0.39	–	-
2	If someone opposes me, I can find means and ways to get what I want.	0.54	–	-
3	It is easy for me to stick to my aims and accomplish my goals.	0.62	0.60	It's easy for me to stick to my aims and achieve my goals.
4	I am confident that I could deal efficiently with unexpected events.	0.58	0.60	I am confident that I can deal with unexpected problems.
5	Thanks to my resourcefulness, I know how to handle unforeseen situations.	0.59	0.64	I can generally work out how to handle new situations.
6	I can solve most problems if I invest the necessary effort.	0.31	–	-
7	I can remain calm when facing difficulties because I can rely on my coping abilities.	0.54	–	-
8	When I am confronted with a problem, I can usually find several solutions.	0.53	–	-
9	If I am in trouble, I can usually think of something to do.	0.55	0.51	If I am in trouble I can usually think of something to do.
10	No matter what comes my way, I'm usually able to handle it.	0.62	0.61	I can generally work out how to handle new situations.
	Cronbach's α	0.84	0.80	

Notes: A three-point response scale was used (1 = Not true, 2 = A bit true, 3 = Very true), ITC: Corrected item-total correlation, original items 5 and 10 were combined for adapted item phrasing, all analyses were performed on selected cases of children 12-15 years from a public data set (Schwarzer, 2006) (n=1,254).

PSYCHOLOGICAL DIFFICULTIES (variable: DCSDQMN)

Adapted from Strength and Difficulties Questionnaire (SDQ) (Goodman et al, 1998) (16 items, $\alpha=0.71$) using items measuring psychological difficulties only

*Item property analyses and selection for the **psychological difficulties** scale (adapted from SDQ)*

Item	Item phrasing and variable names by subscale	ITC pilot	ITC selected items in *EU Kids Online II*
Emotional symptoms (DCSDQepMN)			
1	I get a lot of headaches, stomach-aches or sickness.	0.40	0.36
2	I worry a lot.	0.48	0.35
3	I am often unhappy, sad or tearful.	0.34	0.48
4	I am nervous in new situations, I easily lose confidence.	0.36	0.37
5	I have many fears, and I am easily scared.	0.23	0.40
Conduct problems (DCSDQcpMN)			
1	I get very angry and often lose my temper.	0.61	0.42
2	I usually do as I am told. (reversed)	0.07	0.06
3	I fight a lot, I can make other people do what I want.	0.17	0.27
4	I am often accused of lying or cheating.	0.40	0.41
5	I take things that are not mine from home, school or elsewhere.	0.48	0.26
Peer relationship problems (DCSDQppMN)			
1	I am usually on my own, I generally play alone or keep to myself.	0.43	0.26
2	I have at least one good friend. (reversed)	0.20	0.12
3	Other people my age generally like me. (reversed)	0.32	0.21
4	Other children or young people pick on me.	0.52	0.42
5	I get on better with adults than with people my own age.	0.40	0.28
Hyperactivity (DCSDQhpMN)			
1	I am restless, I cannot stay still for long.	0.36	–
2	I am easily distracted, I find it difficult to concentrate.	0.46	0.37
3	I think before I do things. (reversed)	0.34	–
4	I finish the work I'm doing, my attention is good. (reversed)	0.19	–
	Cronbach's α	0.77	0.71

Notes: A three-point response scale was used (1 = Not true, 2 = A bit true, 3 = Very true); ITC: Corrected item-total correlation; ITCs and Cronbach's αs were computed for the full psychological difficulties scale; the full sample of 9- to 16-year-olds was used for both analyses ($N_{Pilot}=76$, $N_{Data}=25,142$).

SENSATION-SEEKING (variable: DCsensationMN)

From Stephenson et al (2003) (two items, $r=0.64$, $p<0.001$)

Item	Item phrasing
1	I do dangerous things for fun.
2	I do exciting things, even if they are dangerous.

Notes: A three-point response scale was used (1 = Not true, 2 = A bit true, 3 = Very true)

EXCESSIVE USE (variable: DCaddictMN)

Adapted from Šmahel et al (2009) (five items, $\alpha=0.77$)

Item	Item phrasing
1	I have gone without eating or sleeping because of the internet.
2	I have felt bothered when I cannot be on the internet.
3	I have caught myself surfing when I'm not really interested.
4	I have spent less time than I should with either family, friends or doing schoolwork because of the time I spent on the internet.
5	I have tried unsuccessfully to spend less time on the internet.

Notes: A four-point response scale was used (1 = Never/almost never, 2 = Not very often, 3 = Fairly often, 4 = Very often); items were only asked of 11- to 16-year-olds.

References

Currie, C., Gabhainn, S.N., Godeau, E., Roberts, C., Smith, R., Currie, D., Picket, W., Richter, M., Morgan, A. and Barnekow, V. (eds) (2008) *Inequalities in young people's health: Health behaviour in school-aged children (HBSC). International report from the 2005/2006 survey*, Copenhagen, Denmark: WHO Regional Office for Europe.

Goodman, R., Meltzer, H. and Bailey, V. (1998) 'The Strengths and Difficulties Questionnaire: a pilot study on the validity of the self-report version', *European Child and Adolescent Psychiatry*, vol 7, pp 125-30.

Livingstone, S. and Helsper, E.J. (2007) 'Taking risks when communicating on the internet: the role of offline social-psychological factors in young people's vulnerability to online risks', *Information, Communication & Society*, vol 10, no 5, pp 619-43.

Livingstone, S. and Helsper, E.J. (2010) 'Balancing opportunities and risks in teenagers' use of the internet: the role of online skills and internet self-efficacy', *New Media & Society*, vol 12, no 2, pp 309-29.

Schwarzer, R. (2006) 'SPSS raw data with 18,000 participants' (http://userpage.fu-berlin.de/~health/world_24nations_25nov2006.sav).

Schwarzer, R. and Jerusalem, M. (1995) 'Generalized self-efficacy scale', in J. Weinman, S. Wright and M. Johnston (eds) *Measures in health psychology: A user's portfolio. Causal and control beliefs*, Windsor: NFER-Nelson, pp 35-7.

Šmahel, D., Vondráčková, P., Blinka, L. and Godoy-Etcheverry, S. (2009) 'Comparing addictive behavior on the internet in the Czech Republic, Chile and Sweden', in G. Cardosso, A. Cheong and J. Cole (eds) *World wide internet: Changing societies, economies and cultures*, Macao: University of Macau, pp 544-82.

Stephenson, M.T., Hoyle, R.H., Palmgreen, P. and Slater, M.D. (2003) 'Brief measures of sensation seeking for screening and large-scale surveys', *Drug and Alcohol Dependence*, vol 72, no 3, pp 279-86.

Index

Note: The following abbreviations have been used: *f* = figure; *n* = note; *t* = table

A

access locations/platforms 46–7, 50, 61*f*,
  63*f*, 69*n*, 220, 345, 346, 350, 355
  meeting new contacts 181, 182*t*
  mobile access 286–7, 288*f*, 289*t*, 290,
    291, 292*t*, 293
  pornography 168–9, 170*t*
'access rainbow' 259, 260
Acquisti, A. 102
active coping strategies 318, 319*t*, 320*t*
active mediation 220–1, 231, 232, 234,
    236, 264
  digital literacy 265*t*, 267
  parental 223*t*, 224*t*, 225*t*, 237*t*, 238*t*,
    239*f*, 241*f*
activities 69–70*n*, 102, 345–6, 347
  age 74, 75*t*, 79*f*, 80*f*, 83
  average number across countries 76,
    77*f*, 78
  average number of 74, 75*t*, 76
  coping strategies 211*t*, 214*t*
  country comparisons 81*t*, 82*t*, 83
  exposure to online risk/harm 207*t*,
    316
  factor analysis of 130*t*, 131
  gender 78, 79*f*, 83, 133*t*, 134*f*, 135*t*
  range undertaken 88, 91*t*, 92*t*, 94*t*, 129
  types in which children engage 78,
    79*f*, 80*t*, 81
  vulnerability to online risk/harm 318*t*
adult-initiated online activity 6*t*
adverts 89*t*
age
  activities/opportunities 74, 75*t*, 79*f*,
    80*f*, 83
  coping strategies 209, 210*t*, 212, 214*t*,
    215, 216
  cyberbullying 142, 144*t*, 146*t*
  digital literacy 91*t*, 94*t*, 265*t*, 266, 267*t*,
    282
  excessive internet use 198*t*, 199
  experimenting with the self 113, 114,
    115, 117, 118*f*, 119, 120*t*, 121, 123*f*,
    124

exposure to online risk 206*t*, 316*t*, 317
first internet use 64, 65, 66, 346
meeting new contacts 178, 181, 182*t*,
  183, 184, 185, 187
mobile access 287, 290, 291, 292*t*, 293
online access 51*f*, 52, 53*t*, 54, 133*t*,
  134*f*, 135*t*, 346
parental mediation 223, 224*t*, 233, 240,
  257, 258
pornography 167, 168, 170*t*, 171, 172*t*,
  173, 174
sexual images 303*t*
sexual messages ('sexting') 153–4, 155,
  156*t*, 157*t*, 158, 159, 160*f*, 161*t*
social networking sites (SNS) 101*f*,
  104, 346
teacher/peer mediation 246, 249*f*, 254
vulnerability to online risk/harm 299,
  300*t*, 301, 302*t*, 304*t*, 305, 306, 318*t*,
  332, 347
agency 73, 138, 254, 335
Appadurai, A. 99
Austria 38, 253, 261, 333
  access location 60, 61*f*, 63*f*, 69*n*
  cyberbullying 145*f*, 297–8
  digital literacy 92*t*
  excessive internet use 197*t*
  experimenting with the self 115, 116*t*,
    117
  meeting new contacts 185, 186*f*
  mobile access 288*f*, 292*t*
  online access 49*f*, 50*f*, 51*f*, 53*t*
  online opportunities 77*f*, 78, 81*t*, 84*f*
  online usage 60, 64, 65, 136, 137*t*, 276*t*
  parental level of education 263*f*
  parental mediation 225*t*
  response rates 29*f*
  sexual messages ('sexting') 156*t*, 159*f*
  social networking sites (SNS) 105*f*
autonomy and independence: desire
  for 179
avatars 39, 75*t*, 80*t*, 89*t*, 130*t*, 132*t*, 133,
  356

B

C